Emanuel Goldberg and His Knowledge Machine

Emanuel Goldberg.

Emanuel Goldberg and His Knowledge Machine

Information, Invention, and Political Forces

Michael Buckland

New Directions in Information Management

A Member of the Greenwood Publishing Group

Westport, Connecticut • London

Library of Congress Cataloging-in-Publication Data

Buckland, Michael Keeble.
   Emanuel Goldberg and his knowledge machine : information, invention, and
political forces / Michael Buckland.
      p. cm. — (New directions in information management)
   Includes bibliographical references and index.
   ISBN 0–313–31332–6
      1. Information technology—History. 2. Goldberg, Emanuel, 1881–1970. 3.
Inventors—Biography. I. Title. II. Series.
T58.5.B83 2006
004.1'9—dc22   2005034357

British Library Cataloguing in Publication Data is available.

Library of Congress Catalog Card Number: 2005034357
ISBN: 0–313–31332–6
ISSN: 0887–3844

First published in 2006

Libraries Unlimited, 88 Post Road West, Westport, CT 06881
A Member of the Greenwood Publishing Group, Inc.
www.lu.com

Printed in the United States of America

The paper used in this book complies with the
Permanent Paper Standard issued by the National
Information Standards Organization (Z39.48–1984).

10 9 8 7 6 5 4 3 2 1

Contents

Illustrations

Preface

This book has a very specific origin. In 1988 I began to realize that there had been much more sophisticated ideas about information and information systems in continental Europe before World War II than I, or, it seemed, most others, had realized. One day in December 1989, provoked by reading one too many uncritical references to Vannevar Bush and his famous essay, "As we may think," as the origin of Information Science, I decided to probe a little deeper. I started by reading a 1958 essay by Robert Fairthorne, who had been active in the development of Documentation in the 1930s.[1] After referring to Bush's document retrieval device, the Microfilm Rapid Selector, the technological background for the "As we may think" essay, Fairthorne noted that Bush's rapid selector had been anticipated "by E. Goldberg of the Zeiss Company." But I found nothing about this claim in the usual reference works and Mr. Fairthorne, when contacted, no longer remembered how he had come to know about Goldberg. One clue led to another and to evidence that Fairthorne's "E. Goldberg" was Emanuel Goldberg, founding head of the Zeiss Ikon company in Dresden and that, in the late 1920s, he had indeed designed what he called a "Statistical Machine," a document retrieval machine using microfilm for storage and pattern recognition for searching.

The trail also led to Emanuel Goldberg's son, Dr. Herbert Goldberg, and to his daughter, Mrs. Chava Gichon. Dr. Goldberg and I presented papers about his father's life and his Statistical Machine at the Annual Meeting of the American Society for Information Science in 1991 and, in 1992, an article concerning the machine was published.[2]

But the life and the times of Emanuel Goldberg has a much broader interest than a single, forgotten invention by a forgotten inventor. First, there is the human interest in the remarkable efforts and adventures of an extraordinary man. Second, his work and interactions with others provide a window into the intellectual and social history of a formative period in the development of documentation and information technology, a neglected theme. Third, his life is a striking example of how thoroughly the career of a man with little interest in politics was shaped by political forces.

---

1. Fairthorne, Robert A. Automatic retrieval of recorded information. *Computer Journal,* 1 (1958):36–41. Repr. in Fairthorne, Robert A. 1961. *Towards Information Retrieval.* London: Butterworths, 1961, 135–146.

2. Buckland, M. K. Emanuel Goldberg, electronic document retrieval, and Vannevar Bush's Memex. *Journal of the American Society for Information Science* 43, no. 4 (May 1992):284–294. http://www.sims.berkeley.edu/~buckland/goldbush.html

Fourth, his story is a case study in social memory: how and why did the record of a famous man of considerable achievements come to be so thoroughly erased?

The story is complex because it ranges across distant social contexts, obsolete technologies, and incomplete evidence in various languages. Tracing Goldberg's work and influence requires attention to the now-distant worlds of Tsarist Russia, the Germany of Kaiser Wilhelm, World War I, the Weimar Republic, the rise of Hitler's Third Reich, World War II, Palestine under the British Mandate, and the emergence of the State of Israel. Powerful political and military pressures influenced greatly and directly what he could and could not do. Goldberg's life and work can be viewed as a case study of how thoroughly inventors, invention, and the received history of invention can be affected by political and social pressures.

Finding out about Goldberg was not easy. His activities, and the records of them, were affected by the most turbulent events of the twentieth century: World War I, the Russian Revolution, the Third Reich, and World War II. Contact with his family in Russia was lost in the 1930s. The records of his firms were destroyed by bombing, fire, or flood. His successors in Dresden, first Nazi and then Communist, were not motivated to honor a Jewish industrialist. Personal ambition induced others to take credit for his work, or, at least, to withhold acknowledgment. Successive corporate histories of Zeiss Ikon failed to acknowledge achievements of the founding director. Goldberg rarely reminisced, even to his children, and, in the end, he burned most of his own papers and memorabilia. Much of what follows had to be reconstructed from scattered fragments in archives, interviews, and the technical literature of the early twentieth century. The details of these sources are provided unobtrusively at the back of the book. To make this account more accessible, more background has been provided than specialists would need, and a single form of name has been used in the several cases in which persons had multiple names. Some quotations have been translated into English, with the foreign-language original provided in the endnotes.

Exploring these issues would have been much less successful, and far less pleasant, without the help of Goldberg's son, daughter, and son-in-law: Dr. Herbert Goldberg of Concord, Massachusetts, and Mrs. Chava Gichon and Professor Mordecai Gichon of Tel Aviv, Israel. Their invaluable friendship and helpfulness made all the difference, especially given the destruction of so much of the documentation. The University of California, Berkeley, provided support for sabbatical leave and the School of Information Management and Systems and the Academic Senate Committee on Research provided support for incidental expenses, which was very helpfully supplemented by the Harold Lancour Scholarship for

Foreign Study, from Phi Beta Mu, the International Library and Information Science Honor Society, and two unrestricted research grants from Ricoh Silicon Valley, Inc. I am very grateful to them and to the many other people acknowledged elsewhere who have provided so much encouragement and assistance.

Michael Buckland

1

Origins

The Memex project... developed... into the Rapid Selector. The Rapid Selector itself had probably been realized as a workable device by E. Goldberg of the Zeiss Company around 1930.

—Robert A. Fairthorne, 1958

The Origins of Information Science

It is widely assumed that information science and modern information technology were developments that followed World War II, largely originating in the Northeast United States, with 1945 commonly given as a starting date. The development of cybernetics, digital computers, mathematical models of signaling efficiency, the transistor, and the widespread adoption of electronics after World War II were very important developments. And for the organization of information for personal use, the name of Vannevar Bush and his celebrated speculative essay, "As we may think," published in the *Atlantic Monthly* in 1945, has a unique status. In the fields of information retrieval and the development of digital libraries, it is constantly invoked as both the inspiration and the effective starting point for the field.

Nevertheless, a wide range of developments in information technology, including radio, television, movies, punch cards, microfilm, digital circuitry, and photoelectric sensing devices, were already well developed by 1945. So, treating 1945 as the birth year for information science is historically implausible. If one looks, one can find sophisticated ideas about organizing information well before 1945. A little reading of the writings of Paul Otlet, Suzanne Briet, and other largely forgotten pioneers of what was then known as "Documentation," and now often called Information Management or Information Science, shows that much more was achieved in the period from the 1890s to mid-century, the period during which most of modern information technology originated, than has been remembered.

Robert Fairthorne, a man of penetrating insights, was active in the development of Documentation both before and after 1945. In 1958, he wrote a critique of Bush's "As we may think." Referring to Bush's document retrieval device, the Microfilm Rapid Selector, the technological background for the essay, Fairthorne wrote: "Bush's paper was timely even though few of his suggestions were original. The Rapid Selector itself had probably been realized as a workable device by E. Goldberg of the Zeiss Company around 1930." If so, who was E. Goldberg? Which Zeiss company was this? What exactly had he developed? And who knew about it? Mr. Fairthorne, when contacted in 1990, no longer remembered how he had come to know about Goldberg so many years before. Nothing was found in standard reference works on the history of technology, but Berkeley's rich library collections did contain a doctoral dissertation in chemistry completed in Leipzig in 1906 by an Emanuel Goldberg. As is customary in German doctoral dissertations, the last page contained the student's vita, which began: "I, Emanuel Goldberg, of the confession of Moses, was born in Moscow, son of an army doctor... " Eventually, it became clear that this Emanuel Goldberg was the same as the E. Goldberg mentioned by Fairthorne, but what was the rest of the story?

Goldberg's lifetime, especially from the 1890s through the 1940s, was a renaissance period in which the arts, sciences, technology, and society were all transformed. It was a particularly pivotal period for the maturing of modern information technologies: Movies were born, became the "talkies," then Hollywood extravaganzas, and grew into a massive commercial and hobby industry; radio and television were invented; the chemistry, optics, and mechanics of photography evolved from awkward, clumsy, and, often, homemade cameras using glass plates to the technical brilliance of the Leica and Contax 35 mm cameras; color and halftone printing matured; and much more. Emanuel Goldberg was active in each of these areas, and contributed to advances in several. It was a wonderful time to be an engineer and an inventor. It was the dawn of modern precision engineering, the slow transition from instruments made of brass, glass, leather, and egg whites to electronics. Goldberg foresaw and actively sought to develop the new technology of electronics, so very different, so very promising, and, in his day, so much less adequate and reliable than brass or glass. Yet Goldberg, well known internationally at the peak of his career, had somehow been largely forgotten in spite of his achievements.

Technology trends and their social impacts can be described in broad terms, but such summaries are extreme simplifications, imagined aggregations of the myriad details of any number of individuals, their actions, and the consequences. And each detail involves a personal history far too rich and detailed to be fully comprehended. It is only by attempting to reconstruct the details of specific developments, and of actual persons in their complex and ever-changing contexts, that one can begin to comprehend what was going on.

In this examination of one invention, Bush's "Rapid Selector," and of one inventor, Emanuel Goldberg, we begin in the cultured, cosmopolitan world of the upper middle classes in late nineteenth-century Moscow into which Goldberg was born, and with his father, a medical officer in the Tsar's Army.

Colonel Grigorii Goldberg

Grigorii Ignat'evich Goldberg, born in 1853, was a distinguished and decorated Colonel *(Polkovnik)* in the Medical Corps of the Tsar's Army. He is remembered by his grandchildren through a fine portrait of a dignified gentleman in military uniform, proudly wearing an array of medals (See Figure 1.1.)

The Order of St. Stanislaus (a Polish order taken over by Russia) was conferred for military valor ("with swords") or for merit ("without swords"); when awarded to non-Christians, it bore the Imperial Russian eagle instead of the SS cipher of St. Stanislaus. In 1878, the Order of St. Stanislaus, third class, for non-Christians, with swords, was conferred on Grigorii Goldberg following active service in the Russo-Turkish War of 1877–78. Worn next to it in a row are a dark bronze medal in memory of the war of 1877–78 and a medal for the coronation in 1883. Worn centrally at his neck is the Order of St. Anne, third class, for non-Christians, conferred on the Colonel in 1880 "as a reward for outstanding, assiduous service and efforts in the stopping of a typhus epidemic in the troops of the active army." The Order of St. Stanislaus, second class, for non-Christians, conferred without swords for merit, in 1886, is worn centrally below the white diagonal strap.

Grigorii Goldberg married Olga Moiseevna Grodsenska, born around 1859 in Kovno (now Kaunas in Lithuania). Kovno, then a town of about 24,000, was part of Russia and close to the border with the German state of Prussia. At that time, there was wide cultural, linguistic, and religious diversity within the Russian Empire. State policy during the second half of the nineteenth century sought consolidation of this heterogeneous realm through an emphasis on Russification, which favored membership in the Russian Orthodox Church. Catholics, Protestants, Muslims, and, especially,

Figure 1.1. Colonel Grigorii Ignat'evich Goldberg. Emanuel Goldberg's father.

Jews, were regarded with disfavor. However, the Jewish community in Kovno, and Slobodka, across the river, fared relatively well. It was largely Orthodox, relatively secularized, a major center of Jewish culture and, later, of Zionism. Olga Goldberg is said to have kept a kosher kitchen but only until her mother died.

The appointment of Jews who had not converted to Orthodox Christianity to the military medical service was severely restricted. However, a shortage of qualified army doctors during the Crimean War led to the acceptance, after 1862, of those who held a certificate in medicine *(lekar)*, including Grigorii Goldberg. He rose through the ranks to become a highly decorated Colonel *(Polkovnik)*. Such promotion was very unusual

Figure 1.2. Goldberg's family group, circa 1900. The young man in a student uniform, center, next to Colonel Goldberg, is probably Emanuel Goldberg.

for Jews who, like him, did not convert to the Russian Orthodox Church. Another was Joseph Trumpeldor, the highly decorated, one-armed war hero of the Russian-Japanese War, who joined the Zionist Mule Corps to help the British in Gallipoli and founded a Zionist political party with Vladimir Jabotinsky. Goldberg and Trumpeldor were highly exceptional. One of the first actions of the Provisional Government after the February revolution of 1917 was to issue a special decree removing restrictions on the promotion of Jewish military men.

   The military rank of Colonel *(Polkovnik)* automatically conferred on Grigorii Goldberg the civilian status of *Dvorianin,* a hereditary, untitled class of nobility; he also received the title of Court Counselor. A son, Raphael, was born in 1880, and Olga Goldberg now wanted a daughter. But when the next baby arrived on September 1, 1881 (August 19, 1881 in the Old Style Julian calendar then in use in Russia), it was another son, who felt for the rest of his life that his mother would have liked him better if he had been a girl. This second son they named Emanuel. In May 1884, a third child was born, a girl, Tamara. (See Figure 1.2.)

Emanuel Goldberg's Education

In some ways Emanuel Goldberg was a slow learner. He had difficulty memorizing and was late in beginning to talk, but he was quick to decide that he wanted to become an engineer. He later recalled: "At the age of six, I was shown by a friend of the family how a lever can be used to lighten work. Since then I have been obsessed by the idea that by using a tool, life can be made more pleasant. To be an engineer seemed to me the highest goal. It was not easy for a Jewish boy in Czarist Russia to reach this goal. Instead of playing with my tools, I had to learn the irregular verbs of Russian, German, French, English, Greek, Latin, [Church] Slavonic and, last but not least, Hebrew for the Bar-Mitzva. I hated learning languages... "

He was interested in the natural sciences, especially geology and zoology. He learned German and read about animals in Brehm's *Tierleben,* a multivolume German encyclopedia about animals. He collected minerals, and used the wide sill between the double windows of his room as a space to do chemical experiments. His mother did not appreciate these experiments, but, otherwise, his parents appear to have emphasized learning.

Nicholas II, the last of the Tsars, came to the throne when his father, Alexander III, died on November 1, 1894. The formal coronation was 18 months later on May 26, 1896. As part of the festivities, a popular fête was organized, as usual, in the Khodynka field, a large open space in a Moscow suburb. Colonel Goldberg decided to go, and he took Emanuel with him. At 10:00 A.M. food and souvenirs, including mugs bearing the new Tsar's portrait, were to be given out. The location of the booths was unsuitable, near uneven ground, trenches, and wells. A crowd of more than half a million had assembled without sufficient police or adequate planning for crowd control. As those at the back of the crowd pushed forward to get their gifts while supplies lasted, there was a deadly crush. Many fell, were trodden on by those behind them, and crushed or trampled to death. Estimates of the injured ranged from 9,000 to 20,000, and 1,282 corpses of men, women, and children were carried away. Colonel Goldberg, being a doctor, stayed to tend to the wounded as best he could. Fifteen-year-old Emanuel retained a vivid memory of this dreadful experience. The Tsar was distressed by the disaster, but nevertheless attended a particularly lavish ball that evening, because his advisors insisted that the French hosts would be offended if he did not.

In order to gain admission to the engineering program at the prestigious Imperial Technical School of Moscow, Goldberg needed to study a broad range of subjects in secondary school and to do particularly well in his examinations because the number of Jewish students admitted was severely limited. This meant that instead of indulging his passion for engineering he had to study diligently subjects that were of little or no interest to him. He developed an additional lasting resentment against his mother because she made him attend to these studies. Nevertheless, he did well. His secondary school leaving certificate records primarily "excellent" grades in two sets of exams and reads:

> ... This [certificate] was given to Emmanuil GOL'DBERG, the son of a Court Counselor, of Jewish faith and born in Moscow on 19 August 1881, educated at the 3rd Moscow Gymnasium from 1891 on and having spent one [ycar] in its 8th grade.
>
> First, based on observations during the entire course of his schooling at the 3rd Moscow Gymnasium, his behavior was generally excellent, his assiduity in attendance of and preparation for classes and also in the execution of written assignments was very laudable, his diligence indeed zealous, and his inquisitiveness highly developed for all subjects, especially for physics; second, he acquired the following knowledge:

Subjects in Gymnasium	Grades	
	At the Pedagogical Council according to section 74 of the rules at exams for students at the gymnasiums at the Ministry of Public Education	At the examination of May of 1899.
Religious Instruction	—	—
Russian language with Church Slavonic and literature	4 (good)	4 (good)
Logic	5 (excellent)	—
Latin	4 (good)	4 (good)
Ancient Greek	5 (excellent)	5 (excellent)
Mathematics	5 (excellent)	5 (excellent)
Mathematical Geography	5 (excellent)	—
Physics	5 (excellent)	—
History	4 (good)	5 (excellent)
Geography	5 (excellent)	—
French	5 (excellent)	5 (excellent)
German	5 (excellent)	5 (excellent)

In view of the permanently excellent behavior, the diligence, and the excellent successes in the sciences, particularly in Ancient Greek and Mathematics, the Pedagogical Council has ordered to award him a silver medal...

The silver medal indicates that Goldberg ranked second in his graduating class. He then applied for admission to the engineering degree program at the Imperial Technical School of Moscow.

2

University Studies

The years I spent in Leipzig at my alma mater belong to the most beautiful of my memories ... A new science was being born. Young scholars from all over the world gathered there to be introduced to the relationship between chemistry and physics by Wilhelm Ostwald and the relationship between body and soul by Wilhelm Wundt.

—Emanuel Goldberg, 1956

A Quota

The Imperial Technical School of Moscow had a restrictive admissions quota. No more than 3 percent of admissions were allowed for Jewish applicants, meaning, in practice, that no more than one Jewish student would be admitted for Engineering. Goldberg performed excellently in the entrance examination.

A handwritten certificate bearing the seal of the Imperial Technical School survives (Figure 2.1).

In translation, it reads:

CERTIFICATE

After completion of his studies at the 3rd Moscow Gymnasium, Emmanuil Grigor'evich Gol'dberg in 1899 underwent the competition to join the group of students of first-year studies at Moscow's Imperial Technical School's [*Uchilishche*] Chemistry Department and received the following grades on a five-grade scale [5 being the highest]:

Russian language. 4
Algebra 5

9

Geometry............... 5
Trigonometry........... 5
Physics................ 5

Grade sum   24

Do not accept as student due to the 3% acceptance limit for Jews. [Seal] Signed by the Assistant to the Director of the educational section.
12 October 1904 Signature: A. Gavrilenko

His performance in the entrance examination is evidence of high academic achievement, a score of 24 out of a maximum of 25, and with perfect scores on the four scientific subjects. No other applicant outperformed Goldberg, but another candidate had done as well and he was also Jewish.

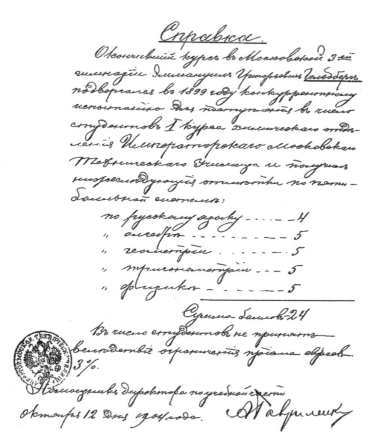

Figure 2.1. Certificate of nonadmission to the Imperial Technical School, Moscow, because of the 3 percent quota for Jews.

The choice between them was made by lot, and, on this basis, the other student was admitted and Goldberg was denied. All the other places were given to non-Jewish students who had performed less well than he had. Deeply disappointed by this discrimination, Goldberg enrolled instead at the University of Moscow to study Chemistry. It was a bitter experience, still recounted whenever his family talks about his life. The examination was taken in 1899, but the certificate is dated 1904, and refers to admission for Chemistry rather than Engineering. A likely explanation is that Goldberg obtained the certificate in 1904 to strengthen his application in that year for admission to the Institute for Physical Chemistry at Leipzig University.

Electro-Plating Zinc

Goldberg was an exceptional student, and he collaborated in research in electro-chemical reactions with Alexander W. Speranskii, a faculty member who specialized in physical chemistry. Together they wrote a paper, "Electrolysis Using Some Inorganic Salts in Organic Solvents," which they presented at a meeting of the Russian Physical-Chemical Society in St Petersburg, and was published in that prestigious society's journal "by A. W. Speranskii and student E. Goldberg." A summary appeared in a major international journal for applied chemistry, the *Zeitschrift für angewandte Chemie,* the following month. The paper had to do with galvanizing, adding a coating of one metal on to another, usually zinc on iron.

Galvanized iron was, and still is, very useful for a multitude of iron products, including nails, pails, gutters, and roofing. The iron provides strength and zinc coating protects the iron from rusting. There were two different production techniques: A "hot dip" process of immersing the iron in molten zinc; and electro-plating, in which zinc is deposited electrolytically on iron objects placed in a liquid solution, 10 percent of which was crystallized zinc sulphate. Each process had disadvantages. Molten zinc required very high temperatures. Electrolyzed zinc surfaces did not adhere as well and had a dull appearance. The use of electrolysis for electroplating with nickel, tin, and zinc depended on affordable electrical power and developed rapidly after 1869. It was, arguably, the first modern chemical industry.

Goldberg and Speranskii had experimented with the composition of the liquid solution in which the electrolysis was performed. They found that using pyridine, a clear, smelly liquid derived from coal-tar, instead of water gave superior results when adding a coating of silver. By the end of 1900, Emanuel Goldberg, still a teenager, had already made a good start as a scientist and as an engineer.

Goldberg also investigated different solutions for electroplating zinc on to iron and found an improvement when pyridine and inorganic salts were added to a water-based solution. The zinc coating adhered better and had a brighter appearance. Early in 1902, he submitted successful patent claims, first in Russia, and then in Germany, Britain, and the United States, for use of this chemical solution. These patents were all in Goldberg's sole name, indicating that it really was his own personal invention. Goldberg also obtained a related patent in Germany for the design of an improved vat for the electrolytic process.

Germany was then the leading producer of zinc, and most of the zinc was used for plating. Goldberg learned that a German firm was using his patented zincing solution without his permission, so he visited the firm to assert his rights. He was in a strong position and negotiated an exclusive contract on August 15, 1904, with Dr. G. Langbein & Co., in Leipzig-Sellerhausen. The terms were 1,730 Reichsmark in cash as soon as German patent 151,336 was formally assigned to Langbein and a 20 Pfennig license fee for every kilo of prepared solution sold in Germany. At the end of the meeting, the manager observed that, given the money receivable under the agreement, Goldberg could afford to travel home in a carriage. Langbein later wrote him a glowing testimonial concerning the vat that he had designed:

Dr. G. Langbein & Co. Elektrochemische Fabrik, Dynamo- und Maschinenbauanstalt.
Branches: Berlin, Solingen, Milan, Utrecht, Brussels, Vienna.
Leipzig-Sellenhausen, February 25, 190[?4].
Mr Emanuel Goldberg, Physikalisches Institut, Leipzig, Lineestrasse.

Herewith we confirm that we have acquired your patent for the "Production of zinc galvanization." We use the process ourselves, and have already widely delivered the vats for the process to others. To date we can only express praise for the effectiveness of the process. The advantages are so impressive, that we regularly recommend the purchase of these vats to our customers.

Respectfully yours.

A similar letter, dated October 1, 1903, from a Russian firm, Russische Metalhandelsgesellschaft Isnoskow, Suckau & Co., in Moscow, stated that Goldberg's patented process was being used, that this process was superior to other methods because it gave a better appearance, required 55 percent less energy than other processes, and caused the zinc to adhere better where there were deformities in the surface being coated.

The royalties from his patents gave Goldberg some financial independence. How he financed his studies prior to the royalties is not known. His father would have been able to support him.

Studies Abroad

At the beginning of the twentieth century, the best choice for any ambitious student was go to the universities of Germany, then at the peak of their prestige. The more famous, such as Leipzig and Berlin, were generally regarded as the best in the world, and, worldwide, students who wanted the best education went to Germany. From the United States, for example, some 10,000 students went to study in German universities before World War I and, after their return, they transformed the universities of the United States along German lines. Students came in large numbers from Russia. At the University of Berlin in 1910, there were more students from Russia than from any other foreign country. Goldberg was fluent in German. Study in Germany was the obvious course of action for him.

Germany universities had an additional attraction, the traditional "freedom to learn" *(Lernfreiheit)*. It was customary for students to move freely, semester by semester, from one university to another, composing a program of study through their choice of teachers and courses, not just from the departments ("Institutes") of one university, but of all the universities. Students would then settle at one of them for the final stage of writing their dissertation and graduate.

During the second half of the nineteenth century, German Jews acquired substantially equal legal status. Despite continuing antagonism in some circles and discrimination in the higher governmental appointments, German institutions were considered to be relatively liberal and Jewish students from abroad were allowed to study and to research freely.

Because German universities had large numbers of applicants from Russia, they tended to be more selective when reviewing Russian applicants. Jewish Russian students, like Goldberg, were especially motivated to study in Germany because of the restrictions on them at home. But Jews from Eastern Europe, especially Jewish students from Russia, were sometimes regarded with distaste. They were criticized for their poor German, for being radical, for endangering Germany's competitive edge, and so forth, and they were discriminated against in various ways. Anti-Semitism was especially common in universities. Further, Russians could be summarily deported. Two thousand Russian families were expelled in 1905–6, including prominent businessmen and engineers. The cultured, cosmopolitan Goldberg, fluent in German, appears to have escaped the harassment.

The winter semester in Germany corresponded to today's fall semester in the United States, but typically started later. Likewise, the German summer semester corresponded to the spring semester in the United States, but started after Easter and included a four-to-five week summer vacation. After having been rejected by the Imperial Technical School, Goldberg enrolled, in the fall of 1899, in the University of Moscow and studied there intermittently through the summer semester of 1904, with extended visits to Germany.

Goldberg spent the summer semester of 1900 at the University of Königsberg in Preussen, a major naval and military fortress town at what was then the very northeastern corner of Germany. Königsberg is now Kaliningrad, part of Kaliningradskaia Oblast', a parcel of Russia cut off from the rest of Russia and surrounded by Lithuania, Poland, and the Baltic Sea. But at that time, with Poland having been divided between Prussia, Russia, and Austria-Hungary, Königsberg was part of Germany, on the Baltic Sea, not far from the Russian border and only about 150 miles from Kovno. It was the capital of the province of East Prussia and occupied both banks of the river Pregel, four miles inland from the Baltic Sea. After the coming of the railroad, it had become a major port for the export of Russian grain. When Goldberg studied there it had a population of about 150,000.

Goldberg studied under Professor Wilhelm Lossen, the Director of the Chemical Laboratory. At the end of Goldberg's stay, Lossen gave him a memorandum, which, translated, states:

The Directorate of the Chemical Laboratory at the Albertus University
Königsberg i. Pr., 27 July 1900
Drummstr. 21

Mr. Emmanuel Goldberg during the month of July worked here at the University's chemical laboratory and particularly worked on quantitative analyses. He was always indefatigably diligent and showed a really good understanding and skill for the [illegible, perhaps "careful"] work.

The Director of the Chemical Laboratory

Prof. Dr. W. Lossen

Goldberg presumably returned to Moscow University for the winter semester of 1900 to write the paper that he co-authored with Speranskii. For the summer and fall semesters of 1901, he returned to Germany, this time to the Institute for Physical Chemistry, at the University of Leipzig. The director of the Institute was Wilhelm Ostwald, who received the 1909 Nobel Prize in Chemistry for his pioneering work in the new field of physical chemistry. Ostwald had enormous energy and wide interests, including the organization of scientific knowledge Like Goldberg, he was from Russia, having been born in Riga, now in Latvia.

Temperature and Photochemical Reactions

In the 1900s it was well known that the rate of chemical reactions increased as temperature increased. Typically the reaction rate would double or triple if the temperature increased by 10° Centigrade. More formally stated, the temperature coefficient was 2.0–3.0 per 10° Centigrade. Goldberg, who was fond of hiking, was puzzled because photography did not seem to follow this law. He had noted that the exposure could be the same at the top of a mountain, where it was freezing, as it was for a meadow, below, where it was hot, if the light was bright in both places. The nineteen-year-old student suggested to Ostwald that the effects of heat and of light on chemical processes—thermochemical effects and photochemical effects, respectively—were in principle different. Ostwald thought that increased light merely enhanced the effects of increased temperature but expressed interest in Goldberg's perception. He commented that photographic sensitivity resembled the synthesis of starch in trees by chlorophyll, and he encouraged Goldberg to investigate.

In an experiment in Ostwald's Institute in the fall of 1901, Goldberg showed that the oxidation of quinine using chromic acid was a temperature-independent reaction governed by the intensity of the light it receives. With a temperature coefficient of 1.0, meaning that heat did not increase the rate of the reaction, this photochemical reaction was clearly untypical. His findings were published early in 1902 as "A study of the kinetics of photochemical reactions: The oxydation of quinine using chromic acid" (*Beitrag zur Kinetik photochemischer Reaktionen: Die Oxydation von Chinin durch Chromsäure*) in a leading scientific journal, the *Zeitschrift für physikalische Chemie.* The scientific and practical significance of this revolutionary finding—that photochemical processes were effectively independent of temperature—was immediately recognized. The leading annual review of advances in photography and reprographics, the *Jahrbuch für Photographie und Reproduktionstechnik,* noted the important implication that photochemical reactions were different from other chemical processes. The *Zeitschrift für wissenschaftliche Photographie* published an extended review on the grounds that "the rather detailed summary may be justified by the value of this work for scientific photochemistry, for which it undoubtedly demonstrates one of the first systematic applications of chemical kinetics, at least for fully homogeneous light-sensitive systems." Other studies began to appear, with similar findings. There had been scattered earlier observations, but a major literature review in 1920 by Johannes Plotnikow, a leading authority on this topic, identified Goldberg's paper as the first to draw attention to the fact that temperature had little effect on photochemical reactions. The Sub-Director of the Institute, Robert Luther, (Figure 2.2), certified Goldberg's work with the following statement: "In this way Mr. Goldberg has proven to be a good experimenter with advanced physical-chemical, especially photochemical knowledge."

Goldberg returned to Moscow for the summer semester of 1902, then went to the Institute for Physical Chemistry at the University of Göttingen where he registered for the winter semester of 1902 and resumed his study

Figure 2.2. Robert Luther, 1868–1945.

of zinc coating under Professor Walter Nernst, the 1920 Nobel Laureate in Chemistry. Nernst was the inventor of the Nernst lamp, the only incandescent lamp to be produced in quantity as an alternative to carbon filament lamps.

For the summer semester of 1903 and through the summer semester of 1904, Goldberg was probably back in Moscow, where he graduated on May 24, 1904. "When I was a student," Goldberg later wrote, "I used all the longer vacations to acquire technical knowledge, and towards this goal I worked in electro-chemical and reprographics firms." He spent the summer of 1904 in England at the School of Photoengraving and Lithography, established by the London County Council in Bolt Court to meet the needs of the newspaper industry in nearby Fleet Street for illustrations. The Principal, A. J. Newton, had had broad industrial experience and emphasized research.

Here Goldberg established an important friendship. "I was working on photochemical problems in Leipzig and spent my vacations in London studying photoengraving. Here my boss, the late A. J. Newton, . . . introduced me to a young chap who was working with a friend [Samuel A. Sheppard] in a home laboratory on the theory of photography. He was a young graduate of London University named Dr. C.E.K. Mees. He showed me around his place and soon we were discussing our common problems." The personal friendship with Mees was deep, and their interaction on technical topics continued.

Ostwald had suggested that Goldberg develop his work on photochemical reactions into a doctoral dissertation and so, after his summer in London, Goldberg returned to Leipzig and enrolled as a student for the winter semester of 1904 and the spring semester of 1905. Robert Luther, the Sub-Director of the Institute, who had also grown up in Moscow, the son of a German lawyer working there, became Goldberg's mentor.

During his prior study at Leipzig, Goldberg had shown that the speed of a light-sensitive chemical reaction was essentially independent of temperature, and this finding had been corroborated by other studies. Now Luther pointed to an anomalous result, a photochemical reaction significantly affected by temperature, and proposed that Goldberg investigate it as a doctoral dissertation topic.

Arthur Slator, also working in Ostwald's Institute under Luther's direction, had investigated the reaction between chlorine and benzene, which produced benzene hexachloride. Using the methodology developed by Goldberg, he found that an increase of 10° Centigrade increased the reaction rate by 50 percent, a temperature coefficient of 1.5. Goldberg carefully developed a very rigorous experimental design to test this finding. He designed and built a set of shallow cylindrical vessels by cutting circular holes 60–70 mm in diameter in thick mirror glass, then cementing a thin pane of glass on one side, which would be toward the light, and a thicker pane on the other side as a backing. He drilled a thin hole in from the back at an angle for adding or removing liquids. The vessels were almost airtight, so few or no air bubbles formed. Four such vessels at a time were mounted on the side of a wheel slowly rotated by an electric motor at a controlled distance from an arc lamp. Rotation and a small, loose piece of glass rod in each vessel kept the solution well mixed.

The project became an experimenter's nightmare. The measured results were wildly inconsistent and made little sense. Sometimes it seemed as if two contradictory effects were at work. Goldberg varied everything he could think of. In case the cement was contaminating the results, he tried substituting other adhesives. Thinking that radiant heat from the arc lamp might be affecting the reactions, he inserted a heat filter, composed of two panes of glass with water in between, in front of the arc lamp. He substituted other light sources. Nothing helped. In the end, the only relationship he could sense—between the speed of the reaction and the presence of air bubbles of varying sizes in the vessel—seemed irrelevant. Then he took a closer look and found that a fully filled vessel behaved differently from an incompletely filled one. For lack of a better explanation, he undertook controlled experiments varying the size of the bubbles of air and eventually determined that the reaction between chlorine and benzene was extremely sensitive to even tiny traces of oxygen that would be present in air bubbles and that could also be leaching from the glass. Oxygen, he found, was absorbed by the chlorine and, until fully absorbed, severely slowed the chlorine's reaction with benzene. In an extreme case, if the chlorine and benzene were in a vacuum—the nearest he could get to excluding all oxygen—the reaction was completed in two minutes; but if, oxygen were added at 3-1/2 atmospheres of pressure, the same reaction would take two and a half hours. It was a very unexpected finding. Slator had not controlled for oxygen and so his anomalous result was invalid. Goldberg found that oxygen also retards chlorine reactions with some other substances and that his careful analysis of the mechanism removed the credibility of some speculative explanations of photochemical reactions that had been advanced by others.

He then presented a more sophisticated analysis of his earlier work on the photochemical reaction of chromic acid with quinine. He developed a set of equations for modeling photochemical reactions, enumerated the assumptions made, and demonstrated the validity of each assumption empirically. Results derived from these equations were then compared with experimental results, finding a close match. Finally, he showed that his theories and his experimental results were consistent with the few other published studies, as well as compatible with Ostwald's idea that photochemical reactions would become more similar to other reactions when the latter are at very high temperatures. All of this was clearly and compactly stated in 47 pages. Entitled *Beiträge zur Kinetik photochemischer Reaktionen* (Studies on the Kinetics of Photochemical Reactions), Goldberg's dissertation was approved on February 5, 1906. The part dealing with the inhibiting effect of oxygen was revised with Luther and published as a co-authored article in the *Zeitschrift für Physikalische Chemie*. A leading journal, the *Zeitschrift für wissenschaftliche Photographie,* judged Goldberg's work so important that it reprinted his dissertation in its entirety.

Goldberg's Doctor of Philosophy degree was awarded with highest honors, *summa cum laude* on April 21, 1906. The dissertation ended with an acknowledgment: "The present work was carried out in the Physical-Chemical Institute of Prof. Ostwald. It is my pleasant duty to express my deepest thanks to Sub-Director Prof. Luther for the inspiration for this work and his many suggestions."

Goldberg was also influenced by Wilhelm Wundt, a professor of philosophy who became interested in controlled experiments of physical stimuli, such as hearing and vision, in relation to the action of the mind. His studies were important because they helped to undermine the traditional separation in scientific thought since Descartes between mental processes ("reason") and physical processes ("cause"). Goldberg developed a sustained interest in the physiology of visual perception and the importance of human factors in the design of equipment.

Many years later, Goldberg wrote nostalgically:

> The years I spent in Leipzig at my alma mater belong to the most beautiful of my memories. It was an unusual time as I, a poor Russian-Jewish youth, crossed the entrance of the Physical-Chemical Institute in the quiet Linné Street for the first time. A new science was being born. Young scholars from all over the world gathered there to be introduced to the relationship between chemistry and physics by Wilhelm Ostwald and the relationship between body and soul by Wilhelm Wundt. The colloquia, in which the most famous scholars in the world participated, provided us with the guiding principles for lifelong creative work.

3

Berlin

We have conquered upon the field of battle in war; we are now conquering upon the field of battle in commerce and industry.

—Crown Prince Friedrich at the inauguration of the Museum for Industrial Art in Berlin, 1871

German Higher Education

The state policy of Russification in Tsarist Russia had disadvantaged Goldberg because he was Jewish. In contrast, he was to benefit from state policies of Imperial Germany. After major military defeats in 1806, reformers in Prussia, the large German state in the northeast, had regarded national security as depending on education and on technical expertise. After centuries of fragmentation, the many German states had been gloriously united in 1871 into a new German Empire under Prussian leadership. This new, united German state had an active policy of fostering industry, technology, technical education, and the military. German technology, German universities, and German industries were major beneficiaries. University policy was based on four principles: The university should serve the needs of state; university scholars should be free to study whatever they wanted; the state should support the universities; and students could move freely from one university to another. It was a brilliantly successful policy for the century that it lasted. By the late nineteenth century, German universities were the best in the world and a magnet for students from all over the world. In the first 14 years of Nobel prizes, Germany won 14 of the 48 awards for science, France won 11, and England 5. Russia, the Netherlands, and the United States each received 2. Nearly half of all research articles in chemistry were published in German journals.

21

Germany also had an exceptionally well-developed and effective system of technical education. One component was the development, largely in the 1820s, of a second type of university, which was called the "technical university" to distinguish it from the traditional or "classical" universities. The technical universities lacked the prestige of the traditional universities; their mission was to give the highest-possible training in architecture, engineering, chemistry, and general science, and to address the practical and educational needs of industry. At the inauguration of a new technical university in Danzig in 1904, the German Emperor expressed his support for technical universities because of their importance in the struggle among the nations for industrial supremacy. By 1907, there were 11 technical universities. Favored by the government and well funded, they were expanding rapidly. They had as few as nine students per faculty member and attracted students from many other countries.

Edwin G. Cooley, the Superintendent of Schools in Chicago, made a detailed study of technical education in Europe after he retired. In 1912, he reported admiringly on the German technical universities: "They enjoy at the present time an extraordinary prosperity and attract numerous students from other countries. No other institutions seem to have been more important in promoting the great industries of Germany. They illustrate Germany's patient toil and tenacity in seeking success in the industrial world by rational means and scientific methods. They are institutions devoted to the adaptation of science and education to the necessities of economic life."

The largest of the German technical universities was the Technical University of Berlin in Charlottenburg, which had some 2,500 students. Praised in the *Encyclopaedia Britannica* of 1911 for its "magnificent buildings erected at a cost of £100,000 ... equipped with all the apparatus for the teaching of science," it was also the best situated. Charlottenburg, a town on the river Spree, formed the western suburb of Berlin. The population and amenities of the Berlin area were expanding very rapidly. The dignified capital of Prussia, Berlin had acquired an enhanced status in 1871 as the center of government of the new German Empire. Its population had increased rapidly from 826,341 in 1871 to 2,033,900 by 1905. As in all large cities at that time, there were grim industrial areas and low-quality housing; but as the Imperial capital, it was graced with many large and impressive public buildings, palaces, churches, squares, and pleasant neighborhoods. From 1880 to 1914, Berlin was also the high-technology center of the world. In this regard, London was then a pale shadow of Berlin. In Charlottenburg, in addition to the Technical University and many flourishing industries, there was the famous royal palace, the Imperial Bureau of Standards *(Physicalisch-technische Reichsanstalt),* wide, well-laid out thoroughfares, and quiet streets with pretty villas.

In 1906, Emanuel Goldberg went to Charlottenburg to work at the Technical University as an assistant to Professor Adolf Miethe, head of the

Photochemistry Laboratory in the Faculty of Chemistry and Metallurgy. Miethe was an adventurous man with wide-ranging interests. He did pioneering work on aerial photography, color photography, the design of telephoto lenses, photography using ultraviolet light to bring out details not visible using daylight, and much else. His efforts at outdoor flash photography near Potsdam in 1887 had generated newspaper reports of lightning from an unseasonable thunderstorm. Goldberg started work in Miethe's laboratory just as a major remodeling was being completed, late in 1906. In a curriculum vitae dated 1917, he stated that he went "to work with Prof. Miethe, particularly in the areas of reprographics and the science of photography."

Photography was still largely a craft activity, but it was undergoing a rapid transition. Amateur photographers, who had been building their own cameras and mixing their own chemicals, were increasingly buying manufactured retail products instead. The photographic industry was undergoing rapid consolidation as larger firms took over numerous little workshops. There was a torrent of technical publications on new advances, such as color photography and telephoto lenses, and on new applications, such as aerial photography and photoengraving. Above all, photography was becoming "scientific" as the nature of the chemical and physical processes involved were investigated, analytically and experimentally, by researchers such as Robert Luther and Adolf Miethe. It was all part of the great advance in chemistry, chemical engineering, and physics at the turn of the century.

Photoengraving and Halftone Printing

Photography was especially important in relation to printing. Instead of engraving a printing plate by hand, an image could be transferred to a metal printing plate photographically. The surface would be coated with a light-sensitive emulsion and an image projected on to it. When the exposed emulsion was processed, the coating in areas receiving light would be developed and removed, leaving the metal plate exposed; areas not receiving light would retain the coating. If the surface was then coated with an acid, the metal would be etched away in the exposed areas, but in the dark areas, where the coating remained, the metal surface remained intact. The acid and remaining coating would then be cleaned off, and the plate retained an etched version of the image. Ink applied to the intact surface of the dark areas would transfer on to paper during printing, creating dark areas. Because the etched light areas were recessed, they would neither receive ink nor be in contact with the paper during printing.

Photoengraving is binary. It divides the printing surface into two areas, the dark areas where ink would be applied and light areas where it would not. Reproducing intermediate, gray tones ("halftones") is more difficult.

The solution adopted was to place a very fine mesh screen over the coated surface of the plate so that the projected image and the etched result would be composed of a grid of very small areas, or "picture elements." In each tiny area would be a dot, the size of which depended on the amount of light received. Printing is still black and white, but, as long as the dots are small enough, the human eye perceives shades of gray proportionate to the size of the printed dots. This effect, and the individual dots, can be easily seen in the reproduction of photographs in newspapers.

Color printing could be achieved by using one or more printing plates and colored inks. For full-color printing, three halftone plates were used with blue, red, and yellow. Any shade of any color can then be reproduced by combining these three colors in different strengths. A visually superior effect is achieved through the use of a fourth plate with black ink to strengthen the darkest areas.

Goldberg studied these processes in detail, including the nature of visual perception, and used a microscope to examine the precise effects of acid in etching the metal surface.

The Moiré Effect

When two or more plates are used, as in color printing, each plate leaves its rows of dots on the paper. However, unwanted patterns of lighter and darker zones can appear. The physicist Lord Rayleigh used the term *moiré* to describe these ripples, because they resemble, in appearance, the patterns in watered silk, also known as moiré. It is an optical phenomena resulting from the superimposition of two or more periodic patterns, such as two rows of evenly spaced dots or lines.

Imagine two rows of dots separately printed on the same piece of paper, with one row at a slight angle to the other. If a dot from the first line were superimposed *exactly* on top of a dot from the second line, they would overlap perfectly. At another place, they might be next to each other but not overlapping at all. Where they overlap completely, the area of visible ink is minimal, the area of one dot. Where two dots overlap partially, the area of visible ink is larger and so that area will appear darker to the eye. When two dots are adjacent, not overlapping, the area of visible ink is maximal, the area of two dots, and so that small region will appear even darker. In this way, the rows of dots interact with each other in an unintended way determined by an accidental relationship in the alignment of the two sets of rows and, so, a second order periodic pattern emerges. This effect can be seen in Figure 3.1, a portrait of Goldberg posing with a lathe.

Goldberg's investigation of the moiré effect is a good example of how he worked. In order to analyze the moiré effect empirically, Goldberg built an experimental device to simulate halftone printing. He made a photographic

**Figure 3.1. Moiré effect on a portrait of Goldberg posing
with a lathe.**

transparency of the rows of dots used in halftone printing to print gray and
mounted it in front of a translucent surface lit from behind. He then added
another identical photographic transparency on top of the first. The light
would now have to come through both transparencies to reach the eye. He
then rotated one transparency relative to the other to simulate the effects of
different alignments of two halftone printing plates.

Rotating one plate demonstrated that:

1. The moiré effect was largest and most noticeable when the printing plates were ever-so-slightly out of alignment;

2. The difference in the alignment of the two plates, and, therefore, of
   the lines of dots, determined the distance between the ripples of

light and dark areas: the closer the alignment, the longer the distance, the "period." With perfectly parallel alignment, the interval between ripples would in theory be infinitely long and there would be no visible interference between the two plates, and so no visible moiré effect. Unfortunately, perfectly parallel alignment cannot be achieved in practice;

3. Because perfect alignment is impractical, the best practical course of action is to maximize the *mis*alignment. This would shorten the period. Systematic moiré interference would be present, but minimally noticeable to the human eye;

4. Because in halftone printing plates the dots are aligned in rows and in columns, rotating the second plate by 90° would again produce a close-to-exact alignment. Therefore, the maximum feasible misalignment, when printing with just two plates, would be when the rows of dots on the two plates diverge at 45°, yielding the shortest periodicity and the minimal visual moiré effect. For the same reason, in the commoner case of three plates used in color printing, the maximum offset and optimal result is when the plates are offset by 30°. With a fourth plate adding black ink to accentuate dark areas, the maximum offset would be 22.5°. More generally, the optimal angle of alignment in multiple-plate halftone printing to offset each successive plate is derived by dividing 90° by the number of plates to be used.

Goldberg published some additional empirical findings in a short paper in *Deutscher Buch und Steindrucker*, a journal on printing. He showed that the mathematical principles given above should be modified in color printing because of the differential visual impact of different colors. Following the principle of maximum offset, the three color plates—blue (cyan), red (magenta), and yellow–should be set at 15°, 45°, and 75°, but the blue and the red dots appear far darker to the eye than the yellow dots. So, while the impact of a moiré interaction between the blue and the red plates is visually very disturbing *(sehr störend)*, a moiré pattern between yellow and red is little noticed by the eyes *(vom Augen wenig empfunden wird)*. In order to take this factor into account, Goldberg recommended unequal angles, allowing a larger angle between red and blue plates, and a smaller angle between the yellow and blue plates and also between the yellow and red plates. His observations led him to recommend that, for the best visual effect, the darkest plate—blue, or black, if used—should be set at 45°. He also found that the visual impact varied with the moisture content of the paper during printing. With moist paper, the inks of the dots diffuse more into the fiber of the paper. Although this does not change the moiré period, it moderates the visual impact.

Modern printing practice follows Goldberg's findings: Black or a single plate is set at 45°, blue at 15°, and red at 75°. Yellow is set vertically at 0°, which is only 15° from blue and from red. This procedure is visually better than the mathematically derived optimal solution for four plates of 90° / 4 = 22.5°.

Frederick E. Ives, who invented halftone printing using dots of variable sizes, has been credited with also being the first to discover that offsetting three halftone plates by 30° would minimize the moiré effect. Goldberg's analysis was prominently published, republished in French, and cited by subsequent writers, which implies that he had added significantly to what was already known. However that may be, his moiré analysis is very characteristic of his work. A practical problem is identified. A theoretical model is adopted, but the analysis is done pragmatically, by practical experimentation. Solutions are assessed in terms of how convenient they would be for human users. Instead of seeking to achieve unattainable perfection, he sought to diminish the disadvantages of practical solutions.

Military Officers

During the 1906–7 academic year, Miethe's institute offered a special course on photography for students in the nearby Military Technical Academy. This academy, established in 1903, was responsible for providing a four-year educational program in science and technology relevant to weaponry, engineering, and logistics for officers in all branches of the armed services. Military and civilian instructors provided classes on a wide range of basic and applied courses on science, technology, and military technical topics. The Academy was in Charlottenburg, in the Fasanenstrasse, deliberately located close to the Technical University, so that its students could also attend lectures there.

According to family tradition, the Academy had approached Miethe, requesting such a course, and Miethe obliged by assigning it to his young assistant. The class was composed of four young officers from infantry regiments. Goldberg's upper class and family military background would have helped him to relate to the young officers, and it appears to have been a very pleasant experience for all five young men. Goldberg kept a photograph of himself with the four young officers. At the end of the year, they presented him with a small silver goblet, inscribed:

> For our respected teacher, Dr. E. Goldberg, in thankful memory of our work together, 1906–1907.
> Oblt [Oberleutnant] Quickard, Infantrie Leibregiment Grossherzogin.
> Oblt [Oberleutnant] Odlé, Grenadier Regiment König Karl.

Lt [Leutnant] von Kempen, Infantrie Regiment 171.
Lt [Leutnant] Tobich, Infantrie Regiment 197.

After the end of his year at Charlottenberg, Miethe wrote a glowing testimonial:

> Herr Dr. Goldberg has been working in my laboratory for a year. I recognized within a few weeks that he is far above average as a gifted chemist with unusually broad knowledge and so I quickly assigned part of my teaching to him, since he showed himself to be outstandingly qualified in the area of photochemistry and reprographics. Goldberg performed a series of very elegant and original pieces of work in my laboratory, which clearly shows his ability to undertake his own research and, through his ideas, he repeatedly gave me evidence of his many-sided and active intellect. In the past semester G. conducted the instruction of the officers from the Military Technical Academy, particularly in the field of reprographics and, in this way, showed that he is an excellent teacher of untiring diligence, who knows how to maintain his authority over his pupils and is lively and successful in stimulating them. I consider him to be very well qualified to lead a large research institute and also to make it a fruitful teaching institution, and also, through his research, to influence the progress of photochemical and photomechanical technology.

But photochemical and photomechanical technology was not Goldberg's only interest. His doctoral dissertation contained a dedication:

Sonja Posnjak gewidmet
[Dedicated to Sonia Posniak]

4

Sophie Posniak

Ειν το παν, One the All.

—Axiom of Cleopatra the Alchemist

Early Life

"Sonja Posnjak" was the younger sister of one of Goldberg's fellow students, George Posniak, also Russian and also Jewish. *Sonja* was a diminutive for Sophie (or Sofiia). Sophie was born on August 28, 1886, which made her five years younger than Goldberg. In official documents, however, the year of birth is given as 1890 because her parents registered her birth four years late.

Little is known about Sophie's early life. Her father, Vladimir Gershonowitsch Posniak (also known as Wulf), had the status of a Merchant of the First Class of Moscow, which entitled him to live anywhere in Russia. Her mother, born Lea Sheftel, was born in Mohilew, northeast of Warsaw, in 1860, then part of Russia. They lived in Nizhnii Novgorod, some 300 miles east of Moscow, where her father owned a soap factory.

Nizhnii Novgorod—named Gorkii from 1932 to 1990 in honor of writer Maksim Gorkii, who was born there—was a provincial capital and one of the biggest industrial centers of Russia. It was an important trading center for areas farther east and Sophie spoke of some of her relatives being active in the fur trade. The Jews in Nizhnii Novgorod were relatively integrated with the Russian population. Sophie's family was proud of the rabbis in their family. Her parents attended the 2nd Zionist Congress in Basle in 1898 and had visited Palestine twice, in 1903 and 1905. In contrast, Emanuel Goldberg's father, the Colonel, had no known Zionist inclination.

29

**Figure 4.1. Sophie Posniak,
circa 1907.**

Sophie performed brilliantly in high school. Her high school certificate, dated June 1, 1903, Old Style, stated:

> This year, at the final examination of seventh-grade students, she
> showed the following knowledge in the Gymnasium course of
> study's mandatory subjects:

1) Religious Instruction		( )
2) In Russian language with		
Church Slavonic and literature	Excellent	(5)
and Composition in Russian	Good	(4)
3) In Mathematics	Excellent	(5)
4) In General and Russian Geography	Excellent	(5)
5) In Natural History	Good	(4)

Figure 4.2. Sophie Posniak and Emanuel Goldberg at the time of their engagement, circa 1907.

6) In General and Russian History	Excellent	(5)
7) In Physics	Excellent	(5)
8) In Mathematical Geography	Excellent	(5)

From all these subjects she received the overall grade 4 6/7

Apart from that, she studied proper script-writing and handiwork with good results.

Moreover, from the non-required subjects of the Gymnasium course of studies she took German, French, and Pedagogy, all with excellent results.

... based on paragraph 30 of the Regulations on women's Gymnasiums and Progymnasiums of the M[inistry] of P[eople's] E[ducation], Sofiia Pozniak has been awarded a gold medal.

The gold medal meant that she graduated top of her class. After high school, she went to Leipzig to study at the Royal Conservatory of Music. She had wide-ranging cultural interests and studied widely in addition to her principal subjects, which were music theory and composition and piano performance.

One day, her mother, visiting her in Leipzig, saw Sophie holding a bouquet of flowers and demanded to know where it had come from. Sophie said that she had found it lying on a bench, but she was not telling the truth. What Sophie's parents had not known was that, in the hostel for young women in which she lived, guests were allowed at meal times, male as well as female. Goldberg had been a dinner guest at her hostel, possibly taken by Sophie's brother George, who had also gone to Leipzig to study. In that way they had met. The bouquet of flowers was from Goldberg, but Sophie was not yet ready to tell her mother about him. (See photos of Sophie and Goldberg, Figures 4.1 and 4.2.)

Love and Warsaw

Goldberg fell in love with George's sister, Sophie, and George fell in love with Sophie's friend and cousin, Sonja Koppelmann, also known as Sara, another student in Leipzig. Sophie and Goldberg became engaged, and, on April 27, 1907 (in the Old Style Russian calendar) in Nizhnii Novgorod, Sophie and her father recorded the official declaration that she intended to marry Emanuel Goldberg, "hereditary honorary citizen of Moscow" *(Moskauer erblicher Ehrenbürger),* and that she was eligible to do so.

Sonja Koppelmann's brother, Max, had attended a wedding at which he was captivated by one of bridesmaids. He thought she looked so wonderful that he had gone straight up to her and kissed her. He explained later that, although she did not kiss him back, she did not resist him, and so he persisted, and, in time, she agreed to marry him. Sonja's sister, Sasha, meanwhile, had become engaged to Lew Jakub.

These romances resulted in four related weddings. Sonja Koppelmann married her cousin George Posniak in Berlin in February 1907. Then, in June, her brother Max married the wonderful bridesmaid, Sima Zetlin, who was also a cousin of Sonja. Her sister, Sasha Koppelmann, married Lew Jakub, and her cousin, Sophie Posniak (now also her sister-in-law), married Emanuel Goldberg.

For the convenience of the extended families, the last three weddings were held within a few days of each other in or near Warsaw. Goldberg and Sophie were married in Warsaw on June 28, 1907, in the modern Gregorian calendar (15 June in the Julian Old Style Russian calendar then used in Warsaw). The other two weddings took place a few days earlier at Wulka, a Koppelmann family home near Pulawy, southeast of Warsaw. Warsaw would have been a convenient location for people coming from Nizhnii Novgorod, Moscow, Leipzig, and Kovno, given the railroad network. Another consideration was that civil marriages in Germany were often not recognized as legal in Russia, which required religious ceremonies by state-sanctioned clergy, so Russians living in Germany commonly returned to Russia to be married. Poland had been divided between the adjacent great powers and much of it, including Warsaw, had become Russian territory.

The Koppelmann, Zetlin, and Posniak families were already connected to each other, and it is quite possible that all eight marriage partners were at least distantly related to each other. They were not to know it, but it was the last large gathering of the Koppelmanns and their relatives.

Goldberg was 25 when they married and Sophie was 21. Both families disapproved of the match. His parents thought that their son was marrying beneath himself, because she was a tradesman's daughter. Her parents thought that their daughter was marrying beneath herself. She, a wealthy manufacturer's daughter, was marrying a mere photographer, who, moreover, had shown up for the wedding without a greatcoat. (Why they thought that he should have a greatcoat in the midsummer heat of Warsaw is unknown.)

The three newly married couples traveled together by train from Warsaw to Berlin, then went their separate ways. Sophie liked the cold northern regions. One of her heroes was Fridtjof Nansen, the Norwegian zoologist, oceanographer, statesman, and recipient of the 1922 Nobel Peace Prize. Nansen had designed a ship, the *Fram*, to survive Arctic ice pressure and drift with the ice flows. In his honor, Sophie named each of her successive dogs Fram. For their honeymoon, Goldberg and Sophie went north, all the way to North Cape, in Norway, traditionally, though not quite geographically, the northernmost tip of Europe, and then a resort destination, noted for its fine cooking and good French wines.

Ouroboros

Goldberg and Sophie shared an interest in music. They went to concerts together and would play duets: She played the piano and he the flute. They also liked to buy good books, handsome editions of the classics of Western literatures, often in the original languages. Sophie, fond of the Arctic north, had a bookplate bearing a stylish picture of a polar bear (Figure 4.3).

For his bookplate, Goldberg, the chemist, reached back into the history of chemistry to the days when chemistry was alchemy and alchemy was concerned not only with the transmutation of base metals into gold but with cosmogony, with the nature and creation of the universe and the unity of the conscious mind with the deeper mysteries of life. His bookplate at this time was a crude drawing of a legless serpent biting its own tail and encircling a fragment of Greek (Figure 4.4).

In 1889, the French scholar, Marcellin Berthelot, had published a book on chemistry in ancient and medieval times. A German edition was

Figure 4.3. Sophie Posniak's bookplate.

published in Leipzig in 1909. It includes a page of diagrams and axioms about making gold by a fourth-century Egyptian alchemist named Cleopatra. The axioms are "One is the All and by it the All and in it the All and if it does not include the All it is nothing" and "The Serpent is One, he who has the Venom with compositions." In it one recognizes the source of Goldberg's bookplate serpent. It is a photographic reproduction, from an eleventh-century manuscript, of one of the diagrams of the alchemist Cleopatra, showing the serpent Ouroboros encircling the Greek axiom Ειν το παν, *Hein to Pan,* "One the All."

Serpents, snakes, and dragons occur repeatedly in the creation myths of the ancient Near Eastern civilizations, playing a role in the creation of the universe out of the primordial chaos, and, sometimes, holding the universe in its place. The primeval serpent holding its tail in its mouth is found especially in Egyptian sources and was a favored emblem of continuity.

Figure 4.4. Early bookplate of Emanuel Goldberg.

The juxtaposition of the tail and the mouth signified that the end is at the beginning and the beginning is at the end, thus denoting change, continuity, and eternity. It symbolized all cyclic systems: unity, multiplicity, and the return to unity; birth, growth, decrease, death; and the duality of the individual and the cosmos. The serpent Ouroboros, literally "tail-eating," became an important symbol among Gnostics and was taken up by alchemists as symbolizing their work. Goldberg would also have known that snakes seizing hold of each other's tails had also advanced modern chemistry when, in 1865, Friedrich Kekulé had had a vision of tail-biting snakes that led him to formulate his theory of the benzene rings.

By 1911, Goldberg had had his Ouroboros bookplate redrawn with a vaguely Oriental appearance, now with legs and without the axiom (Figure 4.5).

Figure 4.5. Later bookplate of Emanuel Goldberg.

Why he chose Ouroboros is not known. One speculation is that he saw Ouroboros as symbol of the importance of an orderly, responsible social structure, for if Ouroboros were ever to abandon its role and release its tail, the universe would destroyed, the creation would be undone, and all order would dissolve back in to dreadful, primordial chaos.

5

Graphics

> *A well-known scholar with a most lively researcher's spirit.*
>
> —J. Zeitler, 1914

Goldberg's reputation grew through a stream of published research. He authored some 70 publications in the years 1906 through 1917, only two of them co-authored. Many covered the same material, being summaries, popular explanations, or versions translated into English or French. Nevertheless, they covered a broad front and constituted a prodigious output by any standard. Hard work, his analytical powers, his skills as a craftsman, his interest in solving practical problems, and his flair for concise explanation found a series of opportunities in the evolving and rather unsystematized state-of-the-art of imaging techniques.

Graphics and Industrial Design

Nineteenth-century European art and architecture were largely dominated by historicism, the use of styles copied or derived from the past, especially Greek and Roman. Their influence can be seen in so much of the monumental civic architecture of museums, courthouses, and government buildings of the time. However, by the end of the century, the dramatic new developments in science and engineering were matched by comparably dramatic developments in the arts. The Impressionists, in particular, inspired a series of fresh movements in painting.

In Britain, the Arts and Crafts movement led by William Blake was a turning away from industrial practices and toward personal craftsmanship and medieval themes. It was followed, internationally, by a decorative style known as Art Nouveau that flourished from 1890 to 1910. German Art Nouveau was generally referred to as *Jugendstil*, a name derived from a periodical started in Munich in 1896 called *Jugend*, meaning "Youth," which made lavish use of Art Nouveau designs. Instead of reacting against industry, Jugendstil combined artistic sensibilities with the needs of industry for designs that were functional. It emphasized graceful flowing lines, often featuring plants and female forms, and had several sources, including Japanese art and psychoanalysis. Viennese Jugendstil was significantly inspired by Freud's discovery of the subconscious. The flowing forms were supposed to express subconscious erotic underpinnings.

Art Nouveau influenced all of the design arts: architecture, furniture, product design, fashion, and graphics. It affected all aspects of the man-made environment: posters, packages, and advertisements; teapots, dishes, and spoons; chairs, doorframes, and staircases; factories, subway entrances, and houses. Art Nouveau was a pivotal transition from nineteenth-century historicism to twentieth-century modernism, and constituted a fundamental change in design philosophy. It moved away from mere decoration to the pursuit of unity in decoration, structure, and purpose. Form should follow function. Efficiency and effectiveness were sought, as well as elegance.

Graphic Arts Education

Specialized vocational schools for secondary and continuing education were a significant component of the German system of technical education. By 1900, there were 16 large schools of graphic arts in Germany, where, as elsewhere, schools concerned with art trades had been stimulated by the great International Exhibition of 1851 in London.

In vocational education, the competition and tension between the traditional, small-scale, craft workers and the new, mechanized, large-scale, mass-production were moderated in two ways. Some educators believed some of the traditional skills would and should be replaced by modern mechanized methods. At the same time, leading industrialists valued the role that some skilled craftsmen still played in the factories. The largest of the graphic arts trade schools was the Royal Academy in Munich, with more than 500 students. The second largest, with more than 400 students, was in Leipzig, where, in 1764, the Court Painter of Saxony, Adam Friedrich Oeser, had established an Academy of Drawing, Painting, and Architecture *(Zeichnungs-, Malerei-, und Architektur Akademie)* and served as its director until his death in 1799.

Most of the graphic arts trade schools had courses for engravers, etchers, lithographers, book designers, and bookbinding technicians, often with workshops where the students could gain supervised experience. For centuries, Leipzig had been the major international center of the book trade and famous for the Leipzig Book Fairs *(Leipziger Buchmesse)*. The desire to bring art and industry together was strong, so the Leipzig academy for graphic arts had developed a special interest in the techniques of book production. Ludwig Nieper, director from 1871 to1900, added printing to the curriculum and established workshops for wood engraving, for lithography, and for etching. In 1883, a Department of Photography was established, and, in 1893, a class in Reprographics, concerned largely with making book illustrations, was added.

The idea was that bookmaking needed to mature as an industry and that the Leipzig academy should assist in this process, so a major redirection was undertaken. The programs in architecture, monumental painting, and sculpture were transferred to the art school in Dresden, and, in 1900, the Leipzig academy was renamed to reflect its new direction, becoming the Royal Academy of Graphic Arts and Bookcraft *(Königliche Akademie für graphische Künste und Buchgewerbe)*. A correspondingly revised curriculum was implemented in 1903. This combination of graphic arts and book technology, perhaps unique to Leipzig, flourished under Max Seliger, the director from 1901 to 1920. It attracted students from all over Germany and abroad.

The Year 1907

A notable development in 1907 occurred when the German General Electric Company *(Allgemeine Elektrizitäts-Gesellschaft, or AEG)* in Berlin, hired an expert in design arts, Peter Behrens, to take charge of all aspects of AEG's visual image: architecture, graphics, and industrial design. He is considered to be the first industrial designer.

Also in 1907, Behrens, with Hermann Muthesius and others, founded an influential association, the Deutscher Werkbund. Vigorously concerned with elevating standards of design and of public taste, the Werkbund attracted architects, artists, industrialists, public officials, educators, and critics to its ranks. Recognizing the need for standardization and the value of machines, simplicity and exactness were welcomed. The Werkbund sought to forge a unity of artists and designers with industry in order to elevate the functional and aesthetic qualities of mass production, particularly of low-cost consumer products.

The year 1907 was also significant because in March of that year, Professor Georg Aarland, head of the Department of Photography in the Leipzig academy, died, and, on September 15, Goldberg took up his appointment as Aarland's successor. It might seem odd that Goldberg, who had already started a scientific career, would have left the Technical University of Berlin to teach photography in a graphic arts trade school in Leipzig, but reasons are not hard to imagine. Leipzig was a beautiful old city with a long tradition of music and culture, more so than Berlin. Sophie and he could return to a circle of friends. In Berlin, he was merely an assistant in Miethe's institute; in Leipzig, he would be employed as a teacher and as head of a department. Not only that, but reprographics *(Reproduktionstechnik)* was pivotal to the new strategic development of the academy.

Reprographics combined the old tradition of artistic skill with the modern application of science to industry. It was an exciting and important area of innovation in the book trade and very much part of the emerging high technology of that time. Its key areas of development, notably color photography, halftone printing, and photoengraving, drew directly on Goldberg's specialties, photography and photochemistry. At that time, scientific photography was as important for graphics as digital techniques are now, and director Seliger would have seen the importance of reprographics for achieving the revised mission of the academy. It was a promising area in which science could be used to achieve practical progress in the book industry, and to increase the prestige of the Leipzig academy. He needed someone with a scientific background who would understand the underlying technologies of chemistry and optics, and Goldberg was appointed.

The academy had programs for different categories of students. In the evening courses, the students were usually 17 to 19 years old. Day students had a broader age range, from 17 to 25. Many were apprentices who came in the evening or had release time during the day. The academy's classes were intended to complement what they learned in the workplace. This alignment of teaching with practice would have appealed to Goldberg.

The academy had occupied a fine new building, constructed from 1887 to 1890 (Figure 5.1).

It was part of a substantial cluster of new cultural and educational buildings erected just outside the old inner city. The streets had been named after musicians, and the area came to be called the Music Quarter. The academy occupied the northern half of a small block, back to back with the new university library, and a large museum and a music auditorium stood nearby. The building has an imposing facade on the Wachtlerstrasse, facing north, and, inside, three wings form two courtyards in the shape of the letter E. Large windows on the top floor admit suitable northern light into studios. The building's exterior is of brick, generously framed with stone around the windows, doors, and edges, and its architect achieved a lightness of style and an uplifting mood that contrasts favorably with the ponderous, historicist architecture of its neighbors. Looking at it from across the Wachtlerstrasse, one can well imagine that this inviting building would have been part of the attraction for Goldberg.

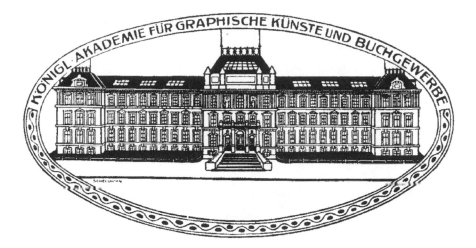

Figure 5.1. Academy for Graphic Arts and Bookcraft, Leipzig.

Goldberg and Sophie, shown in Figure 5.2, made their home in a pretty semidetached villa, Südstrasse 10, in Oetzsch bei Leipzig, then a village on the southern fringe of the city, now part of Markkleeberg, a suburb. It had a deep garden leading down to a railroad line, and a station was conveniently nearby.

Professor Goldberg

Goldberg was unusual. Not only was academic talent accompanied by skill as a craftsman, but he evidently had a flair as a teacher. Here in this beautiful building, in a vibrant city that he liked, he would have the opportunity and the resources to examine, through research, experiment, and instruction, what he was most interested in: the challenges of scientific applied photography. As a department head under the able director Max Seliger, he would have a degree of independence and responsibility that he would never have had as an assistant in another professor's institute. It must have been a pleasing and exciting challenge for the young Goldberg, who took up his position at the academy a few days after his 26th birthday. His impact was immediate. A history of photography in the academy, written more than 80 years later, states, "His immense writing and teaching talent immediately gave the Leipzig Academy prestige in the field of the reprographics: within a year student enrollment in his laboratory classes increased to four times Aarland's average." His courses included: "Chemistry and Physics," "Survey of Reproduction Techniques,"

Figure 5.2. Emanuel and Sophie Goldberg, circa 1909.

"Photography for Photographic Printing Plates for Reprographics Technicians," and "Production of Photographic Printing Plates for Reprographics Technicians." He was active and visible on many fronts, and, for example, helped found the Deutsche Buchgewerbekünstler (German Association of Book Artists).

A surviving letter, dated October 23, 1911, reveals a job offer to work in England with C.E.K. Mees, whom he had met when studying engraving in London in the summer of 1904. Mees had completed his Doctor of Science degree at University College London, working on photographic chemistry and color photography under Sir William Ramsay. Mees had intended to become a high school science teacher, but Ramsay persuaded him that in Britain the need for qualified scientists in industrial research was even greater than in high schools. But Mees was unsuccessful in finding employment in industrial research. In 1906, he went to visit a friend, S.H. Wratten, the manager of Wratten and Wainwright, a small firm in Croydon owned by Wratten's father, which manufactured dry photographic plates. Instead of offering Mees a job, the Wrattens proposed that the firm be incorporated and that, for a small sum, Mees become a partner and joint managing director. The firm needed to develop new products, especially in color photography and filters, for which Mees had just the right kind of expertise. Mees accepted the offer. New products were developed and by 1911, business had increased fourfold. Mees then asked Goldberg to join him in building up Wratten and Wainwright.

Mees's offer apparently induced the academy to make Goldberg a counteroffer in order to keep him: a significant raise, promotion to the rank of Professor effective October 1, 1911, and additional responsibilities. Goldberg decided to stay. Mees responded graciously:

My dear Goldberg,

...I am, of course, sorry for our sake, and especially for my own sake, that you will not be able to come to us, but on the other hand I am delighted that your position is improved so much that you feel you should stay in Leipzig. I hope that the advantages of position and remuneration which Leipzig can offer will prove to your entire satisfaction, and that you may be enabled to do better work in the cause of photo-chemistry there then you could with us.

Should at any time in the future our financial position be such that we could afford to make an offer commensurate with the position which you will then have obtained, and should you at that time feel that the burden of official life was heavy and that you would prefer a change, we may perhaps be able to re-open the subject. In the meantime, I shall, of course, be delighted to have you here for a part of your vacation, and will look forward eagerly to the possibility of doing some research work with you, and of looking into some of those problems in which we have so much in common.

Evidently the offer and counteroffer was not a secret. The November 22, 1911, issue of the trade journal *Die Photographische Industrie* reported that Goldberg had been promoted to Professor, adding: "The news that recently spread in photographic circles, that the researcher and teacher, also well-known to our readers as a contributor to our newsletter, wanted to leave his position, must thus become groundless, which we report with pleasure."

During 1911–12, a new Reprographics Department *(Reproduktion-stechnische Abteilung)* was established under Goldberg; and in 1913–14, the academy took over the west wing of the building, previously occupied by the Royal School of Building *(Königliche Bauschule)*. A large part of the newly acquired space was assigned to Goldberg's new Reprographics Department, and he showed ingenuity in expanding its resources. The academy's report for 1908–10 had reported that in Goldberg's department alone new equipment valued at 10,613 Marks had been added, bringing the total value of that department's equipment up to 48,833 Marks. In contrast, the Department of Nature Photography had acquired a mere 1,674 Marks worth.

In the autumn of 1913, Goldberg asked the academy to buy a lathe. It was an unusual request for an instructor in graphic arts, and there was no provision in the academy's budget for such equipment. There was, however, funding for furniture, so Goldberg shortened the German word for a lathe, *Drehbank* (literally a "turning bench") to *Bank* (bench) and submitted it as a request for an item of furniture. However, he wanted a particularly high-quality lathe from a manufacturer called Lorch, Schmidt & Co., and the price was too high. In the end, he was allowed to spend 1,000 Marks on the lathe itself, and he himself spent "a few hundred" *(einige Hunderte)* Marks on the accessories needed to use it. It may be the machine in Figure 3.1.

Goldberg's successful acquisition of equipment caused a stir in 1911, when an anonymous allegation was published that the academy's annual report was dishonest. It claimed that the amount of equipment reported had been exaggerated and that the academy's budget was insufficient for acquiring so much equipment. The anonymous complaint was traced to G. H. Emmerich, director of the rival academy in Munich. With pride, Director Seliger published a statement confirming that his annual report was correct and noting that much of the equipment had been donated by industry for Goldberg's use.

Dr. Mees Again

Early in 1912, Mees had arranged to visit Goldberg in Leipzig, but instead sent a telegram, followed by a letter, explaining that he had had to cancel his visit because "some very important business negotiations have suddenly arisen and it is imperative that I should remain in England."

George Eastman, the founder of Kodak, had invited Mees to move to Rochester, New York, to establish and direct a Kodak research laboratory. It was to be an unprecedented center for applied photographic research and one of the first major industrial research and development laboratories. Mees declined the invitation, explaining that the Wrattens, father and son, had been so generous to him that he felt an obligation to remain with Wratten and Wainwright. They still needed him.

George Eastman soon wrote to one of his managers: "Since I returned to London I have made a deal to buy out Wratten and Wainwright. I did it in order to secure the services of Dr. Kenneth Mees, who is to come to Rochester the latter part of this year to take charge of our research laboratory, which is to be worked there now on a bigger scale." When Goldberg heard this exciting news from Mees on February 4, 1912, he wrote back immediately:

Dear Dr. Mees!

Your letter today hit me like a "bolt from the blue." I would have expected anything except the news that Wratten & Wainwright were ending their existence as an independent firm and that you would be leaving

England to seek a new home in America. Because you write that your position will be "remunerative and satisfactory," I must sincerely congratulate you, although I certainly cannot hide from you the fact that your news is truly distressing to those who are still fond of our Europe. I would like to see Callier's face when he receives your news. On the other hand, I personally envy you, because America is my old dream, and you should still be able to remember how I have always defended America's merits against you. If you ever need an assistant there, please think of me. Perhaps there will be a possibility later on to work together. The one who I really feel sorry for is Mr. Newton, who has certainly left Bolt Court in order to help *you*. I would be very interested to hear when you plan to leave England. With best wishes [to you and] also to Mrs. Mees,

Yours, E. Goldberg

Mees must have responded by inviting Goldberg to come to America with him, because on March 3, Goldberg wrote again to Mees.

Dear Dr. Mees!

Unfortunately I must write today that I cannot go with you now to Rochester. My wife's parents do not want to hear anything about these plans, so now my wife is also opposed. I hope that you will find a much better colleague than I could have been, but nevertheless want to express my hope that if not now, perhaps in future years, we will be able to work together sometime. I would appreciate it very much if you would write me sometimes how it is going for you in America. In the meantime, I wish you a happy trip and send my regards to your wife.

With best wishes

[signed E. Goldberg]

Goldberg's explanation was probably a diplomatic excuse. It is unlikely that he cared much what Sophie's parents thought, least of all about a major career decision. Goldberg would have understood the potential of the new lab. On the other hand, he and Sophie had developed a strong attachment to Germany as their adopted homeland, he already had a wonderful situation, and they were happy where they were. He admired American ways, but, in 1912, viewed from the rich cultural milieu of Leipzig, Rochester probably seemed rather bleak as a place to live. Mees responded politely:

My dear Dr. Goldberg,

I am much obliged for your letter of the 3rd. While, of course, I am very sorry that you cannot come to America, I am not surprised to hear from you to that effect, because I realised when I was in Leipzig that it was very probable that you would not be able to come. Such a step is a grave one and there are always many considerations which must be dealt with before it can be taken and while I believe that we should work happily together and that in many ways it would be even advantageous for you to go to Rochester, at the same time I should not wish you to come feeling any doubt about the matter and under the circumstances I think that you are doing right not to come.

I shall have to make my staff there fresh from beginning to end and I am afraid that for some time publications will not only be small in quantity but poor in quality, but I must look forward to the time when I shall again have succeeded in training a satisfactory staff and shall be able to do work of the standard which you and I always desire to retain.

With kind regards to your wife and yourself,

I remain,

Yours very sincerely

[Mees]

Goldberg would have been well aware that if he had accepted Mees's invitation the previous year to join him in London in 1911, he would most likely have been in the group assembled by Mees to build the Kodak Research Laboratory. Years later, Goldberg said, "Looking back I sometimes regret not having followed them when a call for collaboration came from London."

Exhibitions

In addition to his teaching and research, Goldberg was also active in the design and creation of instructional exhibits, well before radio, movies, and television developed as educational media. In 1909, an International Photographic Exhibition was organized in Dresden in conjunction with a large international congress on photography. The exhibition, open from May through October, included a special section "for instruction and entertainment." It was a series of educational devices that the public could use by themselves. The idea was to demonstrate visually, as far as possible, the fundamentals of photographic optics, the principle of color reproduction, the photographic process, and related topics. Those primarily responsible were Goldberg, Dr. Scheffer of Carl Zeiss, Jena, and the Institute for Scientific Photography at the Technical University in Dresden, which was now under the leadership of Goldberg's dissertation director, Robert Luther, who had moved there from Ostwald's Institute in Leipzig the previous year.

A set of nearly 50 educational exhibits was described in the official catalogue as " 'Lessons on vision and color as the foundations of photography.' A collection of devices for doing your own experiments in field of optics and color theory, produced by students... under the direction of Dr. E. Goldberg." The ingenuity and effectiveness of the exhibits attracted international attention. "Perhaps the most eloquent testimony to the cleverness of Dr. Goldberg and his students at the Leipsic School of Graphic Art, where the models were made," concluded an admiring account in the *British Journal of Photography,* "was the interest with which ladies and children were seen to make the tour of the cabinets." The chairman of the organizing committee wrote to Goldberg to inform him of the deep regret of the Prize Awarding Committee *(Preisrichter-Kollegium)* that the committee was unable to confer on him the appropriate Grand Prize for Outstanding Performance in the area of the teaching of "Vision and Color as the Foundations of Photography," because he was ineligible on bureaucratic grounds *(geschäftsordnungsmässigen Gründen).* They conferred on him instead an extraordinary certificate of appreciation. (See Figure 5.3.)

Under the highest protection of his Majesty King Friedrich August of Sachsen. International photographic exhibition Dresden. MCMX.
Herewith it is declared that the panel of judges in the plenary session of September 16, 1909 has expressed its regret that it is not possible to bestow the proper award for outstanding performance in the art of scientific photography to Herr Dr. Emanuel Goldberg, Leipzig Oetzsch, due to administrative policies. The Exhibitions Directorship.

The explanation is that in the regulations of the competition, it had been specified that exhibits submitted by academic departments of photography were ineligible for prizes, and Goldberg's department counted as a department of photography.

Goldberg also received and retained a letter of praise from Oskar von Miller, the enterprising founding director of the Deutsches Museum in Munich, the most important technology museum in the world at that time: "[Having] returned to Munich, I do not want to neglect to express again my joy that I was able to admire your exemplary organized demonstration of the phenomenon of various color theories." Miller sought help for the Deutsches Museum. Goldberg sent some material to him and, in 1912, tactfully declined a request from Miller to design a planetarium for the Deutsches Museum, modestly declaring that it was outside his expertise.

Goldberg published numerous guides to, and reports on, exhibits. Already at the International Exposition of 1910 in Brussels, he was appointed a judge for the section on Photography and Reprographics. He also contributed to exhibits in Turin, Munich, and, especially, the huge

**Figure 5.3. Certificate expressing regret that
Goldberg was ineligible for an award.**

International Book Trade and Graphics Exhibition "Bugra," *(Internationale
Ausstellung für Buchgewerbe und Graphik)* on a hundred-acre site in
Leipzig from May to October 1914.

Many years later Goldberg spoke of founding a museum but what happened is not clear. The archives of the academy contain an outline for a
proposed permanent teaching museum of reprographics *(Vorläufiges
Program eines technisch-lehrenden Museums für die Reproduktionstechnik).*
Undated and unsigned, it was probably an initiative by Goldberg around
1913, but nothing seems to have resulted. In 1915, *Photographische
Rundschau,* the photographic trade magazine, announced that a museum of

photography was to be established in Leipzig: "As is known, Prof. Dr. E. Goldberg, both in Dresden in 1909 and also in last year's [Bugra] exhibition in Leipzig, organized a most remarkable collection of objects in the areas of scientific and technical photography.... These objects will now form the foundation for the establishment of a photographic museum. Prof. Goldberg is certainly a qualified person to set such an undertaking into action and to lead it with success." The *Deutsches Buchverein* (the German Book Union), based in Leipzig, greatly increased its collection, known as the German Museum for the Book Industry and Writing *(Deutsches Buchgewerbe- und Schriftmuseum),* at this time, acquiring almost all of the "technical-teaching materials" from the 1914 Leipzig Bugra exhibition. Goldberg had close ties to the Deutsches Buchverein, and it is likely that he contributed his materials to this expansion of the museum, which became open to the public on May 1, 1915.

The Deutsches Buchverein also founded a training program for librarians and museum staff, the *Deutsche Bibliotekar- und Museumsbeamten-Schule,* with Goldberg as one of the instructors. In the school's first semester, starting November 1, 1915, Goldberg taught a course on Monday evenings entitled "Photography, with a Practical Introduction to Taking Photographs" *(Photographie mit praktischer Einführung in das Photographieren).* The other four courses offered were: "The Care of Public Art, Collecting and the Duties of Art Museums and Industrial Museums," "The History of the Book," "The History of Writing," and "Introduction to German and Foreign Literature of the Past Decade from the Point of View of the Public Library Director."

Progress under wartime conditions seems to have been limited. On March 3, 1917, a new organization was formed, the German Association for the Book and Writing *(Deutsches Verein für Buchwesen und Schrifttum),* specifically to organize a major museum and educational program out of what was left of the 1914 Bugra exhibits. Despite the wartime difficulties, a new German Museum of Culture *(Deutsche Kulturmuseum)* was opened on October 12, 1917. Goldberg was a member of its Technical Committee. Scarcity of resources during the war impeded the plan for a separate museum of photography, and, after the war, the museum lacked the resources to sustain an expanded scope. It still exists today as the German Book and Writing Museum *(Deutsches Buch- und Schriftmuseum),* part of the Deutsche Bibliothek, the German national library. The Leipzig Bugra exhibits of 1914, including, presumably, those made by Goldberg and his students, were displayed again in 1932 at the German and First International Photographic Exhibition held in Leipzig. Unfortunately, the World War II bombing of Leipzig destroyed much of the museum's collections and the records that could have documented Goldberg's role.

Progress

Goldberg was prodigiously active from 1906 onward. In addition to his research, his teaching, and his involvement in didactic exhibits, he wrote extensively and authoritatively across the entire field of reprographics: reviews of new developments, articles on specialized topics, and popular introductions providing a technical overview for a wide audience. In 1908, he published *Farbenphotographie und Farbendruck* ("Color Photography and Color Printing") and, in 1912, *Die Grundlagen der Reproduktionstechnik: In gemeindverständlicher Darstellung* ("The Foundations of Reprographics: An Easy to Understand Description"). In 1910, he contributed a chapter on photomechanical processes for illustrations to a luxury volume on "the modern book," illustrating his text with more than 30 plates provided by leading printers showing the very finest examples of different processes.

The academy also flourished. In 1913, Seliger tried to persuade the government of Saxony to fund a Research Institute for Graphics and Book Arts *(Versuchsanstalt für die graphischen Künste und Buchgewerbe)* with two divisions: A Department for Graphic Arts, including copperplate engraving, woodcuts, lithography, and bookbinding *(Abteilung für Kupferstich und verwandte Künste, Holzschitt, Lithographie, Buchbinderei)* under the leadership of Dr. Böttger, Professor of Chemistry at the Leipzig University; and a Department of Photography and Reprographics, including microphotography and spectrophotography *(Abteilung für Photographie und Reproduktionstechnik [einschliesslich Mikrophotographie, Spektrophotographie])* under the leadership of Goldberg. Seliger argued, without success, that such an institute was necessary if Saxony was to sustain technical leadership within Germany against competition from Bavaria; more specifically, Leipzig's status was threatened by Emmerich's Teaching and Research Institute for Photography and Chemigraphy *(Lehr- und Versuchsanstalt für Photographie und Chemigraphie)* in Munich.

The 150th anniversary of the academy's founding was celebrated vigorously in March 1914. The students produced the first issue of a new magazine, *Minerva,* to appear "only every 150 years." It included a quiz: "Who's who?" with cartoon portraits of six faculty members, including, bottom right, Professor Goldberg (Figure 5.4).

Another celebratory production was a book about the faculty printed in an avant-garde type font, Steiner-Prag-Schrift, designed by faculty member Hugo Steiner-Prag. It contains a fulsome account of Professor Goldberg as "a notable scholar with a most lively enthusiasm for research" *("ein namhafter Gelehrter von lebendigsten Forschergeist").*

In 1914, as a supplement to its formal journal, the *Archiv für Buchgewerbe,* the academy launched a magazine, *Mitteilungen,* edited

Wer Ist's?

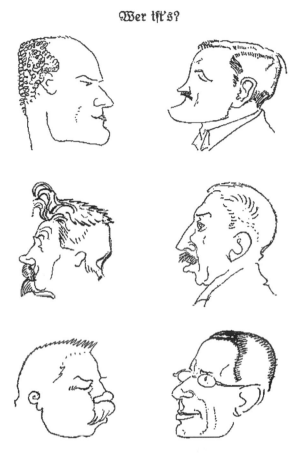

Figure 5.4. Wer Ist's? Cartoon of academy
instructors. Goldberg is at bottom right. Continuing
clockwise: Prof. Hermann Delitsch; Prof. Paul
Horst-Schulze; Prof. Walter Tiemann, later Director,
1920–1941; Hans Dannhorn (?); Prof. Fritz Rentsch.

jointly by Goldberg and a colleague, Dr. M. Bernatt. It was among the first
publications to adopt the new "World Format" *(Weltformat)* standard paper
size proposed by Wilhelm Ostwald. Because efficient systems require
standards and most documents were on paper, Ostwald had proposed a
system of standard paper sizes based on two principles: use of a consistent,
rectangular format, and making each size double the surface area of the
next smaller size. Ostwald used a width to height ratio of $1 : \sqrt{2}$, approximately $10 : 14$. The $1 : \sqrt{2}$ ratio has the property that, when folded in half,

the outline of the smaller, folded paper also has a $1 : \sqrt{2}$ ratio. And, after examining the page sizes of existing publications, he recommended a series of paper sizes. Goldberg used Ostwald's World Format size VIII, 16 cm × 22.6 cm, for the *Mitteilungen*. After six issues, publication was discontinued, a victim of the exigencies of World War I, but Ostwald's $1 : \sqrt{2}$ World Format design eventually became the basis of the present-day international standard paper sizes (A4, etc.).

6

The Goldberg Wedge

The device universally known under the name of "GOLDBERG wedge."

—Emanuel Goldberg, 1926

The Characteristic Curve

Photographs are created by the effect of light on light-sensitive material. Goldberg explored, systematically and persistently, the nature of the photographic image. Early in his research, he decided that a complete theory of image reproduction had to include both the reproduction of tones, the accurate replication of shades of light and dark, which he called "details of brightness" *(Helligkeitsdetails)*, and image resolution, the clear and exact reproduction of points, edges, and lines, which he called "details of sharpness" *(Schärfendetail)* or the "rendering of details" *(Detailwiedergabe)*. There was also the design and manufacture of cameras and other equipment capable of supporting high-performance image-making. He worked on all of these issues and, in addition to reporting his research, he also wrote about photography for a general audience.

Tone reproduction is concerned with the varying degrees of light and dark, of brightness and shade, that occur in between the extremes of black and white. The central technical concern is with the nature of the darkening of a light-sensitive material when exposed to light. To which wavelengths is it sensitive? How little exposure to light results in a perceptible change? How much light will saturate the light-absorbing capacity? These questions are aspects of two central technical problems: how light-sensitive materials change with increased exposure to light; and how the darkening should be measured.

As the film becomes darker, it becomes more opaque, and less light travels through it. So, one can place darkened film in front of a light and observe how much of the light is blocked ("absorbed") or how much is transmitted through to the other side. The proportion of light blocked is known as the Opacity of the film. A logarithmic scale of Opacity is used, and called Density, rather than a percentage, because a logarithmic scale corresponds better than a linear scale to both the behavior of films and the physiology of visual perception.

How any particular film responds to increasing exposure to light can be shown by plotting the increase in its Density relative to increased exposure to light. On a standard graph of photographic sensitivity, Density is the measure on the vertical axis, and exposure to light on the horizontal axis, also using a logarithmic scale. So, for example, exposure to an illumination of 200 Lux (a standard measure of light) for one-tenth of a second would be recorded as the logarithm of $200 \times 0.1 = \text{Log } 20 = 1.3$. This plotted line is known as the "Characteristic Curve" of the film, or as the "H & D Curve," from the names of the pioneering British researchers Ferdinand Hurter and Vero C. Driffield. Because this curve describes how the film reacts to light, knowing the Characteristic Curve of a light-sensitive material is fundamental for reliable photography. Figure 6.1 shows a typical Characteristic Curve. Conventionally, the underexposed low end of the Characteristic Curve is called the "toe," and the high, overexposed end is the "shoulder."

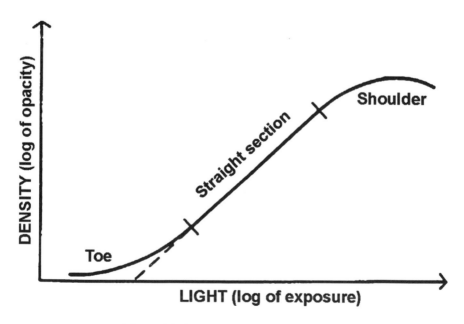

Figure 6.1. A typical Characteristic Curve.

Unfortunately, determining the Characteristic Curve for light-sensitive material was a difficult, delicate, and tedious task. Portions of the film had to be subjected to numerous exposures at different intensities of light, under closely controlled conditions, and then developed and fixed, also under closely controlled conditions, so that the effect of each different level of light could be established precisely. The shape of the Characteristic Curve could then be plotted from these results, but the fact that film sensitivity follows an S-shaped curve, not a simple straight line, greatly increases the complexity of the task. In August 1910, Goldberg announced that he had invented two devices to make this measurement much less difficult and much less expensive.

Every few years, the International Union for Photography organized an international congress: Paris in 1889, Brussels in 1891, Paris again in 1900, and Liège in 1904. (The Dresden Congress in 1909 at which Goldberg's exhibits had attracted attention was separate from this series.) In 1910, an international exposition was held in Brussels and numerous scholarly and scientific societies, including the International Union for Photography, held their meetings in Brussels in conjunction with it. Goldberg and Sophie went to Brussels for the exposition and for the Fifth International Congress of Photography, at which he presented papers on two related inventions that brought him international acclaim: the Goldberg Wedge and the Densograph.

The Goldberg Wedge

Measurement of the sensitivity of emulsions to light, sensitometry, depends on an ability to expose an emulsion to varying amounts of light in a carefully controlled way. Varying the amount of light by increasing the intensity of a light source, however, ordinarily increases the temperature of the source, which is unsatisfactory because it changes the color of the light. A better way to vary exposure to light is to use a stable light source and to insert a filter to reduce the amount of light reaching the emulsion. Controlled experiments require a graduated filter, one which could vary systematically the amount of light transmitted, from none being blocked to all being blocked. There were two kinds of graduated filter: a "step filter" would have a series of different degrees of opacity; and a wedge-shaped filter with flat faces providing a continuous gradient from clear to opaque. The intensity of the light transmitted decreases exponentially as the wedge thickness increases, which is important because a 1 : 1,000 range of intensity, a range quite likely to be encountered in outdoor photography, can be accommodated. A scale of this kind matches human physiological perceptions in which exponential increases of light, sound, and distance are perceived as linear differences.

Graduated filters can be used both for photometry and for sensitometry. Photometry measures the amount of light passing through, or reflected by, any medium. The amount of light that passes through the medium is measured by comparing it with the amount passing through different thicknesses of a filter. Sensitometry measures the effects of different light exposures on a light-sensitive emulsion, and a wedge filter placed between a light source and the emulsion can provide the requisite range of light intensities. A filter, when used for this purpose, needs to be optically neutral, meaning that it blocks evenly and equally light of all colors (all wavelengths) to which the film being tested is sensitive. At the congress, Goldberg presented a simple technique for making relatively inexpensive neutral wedge filters.

The idea of using a neutral wedge filter was not new. For example, the 1911 *Encyclopaedia Britannica* describes a wedge photometer "constructed on the principle that the absorption of light in passing through a uniform medium depends, *caeteris paribus,* upon the thickness. On this principle a thin wedge is constructed of homogeneous and nearly neutral-tinted glass." Glass wedges, however, were expensive, fragile, and not really neutral. Further, as glass is brittle, the thin end of a glass wedge could be not really thin, and the thickness range between the thin end and the thick end was much too small to generate the 1 to 1,000 range in Density required for general photography. Goldberg's achievement was to develop a reliable technique for making inexpensive, neutral wedges of gelatin instead of glass.

There were both advantages and problems in making gelatin wedges. Solid gelatin flakes were dissolved in water to make a solution to which ink or other light-blocking material could be added. As the gelatin dries, it shrinks substantially, to about the thickness of a sheet of paper at the thick end, resulting in wedges that were accurate and practically flat. However, gelatin adheres tenaciously to the sides of a mold, making usable gelatin wedges difficult to produce. Unless the gelatin happens to adhere to only one side of the mold and separates from the other, it does not dry and shrink evenly. So the principal technical challenge was to find a releasing agent that would release the gelatin, once set, from one side of the glass mold, or from both.

Goldberg had a highly restricted diet, with minimal fat and oil. He ate roast potatoes and chicken, but no salads or uncooked vegetables. He ordinarily had two eggs for breakfast, and he had noticed that the eggshell and the thin membrane enclosing the egg could be removed cleanly from the white part of a boiled egg. This observation led him to experiment with the use of egg white as a releasing agent. Egg white had already been used extensively to coat photographic paper and to make "albumen" emulsions in which light-sensitive particles were suspended. Dresden was, in fact, the world center for manufacturing albumen photographic products; in 1888, one factory alone used the whites of more than six million eggs.

After years of experimenting, Goldberg found that a cast gelatin wedge could be removed from its mold if one side of the mold had been coated with a properly prepared solution made of egg white and distilled water, but only if the eggs were fresh. Only one side of the mold needed to be coated, because the gelatin could be allowed to adhere to the other piece of glass, which could then provide a mounting for it. Goldberg used two glass plates set at a small angle to form a wedge-shaped casting mold in which the tinted gelatin would set. The thin end of the wedge could be formed very precisely because the liquid gelatin would fill the mold through capillary action. Only one mold was necessary, because stronger (denser, more opaque) or weaker wedges could be achieved by increasing or decreasing the concentration of light-blocking material in the gelatin.

The wedges used for photometry or sensitometry need to be optically neutral or "gray," blocking light across the spectrum equally for all relevant wavelengths, otherwise the measured results would be misleading. Glass wedges were not entirely neutral. At first Goldberg used a watercolor tint called "lampblack." However, inks and tints, while blocking blue light, generally transmit infrared rays freely and also, to some extent, red rays and so were not perfectly neutral. He determined that adding exposed silver grains to the gelatin, instead of a tint, achieved highly neutral wedges.

Goldberg's first paper at the 1910 Brussels Congress, "On the preparation of neutral gray wedges and filters for photographic purposes" (*Über die Herstellung neutralgrauer Keile und Schichten für photographische Zwecke),* was extensively reprinted and summarized in German, English, and French technical journals during the next two years. The *British Journal of Photography* published a translation the very same month, entitled "The preparation of prismatic wedges of neutral colour for photometric work," with the following editorial note:

> The two papers by Dr. E. Goldberg which we publish this week, are among the most notable scientific communications to the Congress, since they describe new methods of sensitometric measurements which will bring such work more nearly within the powers of workers who have not an elaborate set of instruments at their disposal. It will, perhaps, be remembered that it was Dr. Goldberg who devised the extremely ingenious collection of working demonstration models shown last year at the Dresden Exhibition. . . .

Neutral wedges have a very wide range of applications in photography, photometry, and sensitometry. One important use is to measure the intensity of any light source by comparing it with another light source of known intensity. When a wedge is moved across the brighter of the two lights until both are equal brightness, the point on the wedge at which equality is achieved indicates the intensity of the unknown light relative to the known light.

Wedges in Sensitometry

Goldberg had remained in close contact with his former teacher, Robert Luther, and both of them presented papers at the congress on how wedge filters could be used to ascertain the Characteristic Curve of light-sensitive emulsions. Their work was based on a penetrating insight: When a film is exposed to light through a wedge, the resulting image will be a product of the combined effects of both the wedge and the characteristics of the film. Therefore, if the known effects of the wedge could somehow be subtracted, or separated out, from that image, what remained could be attributed to, and would reveal, the characteristics of the of the film. More practically, a direct comparison of the linear increase in Density of the wedge with the s-shaped increase in Density of the image should reveal the Characteristic Curve of the film.

Luther presented an account of the "crossed wedge method," which he and Fritz Weigert had developed in collaboration with Goldberg. They used a square wedge, 8cm $\times$ 8cm, through which a square photographic plate of the same size was exposed. The tone gradation of the processed image would necessarily have been determined by the effects of the wedge and the characteristics of the film. They would set down the processed plate with the darkest edge to the left and the lightest edge to the right, then place the wedge on top of it, but rotated by 90 degrees, with the densest edge at the top and the clearest edge at the bottom. As a result the combined tonal graduation would run diagonally from the top left corner where the darkest edges of both overlapped to the lower right-hand corner where the two lightest edges overlapped. The other two corners (power left and upper right) would have a midtone. In the lower left was darkest edge of the plate and the lightest edge of the wedge, and in the upper-right corner, the lightest edge of the plate and the darkest edge of the wedge. If the Characteristic Curve of the plate had been perfectly linear and identical to the increasing density of the wedge, then the combined effects of plate and wedge would result in contours of increasing darkness ("isopaques") forming in straight diagonal lines running from lower left to upper right. But to the extent that the Characteristic Curve of the film was s-shaped and differed from the slope of the wedge, these diagonal isopaque lines would deviate from straightness and create s-shaped forms. Better yet, a photographic paper exposed under the plate and wedge could capture graphically the s-shaped Characteristic Curve of the film.

Goldberg developed a variation on this "crossed wedge" approach for testing photographic papers. The paper to be tested was exposed through a wedge and processed. Another, opaque print, with evenly graduated bands from light to dark, was laid on top of the test print, again with the tonal gradient at a right angle. The second, top print had numerous, evenly spaced holes through which the lower paper could be seen. Sometimes, the darkness on the lower, test print, visible through the holes, matched the darkness around the hole on the top paper. Drawing lines connecting the holes where the darkness of the two prints were equal would indicate the Characteristic Curve. Goldberg called the upper sheet a "detail plate" *(Detailplatte)*.

The Densograph

Luther's presentation of a clever way to derive a rather crude image of a Characteristic Curve was upstaged by Goldberg's second paper at the congress, revealing an ingenious mechanical device, the densograph, to plot precise graphs of the Characteristic Curves of photographic plates. It used the same principle of comparing an emulsion exposed through a Goldberg Wedge with the wedge. The densograph, unlike the technique presented by Luther, used direct visual comparison to establish the Characteristic Curve.

The observer looks through an eyepiece at a light source diffused by a ground glass screen. The view of the light source is split in half by a mirror within a glass cube, such that half of the image is the light source seen through the plate being tested and the other half is seen through the wedge with which it is being compared. In the version of a densograph drawn in Figures 6.2 and 6.3, the comparison wedge *(Vergleichkeil)* lies flat, ahead of the eyepiece (a), with the clear end toward the viewer and the dark away. Turning the knob at the right (l) moves the comparison wedge forward or backward, and brings any point of it into the field of view of the eyepiece. The plate to be tested (u) is held vertically on a mounting (k), with the clear end to the right and the dark end to the right. A knob (r) is used to slide the mounting sideways to the left or to the right. Both knobs (l and r) allow the viewer to adjust the machine to see any point on the test plate in one half of the viewer and any point on the comparison wedge in the other half of the viewer. When a sheet of graph paper (m) is laid flat on the top of the machine, its vertical axis corresponds to the point at which the comparison wedge is being viewed in the eyepiece, and its horizontal axis to the point at which the test plate is being inspected through the eyepiece.

To plot the Characteristic Curve of a test plate, the observer starts with the eyepiece, viewing the clear ends of both the test plate and the comparison wedge. The test plate in its holder is pulled in steps from left to right, changing the view in the eyepiece progressively from the clear

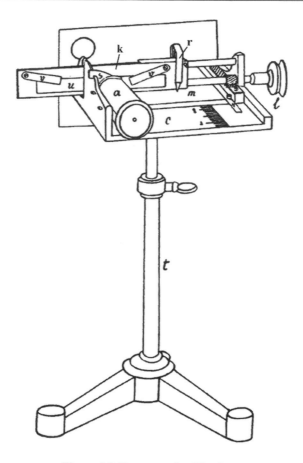

Figure 6.2. Densograph: side view.

(light) end of the test plate all the way over to the dense (dark) end of the plate. At the same time, the knob (l) is turned so that the view in the eyepiece of the comparison wedge is adjusted to the same Density (darkness) as the part of the test plate that is being viewed. Each time the Density appears to be the same, a pointed stylus is depressed to prick a hole in the graph paper, thereby plotting points at which the test plate and the comparison wedge are of equal Density. In a later version, made around 1930, the eyepiece was mounted more conveniently, at an angle. (See Figure 6.4.)

The pricks on the graph paper can then be smoothed by hand into a curved line to show the Characteristic Curve of the test plate. The densograph established the Characteristic Curve point by point.

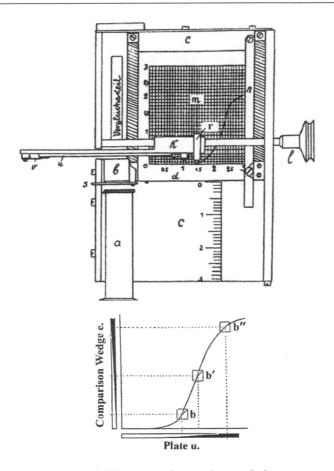

Figure 6.3. Densograph: top view; and plot.

In December 1909, Goldberg had applied for a German patent for his densograph, and in August 1912, Patent 250,062, "Apparatus for the automatic recording of local differences in the light-absorption or light-emission of objects," was issued. However, a few weeks later, in October, the German Patent Office revoked this patent and replaced it with a Gebrauchsmuster, a special kind of patent then issued in Germany for mechanical devices: G.-M. 527,621, "Photometer for the evaluation of local differences in light intensities, especially for the measurement of the darkening of photographic emulsions."

The repetitive photometric matching process needed for every single observation, for every single prick of the graph paper, when using the densograph, was demanding and tiring work, but it was by far simpler and better than any other system available for a quarter of a century.

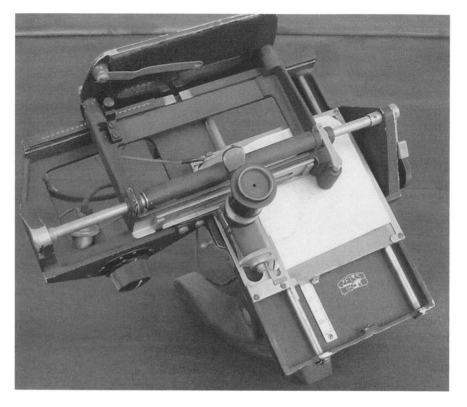

Figure 6.4. Densograph with angled eyepiece and Zeiss Ikon logo, circa 1930.

The Spectrodensograph

The densograph measured the Characteristic Curve of an emulsion with respect to the intensity of any given source of light. But light comes in a range of wavelengths, from short ultraviolet rays through the rainbow hues of visible light to the longer infrared rays. For many purposes, the specific parts of the spectrum to which an emulsion is sensitive needs to be known. For most photographic purposes, for example, an emulsion should be panchromatic, meaning sensitive to all the wavelengths of visible light. To measure the sensitivity of emulsions to specific wavelengths, Goldberg and his Belgian friend, André Callier, developed a device in 1913 that measured the intensity of light of different wavelengths, one at a time. A series of measurements gives a profile of how the intensity of the light source varied across the spectrum of wavelengths. They called it a spectrodensograph. It could also work with reflected light, so it had a wide range of uses, including the measurement of the effects of dyes on fabrics, paper, and other solid materials, as well as films and filters.

Paul Otlet and Microfiche

One of the organizers of the Brussels Congress of Photography was Paul Otlet, an idealistic Belgian who, with Henri LaFontaine, had cofounded the International Institute for Bibliography, in 1895, to promote the efficient organization and dissemination of knowledge. As a storage medium, paper is bulky and heavy, and, at that time, making copies was cumbersome and expensive. Otlet was interested in the use of photography for microfilming documents. Microfilmed documents are extremely compact and, because they are easy to copy and to transport, they could be disseminated economically. In 1906, Otlet and Robert Goldschmidt, an inventive chemist, had proposed "microfiche" as a standard format for a "microphotographic book." Seventy-two pages in 12 columns of six frames were recorded on a sheet of film 75 × 125 mm, the size of a standard catalog card *("fiche")*, with a humanly legible heading across the top giving the author, title, publication details, and subject classification number. Using this size meant that standard library catalog cabinets could be used to store them. Indeed, the texts could be interfiled with the catalog cards, or even serve as catalog cards, thereby overcoming the inconvenience of the physical separation of a catalog from the documents it lists.

Later on, as 35 mm film came into widespread use, Goldschmidt and Otlet proposed a portable library of "microphotic books," a wooden carrying case containing, on spools of 35 mm film, the equivalent of 18,750 volumes which, on paper, would have required 468 meters of shelving.

There were, however, unsolved technical challenges. A convenient and efficient copying camera was needed to film paper documents, as well as affordable, effective microform readers. A more difficult challenge was that, although one could find any particular frame if its location on the film were already known, there was no search engine capable of identifying relevant documents on a long spool of microfilm if their existence and their locations were not already known. Goldberg became interested in copying camera design and also in the challenge of building "selection" machines for finding and displaying relevant documents on microfilm.

Ostwald and Hypertext

Wilhelm Ostwald, who had received the Nobel Prize for Chemistry in 1909, also attended the international exhibition in Brussels in 1910. While there, he met Paul Otlet. Ostwald had a longstanding interest in the organization of science, the relationship between science and society, and the effective publication and use of science literature. He was captivated by the efforts of Otlet and his partner LaFontaine, who had developed a highly sophisticated "Brussels Expansion" to Melvil Dewey's Decimal Classification to create what they called the Universal Decimal Classification, and they had set out, with prodigious energy, to build a Universal Bibliographic Repertory, a catalog of all documents of all kinds, including images. Ostwald was so inspired by Otlet's institute that he resolved to establish a comparable initiative in Germany.

Ostwald was a man of action, the author of 45 books, some 500 articles and 5,000 reviews, the editor of six journals, and the initiator of a series of reprints of classic scientific works, *Ostwalds Klassiker der exakten Wissenschaften,* in which 267 volumes have been published. Returning to Germany, he formed a partnership with Adolf Saager, a German author, and with Karl Wilhelm Bührer, a Swiss businessman, who had also met with Otlet. In June 1911, using Ostwald's Nobel Prize money, they founded, in Munich, an organization they called "The Bridge: International Institute for the Organizing of Knowledge Work" *(Die Brücke: Internationales Institut zur Organisierung der geistigen Arbeit).* The bridge symbolized their view of the nature of intellectual work. Administrative, agricultural, commercial, industrial, and military work was ordinarily conducted within a geographical area, or, at least, within the structure of political jurisdictions, such as a town or a nation state, they said. But science and intellectual work was more the result of the efforts of individuals who were geographically and otherwise isolated from each other. In this sense, the intellectual world was like an archipelago of islands and to enable lonely thinkers to become a coherent, effective system, bridges were needed to connect them. It was not only a matter of linking intellectuals with each other, but also of making their work available and accessible for the rest of society. Ostwald, like Goldberg, Otlet, and others, believed fervently in the need for creative interaction between science and society, especially for technological innovation in industry. Efficiency, standards, systems, and documentation went hand in hand as the essential ingredients for collective progress in their powerful modernist vision.

Ostwald, Bührer, and Saager advanced a modernist approach to the efficient management of knowledge by seeking to atomize literature into small components of recorded thoughts, much smaller than books, articles, and technical reports. In principle, these individual single chunks of recorded knowledge, of "facts" or "micro-thoughts," could then be arranged, rearranged, and linked in multiple ways, using the expanded decimal classification for the especially important and difficult task of linking each chunk with other chunks on the same topic and, also, those on related topics.

The use of printed cards as an advertising device provided inspiration. Collectible sets of cards were already being issued with a picture on one side and an advertisement on the other. In Germany, these cards were called *Monos,* meaning "single units" and, in 1905, Bührer had established the *Internationale Monogesellschaft* ("International Mono Company"), in Winterthur, Switzerland, with, later, a branch in Munich, to develop this kind of advertising.

Bührer, Ostwald, and Saager reasoned that one could easily issue collectible sets of cards bearing units of recorded knowledge. This approach would be extremely cost-effective, because, by issuing, revising, selecting, collecting, and retrieving cards as needed, the enormous duplication, redundancy, and obsolescence of existing publication practices could be greatly reduced. Information offices, such as Otlet's Institute in Brussels and their Bridge in Munich, could organize the production and distribution of the cards.

Anyone could then assemble, selectively, the set of cards that would constitute a concise summary of any field of interest. A complete set of all cards would provide a comprehensive, dynamically updated, easily distributed encyclopedia of all recorded knowledge, which, already in 1912, Ostwald was describing as a "world brain." Based as it was, on the "mono" advertising cards, they called their approach the Monographic Principle *(das Monographprinzip),* and they saw this ability to manipulate and rearrange knowledge in creative new ways as analogous to the invention of moveable type by Gutenberg. With moveable type, for example, the letter "a" could be deployed as part of the word "apple" this week, part of "Bavaria" the next week, part of "zebra" the following week, and so on.

The prospect of creatively, efficiently redeploying micro-thoughts was very exciting. In an attempt to bypass the Babel of languages, they published a manifesto in Esperanto, "everybody's second language," as *La organizado de la intelekta laboro per la Ponto* ("The organizing of intellectual work by the Bridge"). After a brief but vigorous existence, the Bridge collapsed when Ostwald's prize money ran out. Their use of the monographic principle was a form of hypertext and the sophisticated structure of links between documents using the Universal Decimal Classification could have been called trails, but, prior to the use of digital computers, hypertext was cumbersome and laborious.

Josef Maria Eder and Franz Stolze

Josef Maria Eder, a professor in Vienna, was a leading authority on photography and editor of the most widely read annual survey of advances in photography known as "Eder's *Jahrbuch.*" Eder self-righteously drew attention to the prior development of a neutral gelatin wedge by Franz Stolze in 1893: "In 1911 Prof. Emanuel Goldberg detailed an improved method for the production of these gray wedges, which later found wide acceptance and was acclaimed as a great step forward in production. However, the priority of Stolze, who was long dead, had been forgotten about; so that Eder had to take his position."

Stolze had used an open mold to cast wedges. He laid a thin sheet of glass, 22 by 12 cm, on a flat surface, then raised one edge so that the surface sloped. He then created an open reservoir by pasting vertical walls around it made of paper or wood. Into this container, he poured gelatin crystals dissolved in water, tinted with Indian ink, with some sugar added to make the gelatin adhere to the glass base. After the gelatin had set, the walls could be removed. A layer of collodium was added to the surface to keep moisture out and the wedge was cut into two narrower wedges. Lacking an effective release agent, a precise closed mold could not be used and, unfortunately, Stolze's process did not result in accurate wedges. In an open well, the surface of the gelatin would not necessarily set evenly and the thin edge, on an open slope, would not be precise. The collodium coating would also add some interference. The Stolze wedge appears not to have been adopted. Goldberg was probably well aware of the Stolze wedge and its defects. His achievement was not the idea of gelatin wedges, but the development of a superior and practical process for making them.

In 1919, Eder and Walter Hecht developed and marketed a very successful commercial adaptation of the Goldberg Wedge in a form known as an "exposure tablet." A neutral gelatin wedge was mounted on a celluloid card across which numbered lines were printed, calibrating the increasing Density of the wedge as it became thicker. The more opaque the wedge, the higher the number. The "Eder-Hecht Neutral Wedge Photometer" would be placed on top of film to be tested and exposed to a controlled amount of light. After exposure, the film would be developed and the printed line with the highest number visibly recorded on the material would indicate how sensitive the material is, how little light would create an image. As an additional amenity, four more columns were provided with color filters for red, gold, green, and blue, so that the sensitivity of the film to each of these four wavelengths could also be tested separately at the same time. A modified version was marketed for testing photographic papers.

The Eder-Hecht photometer was a calibrated Goldberg Wedge, which led to an undignified dispute. Goldberg was displeased that Eder had renamed it for himself and Hecht, and he protested in a footnote in his book *Der Aufbau:* "It should not go unmentioned that Eder and Hecht chose to have what is known *throughout the entire* technical world under the name the Goldberg Wedge designated under their own names." This complaint carried over into the French edition: "The author is concerned to point out that Eder & Hecht have preferred to give their own names to the device universally known under the name of 'GOLDBERG wedge.'"

Goldberg's irritation may have been increased because his own initial attempt to make his wedge into a commercial product had not worked out. In October 1912, Goldberg had negotiated a contract giving Ilford Ltd, of London, exclusive U.K. manufacturing rights and worldwide sales rights. A letter from Ilford, dated October 23, 1912, offered to buy exclusive worldwide rights to the wedge, with an immediate £20 royalty payment on signing. But Goldberg had previously made arrangements for his Belgian friend André Callier to manufacture his wedges in Belgium. In 1913, he found that Callier had not only invested in expensive equipment but was already supplying wedges to customers in the U.K., undermining Ilford's expectations, and so Goldberg's agreement with Ilford could not be honored.

Eder was also the author of the leading encyclopedia of photography, the *Ausführliches Handbuch der Photographie,* a multivolume work that was continuously revised. In the first volume, on the history of photography, Eder again emphasized Stolze's priority, publicized Goldberg's failure to commercialize his wedge, and noted his own commercial success with the Eder-Hecht wedge photometer, which was widely used until the adoption of the DIN film speed standard in 1934. Eder even included in his encyclopedia the text of a letter from a satisfied purchaser of an Eder-Hecht wedge that contained a gratuitous personal attack on Goldberg.

Goldberg Wedges eventually become available commercially and thousands were sold. It was used in a popular visual light meter, the Ica Diaphot, which contained a circular wedge behind a peephole. The user would look through a peephole at the scene to be photographed, then rotate the wedge until the view darkened to the point of looking like a landscape in moonlight. The exposure setting for various film speeds could then be read off a scale.

Recognition

The availability of reliable, easily manufactured neutral wedges was of central importance in photography and authoritative accounts agree that Goldberg invented a superior technique for making them. Wolfgang Baier, for example, wrote in his history of photography of the importance of the Eder-Hecht wedge "after Goldberg, independently of Stolze, in 1911 published another better method for making neutral wedges." Similarly, 20 years after Goldberg had announced his gelatin wedge in Brussels, the Peligot Medal Committee of the French Photographic Society declared it to be his most important invention:

> But the most important of the discoveries of Professor Goldberg, which has made his name familiar among photographers is that of the sensitometric "wedge" which he presented at the International

Congress of Photography of 1910. You all know what assistance this wedge has brought to sensitometric studies and what a valuable aid it is in a large number of photometric devices. An immediate use of the wedge in his "Densograph" placed at the disposition of sensitometric laboratories a rapid method for photometric measurements and for the automatic tracing of the characteristic curves of emulsions.

By the end of 1910 Goldberg was not yet 30, but he could be proud of his achievements. His work was both widely published and extensively reported. In a culture that respected age and seniority, a biographical article on him had already been included in a scholarly encyclopedia, Emmerich's *Lexikon für Photographie und Reproduktionstechnik (Chemigraphie, Lichtdruck, Heliogravüre)*. Further evidence of international recognition came in July 1914 when the Secretary of the Royal Photographic Society of Great Britain wrote to Goldberg requesting that he give the society's prestigious Traill Taylor Memorial Lecture and that he talk about his work on wedges. This annual lecture commemorated John Traill Taylor, the former editor of the *British Journal of Photography*. The invitation was a significant honor, but with the outbreak of World War I, it could not be accepted. When the war began, Mees wrote to Goldberg again inviting him to come to work in the Kodak research labs in Rochester.

7

The Great War

And I am as tough as leather.

—Emanuel Goldberg, 1916

Professor Luther Goes to War

The rank of full professor had a high prestigious status in Germany. It was a civil service appointment and citizenship was routinely conferred when a foreign national became a professor. But Saxony had a longstanding administrative order banning the naturalization of foreign Jews and few exceptions were allowed. So the thoroughly assimilated Goldberg had had to remain a Russian citizen even though a professor, and, with the outbreak of war, he had become an enemy alien.

Goldberg complained bitterly to Director Seliger: "In the present very serious time I feel the need to most loyally ask the Royal Ministry to rescind the restriction inserted into my appointment letter of 25 November 1911 denying conferral of Saxon citizenship. As the son of a German mother, who lost her Prussian citizenship through marriage, I have endeavored since 15 September 1907 to serve the state of Saxony faithfully and to the best of my ability. Even before then, I had the honor of conducting the education of the officers of the Royal Military Technical Academy in reprographics. It is extraordinarily painful for me to be, nevertheless, treated as a citizen of an enemy state." The restriction was removed and citizenship conferred.

At the outbreak of war, Sophie was expecting a baby, and a boy, Herbert, was born on November 20, 1914. Goldberg had high hopes. A printed birth announcement card was sent out with the words *Ingenieur in spe,* meaning "An engineer, we hope." They moved into an elegant apartment building in the city, Hardenbergstrasse 19, within walking distance of the academy.

Goldberg had his 33rd birthday that year. He would have been eligible for military service, but he received a series of deferrals because he was quite nearsighted, and he was never called up. Perhaps he was considered to be in a privileged occupation. The son of an army officer, Goldberg could be expected to be interested in military applications of optics and imaging. Germany was engaged in an awesome international arms race, and engineers could see that many new technologies, such as the internal combustion engine, new chemicals, improved optical instruments, radio, airships, airplanes, and photogrammetry, had the potential to transform warfare.

Goldberg had remained in close contact with his former teacher Robert Luther, the Sub-Director at Wilhelm Ostwald's Institute in Leipzig. Luther's relationship with Ostwald had deteriorated, and he had moved to Dresden in 1908. Dresden was the center of the German photographic industry and the Technical University had an Institute for Scientific Photography *(Wissenschaftlich-Photographisches Institut)*. Following pressure from local photographic firms, the government of Saxony had established the first professorship of scientific photography in Germany and Luther had been appointed. He was eager to use the methods of physical chemistry to advance photography, but he also insisted on his students having workshop skills. The Institute had a well-equipped workshop with a lathe, a drilling machine, and a workbench, and Luther required all students to make their own equipment. As his assistant recalled, "There was always a little rivalry between Prof. Luther and his friend Prof. Dr. Goldberg of Leipzig. Prof. Goldberg was an outstanding design engineer and hobbyist. And when Prof. Goldberg came to visit the Institute, one always found the two friends in the workshop, where they tried, through little ruses, to outdo each other at the workbench."

Luther also had a passion for ballooning. The German military authorities had chosen to invest heavily in rigid airships, Zeppelins, instead of airplanes and, at the front lines, used tethered balloons as military observation posts. On the outbreak of war, even though 46 years old, Luther volunteered for military balloon service, and the direction of Goldberg's life changed when he visited Luther on the Western Front to offer technical advice.

Early Aerial Photography

Photography had two early military uses. It was used to make copies of diagrams and orders, for distribution in the field, and it was also a way of recording enemy positions and activities. Priority in aerial photography is generally attributed to the French photographer, Nadar, who took photographs from balloons around 1860. It was, he declared, like having a mobile clock tower to observe from.

A substantial technical literature, much of it written by military officers, developed in the 1880s, and, from 1891, the principal annual review of scientific and technical advances in photography, Eder's *Jahrbuch,* included a section on aerial photography. Adolf Miethe, who had hired Goldberg at the Technical University in Berlin, published a book on aerial photography entitled *Photographische Aufnahmen vom Ballon* ("Photographic Pictures from a Balloon") in 1909 when free-floating balloons were used. By the time of the second edition in 1916, the title became *Photographie aus der Luft* ("Photography from the air") and Miethe was careful to explain that aerial photography was now ordinarily done from an airplane or from a dirigible. Aerial photography from free-floating balloons, he explained, was now done only for sport or for scientific research on the atmosphere.

Much ingenuity was applied. Tiny, lightweight cameras were strapped to the chests of homing pigeons, for example, and, by 1911, the German Army was using guns to shoot projectiles carrying cameras that would be released at the height of the trajectory to take photos while floating down on a parachute. Prior to 1914, aerial photography was done mostly from tethered or free-floating balloons. The first use of an airplane for aerial photography was in 1909, but none of the combatants had equipment for photography from airplanes at the outbreak of hostilities in 1914. In March 1915, a trench map prepared chiefly from aerial photographs was used with great success by the British and the use of aerial photography developed during the war, initially from balloons, but increasingly, from airplanes.

Aerial photography would seem a natural activity for the smooth-sailing dirigibles. They could head into the wind and remain stationary in the air, but they were vulnerable to bad weather and enemy gunfire, and had other technical problems. The principal account of the German military airship battalion makes no mention of aerial photography.

There was a very basic problem in aerial photographic reconnaissance. The military photographer in a balloon was rather like a boxer with short arms. The effective range of cameras, the maximum distance at which usefully detailed images of the enemy soldiers could be obtained, was less than the effective range of the enemy guns. So a military photographer who went up in a large and slow-moving balloon could expect to be shot out of the sky before any useful photographs could be taken.

Drachen-Photographie

Late in the nineteenth century, there was a renewed interest in Europe in the ancient art of flying kites, popularized by, among others, Lord Baden-Powell, founder of the Boy Scout movement. Multiple kites tied together could raise a human observer. Using a kite to hoist a camera for aerial photography without an observer had significant advantages. A kite was much cheaper and smaller than a balloon. It could be maneuvered with some precision over enemy positions with inexpensive, easily replaceable equipment.

By 1888, successful aerial photography from a kite had been reported in Britain, France, and the United States. There were, however, challenging constraints. The camera needed to be as light as possible, and film was preferred to glass plates because it weighed much less. A fast shutter speed, 1/100th second or faster, was needed because of the instability of the kite, because if the shutter mechanism shook, the camera the image would be blurred. For precise work the camera needed to point vertically downward regardless of the angle of the kite. As with photography from a balloon, if the reconnaissance was being done to support accurate targeted artillery fire, the position of the camera at the moment the photograph was taken needed to be established accurately by triangulation, which could be done using trigonometry if there were two observers in different positions with instruments to estimate the distance, the compass orientation, and the angle of elevation of the kite. To interpret the photograph, the orientation of the camera with respect to the points of the compass needed to be known or estimated, but this was much more of problem with a free-flying balloon than with a tethered balloon or kite. The observers needed to know exactly when the photograph was taken, and tripping the shutter had to be delayed until the kite was in the desired position. Three quite different mechanisms were used to time the tripping of the shutter: an incendiary fuse, a clock-based timing mechanism, and an electric relay controlled by the kite flier. A relay gave maximum control and could be combined with a mercury level switch on the camera such that the circuit was not completed unless the camera was pointing vertically downward, but a relay required at least two metal wires up to the kite, which increased the weight.

In 1899, R. Thiele, an Austrian employed by the Russian Ministry of Communications, had successfully used a cluster of cameras hoisted by kite during a mapmaking survey from the Caucasus to the Persian Gulf. Kite photography was also used for specialized purposes such as photographing an active volcano from above, and the inspection of the exterior of cathedrals and other tall buildings. By 1911, kite photography had been used experimentally by the military, mainly in England, France, and Russia, but not in warfare or even on maneuvers.

Kite photography was just the kind of challenge that would have appealed to Goldberg. It was a practical application of photography requiring precision, reliability, and ease of use. The camera, lens, and shutter control needed to be miniaturized to reduce weight and to minimize exposure to gunfire.

What precisely Goldberg did to help Luther is not clear. Three military documents survive. A handwritten note, dated December 23, 1915, issued by the Field Balloon Unit No. 7 *(Feldluftschifferabteilung Nr 7),* is a pass from Leipzig to Sallaumines. Another, undated, also mentions Sallaumines, which is in northern France, near to Lens, between Lille and Arras, and very close to the German front line in the trench warfare of the Western Front from October 1914 until 1917. The third, a typed statement, issued at Sallaumines, dated January 18, 1916, and signed by Captain Peters, Commander of the Field Balloon Unit No. 7 *(Peters, Hauptmann und Kommandeur der Feldluftschifferabteilung Nr 7),* appears to refer explicitly to photography from a kite: "Professor Dr. Goldberg has very kindly rebuilt, at no charge, the kite-camera *[photographische Drachenkamera]* manufactured by the Braun Company in Berlin and delivered in unusable condition, so that it now functions excellently. In order to test the kite-camera in practice, the Professor went personally to the Front to the Feldluftschiffer Abteilung 7 (Jan 15–18, 1916). The camera functions excellently in every respect, as the practical tests launching the kite have demonstrated."

During the trench warfare on the Western Front, both sides used tethered observation balloons, or "aerostats," large enough to carry two observers in a basket. Spherical tethered balloons could be used only in very calm weather because they would bob to and fro in a wind. To remedy this instability, officers in the Prussian Balloon Battalion in Berlin had developed, in 1893, elongated, aerodynamic balloons with tail fins. An elongated shape reduces swaying. The tail fins added steadiness and kept the balloon headed into the wind. This kind of balloon behaved like a kite and became known as a *Drachenballon* ("kite balloon") or simply *Drachen,* even though "Drachen" ordinarily means a kite. (See Figure 7.1.)

Hundreds of observation balloons were built and deployed along the front by both sides and the "kite camera" that Goldberg repaired was probably for use with a "kite balloon." A field balloon unit *(Feldluftschifferabt eilung)* of the kind that Luther joined would be responsible for a single kite balloon. The unit would need eight wagons, each with six to eight horses, to carry the balloon, reserves of gas for the balloon, fodder for the horses, and the 48 men needed to operate and maintain one balloon. The observer in the basket would use binoculars to monitor enemy movements and to fix the location of enemy batteries and a telephone to guide artillery fire. It was very dangerous work, as the balloons could be shot down. The risk increased as airplanes, initially used only for visual observation, became faster and began to be equipped with guns.

Goldberg is known to have used a 6 × 9 cm camera attached to a balloon with a clockwork device to trip the shutter. It had to be hauled down after each exposure. In 1932, he referred to his "efforts which later led to serial images (cinematography from aircraft) were photographs taken from large observation balloons." Years later Goldberg reminisced

Figure 7.1. Aerodynamic Observation Balloon (Drachenballon).

about automatic aerial photography from a balloon: "I was called upon at the beginning of World War I to improve an automatic camera for aerial photography which would appear infantile nowadays."

At the outbreak of war, Carl Zeiss Jena was the world's dominant manufacturer of military optics: binoculars, gun sights, rangefinders, telescopes, and the like. Ernst Wandersleb, shown in Figure 7.2, then the head of the Zeiss Photo Optics Department in Jena, was also, like Luther and Miethe, a ballooning aerial photography enthusiast.

In 1957, reminiscing about Goldberg, Wandersleb wrote: "In spring 1916 I came across Goldberg's tracks in the German trenches on the Western Front near Douai, . . . where they were full of praise for Goldberg's valuable suggestions. He had recently been there at the suggestion of his longtime friend [and] colleague from the Ostwald school, Prof. R. Luther, then an officer in a balloon battalion."

It seems likely that Goldberg was involved in an experiment with photographic reconnaissance from a "kite-balloon." He himself spoke of putting up a balloon and camera in the dark of night and positioning it where it could photograph the enemy trenches. The shutter was timed to go off as soon as the dawn provided sufficient light, whereupon the balloon would be hauled in before it could be noticed and shot down by enemy fire. It has been suggested that the camera was hauled up and down the balloon's tethering rope. But it is not known precisely what he did, nor why it was considered so

Figure 7.2. Ernst Wandersleb, 1879–1963.

remarkable. Wandersleb spoke of suggestions, in the plural, so, in all likelihood, Goldberg did several different things. Whatever they were, Wandersleb was impressed, sought him out, and urged him to visit Jena after the war, implying the prospect of employment at Zeiss.

Carl Zeiss, Jena

In fact, Goldberg's connection with Zeiss began much sooner. Around 1916, Goldberg, in his research at the academy, had invented an ingenious device for testing all the important characteristics of a lens (aberrations, distortions, resolution, etc.) in a single exposure. A convenient, compact, cost-effective lens-testing device was naturally of great interest to the Carl Zeiss company, the leading maker of camera lenses. A Zeiss representative visited Goldberg in Leipzig to examine it. Zeiss signed a contract with Goldberg in the summer of 1916 for him to supply a copy of the lens-testing device and to go to Jena to train Zeiss employees to use it. The contract explicitly reserved the intellectual property rights to Goldberg. He also supplied one to the Institut d'Optique in Paris.

In November 1916, Goldberg requested permission to reduce his employment at the academy to two days a week so that he could accommodate Zeiss's request for technical assistance in the production by photo-etching of the fine calibration lines ("reticles") in military optical devices such as sniper's sights and naval range finders. In a resume dated 1917, Goldberg wrote: "From summer 1916 to summer 1917, I was given leave, at the request of the Carl Zeiss works to work on military scientific tasks in Jena, but I continued teaching in Leipzig. From fall 1915 to the beginning of 1917 I was an instructor at the Women's University in Leipzig, where I taught courses and held practical exercises on scientific photography and microphotography." The Women's University *(Hochschule für Frauen)* existed in Leipzig from 1911 to 1921. It was a technical college with two-year programs providing an academic education that prepared women to be assistants in medical and scientific institutes and in similar industrial facilities, to be social workers, health-care supervisors, and educators of kindergarten teachers, youth workers, and the like.

Although hired to train Zeiss employees to use his lens-testing equipment, Goldberg was active in solving other technical problems. One of them had to do with imperfections on optical surfaces, which were not necessarily visible to the eye. There were specifications for the allowable size, number, and distribution of scratches and "digs," depending on the application, but in some applications no imperfections were allowed. For instance, many military instruments had scales, grid patterns, or reference marks on internal surfaces, which, when in visible focus, were usually magnified. Zeiss had a serious problem with very small spots on certain naval range-finder prisms. Once noticed, an observer would take them to be a distant airplane and would find it difficult to concentrate on other areas in the field of view. Zeiss staff thought that the spots were defects in the silver-coating process and had the prisms re-silvered. Goldberg secretly marked the flawed prisms and demonstrated that the same prisms were being repeatedly found defective and repeatedly re-silvered. The defects originated in the polishing of the glass prisms prior to silvering. Goldberg stressed the importance of standards, but also insisted on the need for them to be appropriate to the purpose. No optical prism would be perfect. If one looked closely enough, some scratch or blemish could always be found, but, if it did not affect performance, it would not matter. Goldberg explained this by saying that he used prisms for looking through, not for looking at. Another problem involved poor performance of range finders caused by distortions resulting from heat expansion. The glass pentaprisms and the metal with which the range finders were constructed were liable to expand differently when getting hot in the sun. Goldberg recommended replacing the glass pentaprisms with enameled steel plates that could be polished to a mirror-like surface. Being metal, they would expand uniformly with the rest of the range finder. He made some of them. Zeiss took out a patent on this solution and called it a "Goldberg mirror" *(Goldbergscher Spiegel)*.

Moving On

Goldberg, who had previously only been employed in academic institutions, had now seen a different world with wider, different possibilities. He decided to leave the ivory tower for industry. On March 19, 1917, he submitted to Seliger a formal request to have his civil service employment terminated:

Dear Privy Councillor,

As I informed you yesterday by word of mouth, I must to my great regret ask you to forward to the Royal Ministry my termination from State service. For years already, I have been urged from various parts of industry to move over to engineering. The recent period has made me very aware that my abilities are of an unmistakably technical nature. More and more I come to the insight that I can be far more useful in industry, in a general sense, than in my present teaching position. Now, when it is especially important to utilize all available strengths, I could not refuse a renewed offer to be a manager of the "Ica" company in Dresden. There my experience and knowledge can be applied to the service of Saxony's industry, which I know well from years of collaborative work, in the presently extremely important field of military photography. You will believe that it will be very hard for me to leave my workshop in the Academy, which I have built and cared for largely by my own hands in years of work. But I hope that I will be able to be far more useful to the State of Saxony and to the general good in Dresden than in Leipzig.

Because the staffing difficulties in industry become greater day by day, whereas in the Academy activity has necessarily had to be severely curtailed with the outbreak of war, and because through my activities at "Ica" would be concerned with extremely important military tasks, production, and urgent needs (on this written evidence can willingly be supplied), I quite loyally ask for a quick termination for the general good. However, I would gladly spend one working day each week in Leipzig and fully maintain teaching in the Academy, at least until the end of the summer semester, if need be with reduced salary. And afterwards I promise to do all I can by word and deed to support the Academy as may be desired.

With most heartfelt thanks for the support and trust always shown to me, I remain, most honorable Privy Councillor,

Yours sincerely,

E. Goldberg.

Seliger forwarded the request to the Ministry, noting that the loss was a severe blow for the academy, but that Goldberg's contribution to the industrial war effort was some consolation. Because replacing him would be a severe problem, he requested that Goldberg be retained to teach one day a week for the duration of the war. Goldberg, he noted, had not taken any vacation time during his 10 years at the academy. The Ministry approved Goldberg's resignation, noting that, under a law of 1835, his pension rights were thereby forfeited. It was agreed that he would facilitate the transition by returning to teach at the academy one day a week for the rest of the semester. Seliger also requested that the King's next birthday honors list include an order of honor for Goldberg, but this did not happen. And there was the lathe. In October 1917, Goldberg wrote to Seliger, pointing out that although the academy had bought the lathe, the accessories needed to use it belonged to him, as he had paid for them. The lathe was useless to the academy without the accessories, and the accessories were useless without the lathe. With Goldberg's departure, nobody in the academy expected to use it. He asked whether, if he were to reimburse the academy for the 1,000 Marks it had spent on the lathe, he could take possession of it. First Seliger and then the Ministry agreed, and Goldberg took the lathe to Dresden.

Zeiss had appointed Goldberg a member of the management board (*Vorstand*) of the Ica company. The name Ica was an abbreviation of Internationale Camera Aktiengesellschaft (International Camera Company). It was formed by mergers organized by Rudolf Straubel in 1909 and controlled by the Carl Zeiss Stiftung (Carl Zeiss Foundation) in Jena, which consolidated its camera manufacturing operations into Ica, making it the largest camera company in Germany. The head of Ica was a tough, self-taught man, Guido Mengel, who believed in maintaining complete control. The managers who came with the firms merged into Ica soon left. When interviewed for a position at Ica, Goldberg was warned that Mengel was as hard as steel. Goldberg replied that he himself, in contrast, was "as tough as leather." It was an allusion to the steel straight razors (also known as "cut-throat razors") used by men for shaving in the days before modern safety razors. A steel razor could achieve peak performance only when properly honed with a strip of tough leather.

Goldberg's task was to develop improved military products at Ica, which was already the primary German manufacturer of cameras used in military aerial photography. His appointment at Ica was effective April 1, 1917, but his arrival was delayed without explanation while he undertook a secret military mission.

List on Sylt

The German navy had started the war counting on airships, rather than airplanes, and at the outbreak of hostilities, they had only 18 airplanes.

Zeppelin airships did drop some bombs on England, but both airships and airplanes were intended primarily for reconnaissance.

Airships had tremendous symbolic value in Germany. Adolf Saager, Wilhelm Ostwald's collaborator in Die Brücke, wrote a book praising Count Zeppelin as savior of the Fatherland, but, in practice, the military airships were unsatisfactory. They were expensive; they were accident-prone; and the engines were inadequate. Airplanes, meanwhile, were steadily improving, and there was a significant policy shift toward airplanes: 1,346 airplanes were constructed in Germany in 1914; 4,532 in 1915; 8,182 in 1916; 19,746 in 1917; and 14,123 in 1918.

Sylt is a sandy island in the North Sea off the extreme northwest corner of Germany. On Sylt there was an airport for the German Navy's planes. First occupied in 1915, the List airport was built up until it had three hangars, 20 officers, 350 men, and two seaplane slips, one of wood and one of concrete. The only trace found of Goldberg's secret mission is a document stamped *Geheim!* (Secret!). It is a summary of two meetings at List on September 20 and 27, 1917, between the members of the Technical Section of the Special Committee *(Sonderkommission),* a Director of the Ica works (Goldberg), and the head of the Zeiss Photo Department (Ernst Wandersleb). The others present, apparently the members of the Technical section of the Special Committee, are given as Brehmer, Miethe (presumably Adolf Miethe of Berlin), and Mangold. The meeting was concerned with improving the reliability of airplane observers looking for floating mines. The use of polarizing filters to reduce reflection from the surface of the water was discussed and Goldberg reported that he had been doing experiments that led him to recommend searching with a narrow angle of vision. There was agreement on implementing Goldberg's recommendations, and Zeiss undertook to build some telescopic sights with a modest magnification and a narrow field of view.

The only aerial photographs left among Goldberg's personal papers show World War I enemy trenches and are evidently a series taken from an airplane. They are thought to be among the earliest German military aerial photographs. Sophie was very worried by his going up in airplanes.

8

Ica and the Kinamo

He drew on his Greek combining ('Kine-' movement) and Latin ('amo,' I love) to coin the name "Kinamo"—'I love movies.'

—N. Goldberg

Dresden

Saxony had two major cities, Leipzig and Dresden, both ancient Slavic settlements that had became Germanized. Dresden, at a crossing point of the river Elbe, grew in importance and became the capital of the Kingdom of Saxony under the Wettin dynasty. But the nineteenth century brought military and political misfortunes. In 1809, Saxony sided with the Prussians against Napoleon and was defeated. In 1813, it sided with Napoleon against the Prussians and was again defeated. In 1866, Saxony joined with the Austrians against the Prussians and was humiliatingly defeated. In 1870, they helped the Prussians against the French; this time it was a military victory, but a political loss. The French were defeated, but the Prussian success resulted in the subordination of Saxony within the new Prussian-led German Empire.

Nevertheless, Saxony, and especially Dresden and Leipzig, flourished in agriculture, the arts, and industry. "Saxony," declared the 1911 *Encyclopaedia Britannica,* "is one of the most fertile parts of Germany and is agriculturally among the most advanced nations in the world." Good roads, a well-developed railroad system, and a central position within Europe favored commerce.

In Goldberg's time, Saxony was the most urbanized of the larger German states and the one with the fastest population growth. Leipzig and Dresden were then the third- and fourth-largest industrial centers in

81

**Figure 8.1. Announcement of Goldberg's appointment at
Ica, June 1917.**

Germany, after Berlin and Hamburg. Leipzig was the international center
of the book trade and had a precision engineering industry, making player
pianos and other instruments. Dresden was noted for its fine porcelain,
metal industries, machinery (including bicycles, calculators, sewing
machines, and typewriters), and household equipment, such as hair dryers,
vacuum cleaners, and electric water heaters.

Dresden, like Leipzig, had a population of about half a million, with
a similar number in the surrounding areas. With its fine architecture, art
collections, and the famous Opera House designed by Gottfried Semper,
Dresden was sometimes referred to as "the Florence of Germany" or,
sometimes, the "Florence of the Elbe" *(Elbflorenz)*. It was also "Photocity"
(Fotostadt Dresden), the center of the photographic industry in Germany.
Hermann Krone, the outstanding photographer of nineteenth-century

Germany, lived in Dresden, which was the home of several well-known photographic companies, such as Balda, Ernemann, Ica, Ihagee, and Mimosa, and numerous smaller firms. Photographic film, photographic paper, and equipment of every kind were manufactured there.

In June 1917, Goldberg joined Ica and was appointed to the Managing Committee *(Vorstand)*. (See announcement, Figure 8.1.)

Zeiss intended that Goldberg would assist and eventually succeed Guido Mengel as head of Ica. Their immediate task was to develop photographic equipment needed by the military. However, the Treaty of Versailles, the peace treaty imposed on Germany at the end of World War I, included extreme restrictions on military activity and on the production of military equipment, so the expectation that Goldberg would work on military applications of photography could not be fulfilled. Instead, he developed improved commercial products and better manufacturing procedures.

German camera firms had dominated the German domestic market, but, weakened by the war, they now faced growing British, French, and U.S. competition. American manufacturers, in particular, were more efficient.

Innovations

There remained a need to modernize Ica and its products. Goldberg found manufacturing was still at the craft level. They were building cameras without first making drawings. Instead, templates were made and parts were made and assembled from these. He introduced more modern production procedures, and his success in designing improved products is reflected in some 60 German patents issued to Ica during the next few years.

German intellectual property law in this period differed significantly from U.S. law. Under U.S. patent law, only a human being can be deemed an inventor, so U.S. patents are always awarded to, and only to, one or more named individuals, even though the inventors usually assign the rights to their employers under the individuals' terms and conditions of employment. In contrast, in Goldberg's time, German companies owned their employees' inventions outright as it was considered "work for hire." The patent was awarded to the employer, not the employee. In consequence, until German patent law was reformed in 1936, German patents do not ordinarily indicate who the inventor was; and the name of the individual may be identifiable only if there was a companion patent issued in the United States or another country that assigned patents to individual inventors. So, among the Ica patents, one cannot tell which were attributable to Goldberg and which were invented by others, who may or may not have been working under his guidance. In any case, in a team environment the assignment of individual credit tends to be rather artificial. What is clear is that under Goldberg's leadership there was a great deal of attention to innovation and improved design.

The Ica patents were almost all for mechanical improvements across a wide range of photographic equipment: cameras, enlargers, film holders, flash lights, light meters, printing and developing equipment, tripods, and so on. Nearly half were movie camera and movie projector designs. Some reflected Goldberg's interest in improving efficiency through labor-saving devices. "I am lazy to the highest possible degree," he enjoyed saying. "I'm so lazy that I don't want to work. I'd rather spend ten times as much effort inventing an easy way of doing a job than do the job itself." One example was a holder for printing paper that, when it was closed and ready to print, automatically turned on the light to begin the printing process. Another was a self-focusing enlarger designed so that as the projection head was moved up or down to achieve the desired degree of enlargement, the lens also adjusted, automatically, to remain in focus (Figure 8.2).

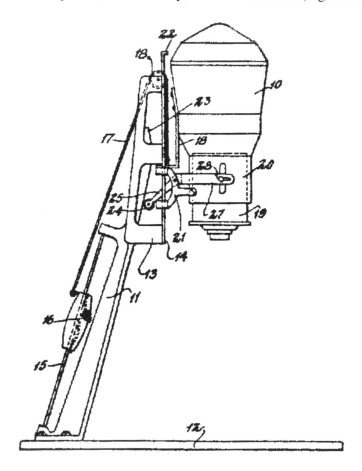

Figure 8.2. Self-focusing enlarger by Emanuel Goldberg and Martin Nowicki, 1926.

Goldberg was also now in a good position to arrange the manufacture and sale of his earlier inventions, including the densograph and spectrodensograph. Thousands of Goldberg Wedges were made and sold, especially in the popular Diaphot, the inexpensive light meter described in Chapter 6.

The Kinamo

Cinematography was still young when the war ended but was growing rapidly in popularity, and the number of movie theaters was increasing rapidly. Ica was already well established as a maker of movie projectors. Its very successful Monopol projector was widely used in schools. Goldberg was one of the founders, in 1920, of the German movie technology society *(Deutsche Kinotechnische Gesellschaft),* and he believed that there would be a large market for cameras for amateurs making "home movies."

After Goldberg had been at Ica for three years, the factory was divided into two separate groups: one group for still cameras, and the other, under Goldberg, for movie equipment, including the Kinamo, a movie camera he had designed. The undated photograph, Figure 8.3, of Goldberg with his staff is probably from this period.

Figure 8.3. Goldberg and his staff, circa 1920.

Ernst Wandersleb remembered taking a four-day skiing vacation with Goldberg and others and relaxing after a day on the slopes: "While we other comrades enjoyed the evening in the cosy hut on the Schwarzwasser Alp, having fun, eating, drinking, smoking, and singing, happy to be far from our jobs, Goldberg unpacked from a backpack an entire arsenal of small tools and worked for hours on the first Kinamo model, which he had brought, a new movie camera that he was developing then in Dresden."

The name Kinamo, derived from Goldberg's early studies of Greek *(kine)* and Latin *(amo),* meant "I love movies." It was the smallest of three competing, compact 35 mm movie cameras to reach the market in or around 1921. It was significantly cheaper than earlier movie cameras and cost no more than a good still camera. Goldberg recognized that a major constraint in film making was the immobility imposed by the tripod, which was necessary to hold the camera steady while the crank was turned. To dispense with the tripod, one had to get rid of the crank. His solution was to design a spring-driven camera. The technical problem was the same as with a clock. The gradually diminishing tension on a wound-up spring as it unwinds had to be converted into a very evenly regulated movement. A wind-up, spring-driven model of the Kinamo was available in 1922, one of the first handheld movie cameras. Initially the spring motor malfunctioned at very low temperatures, so on a trip to the Alps, Goldberg would leave his Kinamo out overnight, then dismantle the spring motor section each morning trying to find the source of the problem.

The Kinamo was designed for ease of use and had several attractive features. It was amazingly small and portable, even though it used standard 35 mm film. For example, the N25 model shown in Figure 8.4, could be loaded with 25 meters of "Normal" (meaning 35 mm) film, yet was only 6 inches high, 5½ inches deep and 4 inches wide (15 × 14 × 10 cm).

The Kinamo could also be used as a still camera, taking one shot at a time. A series of still shots, taken at intervals, permitted special effects such as a film of dramatic cloud movements. A button could be pressed to mark the film at the end of a scene. The film came in cassettes that were easily changed even in sunlight. A particularly useful feature for the home moviemaker was the delayed action mechanism that enabled the camera operator to be included among those being filmed. One inserted a leaf or a scrap of paper in a small clamp on the front, and, in the words of an evaluation in the *British Journal of Photography:* "When the camera is released and the photographer is in the view of the lens he will see the piece of paper flutter to the ground just before the camera mechanism starts up. The mechanism is very quiet in operation and the photographer using the delayed action thus avoids the terrible uncertainty as to when to begin the action for the film."

Standard film, the 35 mm stock used in the movie industry, had disadvantages as a medium for amateur moviemakers. It was bulky, expensive,

Figure 8.4. Kinamo N25 movie camera.

and highly flammable. By the early 1920s, 16 mm movie cameras were being marketed, and they used safety film. About 1924, Ica brought out a 16 mm version of the Kinamo, the S10, and, later, a larger version, the KS 10. Even the larger KS 10, which held 33 feet of 16 mm film, measured less than 4½ × 3½ × 2½ inches and weighed only 3 pounds.

Promoting Amateur Movies

Ica's publicity stressed the Kinamo's small size and ease of operation: "The Kinamo is a practical camera.... Its very compact size will make a strong appeal to those who have always wanted to make movies. The great bulk, excessive weight and complicated mechanism of the average movie camera, not to mention its expense, has heretofore confined motion picture photography to the professional producer." Goldberg's own interests were reflected in Ica's advertising of the handheld spring-driven Kinamo as the camera to use when mountain climbing, skiing, or taking candid photos of children. The Kinamo was advertised for family use: "In the home, movies of the family, the children and friends will be priceless in years to come. What would be more interesting after the children have grown up or the old folks have passed away, than to spend an evening showing a few thousand feet of Kinamo film.... the results will in every way equal most of the best professional motion pictures."

Das Neue Universum, an annual for boys, reported with enthusiasm that the introduction of the Kinamo removed all reservations about making amateur movies. It is no larger than the usual still camera, so "one can easily take it along on outings, walks and journeys.... Operation is extremely simple; one does not need to be an experienced amateur to take good pictures because any good photoshop can process the film. What inviting prospects using a Kinamo offers for the family chronicles!"

Because Goldberg saw amateur movies as an important potential market, he gave talks on the topic and wrote an article on how to film clouds for a magazine called *Bezee-Photo-Mitteilungen.* Unfortunately, this article seems lost. In the only set of this magazine found, in the Leipzig University Library, the pages containing Goldberg's article were destroyed by bombing in World War II.

Nevertheless, sales of the Kinamo were hindered by the widespread assumption that only a professional cinematographer would be able to make movies. In an attempt to reduce this market resistance, Goldberg scripted, produced, and directed short movies of about five minutes using himself, his wife, his children, and their friends as actors. They were black-and-white films in standard 35 mm format, silent, with intertitles. Every intertitle bears the Zeiss Ikon logo and a reference to the Kinamo camera, either "Kinamo-Film" or "Kinamo-Selbstaufnahme," literally "Kinamo shoot it yourself," implying that any amateur could make such movies with a Kinamo camera. Copies were distributed to Zeiss Ikon dealers for promotional purposes. The dealers were expected to use these short, informal films to charm customers into believing that they too could make movies of their own family if they bought a Kinamo. None of these promotional films appears to have survived, but, for four of them, there is a 16 mm copy, made some 40 years later from deteriorated 35 mm originals that no longer exist.

Im Sonneck: Bilder aus dem Kinderleben ("In the Sunny Corner: Scenes from the Children's Life") is the shortest, at 4 minutes, and, probably, the earliest of these films. It is a series of episodes, from waking up to going to sleep, in the day of a little girl about two years old (Renate), looked after by an older brother (Herbert) aged about nine or ten. Some of the scenes were shot indoors, inside the Goldberg home on Wallotsstrasse. For example, soon after waking up, the little girl is shown, still in her nightie, looking out of the window (Figure 8.5). Although these promotional shorts were issued after Zeiss Ikon was formed in October 1926, the age of the little girl suggests that these scenes were probably filmed in

Figure 8.5. Herbert Goldberg helps Renate look out of the window. Still from *Im Sonneck*, circa 1924.

1924. Before the first scene, an intertitle declares in prominent lettering: "Handheld filming with the Zeiss Ikon Kinamo" *(Aufgenommen aus freier Hand mit Zeiss Ikon-Kinamo).* (See Figure 8.6.)

In *Zeltleben in den Dolomiten* ("Camping in the Dolomites"), 9 minutes long, Goldberg stars in his own film. He would set the camera on a tripod, carefully compose the scene, then use the Kinamo's self-timing mechanism to delay the start of filming until he could take up his position in the scene being filmed. He, Herbert, and a young man can be seen setting up a tent in a lush alpine valley next to a stream (Figure 8.7). They cook breakfast, then climb up higher to camp on rocky ground above the treeline, among fine views of rugged mountain peaks and dramatic cloud effects. A rock-climbing scene seems to have been very subtly enhanced by trick photography.

The most ambitious and dramatic Goldberg short to have survived is *Die verzauberten Schuhe: Eine heitere Kinamo-Tragödie* ("The Magic

Figure 8.6. "Handheld filming with the Zeiss Ikon Kinamo." Promotional intertitle in *Im Sonneck*.

Shoes: An Amusing Kinamo Tragedy"), a humorous melodrama about a family on vacation in the Alps. The exasperated father, played by Goldberg, loses his temper at mealtime. He denounces family life, knocks plates on to the floor, and storms off to hike in the mountains, leaving his wife and daughter, played by Sophie and three-year-old Renate in tears. Two boys, played by Herbert and a friend, set off after him, track his footprints in the snow, and find him sleeping in his tent. Noticing that the father had removed his shoes, they decide to teach him a lesson. They tie a long cord to the shoes, hide some distance away, and wait. When the father awakes and reaches for his shoes, they pull the cord and the shoes magically move out of his reach. Repeatedly, the boys pull on the string. The father is obliged to chase after the shoes and is eventually brought home repentant and apologetic. The mood in the story is exactly paralleled by the weather, with shots of a gathering storm, dramatic, billowing storm clouds among spectacular mountain peaks, then calm, and, after the reconciliation, lovely sunshine as the three children play happily in a meadow. The film was made in the Dolomites, where the family spent four weeks after Renate had pneumonia. (See Figures 8.8 and 8.9.)

Figure 8.7. Goldberg and Herbert in a tent. Still from *Zeltleben in den Dolomiten.*

In a fourth, incomplete, and untitled film, lasting nearly 8 minutes, father and son (Goldberg and Herbert) travel by train to a little town in the mountains. They set off cross-country skiing, but, caught by bad weather, they take shelter in an old farm hut. Returning to the town, they find a letter from Mother at the post office and also a parcel of candies. They set off skiing again, then stop to open the parcel, and, in a good-natured way, they each try to seize the tastiest items. (See Figures 8.10, 8.11, and 8.12.)

These short films are charming, humorous, and good-natured. Goldberg, formally dressed with a collar, tie, and hat, tends to play a comic role, dropping things, stumbling, and, for example, trying to rescue the cooked breakfast that he has spilled on the ground.

The implication that anyone who bought a Kinamo camera could make movies like these was quite misleading. Goldberg's short films were far from amateurish. They reveal very skillful composition, crisp editing, and quite sophisticated use of backlighting and shadows. Nevertheless, the Kinamo has been credited with making home movies popular among the wealthy, at least in Germany.

A compact, spring-driven, handheld movie camera could be used in a wider range of situations than a hand-cranked, tripod-bound machine. It could be used unobtrusively, even secretly, and with these advantages, the Kinamo contributed to the development of documentary movies.

Figure 8.8. Goldberg, Herbert, Renate, Sophie, and an unidentified youth (second from left) in *Die verzauberten Schuhe.*

Joris Ivens

Joris Ivens, the pioneer of documentary movies, used a Kinamo camera. In his autobiography, *The camera and I,* Ivens describes how he went to Germany to acquire technical knowledge of photography, first studying in Berlin, then, to learn more about cameras and lens construction, working in the Ernemann and Ica factories in Dresden where, "In the mechanical workshop, one man made a great impression on me: Professor Goldberg. He was an inventor who had just perfected a marvelous little camera, the famous Kinamo, a professional 35 mm spring-driven camera of a robustness and precision that was astonishing for its time. From this man I learned the basic principles of this kind of machine and I meddled with the secrets of manufacture." Returning to Antwerp in 1927, Ivens was pleased with the tonal quality of a film made indoors inside a bar:

> But, even better, with my camera held in my hand, the marvelous Kinamo of Professor Goldberg, I was, naturally, freed from the rigidity of a tripod, and I had given movement to what, normally, would have had to be a succession of fixed shots. Without knowing

Figure 8.9. Sophie weeping, with Renate, in *Die verzauberten Schuhe.*

it, filming flexibly and without stopping, I had achieved a continuity. That day I realized that the camera was an eye and I said to myself, "If it is a gaze, it ought to be a living one."

Ivens made an avant-garde film of a new steel railway bridge over the river Maas in Rotterdam with a central span that would be raised to allow larger ships to pass.

> To me the bridge was a laboratory of movements, tones, shapes, contrasts, rhythms and the relations between all of these.... What I wanted was to find some general rules, laws of continuity and movement.... I used a borrowed camera from my father's store, a Kinamo with three lenses.... The Kinamo is a small spring driven automatic handcamera. It holds a magazine of seventy-five feet of 35mm film. I had worked on this very model in the construction department in the Ica factory. I had learned all its advantages and also its weaknesses from Professor Goldberg, the inventor of the practical little instrument, so that when I took the Kinamo onto the bridge it was already an old friend.

The Bridge is just 12 minutes long, a fast-paced, rhythmic series of patterns and movements in and around the bridge: shadows, girders,

Figure 8.10. Herbert and Goldberg look out from a farm hut. Still from an untitled film.

wheels, steam, seagulls, and boats. It is both a study of movement and also a portrait of the bridge, the steam trains that cross it, the boats that pass under it, and life around it. At the start, the screen is dominated by close-ups of the Kinamo camera itself.

Other moviemakers used the Kinamo. Erwin Anders was a Zeiss Ikon employee who, against Goldberg's advice, gave up secure employment to make films. Bernt Berg, the Swedish nature photographer and author of best-selling travelogues, visited Goldberg and presented him with copies of some of his books as a gesture of appreciation for the Kinamo. Werner Sell, a Junkers aircraft engineer with a taste for travel to exotic places, financed his trips through commercial use of movies and stills taken with his Kinamo.

While Ica promoted the Kinamo for amateur moviemaking and professionals like Ivens explored its potential, Goldberg was busy developing specialized uses for it. In 1925, Ica announced a "Goldberg Mikrophot Microscope Attachment" *(Goldbergscher Mikroskopaufsatz Mikrophot)* for taking photographs through a microscope (photomicrography). It was an attachment that could be clamped to the top of any microscope, with a

Figure 8.11. Son and father (Herbert and Goldberg) receive a letter. Still from an untitled film.

partially silvered mirror set at a 45°angle, reflecting 99 percent of the light from the microscope's specimen at right angles into a camera attached at the side. If the specimen was brightly lit, there would be enough light to take photos and, in addition, the remaining 1 percent could still be seen through an eyepiece at the top of the microscope in the usual way, which provided a viewfinder and enabled the photographer to ensure that the microscope was properly focused. Better yet, if the Kinamo was used, the photographer could take still photos or film the specimen, or do time-lapse slow motion imaging. Goldberg used a partially silvered mirror (or half a mirror) in several of his inventions.

Again a Professor

Despite his responsibilities for developing new products at Ica during the immediate postwar years, Goldberg somehow found the time for popular technical writing, investigations into the nature of the photographic

Figure 8.12. Son and father (Herbert and Goldberg) enjoy a parcel of candies. Still from an untitled film.

process, and part-time teaching. The continued close contact with Luther and the Institute doubtless helped.

He prepared a revised edition in 1923 of his 1912 book *Die Grundlagen der Reproduktionstechnik: In gemeindverständlicher Darstellung* ("The foundations of reprographics: An easy to understand explanation") and, in 1927, he was responsible for a new and revised edition of Carl Kampmann's popular pocket book on the graphic arts *(Die graphische Kunste),* a good example of concise, clear exposition.

Soon after reaching Dresden, Goldberg investigated the effect of atmospheric haze in reducing the clarity of aerial photographs, which had emerged as a significant problem in military reconnaissance during the war. He measured the effect of haze by a series of outdoor observations comparing the luminosity of a nonreflective, black surface close at hand with an identical surface at a distance. The nearby black surface really did look black, but the other, equally black, surface appeared much less black because light absorbed by, or reflected from, particles in the air moderate the tonal range of distant objects. However different they might appear up close, remote objects tend to have similar tones. Haze reduces contrast.

Figure 8.13. Student's cartoon of Goldberg, 1927.

When Goldberg moved to Dresden, he was nominated for a faculty appointment. Director Seliger wrote a letter praising his teaching skills and Luther vouched for his academic record. He was appointed to teach photography, cinematography, and reprographics (*Photographie, Kinematographie, und Reproduktionstechnik*). The initial appointment was as Privatdozent, an instructor who has not yet satisfied the rigorous review *(Habilitation)* for appointment as a full university professor, but, soon afterward, he was appointed Adjunct Professor *(Honorarprofessor)*. His inaugural lecture was titled "Cinematography as Technical Problem." Goldberg regularly taught a course on cinematography, for which his lecture outlines for the summer semester of 1930 survive. Other courses that he taught regularly were Applied Photography in Science and Technology, Sound Movies, and Reprographics. After his lectures, he liked to stay and chat with Luther. They had very similar interests, extending broadly across photography and including physiological and psychological aspects.

Goldberg also went skiing with the students. A university magazine gave a light-hearted account of a skiing trip to Vikartal in the Austrian Alps at Easter in 1927. "Professor Goldberg came. He came with colossal plans and ideas for producing a movie, which was only appropriate for his calling as an expert—but he came without a camera. Or, rather, he brought an experimental camera which would not cooperate. So he sent a telegram to Dresden: *'Sendet bald Apparat an Bald. G.'* ('Send a camera quickly to Bald. G.'). One 'bald' meant that the camera should come immediately, but the other 'Bald' meant that delivery should be to our fellow-student.

So, three days later Adolf Bald went to Innsbruck to pick up the camera and, in addition, more chocolate, shoes, apple juice, and many other lovely things." Some of the students were women, and the movie that was made included a love story. The students presented Goldberg with an album, "Dedicated to Herr Prof. Dr. Emanuel Goldberg in gratitude [by] the original inhabitants of Vikartal, Alpine Ski Course, Easter 1927" and bearing a cartoon of him. See Figure 8.13.

9

The Goldberg Condition

The basic reproduction law of sound cinematography, the so-called "Goldberg condition."

—E. K. Kaprelian, 1971

The Gamma

In photography, sensitivity refers to the darkening of a light-sensitive material when exposed to light. As a film darkens, it becomes more opaque, and so less light can travel through it. So a practical way to assess sensitivity is to measure the light transmitted through the film. As explained in Chapter 6, the percentage of light blocked by the darkening of the film is known as the film's Opacity, usually expressed as Density, the logarithm of Opacity. How a particular film responds to increasing exposure to light is shown by its Characteristic Curve, a graph showing the increase in its Density as exposure to light increases.

The slope of a line can be measured by the angle of the line relative to the horizontal, or, equivalently, by the ratio of vertical movement to horizontal movement. (See Figure 6.1.) This ratio is known as the Gamma (the Greek letter γ) of the line. A line with a 45° degree slope moves vertically and horizontally in equal amounts and so has a Gamma value (ratio) of 1. A steeper slope would have a Gamma value above 1.0 and a shallower slope would have a Gamma value less than 1.0.

The Densograph provided an improved technique for recording the Characteristic Curves of light-sensitive materials, but what form *should* the Characteristic Curve take? What slope or shape should be the goal of the producer of photographic emulsions? And in cases in which the desired slope has not been, or cannot be, achieved, what would be the optimal corrective action? Goldberg addressed these questions by enunciating an engineering principle that became known as the Goldberg Condition.

The most efficient use of the tonal capacity of light-sensitive material occurs when the entire range is fully and evenly used. In other words, as far as the capability of the light-sensitive material allows, small differences in light and shade are recorded and comparably small differences would be equally well recorded across the range: in the bright areas, in the dark areas, and in between. On this principle, an uneven Characteristic Curve would involve a greater loss of small tonal differences in some parts of the tonal range than in others, which would occur, for example, if the reproduced image were to go black in the darker areas more quickly than it should, and small tonal differences in the darker areas, as in the shadows of a landscape, are lost. Or, at the other end of the range, the brightest areas might become solid white ("burned out") too soon, in which case fine details in the light areas, such as the texture of a white wall, would be lost. Intuitively, the Characteristic Curve should not only match the requisite range of luminosity from dark to light, but should also be evenly monotonic, increasing evenly, which means that the ideal Characteristic Curve would be a straight, diagonal line from the origin (bottom, left) to the maximum, in the top, right-hand corner. In an ideal Characteristic Curve, plotted in the standard way, for each increment in exposure (movement horizontally to the right), there would be an exactly equal increment in Density (movement upward), mathematically a slope rising at 45°, with a Gamma value of 1.0.

The Goldberg Condition

Creating a photograph is ordinarily a two-stage process: First, an image is made in which light darkens the photosensitive material, reversing tonal values and creating a "negative." Then, from the negative, a print is made, in which, again, the light darkens the material, reversing the tonal values to yield a positive image resembling the original. Thus the process involves two different light-sensitive surfaces, the negative and the print, each with its own Characteristic Curve. Both stages affect the result, so an imperfect performance at either stage will diminish the quality of the resulting image. Like Hurter and Driffield before him, Goldberg recognized that faithful reproductions could be achieved over a limited tonal range by using negative and positive emulsions with Characteristic Curves having straight line portions sloping at 45°, where the Gamma is 1.0

Commonly, a negative is "weak," in shades of gray, with the darkest part not being much darker than the lightest part. If uncorrected, this will result in a "weak" print in which the tonal range, the contrast, is understated. One remedy for a weak negative is to compensate with a "strong," contrasty printing paper. Conversely, an overly contrasty, stark negative could be balanced by a low contrast paper. More generally, Goldberg pointed out, any deviation at one stage could be compensated by a complementary deviation at another stage.

If the Gamma of the slope of the negative were, say, greater (steeper) than 1.0, then it could be compensated by a paper with a shallower slope, with a Gamma of less than 1.0, such that the two together will have a combined Gamma of 1.0. This relationship can be expressed mathematically by multiplying the Gamma values of the two slopes, the negative (γ_N) and the positive (γ_P). For optimal effect, the product should be 1.0: $\gamma_N \times \gamma_P = 1.0$. For example, a negative with weak contrast and a shallow slope of, say, $\gamma = 0.5$, could be matched with a contrasty, "hard" negative, with a steeper slope of, maybe, $\gamma = 2$. In this example, the pair would balance each other, as $0.5 \times 2 = 1$. This design principle, that the product of the Gammas should be 1.0, became known as the Goldberg Condition *(Goldberg Bedingung)*. As Francke's *Lexikon der Physik* states:

> The Goldberg Condition has to do with the correct photographic reproduction of light density, (intensity, tonal range) during the copying process. It is $\gamma_N \, \gamma_P = 1$ or, more generally, $G_N \, G_P = 1$, where γ_N and γ_P represent the Gamma values of the darkness curve of negative or positive process; G_N, G_P are the slopes of this curve when the points are plotted. Qualitatively, the Goldberg Condition states that for a "weak" negative a "hard" copy paper or a strong development of the positive is needed and vice versa, in order that the light density reflected from the positive or allowed through the transparency of various portions of pictures behave as light density does in nature.

The Goldberg Condition can be stated this way: Other things being equal, every single Characteristic Curve should, in theory, have a Gamma of 1.0, but when that is not the case, the Gamma at one stage can be compensated by the Gamma at another stage to make the overall Gamma equal 1.0.

In practice, other factors do need to be taken into account. In the early 1900s, the dominant uses of photography were professional portraiture and amateur picture taking, and so Goldberg concentrated on these two applications. For amateur photographers, exposure latitude, the ability to produce usable images with faulty exposure, is important, and for this, a negative emulsion with a low, "weak" Gamma slope is preferable. (By definition, any given variation in exposure has less effect on density when the Gamma is low than when it is high. A low Gamma emulsion can accommodate a larger exposure range and can be balanced by a "hard" positive material with a steep slope.) In general photography, a low-contrast negative is often acceptable. The Goldberg Condition can also help professional photographers, artists, and archivists dealing with scenes or objects of unusually low or high contrast, or with achieving special effects, by allowing them to design for a Gamma higher or lower than 1.0. Further, different kinds of applications, such as motion pictures, X-ray imaging, astronomic photography, and printing papers, need differently designed emulsions with respect to film speed, resolution, wavelength sensitivity, and other characteristics in addition to the Gamma.

The Goldberg Condition was occasionally referred to as the Goldberg Constant, although it is a really a normative value rather than a constant. Ordinarily expressed as the simple multiplication of two slopes, it is sometimes criticized as unrealistic because photographic materials invariably have an S-curve, tending to straightness only in the middle range, with a curving toe and shoulder less sensitive than the central straight line portions. So extending the range of linear, or faithful, reproduction beyond the straight line component is questionable. The principle, however, runs more deeply. Goldberg realized that results depend on the products of the Gamma values at all points of the individual Characteristic Curves of every stage of the process and that the Goldberg Condition applies to each point of the Characteristic Curves. Whatever the shape of one curve, it would in principle be optimally balanced when the other curve has a complementary shape. At each and every point, the combined result should in theory have a Gamma of 1.0, whether or not that can be achieved in practice. Goldberg's son Herbert realized that there was a simpler and more general formulation of the Goldberg Condition: The angles of the slopes of the two Characteristic Curves should *at each point* sum to 90°. Because his father did not always appreciate having his ideas improved upon, Herbert never mentioned this refinement.

Movie Soundtracks, Fidelity, and Aesthetic Perception

A very important application of the Goldberg Condition was in movie soundtracks when this was done photographically using the "variable density" technique, in which the soundtrack is a narrow band along the film in which the Density is varied. The variation in Density changes the amount of light transmitted through the track from a light source to a photoelectric cell, generating a change in the flow of electrical current from the photoelectric cell to the loudspeaker.

The Goldberg Condition is applicable to multistage processes with comparable linearity. The product of all the Gammas should ideally equal

1.0, however many the stages, as is reflected in this excerpt from a text-book on cinematography:

> While laboratories can very accurately determine the printer gamma, the ideal projection gamma will be slightly different for each cinema. . . . The contrast of a projected image also depends upon the reflection of the cinema screen and the haze-content of the auditorium. (This is one reason why a "no-smoking" rule is applied in some countries.) The contrast of the image as it leaves the projector (but before it reaches the screen) is in the region of 1.25—but the average reflectivity of the screen is 0.80 and will reduce this contrast to unity. . . .
>
> Although the ideal over-all gamma should be unity, this only yields the most satisfactory result under equally ideal conditions. Such factors as stray light, both in the camera and on the projection screen, together with reflection losses between lens components, all tend to reduce the *apparent contrast* as viewed by the audience. To allow for these reductions the contrast in the final result is often made intentionally higher than would be required in the ideal case. Present day practice is towards an over-all gamma of approximately 1.2, This may be expressed as follows:
>
> gamma of (negative $\times$ print $\times$ positive $\times$ projector $\times$ screen) $= 1.20$
>
> . . . the positive print is a *married* copy carrying both the picture and sound records . . .

The Goldberg Condition provided an elegant design principle for efficient high-fidelity reproduction, but was it also a valid guideline for human perception of what was to be depicted? Goldberg, very aware of human factors in his designs, conducted a two-stage investigation to find out.

The first stage was to identify examples of aesthetically pleasing images, which he did in two ways. "Old masters" selected for exhibition in art museums provided, by definition, a population of aesthetically pleasing images. The judgments of generations of art critics, art historians, and museum curators constituted the authority for that assumption. To select a second population of aesthetically good images, he assembled a set of images and then asked a variety of individuals to pick out images they liked.

The second step was to examine the tonal gradients in these two sets of aesthetically attractive images. He designed a handheld photometer with which he could compare the brightness of the reflected light in the lighter and darker points of a picture relative to a stable light source such as daylight coming through the window. With photometer in hand, he examined the tonal range of old masters hanging in the rich art collections of Dresden. Similarly he examined minutely the tonal range of the images identified as pleasant by the volunteers.

What he found was that both the old masters and the images identified as aesthetically pleasing by the volunteers had good tonal gradation—meaning minimal loss of detail—in the light areas and in the medium areas, but not in the dark areas. Loss of detail in the shadows did not seem to matter. In this, good imaging for aesthetic purposes diverged from high-fidelity reproduction in technical sense. The tendency for acceptable reproduction to differ from strict fidelity also emerged in sound transmission in telephony and movie soundtracks. High-fidelity ("phonographic") recording at the sound source, a faithful reproduction of a specific performance, tends not to provide the most effective, intelligible ("telephonic") effects for the listener.

Der Aufbau

Goldberg, ever the teacher, decided to write a concise introduction to the construction of photographic images, drawing heavily on his own research. He planned two slim volumes: one on tone reproduction, the gradations of light and dark tones in images; the other on resolution, the sharpness and clarity of images. Each was to be a short coherent synthesis that could be read, in his own phrase, "in one pouring" *(auf einem Guss)*.

The first volume, on tone reproduction, was published in 1922: *Der Aufbau des photographischen Bildes. Teil I: Helligkeitsdetails*—"The Construction of the Photographic Image: Part I: Details of Brightness." It was very well received and sold out within a few months. A second edition appeared in 1925. It was published twice in French in 1926, first as installments in a magazine, then separately as a book, and in Russian in 1929. It was not published in English, although Mees is said to have had a translation made for internal use within the Kodak Research Laboratory.

Goldberg wrote about the Goldberg Condition in *Der Aufbau,* but he does not appear to have used the phrase "Goldberg Condition" explicitly, nor to have written any articles specifically on the "Condition." The term does occurs in a published summary of a talk he gave in 1931: "Finally the speaker recalled the studies in sensitometry brought together in his famous work *Der Aufbau des photographischen Bildes.* From these riches, the Goldberg Condition has just recently attained a contemporary importance in sound recordings."

Entries for the Goldberg Condition are commonly found in European technical encyclopedias; in the United States, it is more commonly referred to as "the Gamma rule." Although it is not clear that he himself called it the Goldberg Condition, it pleased him that others did.

10

Microdots

If I were a rich man I would get Dr. Goldberg to build me a library.

—Michael Gesell, 1926

Sharpness of Details

In parallel with his work on tone reproduction, Goldberg worked on image resolution, on how clearly photographic images could reproduce shapes, especially the edges. He thought that just as there is a perception of tone in photos, prints, and paintings, there was also a perception of sharpness depending on factors such as Density level, Density differences at edges, the prevailing level of illumination, and, perhaps, other factors. He thought that research would eventually lead to commercial standards for measuring resolution, just as his work on tone reduction contributed to the adoption of a standard for film speeds.

How precisely would the photographic image match the edge if one partially covered a photographic plate and then exposed it to light? In practice, small amounts of the light get diffused under the edge of the covered area, reducing the sharpness (resolution) of the image. Emulsions were coated on to a glass or celluloid support; and light passing through the emulsion could be reflected by the back surface of the support into areas that were covered from direct light, thereby slightly expanding the exposed area. The result was a halo effect, known as halation. Goldberg investigated the use of light-absorbing coatings on the back of the support to reduce reflection and, thereby, halation.

Refraction also reduced resolution. The direction of light rays coming through the air would be changed by passing from air to the denser medium of the emulsion, thereby exposing areas that unrefracted light would not have reached. This process, known as optical turbidity, diffuses the edge of the image, depending in part on the thickness of the emulsion.

The opacity of the emulsion also influences resolution. The more opaque the emulsion, the more quickly any stray light would be absorbed rather than diffused, an effect known as photographic turbidity. Resolution also depends on the granularity of the light-sensitive emulsion. Enlargements of photographic images tend to appear "grainy." The finer the grain, the more precise the image, but smaller grain sizes have the disadvantage of requiring longer exposure times.

The challenge was to sort out these various causes and effects in order to create crisper images. Goldberg's first scientific paper in this area, "The Reproduction of details in photography" *(Detailwiedergabe in der Photographie),* was published in the *Zeitschrift für wissenschaftliche Photographie* in 1909, and a steady flow of technical papers followed over the next two decades. In 1912, in one of the first quantitative studies of photographic turbidity, entitled "On the resolving power of the photographic plate," he showed that with most emulsions, the diffusion increased with the logarithm of the exposure. But Goldberg gave priority to working on tone reproduction, which he summarized in the first volume of *Der Aufbau* in 1922, and, by then, he had to devote more and more time to his industrial responsibilities, so the planned second volume on resolution never appeared. But in the meanwhile, he had become very interested in very high resolution microphotography and the potential it had for information storage and retrieval.

Microphotography

Microphotography, the making of very small images of objects, depends on high resolution. As resolution is improved, smaller and smaller images can be made; so the challenge of achieving better resolution becomes a challenge to produce ever-smaller microphotographs. In 1917, Goldberg published a paper on how to make "greatly reduced photographs" *(stark verkleinerten Photographien)* using a two-stage process. He describes how to mix an emulsion, coat a glass plate with it, and use a simple camera with a standard lens to take very high resolution photographs at a 30 : 1 reduction. First an object was photographed. Then the small image on the negative was photographed to produce an even smaller positive image of the original. Two electric lamps were placed inside a box and the negative was positioned to fill the box's only window. Light from the lamps, reflected from the back of the box, resulted in evenly diffused light, illuminating the negative from behind and enabling it to be photographed in a darkroom. (See Figure 10.1.)

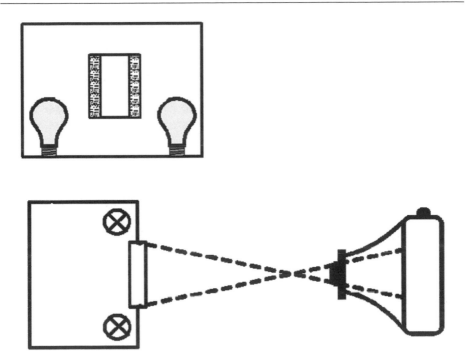

Figure 10.1. Diagram of Goldberg's method of photographing a negative to produce microphotographs, 1917.

Using this technique, a printed page, 30 cm high, was easily legible on a microphotograph only one centimeter high. Glass plate negatives, then still in common use, had the advantages of being rigid and easy to coat with a homemade emulsion. As only simple equipment was needed, a lightly revised version of this paper appeared in 1919 in *Das Neue Universum,* an annual for boys, which published material on "interesting inventions and discoveries in all areas, also travel descriptions, stories, hunting, and adventure. With a do-it-yourself supplement for the home workshop." But this was only the beginning.

Goldberg's interest in microfilm was noted in the diary of Victor Klemperer, who taught French at the Technical University in Dresden. As a child, Klemperer had grown up in what is now Poland. His father was a rabbi, but Klemperer himself was assimilated and, officially, a Lutheran. Introspective and unhappy, Klemperer felt alienated and disadvantaged as a humanities scholar in a technical college and chronicled his daily experiences and discontents in a diary. Trained as a philologist, he commonly noted the accent or dialect of people he encountered. On February 14, 1925, Klemperer morosely recorded his attendance at a university dinner the previous evening.

> Opposite me, speaking Galician German, a Professor Goldberg, director of the ICA works (photographic company). At first we were embarrassed by his strict positivism—one will calculate psyche as an electrical current—but then he spoke most interestingly about progress in microphotography and the assured future of libraries. Already one can place 10,000 print pages in easily legible microscopic writing on the diameter of a dinner plate. One will carry a whole library in a briefcase. There will be microscopes in the reading rooms and one will find a particular page by turning a crank.

Galicia is an historic name for what is now central southern Poland and adjacent areas of Ukraine. In the nineteenth and early twentieth centuries, Poland was entirely partitioned between the Austro-Hungarian Empire, Prussia, and Russia. Galicia was made part of the Austro-Hungarian Empire, and German was the language of a substantial and relatively prosperous minority of the population. The German-speaking population was increasingly Jewish. In a letter to Seliger in 1914, Goldberg had stated that his mother was German, and he kept a letter written to him by his grandmother in excellent German. Possibly Goldberg's mother's family was from the German-speaking community in Poland, and, if so, this might have been an influence on how he spoke. Klemperer was a philologist and should have been able to detect traces of dialect accurately, but others, who knew Goldberg well, say that he spoke without any accent. Goldberg and Sophie were both proud of their ability to pass as native-speaking Germans.

Klemperer's comment is suspect because, in that time and context, the adjective "Galician" had a particularly negative meaning. Germans regarded Jews from Eastern Europe, as being, in general, dirty, greedy, and uncivilized, as well as unable to speak good German. Assimilated Jews in Germany, like Klemperer, regarded immigrant Jews from Eastern Europe, which Goldberg was, with particular hostility from fear that they would undermine the status of the Jewish Germans. The word *Galician* was widely used to disparage the Jewish immigrants.

In April 1928, Klemperer and his wife were dinner guests at the Goldbergs' home and "Goldberg spoke very interestingly about the visit to his factory of an oriental despot, Aman-Ulla." In an entry for May 15, 1928, Klemperer recorded the excellent food and wine at a banquet celebrating the centennial of the Technical University. He was, however, deeply offended by a speech by Erich Bethe, the Rector of Leipzig University, which criticized the existence of humanities departments in technical universities. Bethe stated that technical colleges should stick to technical education and leave the humanities to the traditional universities. Klemperer noted angrily that this speech had been well received by engineers present and, afterward, praised as correct by "Goldberg, the Icarusman." Goldberg, himself cultured and broadly educated, did support Bethe's view, which he regarded as an efficient division of labor. "Icarusman," an allusion to Icarus, the mythic Greek who was overly confident in technology, is presumably a pun on Goldberg's firm, Ica, and the fact that he was a Russian man.

Goldberg-Style Microdot

Goldberg had a more public platform to talk about microphotography in the summer of 1925. World War I had left Europe devastated, with more than 8 million combatants killed, another 21 million wounded, and massive dislocation. The Germans were blamed for the war and the victorious Allies imposed punishing conditions on Germany in the Treaty of Versailles. There had not been an international congress of photography since the Fifth Congress in Brussels in 1910, but, finally, one was to be held in Paris in 1925. Germans were being excluded from international scientific activities, and Georges Labussière, of the Permanent Committee for International Congresses of Photography, in Paris, wrote to Mees in Rochester for advice on the delicate question concerning whether Germans should be invited to participate. There was a desire for international scientific discussion, but there was opposition to inviting Germans, and it had been suggested that the presence of Germans in Paris might provoke incidents. Labussière's plan was to send only personal invitations, and only to a limited number of selected individuals, including Goldberg and Luther. Mees replied, "With respect to the Germans, I am glad that you are going to ask some to come to the convention. If, however, you ask Luther I see no reason for excluding any particular German.... I think that you ought to ask some more.... I suggest that you write to Dr. Goldberg who, incidentally, is not a German but a Russian and ask him to make suggestions."

Goldberg went to the congress and became the center of attention when he distributed copies of a keepsake, a small case of grained leather containing a microscope slide bearing a small dot. It was a portrait of Nicéphore Niepce to mark the centenary of Niepce having made the first photograph using asphalt (Bitumen of Judea) in 1826. The portrait is sur-rounded by a circle of 360 1-degree divisions, every tenth numbered. The interval between the divisions was about 1 micron, which is one-thousandth of a millimeter. Goldberg called his image a *Mikrat,* more especially, a *Mikrat nach Goldberg,* a "Goldberg-style microdot." See Figure 10.2.

Goldberg had devised a technique that was both ingenious and simple. It was an elaboration of what he had written about in *Das Neue Universum.* It was still a two-stage process, but now, in the second stage, photograph-ing the intermediate negative, an ordinary microscope is used as a camera, as shown in Figure 10.2. As before, the object to be reproduced in the microdot was first photographed on to a glass plate. The resulting negative

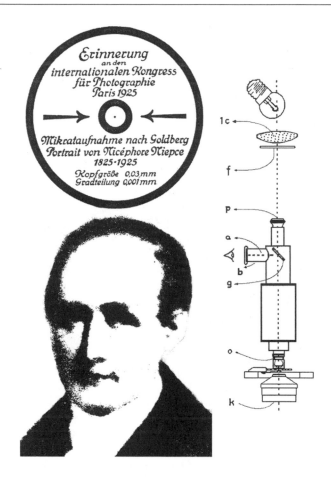

Figure 10.2. Goldberg's 1925 Microdot. The dot in the center of the 1925 Congress souvenir contains a portrait of Nicéphore Niepce only 0.03 mm high and surrounded by a circle of 360 compass lines 0.001 mm apart. Right, the image on a negative (f) is projected in through what is usually the eyepiece (p) of a microscope and focused on to an emulsion on a mount (k) below the objective (o). A partially silvered mirror (g) provides a view of the emulsion from an eyepiece at the side (b).

image was placed above the microscope where the user's eye would ordinarily be, and a slide coated with Goldberg's emulsion was placed where a specimen would ordinarily be.

The light from a small incandescent lamp, placed where the back of the viewer's head would normally be, shone through the negative and was focused by the optics of the microscope into a tiny image on the emulsion. Ordinarily such a small image would be unsatisfactory because of the grain in the emulsion, but Goldberg used an old-fashioned collodion emulsion, the use of which had long been discontinued, but which was essentially grainless. It also created a visible image ("printout") during the exposure and so it did not need to be developed, which would have reduced the resolution. Because the image being projected was already a negative of the original, a new negative would be rendered as a positive image.

This antiquated emulsion was very slow, but that was not a problem precisely because of the extreme reduction. All of the light coming through the negative was concentrated on to a very small area of film. The exposure time using a 6 Volt 30 Watt incandescent automobile lamp was about 10 seconds.

But how would one know when it was in focus and the correct length of exposure? Goldberg used the same technique that he had used in the visual photometer for studying light and dark tones in paintings. He inserted into the barrel of the microscope a partially silvered mirror set at 45° such that some of the light reflected back from the emulsion would be diverted into an external eyepiece set into the side of the microscope barrel. This approach served two purposes. First, one could see, prior to exposure, whether the image to be copied was sharply focused. Second, because the emulsion formed a visible image during exposure, by looking in through the eyepiece at the side, one could see when a sufficient image had been formed and, therefore, when no further exposure was needed. The exposure could be interrupted during inspection by temporarily inserting under the light source a filter passing a red or yellow light to which the emulsion was not sensitive, but that was visible to the human eye.

Goldberg proudly announced in his paper to the congress, that "by the aid of the method described below it was easy to make reductions of printed matter in which the letters were of from 1 to 2 microns size in such a way that the 50 lines of a page of an ordinary book could be legibly photographed on a surface of 0.01 sq. mm." Microphotography was not new, but such extreme reduction, using such simple equipment, created a sensation.

Although Goldberg described his method more than once, he did not provide a detailed explanation of his results. G.W.W. Stevens, an authority on extreme resolution photography, reconstructed his claim:

> One of the smallest recorded images was made by Goldberg, who produced a legible image of a page of fifty lines of print with a height no greater than 0.1 mm (0.004 in). Now the area occupied by the text must have been about 1/140 of a square millimeter, and it follows that no fewer than 87,500 such pages would be needed to fill a square inch. The text of rather less than two such pages is likely to be equivalent to the text of a page of the Bible, so that Goldberg's image was reduced to a scale corresponding to about 50 *complete* Bibles in a square inch.... With this process Goldberg produced images whose fineness has been a challenge to all subsequent workers.

Goldberg himself disliked "Bibles per square inch" as a measure. He thought it unscientific, but it became popular. For example, an article entitled "Communications engineering approach to microforms" appeared in 1961 in *American Documentation,* a technical journal that Goldberg used to read. The author, Laurence B. Heilprin, refers to a photograph of the first page of Genesis at a linear reduction of 1000 to 1 in which some, but not all, of the letters were legible when enlarged. Heilprin comments, "The reduction in area is so great that the entire Bible could be stored at this scale on one quarter of a square centimeter, i.e., on about the area of a baby's fingernail. Even this feat was surpassed by Goldberg who achieved 50 Bibles per square inch."

Goldberg's statement that a page of an ordinary book could be legibly photographed on a surface of 0.01 sq mm implies that 100 pages could photographed on 1 sq mm, and, therefore, 10,000 pages on 1 sq cm. One square inch is about 6.45 sq cm, which implies 64,500 pages per sq in or 50 books each of 1,290 pages, which is a realistic size for a Bible.

The Goldberg Emulsion

The collodion emulsion that Goldberg developed for making micro-dots was made in stages. First, three solutions were prepared:

A. 5 grams of anhydrous lithium chloride in 22 cubic centimeters of distilled water and 70 ccs of alcohol;

B. 24 grams of silver nitrate in 30 ccs of distilled water and 60 ccs of alcohol; and

C. 12 grams of citric acid in 50 ccs of alcohol and 50 ccs of ether.

Then three different collodion mixtures were prepared by mixing 11 ccs of A, B, and C each with 100 ccs of 2% collodion.

Finally, when a plate is to be coated, 3 ccs of the collodion mixture with A is combined with 3 ccs of that with B and 4 ccs of that with C. If it is intended that the emulsion remain on the glass plate after exposure, the plate is first given a weak coating of gelatin to serve as a cement. This "Goldberg Emulsion" is occasionally found in technical publications under that name.

A National Library in Your Pocket

Goldberg's microdots attracted attention. One lyrical essay published in a magazine envisaged the possibilities for a personal library. (The German original is in Appendix A.1):

If I were a rich man I would get Dr. Goldberg to build me a library.

Dr. Goldberg is no architect. Dr. Goldberg is a photographer. And this photographer has invented the library of the future.

His invention allows one to carry a library of a thousand books, each of a thousand pages, in one vestpocket. The entire *Brockhaus* encyclopedia takes up not even five square centimeters of space and all the German classics from Ulsilas to Klabund can be comfortably housed in the same amount of space.

Dr. Goldberg demonstrated his microphotographic process at the International Congress on Photography in Paris. It is proven technically, and only questions of cost cause some difficulties. Dr. Goldberg stored on a glass plate of nine by twelve centimeters the content of a thousand books each of a thousand pages. With the help of a specially built microscope one can, with some time, if one had it, read all the text on this plate.

If I were a rich man, I would have Dr. Goldberg build me a workroom. It should be eight-sided, have a comfortable revolving chair in the middle, at which the microtelescope would be installed, and the walls should be made of glass plates.

This workroom needs only a modest space of eight by five meters and five meters high. I would then have precisely 200 square meters of library surface available. On it, as anyone can verify, one could accommodate about twenty million books, each of a thousand pages. I would sit in my revolving chair and start to read. No State Library would be able to irritate me anymore, as I would have the most important of world literature at hand, even if a couple of square meters of my library had to remain empty in the absence of some works.

Seriously: What is radio or aviation compared with this invention? ... If the process can be done practically, one should expect from it a revolution, whose consequences must leave Gutenberg's invention standing far back in the shadows. It is entirely reasonable and imaginable that entire fields of scholarship could be brought together in such a small glass library. The creating of the first copy would be an enormous task and enormously expensive. But one would easily find a way to replicate the original at will, so one could supply copies of the photographic plates in unlimited numbers. One need only buy just a copy in order to be able to carry that field of knowledge with you.

Our desk will experience a small change. We will work with a microscope and a spotlight. Our libraries will no longer need massive stacks; a file, in which a few hundred copies of the original plates of each field of knowledge are stored, will suffice. One action by the staff suffices to put the entire Goethe literature at your disposal if you are not in a situation to buy a copy of it. A pair of knobs at your microtelescope—and this marvel functions in the sizzling searchlight. Fine gears that work in hundredths and thousandths, allow you to browse through your miniature library. It would be a pleasure to be a linguist.

Of course, bibliophiles will not have much joy in this kind of glass bookset or library books. But the times and civilization shrug off the old romance to create a new one. Dr. Goldberg's invention is necessary. It corresponds, one might say, with airplanes and radios. Just as those have made the planet very small, so microphotography has reduced the intellectual and spiritual achievements of mankind to the smallest possible space and created the possibility, which was at risk of being lost, to look over and make use of this achievement. Metaphysics winks.

It was the same theme that H.G. Wells was to popularize in the late 1930s: "The time is close at hand when any student, in any part of the world, will be able to sit with his projector in his own study at his or her convenience to examine *any* book, *any* document, in an exact replica." Wells, like Ostwald two decades earlier, referred grandly to this indexed collection of texts on microfilm as a "world brain."

On September 10, 1938, the *Prager Tagblatt,* a German-language newspaper in Prague, printed an article under the headline "The National Library in the Waistcoat Pocket. A Professor's Dream and the First Steps to Its Achievement" *(Die Nationalbibliothek in der Westentasche: Ein Professoren-Traum und die ersten Schritte zu seiner Verwirklichung).* The article reported that American libraries are increasingly using 35 mm microfilm to store printed material. Microfilms saved storage costs and could copied and transported easily. Workstations are being developed for use in the offices of large American firms where microfilmed images of, for example, construction blueprints could be stored inside a box or desk and projected on to a desktop screen. Some of these workstations are mechanized: The user could dial or key the code for the desired image if its location on the microfilm was known and that image would be displayed. (Figure 10.3 shows a example from 1936.)

The article continued:

> With the construction of this wonderful table, in which entire libraries are found on film, is the first step to the realization of an idea that was demonstrated seven years ago ... by the Russian scientist Goldberg. At that time people laughed at the dreams of the professor, who was known not only as a film and cinema engineer but was also a passionate inventor.
>
> The library of the future, so claimed Professor Goldberg, would have only projection tables in its reading rooms, and in each of these

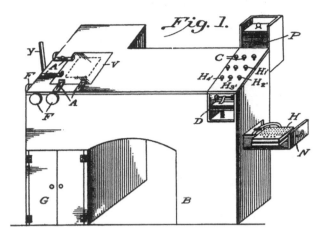

June 21, 1938.   L. G. TOWNSEND   2,121,061
METHOD OF AND APPARATUS FOR THE INDEXING
AND PHOTO-TRANSCRIPTION OF RECORDS
Filed July 3, 1936   5 Sheets—Sheet 1

Figure 10.3. Mechanized desktop microfilm reader. Diagram
from U.S. patent 2,121,062, filed by L. G. Townsend in 1936,
issued June 21, 1938.

tables the entire library collection would be found on film. Hundreds
of readers could simultaneously study one work, of which today
there is only one copy. People laughed then about this prophetic declaration. As the professor demonstrated to his colleagues the first
model of the projection table, in his workshop, they became thoughtful. Nevertheless, people thought that the professor's prophecy was
a great exaggeration. If every page of a book could be transferred to
an 8 mm machine, how many such exposures could find a place in
the inside of such table? The visitors began to calculate, but with a
triumphant smile, the professor interrupted. He led his colleagues to
a microscope and requested that they look through the instrument. In
the field of vision one could see a complete page of a publication of
the professor's in the *Zeitschrift für technische Physik*. Every single
letter was clearly recognizable. The professor had reduced one page
and still, when one looked through the microscope—one could see
that every detail could be exactly discerned. The professor's colleagues, all experienced photographic engineers, could not believe it.
According to their experiences with microscopic reduction, the grain
of the photographic material would wipe out all details, rendering
them unrecognizable. In the microscopic picture, however, there was
no trace of the photographic grains to recognize. People besieged the
professor with questions. The small professor with the endearing,
wrinkled face chewed on the filter of his cigarette and enjoyed his

triumph completely. "Look through the microscope again," he asked with a sly smile, "and read my publication. Then you'll know my entire secret." The publication was about the characteristics of collodion emulsions and proved that these emulsions are practically grainless and therefore could be used for any desired reduction. The collodion emulsions, which can only be used when wet, were in general use before the introduction of gelatine dry plates, but were overlooked until Professor Goldberg pointed out new possible uses.

New optical apparatus is not necessary for the production of reductions because these only require an inverted microscope. And, as Professor Goldberg emphasized, the magnification of the microscopically small exposures by the projection is not an insoluble problem. "And now, gentleman," the professor ended his demonstration, "you can calculate whether an entire library can be housed in a table or not. I can reveal that the printed page that you are reading through the microscope on the film has a distance between lines of a thousandth of a millimeter. A page of approximately 50 lines can easily be stored on a hundredth of a square millimeter—that makes for one 300 page book 3 square millimeters. On a square centimeter, then, come 33 books, on a square decimeter 3,300 and on a square meter 330,000. In roll form it would be possible to accommodate a film a meter wide and 1,000 meters long inside the table; on this film 330 million books should be accommodated. The gentlemen had to admit that in this regard no difficulties could stand in the way of the project of the professor. One remained skeptical, however, regarding the automatic locating of the desired position of the film in the projection table. But also in this regard the professor was firmly convinced of the feasibility of his project. With a punch card system in connection with photocells this problem would also be solvable in his opinion. He demonstrated a small model to his visitors that in principle completely corresponds with what is used in the American projection tables now.

"That my dream will one day be carried out, I do not doubt," explained the professor, "but I am not convinced that I will live to see it."

When Professor Goldberg was asked about the progress of his project three years ago on the occasion of a Paris congress, he was not very confident. "I heard that my microscopic reductions have found entry in the espionage service of different powers," he explained. "But that is nothing new. Already in 1871, the French, besieged in Paris, used photographic reductions with homing pigeons for the transmission of news. It is new that the detective story authors jumped at my idea. But that is already all that I have to report about its progress."

Today, the way to the fulfillment of the dream of the small professor is still distant. But with the developments in America we are a large step closer to the goal.

The above is almost the only surviving informal account of Goldberg, and it is puzzling in several ways. Most likely, it is based on a demonstration in the laboratory *(Versuchsraum)* next to his office at the Ica works for delegates to the International Congress of Photography held in Dresden in the summer of 1931. (The original German text is reprinted in Appendix A.2.)

There is some journalistic exaggeration. "Workshop" in the original text is *Bastlerwerkstatt,* which implies a hobbyist's den rather than a corporate laboratory. Goldberg's face was hardly wizened *(zerknitterten)* in 1931. He occasionally smoked a pipe on vacation, but never at work and never cigarettes. The article is unsigned. Who wrote it? And why was it published in 1938, seven years after the demonstration?

The *Prager Tagblatt* was editorially opposed to Hitler and went out of business when Hitler invaded Czechoslovakia shortly after this article appeared. This article itself is hard to find because it appeared only in an early edition of that day's paper. It was replaced in later editions by news of political developments in the threat of invasion by Nazi Germany. A microfilm copy in the Library of Congress in Washington, D.C., is of the early edition in which Goldberg's achievements are described. Only four other copies of the *Prager Tagblatt* of September 10, 1938 have been located and at least three of them are of a later edition in which there is no mention of Professor Goldberg and his library dream. It is easy to imagine something symbolic and ominous in this: The peaceful little inventor displaced and eclipsed by the aggression of the mighty Nazi regime.

As with his moiré, wedge, and other work, Goldberg had evidently learned a good deal from practical experimentation. He reported, for example, that vibrations from traffic on the Schandauer street outside the Ica works building could ruin the clarity of the image. His paper on making microdots was reprinted in English, French, and in various German versions, and included quite practical advice. For example, "it is very difficult to identify the image in the case of great reductions (the image measures only one or two hundredths of a millimeter and is scarcely distinguishable from particles of dust, etc. on the plate ...)." His solution was the use of a preprinted grid on the emulsion as an aid to location.

Goldberg's mention of microdots in detective stories was probably a reference to an episode in Frank Thiess's epic cycle of novels called *Jugend* ("Youth"), set in the turbulent events in Germany from 1909, through World War I, and on into the Weimar Republic. The fourth and final novel, *Der Zentaur,* published in 1931, involves a young flying enthusiast involved in the development of aerial military equipment and features Goldberg's microdot, referred to as "Dr. Goldberger's cute invention" *(Dr. Goldbergers hübsche Erfindung),* as a vehicle for smuggling industrial secrets out of a factory:

> My God, I'm used to quite a bit, I know of the ways in which people have sought to resist Dr. Goldbergers cute invention—the photographic plate 1 square millimeter large, almost grainless paper, and what does one build? A room with penetrating light that destroys all the plates. Visitors and staff must transverse this room in order to exit the factory. I wouldn't have feared such punishment. But what did I notice? That the instruments were wrongly adjusted! Not each one, you understand, and not every one in the same way . . .

But even if distinguishing between dust specks and microdots were not a problem, the problem of locating the right microdot record when 800,000 different microdot records could be stored on a 5 × 3 in card brought a new challenge: How would one identify the records that contained the information needed? Compact documents were all very well, but how, and with what tools, could relevant microfilmed records be identified, located, and viewed? Goldberg was up against the central library problem of organizing and indexing very large collections of documents in ways that could support searching, selection, retrieval, and display. His use of micro-images meant that a search engine was required. The most advanced existing microfilm workstations could "locate" documents, meaning that they could display any image if the user specified its location, but they could not search and select documents with any particular characteristic. Goldberg was designing an ingenious solution to that problem also.

11

Zeiss Ikon and the Contax

Under his leadership Zeiss Ikon grew into one of the leading German manufacturers.

—Oskar Messter Memorial Medal citation, 1932

Zeiss Ikon

In 1920, Ica formed a business alliance *(Interessengemeinschaft)* with Contessa-Nettel AG, a camera manufacturer in Stuttgart, and the Carl Zeiss Stiftung, which controlled Ica, acquired the majority of Contessa-Nettel shares. Similarly, in 1925, Optische Anstalt C. P. Goerz AG, a manufacturer of optical and business equipment in Berlin joined the alliance, followed by Ernemann-Werke AG, a camera maker in Dresden, famous for its movie equipment.

On October 9, 1926, these four firms—Contessa-Nettel, Ernemann, Goerz, and Ica—announced a "fusion" into a new company to be called Zeiss Ikon AG. Use of the German word *Fusion* was diplomatic: It meant that all parties joined together and nobody would be laid off. The underlying reality, however, was that the Contessa-Nettel, Goerz, and Ernemann companies were failing. Germany lacked antitrust legislation at that time and the Carl Zeiss Stiftung, although very attentive to its corporate image, used manipulative business practices to achieve its ends. For example, a secret agreement between the Stiftung and two leading camera shutter manufacturers, Deckel and Gautier, to control prices and availability in the German shutter market had a lasting negative effect on some camera manufacturers and on the German shutter industry itself. Of the four firms in the Fusion, only Ica, which paid the lowest wages, was relatively prosperous. Goldberg was very proud of the fact that under the terms of the Fusion, one Ica share was exchanged for a new Zeiss Ikon share, but two Ernemann shares were needed for a Zeiss Ikon share. The other three companies were substantial, long-established firms, but they were going bankrupt. Goldberg had to bring together and win the continued support of the proud owners: Heinrich Ernemann, Helmuth Goerz, and August Nagel.

The challenge in choosing a name for the new company was twofold. First, there would be an obvious marketing advantage in capitalizing on the enormous prestige of the Zeiss trade name; second, the name had to be differentiated from Carl Zeiss in Jena because the new enterprise was, legally, a separate firm. Once again, as with naming the Kinamo, Goldberg drew some benefit from the classical studies that he had so disliked as a schoolboy. He proposed playing on the ambiguity of the Greek word *icon*, in German *Ikon*, which means an image, a picture, which was apt for a photographic firm, but also has a secondary sense of something exemplary, leading, outstanding. The name Zeiss Ikon achieved both objectives: It made the Zeiss connection very prominent, it was apt, it was short, and both words projected an aura of excellence.

Zeiss Ikon's name is sometimes said to have been derived from the names of the firms that joined the Fusion, with I for Ica and Con for Contessa. This formulation is given in the 1937 company history, but it was not the origin of the name. The four letters of "Ikon" cannot be interpreted as representing all of the constituent firms and a name derived from just two of the firms' names, Ica and Contessa, would, in 1926, have been unacceptable to Ernemann and Goerz.

The Goerz component, located in Zehlendorf, a suburb of Berlin, was known as the "Goerz works" *(Goerzwerke)* and the Contessa-Nettel plant in Stuttgart became the "Contessa works." August Nagel, who had owned Contessa, was in Stuttgart, a 10-hour train journey from Dresden, and too far away to participate in the management of Zeiss Ikon as intended. He soon withdrew from the Fusion and started a new camera manufacturing business, which was eventually acquired by Kodak.

Zeiss Ikon was established as a legally independent firm with publicly traded stock and several shareholders. Nevertheless, the majority of its shares were held by the Carl Zeiss Stiftung, which was clearly in control. The Stiftung was a for-profit foundation chartered to support the public interest, and had been established to avoid the instability of family ownership of the Carl Zeiss optical firm. The Stiftung also controlled the important glass-making Schott company, Ica, and numerous other companies. Rudolf Straubel, now the chief executive officer of the Stiftung, had been instrumental in the formation of Ica in 1909. He helped in the formation of Zeiss Ikon and became the chairman of its supervisory board. It is clear from surviving business records that the managers in Jena maintained close oversight over Zeiss Ikon. Like Goldberg, Straubel was a former professor and they had a good personal relationship. Goldberg felt that Straubel had a much better understanding of what he was trying to achieve than did the other managers.

Zeiss Ikon was the world's largest camera firm, but it also had a variety of other products. In January 1927, a demarcation of interests *(Arbeitsv erteilungsvertrag)* was agreed between Zeiss Ikon and Carl Zeiss Jena. Optical products were in Carl Zeiss Jena's sphere. Zeiss Ikon's photographic product range would be cameras, nonoptical accessories for cameras, and movie equipment. Zeiss Ikon continued to manufacture a range of nonphotographic products, mainly automobile accessories, office equipment, safety locks, and streetlights. The individual factories of the formerly separate companies continued to make their existing products. The Contessa works in Stuttgart continued to make auto appliances, especially gasoline pumps, turn indicators, and windshield wipers, as well as cameras. The Goerz works in Berlin made cameras, but also industrial lighting equipment and streetlights, calculators, scientific equipment, film, and office equipment. The Ernemann works specialized in movie cameras and movie theater projectors. The Ica works made still cameras, movie cameras, and projectors for amateur use.

The ground rules for the new company were summarized in the minutes of the May 10, 1927 meeting of its management committee, the Vorstand. It was agreed that the intended geographical distribution of the workforce would be in the ratio of Dresden 12 : Stuttgart 7 : Berlin 7.

Each of the four partner companies brought its own range of cameras to the Fusion. The inefficiency of having so many different models in production was obvious, but trimming the product range was complicated by decentralized production facilities in multiple factories in three different cities, by the agreed staffing ratios, by the personalities involved, and by the need to develop new products, in addition to dealing with all the other problems to be expected in a merger of four companies. The Zeiss Ikon product catalog of 1930 still listed a confusing array of 45 different still cameras available in 74 different sizes.

The flow of patents that had started with Goldberg's arrival at Ica continued, but now patents were also frequently obtained in France, the United Kingdom, and the United States as well as Germany. Under Goldberg, Zeiss Ikon probably obtained more patents than Carl Zeiss Jena did. As Goldberg later wrote, "I was the source of a great number of Zeiss Ikon patents and engineering improvements."

In keeping with Zeiss tradition, Zeiss Ikon did not have a chief executive officer as such. Instead, a small group of Directors formed a Management Team *(Vorstand)*. Goldberg, technically Chairman of the Management Team, was in effect in charge. He had an agreement with the Stiftung that nobody at Zeiss Ikon would be paid more than he was and that he would have unquestioned access to all files and records.

In 1927, Goldberg's 10-year employment contract with Ica, made in 1917, was renewed for another 10 years through April 8, 1937. It had been decided that the members of the Management Board *(Vorstand)* would all receive the same salary, 36,000 Marks a year. Goldberg pointed out to Straubel that his previous contract with Ica had included additional provisions for profit-sharing in addition to his 36,000-Mark salary. Goldberg was also concerned about widow's benefits for Sophie if he died. Straubel said initially that because of the principle of equal payment for the officers, nothing more could be done, but later suggested that these extra benefits could be handled by memoranda supplementing the contract. However, no such memoranda materialized, despite Goldberg's reminders. Goldberg kept notes on these discussions and became suspicious about the remuneration of the other officers. One evening he was traveling by train from Berlin to Dresden with Eberhard Falkenstein, who handled the company's legal work. Falkenstein commented on the large amount of income tax Director August Nagel was paying. Goldberg inferred from these remarks that Nagel must be receiving payments from Zeiss in addition to his Zeiss Ikon salary, and, therefore, more than he himself was, in violation of the policy that all the officers were to be paid the same. Goldberg changed his itinerary and traveled instead to Jena, where he went directly to Straubel's house, rousing him from his bed in the middle of the night. Straubel conceded that Goldberg was right: Nagel had, in fact, been receiving covert additional payments. There and then, Straubel, who had the personal authority to act on behalf of the Foundation *(Stiftungsbevollmächtiger)*, wrote out by hand and signed an addendum to Goldberg's contract, increasing his salary. Goldberg then resumed his journey home to Dresden.

Sound Movies

Movie equipment was a major product line for Zeiss Ikon. Thanks to its Ernemann division, Zeiss Ikon had a near monopoly in the market outside of the United States for large projectors for movie theaters. The next major development was to move on from silent to sound equipment, but here Zeiss Ikon found itself excluded. In the United States, five firms had formed an oligopoly. Warner Brothers, Paramount, Fox, Loew's, and RKO agreed to act together: All of them would use Western Electric's Movietone sound system. In Germany the principal German sound system, called Triergon, was completely controlled by a small group of companies, and the Triergon patents were broad. For example, film moves discontinuously, frame by frame, through the movie gate, but it needs to flow steadily where the soundtrack is scanned. The usual way of achieving a smooth flow on a rotating shaft is to add a flywheel and Triergon obtained a patent for use of a flywheel on the soundtrack spindle. The patent was surprising because the method was a standard engineering solution; in the United States, Triergon's flywheel patent was eventually invalidated for that reason.

To be shut out of cinematographic sound, the emerging "talkies," would be a devastating blow for Zeiss Ikon, and Goldberg struggled to find a way out. An industrywide committee of firms excluded from the Triergon patents was formed, with Goldberg as chairman, to address the problem. A complaint was lodged with the German government, but without success, so the committee threatened to find ways to engineer around the patents. One problem patent had to do with the amplifier, in which tubes at the last stage were more powerful than those of earlier stages. To get around it, they developed an alternative design with a tube that was a little too big for the first stages and, in the last stage, they put eight tubes in parallel. It was a cumbersome way of making an amplifier, but it did get around the Triergon patent. The committee revealed this work-around to Triergon, suggested that collaboration would be more profitable for both parties, and, in this way, eventually succeeded in breaking the patent lockout.

The Messter Medal

The Deutsche Kinotechnische Gesellschaft, the German Movie Technology Society, awarded the Oskar Messter Memorial Medal to honor individuals who had made outstanding contributions. The medal commemorated Oskar Messter, a leading figure in the development of cinematography in Germany and also in aerial photography from airplanes. In 1932, the medal was conferred on Goldberg, and, 20 years later, an historical account of the Messter Medal explained why the medal was conferred on Goldberg:

> Film technology soon raised important challenges for photochemistry. In their solution, one man deserves special credit. No sound engineer and no image engineer can ignore his work on the control of copying and development processes. It was Emanuel Goldberg, who, as scientist and later as director at Zeiss Ikon AG, laid the foundation for the principles of sensitometric control in copying procedures. In addition, he was also equally successfully engaged as an equipment designer, for example, of the Kinamo, of the portable Zeiss Ikon sound film system [Tonfilmkoffers], and many other inventions. Under his leadership Zeiss Ikon AG grew into one of the leading German manufacturers.

Rangefinder Design

The ingenuity of design under Goldberg's leadership is illustrated in the development of coupled rangefinders in folding cameras. For a sharp image, the camera lens must be focused to the right distance. Rangefinders are important because they measure how far away an object is.

Camera rangefinders work by triangulation. They have two views visible in the same aperture. One view looks straight forward, the other view is offset to the side, reflected by a 45° mirror in the aperture, and then reflected forward again by a second mirror. Rotation of the second mirror changes the direction of the second view. The degree of rotation of the second mirror needed to make the two images of an object exactly coincide, when viewed through the aperture, depends on the distance to the object and, therefore, can be calibrated to indicate what the distance is. Great precision is needed.

The photographer also needed to remember to adjust the focus of the lens to match the distance indicated by the rangefinder. This separate and easily forgotten task became unnecessary with a "coupled" rangefinder connected to the lens mounting such that adjusting the lens also adjusted the rangefinder and vice versa. But many popular cameras folded when not in use to make them smaller and easier to carry, and this prevented a mechanical coupling between the lens mount and the rangefinder. A particularly ingenious design used an optical method to allow a folding camera to have a coupled rangefinder. The base of the rangefinder is built into the camera body, with the second mirror, instead of rotating, fixed at 45° for infinity. On the lens housing, coupled to the lens focusing mechanism, are two wedge-shaped disks. (See Figure 11.1.)

When the camera is unfolded and ready for use, these two disks are in the line of sight of the rangefinder's second view. When the focus of the lens is set to infinity, the two wedges point in opposite directions and their refractive effects cancel each other out. Their combined effect, as a pair, is that of a flat piece of glass. Light passes straight through and the view through them from the rangefinder, set for infinity, is unaffected. But when the lens focusing mechanism is turned, the two wedges are made to rotate in opposite directions, changing the angle of the glass surfaces into a wedge. With the front and back glass surfaces no longer parallel, light passing through is refracted (bent) sideways at an angle. In this way, the rangefinder's second view is deflected as the lens is focused, and one has a coupled rangefinder on a folding camera.

The rotating wedge design is also more precise than a mechanically rotating mirror mechanism. Later, it was realized that sliding a concave prism around a convex prism, the "swing wedge" design, would allow an even simpler mechanism to achieve the same optical effect.

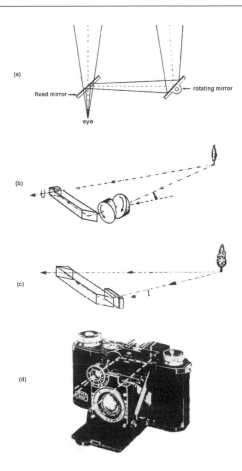

Figure 11.1. Coupled rangefinder for folding camera: (a) conventional rangefinder design with fixed, partial mirror on left and rotating mirror on right; (b) rotating wedge design; (c) swing wedge design; and (d) Zeiss Ikon Super Nettel folding camera with a coupled rotating wedge rangefinder.

The Contax

In the early years of Ica, Oskar Barnack, a Zeiss employee, had suggested to Guido Mengel, the head of Ica, that a small still camera could be designed to use standard 35 mm movie film, with an image area of 24 × 36 mm, twice the 18 × 24 mm area of a standard movie frame. Mengel did not act on the proposal. He developed the larger, best-selling Icarette 6 × 6 cm camera instead. Barnack later went to work for the Leitz company where, about 1913, he developed a compact prototype of his idea, which, in 1925, Leitz began to market very successfully as the Leica (the *Leitz ca*mera). Zeiss Ikon now urgently needed to design and market a comparable high-quality 35 mm camera if it was not to lose market share. It would have to be sufficiently different to avoid Leitz patents. Zeiss Ikon eventually succeeded with the Contax I, successfully introduced in 1932. (See Figure 11.2.) The design included some important innovations that made it easier to use than the Leica:

1. On the Contax the back opened out and was removable, allowing easy film loading. The Leica back did not open. One had to slide the film in sideways from the base and it would sometimes catch during loading.

2. A bayonet lens mounting allowed quicker, more reliable lens changing, compared with the Leica's screw mounting.

3. An all-metal focal-plane shutter avoided the disadvantages of the use of rubber in the Leica's shutter, which would sometimes stick.

4. The rangefinder had an unusually long base relative to the size of the camera, allowing more accurate focusing and used a new dichroic beam combiner, which was about 60 percent brighter, making focusing easier in dim light. The traditional swing mirror mechanism in the original Contax was replaced, first, by the more precise rotating wedge design, and, later, by the simpler, sliding wedge system.

5. With the Contax II (Figure 11.3), a single aperture allowed the photographer to use the rangefinder and the viewfinder at the same time. Up until then cameras had always had separate apertures for

Figure 11.2. Contax Model I, 1932.

the rangefinder and for the viewfinder and one could only look through one or the other at a time.

6. The film support plate had a recess to allow the film to move in precisely the right position. A history of camera technology states: "One of the most significant efforts was the film channel, first seen in the Contax from Zeiss. . . . The resulting film channel has a gap of 0.20 mm, a value that hasn't changed since."

7. Once the lens had been set for infinity, an "infinity lock" kept the lens set for infinity unless the rangefinder was used. The range-finder was actuated by a small knurled wheel. Placing one's finger on the rangefinder would release the lens to move away from the infinity setting when one wanted to focus it. Otherwise, with objects more than 50 feet away, the rangefinder would not be used and the lens was best left set at infinity.

8. The standard 50 mm lens, the Sonnar, specially designed for the Contax, was a brilliant new design. It produced unusually clear pictures and had an exceptionally wide aperture, f1.4, doubling the previously available light-gathering power and allowing the use of slower, high-resolution films.

9. It may well have had the first camera built with a die-cast body.

The Contax was a good example of modernist industrial design. Visually, the starkly rectilinear body was complemented, on the front, by the circularity of the lens mounting and, in its earliest versions, a round

Figure 11.3. Contax Model II, 1934.

speed-setting dial. It also reflected Goldberg's interest in ergonomic design: the focus could be adjusted using the middle finger of the right hand and the shutter tripped by the index finger, both without moving the hand.

The development of this highly complex and innovative camera involved several engineers and designers. Unlike German patents, U.S. patents required that each patent be in the name of the individual who actually did the detailed inventing, so the U.S. patents associated with the individual innovations in the Contax are under the names of a number of different Zeiss Ikon employees. Heinz Küppenbender is on several, Martin Nowicki and Arthur Mende are on some early patents, and Hubert Nerwin on later ones. Goldberg's name is only on the initial patent for the basic design. However, he was always very clear about who was in charge, and he insisted upon making all final decisions about the features of new products. The Contax was a particularly important new product, and he regarded it as his own baby. The innovations listed above, which became standard features of 35 mm camera design, are exactly the kind of user-friendly details that Goldberg, with his emphasis on designing for the public, would have insisted upon, even though he would have been too busy to have worked out the details himself: For that he employed designers and engineers.

An historian of camera design, Norman Goldberg (no relation to Emanuel Goldberg) wrote:

> Among the many cameras for which he had responsibility, the Contax is perhaps the best known. It was Goldberg's direction that brought about such features as the combined rangefinder-viewfinder, removable back, infinity lock that released when the focussing wheel was touched, and others. A young man named Kuppenbender served as the theoretical man—analyzing all the gears, levers, etc., mathematically, while Goldberg served as the practical man on the project.

Heinz Küppenbender was a young engineer, who, like Goldberg, had been recruited by the managers at Jena. An expert on the design of camera shutters, he had been assigned to Zeiss Ikon. He was clearly being groomed for leadership. Sophie and the wives of the management board members met monthly for coffee and Mrs. Küppenbender was invited also, even though her husband was not a member of the board. The Küppenbenders were invited to dinner twice a year by Goldberg and Sophie.

Under the demarcation of interests between Carl Zeiss Jena and Zeiss Ikon, Zeiss Ikon did not manufacture lenses and was not engaged in lens design. Nevertheless, Goldberg was able to make an exceptional arrangement for Ludwig Bertele to work in Dresden on new lenses for the Contax. Bertele came up with a brilliant design called the Sonnar that was built to the exceptionally large aperture of f1.4. In those days, before lenses were coated to reduce reflections, every glass-to-air surface involved some scattering of light, which degraded lens performance, a problem on which Goldberg had published research. Although the Sonnar had seven different glass elements, they were cemented into three groups of two, three, and two elements, respectively, and so it had only six glass-to-air surfaces, an important advantage over other lenses. There was nothing comparable.

The Sonnar was in competition with the Planar lens of Carl Zeiss Jena. One problem for lenses is curvature of field: If one photographs a flat surface, one wants the image to be flat too. Goldberg was angry when he learned that at Jena, a comparative test of the Planar and the Sonnar involved photographing a line of men standing in an arc, instead of a straight line, thereby masking the Planar's weakness in this respect and diminishing the apparent superiority of the Sonnar.

Oeserstrasse 5

Goldberg had a lot of administrative work, especially from 1925 onward. The company chauffeur would drive him to work at 8:00 A.M. He would return home for lunch, take a nap, then return to the office, and come home again at 7:00 P.M. exhausted. He also had business travel. A cartoon captured his habit of leaving for the railroad station at the very last minute (Figure 11.4).

Sophie thought he would wear himself out. The family lived in a third-floor apartment in a handsome house, number 35 on Ludwig-Richter-Strasse, now called Wallotstrasse. A photograph of the inside of the living room is used as an illustration on page 14 of Goldberg's book *Der Aufbau.* Ludwig-Richter-Strasse was part of an elegant new neighborhood near to a large park and located between the city center and the Ica works. Goldberg had his lathe, a smaller foot-operated lathe, a milling machine, and a great many other tools in a workshop. He was possessive about his tools, and nobody was allowed in his workshop unless he himself was present. Even when Herbert, the *Ingenieur in spe,* was 16 years old, he was not allowed to use the power tools.

After the Russian Revolution, Sophie's parents came to Dresden. They lived initially in a small hotel in Weisser Hirsch, an attractive, hillside suburb of Dresden, then moved in with Goldberg and Sophie, but would spend the winters in Nice, enjoying the mild Mediterranean climate. Sophie's father had managed to bring some money out of Russia, but it was lost through unwise investments during the German hyperinflation, and so her parents became dependent on her husband.

Goldberg decided to build a small summer house in Loschwitz, not far from Weisser Hirsch, and bought a plot of land near the top of a hillside overlooking Dresden. It was on Oeserstrasse, named for Adam Friedrich Oeser, who had founded the Academy for Graphic Arts in Leipzig. Goldberg

Figure 11.4. "When the Professor travels." Cartoon of Goldberg going to the railroad station at the last minute.

admired the design of a house he had seen in an illustration in an English gardening magazine. It had a most unusual feature: the roof tiles curved up the sides of a central chimney, continuing all the way to the top. He decided to build a house like it and hired an architect. He later dismissed the architect and completed the plans himself. It was built nine meters (29 feet) square and was completed in 1929.

The land had been for sale for a long time and, when Goldberg put in a low bid of 20,000 Marks, it was accepted. The city of Dresden wanted it at that price and decided to exercise eminent domain. The city cited a law that had been passed during the period of extreme German inflation to prevent foreigners with hard currency from buying up real estate at bargain prices. Goldberg, incensed, pointed out that the city had had plenty of time and opportunity to buy the property, and he threatened to move the administrative headquarters of Zeiss Ikon to Berlin, where the company had unoccupied office space at the Goerz works. Faced with the prospect of the largest firm in town being controlled from Berlin, the city administration backed down.

The new house had a wonderful view, looking out over Dresden. Goldberg decided to expand it and make it his year-round residence. Because of the magnificent view, he incorporated a massive plate glass window, floor to ceiling and 14 feet wide. Despite its size, it could be lowered by an electric motor into a slot in the floor. He spent many weekends designing the structure from which the heavy, steel-framed window was suspended and an automatic clamping mechanism that would press it forward against a sealing frame to keep the weather out when it was closed. In the basement was his well-equipped workshop, with a similar view and with the Lorch lathe brought from the academy in Leipzig.

To reach Oeserstrasse from the Ica works, he would drive away from the city center to the northeast and cross the river Elbe over a famous metal bridge of an extraordinary design, the *Blaues Wunder* (Blue Wonder) Bridge, one of several reminders of Saxony's technological preeminence. Near the end of the bridge, two cable car services transported passengers up and down the steep hillside on the right bank of the Elbe: the Drahtseilbahn, running on rails to Weisser Hirsch, and the Schwebebahn, a monorail using cars suspended from above, running to Oeserstrasse. At the top of the Schwebebahn was a café adjacent to Goldberg's new property. On Sundays, visitors to the café could observe not only the fine view over Dresden but also Dresden's leading industrialist lovingly tending his garden.

Saturday was a four-hour workday at that time. On Sundays, Goldberg enjoyed ski trips to the Erzgebirge, a mountain range southwest of Dresden, and all-day hiking trips in a picturesque, hilly area with dramatic rock formations known as the "Switzerland of Saxony" *(Sächsische Schweiz)*. Both were only about 15 miles away. Occasionally he would use a company car for personal use, carefully making reimbursement based on the number of miles driven. Later, he bought his own car, a Mercedes convertible. He accepted an invitation to join the Rotary Club, which in Dresden, unlike some other German towns, was willing to admit Jewish members; and he was supportively involved in the König-Georg Gymnasium, the high school that his son Herbert attended, and the Landheim, a farm owned by the school for classes to visit. In winter, he liked to go skiing in the Engadine region in Switzerland and at Obergurgl in the Tyrol. In the summer, he liked to go hiking and filming in the Dolomites, staying in mountain huts or small guesthouses. Sophie preferred less strenuous vacations in Florence or Marienbad.

Television

*An economic-technological move of the first order, because
the different firms could make joint use of their differing expertise ... With this, the day of the individual inventor in the small
private lab is definitely gone.*

—S. Zielinski, 1989, on the founding of Fernseh AG

Wireless

Goldberg was interested in radio and, in spite of his responsibilities at
Ica and Zeiss Ikon, he found the time to experiment in his home workshop
with new radio techniques, including the superheterodyne. One of his
friends, Siegmund Loewe, also an inventor and entrepreneur, was a leading
figure in the development of broadcasting in Germany. In 1923, Loewe had
been instrumental in ending a ban in Germany on nonmilitary use of radio
receivers. The same year, he and his brother, David Ludwig Loewe, founded
a radio equipment manufacturing company, Radio AG D.S. Loewe.
Goldberg explained later to his family that the two Loewe brothers
sometimes had difficulty agreeing and, as each owned exactly half of the
company's shares, neither could outvote the other. They approached
Goldberg, made him a director in 1929, and offered him a small stake in
their company. In this way, they explained, they would not only be able to
benefit from Goldberg's advice, but also enable him, as a minority share-
holder, to cast a deciding vote whenever they could not agree.

Radio Loewe was innovative and successful. By building reliable,
inexpensive radios, it came to dominate the retail market for radios in
Germany.

Fernseh AG

Television combined Goldberg's interests in imaging and in radio. Television systems, then as now, were based on copying and reproducing an image one small spot at a time by examining and reproducing the lightness of the original, repeatedly scanning the original in a series of lines, one after the other. Done fast enough, and with enough lines, the dot and the lines cease to be noticeable and a reproduction of the image appears. At first, the movement of the spot across the image in horizontal lines was controlled mechanically when scanning, and also when reproducing the image. A popular approach was to use a large rotating opaque disk, a Nipkow disk, with small holes arranged in a single turn of a spiral circle; as the disk turned, each hole in turn defined the line being scanned or projected. Another approach was to use a rotating stack of slightly offset mirror edges, one mirror for each different line.

When scanning, a photoelectric cell measured the varying intensity of the light in the moving dot area. This varying intensity was then sent by radio to the receiver, where the radio signal would vary the brightness of a beam of light projected through another Nipkow disk, thereby reconstructing the image. The photoelectric cells used in early television cameras were simply not sensitive enough to respond adequately to the very small beam of light of varying intensity admitted by a small hole in a Nipkow disk, and great ingenuity was devoted to overcoming this limitation as well as to improving the cells. One solution was to replace the small holes in the Nipkow disk with lenses. Each lens would have a much larger diameter than the usual hole, thereby gathering more light. The lens would focus this received light on to the same small area, significantly increasing the amount of light reaching the photocell. Goldberg himself received a patent for making Nipkow disks with embedded lenses: U.S. Patent 1,973,203, September 11, 1934, *A Method of Making Nipkow Disks or Plates for Television.* (See Figure 12.1.)

Goldberg could see the technical and the commercial possibilities of television. It appears that he believed, already in the 1920s, that electronic imaging and television would rival or displace conventional photography and cinematography. Consequently, television was both a major threat and a major opportunity for Zeiss Ikon. If commercial rivals came to control the key patents for television, Zeiss Ikon would be shut out of television technology as it had been with sound movie technology. However, to compete in a television equipment industry at this early stage of technical development would require a long-term investment in research and development so large that it would make sense to share the costs with partners.

The British television pioneer John Logie Baird had been frustrated by the lack of interest in television shown by the British Broadcasting

Figure 12.1. Cross section of a Nipkow disk. Diagram from
Goldberg's U.S. Patent 1,973,203, September 11, 1934,
A Method of Making Nipkow Disks or Plates for Television.

Corporation and by the British Post Office. He was attracted by the positive and supportive interest shown by the German Post Office, the government agency responsible for communications in Germany. Two managers of the Robert Bosch company, Erich Rassbach and Karl Martell Wild, impressed by Baird's Nipkow disk-based system, suggested collaboration only to find that Baird had already approached Siegmund Loewe. Because Baird and Loewe both lacked the capital that would be needed, Loewe asked Bosch and Zeiss Ikon, both large companies with substantial financial resources, if they would be willing to become partners. Both agreed to do so. The outcome was the founding, on June 11, 1929, of a new company, Fernseh AG (literally "Television Company"). It was a joint venture by the four companies: Robert Bosch AG of Stuttgart, Radio AG D.S. Loewe of Berlin, Baird Television Ltd of London, and Zeiss Ikon of Dresden. They agreed to share their expertise, their patents, and their capital in order to enter the large expected market for television equipment. Efforts to persuade Denes von Mihály's group to join were unsuccessful.

It was a very powerful combination. Baird was the leader in television technology and would supply expertise in picture scanning. Loewe was successfully pioneering the design and manufacture of improved tubes and wireless equipment. Bosch was a major manufacturer of electric motors, measuring devices, and other high-technology equipment. Zeiss Ikon was a leader in optical and photographic equipment, including movie projectors. In addition, the German government was willing to support Fernseh AG in order to avoid a monopoly within Germany by Telefunken, a subsidiary of AEG and Siemens, which was in partnership with an American firm, RCA. "With this," a historian of media later wrote, "the day of the individual inventor in the small private lab is definitely gone."

Goldberg's enthusiasm for the potential of television was decisive in moving Zeiss Ikon into electronic imaging. With his PhD in physical chemistry and his dissertation on the effect of light on chemical processes, Goldberg had the scientific background to appreciate the possibilities of television. Zeiss Ikon was already concerned with electronics because of the photoelectric cells needed for sound projectors and for camera exposure meters. In the depth of the Depression, when staff was being laid off, Goldberg hired a specialist in photoelectric cells, Paul Görlich, who was to have a long and distinguished research career. Goldberg's view that electronic imaging could rival or eclipse photography was probably not shared by other Zeiss managers, but Rudolf Straubel, the head of Carl Zeiss Stiftung and the real decision maker, often shared Goldberg's views. It was with evident satisfaction that Goldberg reported to the Carl Zeiss managers, "Yesterday in Berlin, after long negotiations, the founding of Fernseh AG was completed following the objectives that I reported to you in detail at the last meeting of the Management Committee."

The board of directors of Fernseh AG was composed of Emanuel Goldberg, Oliver George Hutchinson (for Baird), David Ludwig Loewe, and Erich Carl Rassbach (for Bosch). The Chief Technician of the German Post Office, Dr. Banneitz, was appointed as a consultant, and Eberhard Falkenstein, who did legal work for Zeiss Ikon, was also involved. Goldberg became the first chairman of the board of directors and Paul Goerz was put in charge of the new company, which was assigned space in Zeiss Ikon's Goerz works in Zehlendorf, a suburb of Berlin. Rolf Möller, who had an excellent education and a strong background in optics, became responsible for physics and vacuum technology, and Georg Schubert for high-frequency technology.

Goerz, Möller, and Schubert provided strong leadership. Excellent laboratory and manufacturing facilities were rapidly installed, and the new company was immediately and consistently successful in technical innovation, receiving many patents, and making some commercial progress. In 1931, they had their first export order. George Everson, who worked with television pioneer Philo Farnsworth, visited Germany and commented: "The work of Fernseh was particularly impressive. The engineers of the company were applying the skill for detailed refinement that is so characteristic of German scientists and engineers. Fernseh's laboratories were located in the plant of the Zeiss-Ikon Company and had the advantage of the tradition of fine workmanship that has made them noted throughout the world for optical and precision instruments."

The four founding companies each held a quarter of the shares, but it was an uneven combination: two large firms with strong financial resources (Bosch and Zeiss Ikon) and two small firms with specialized technical knowledge (Baird and Loewe). In 1932, Erich Rassbach, the Bosch representative, wrote a letter to August Kotthaus, a fraternity brother, now the production manager at Carl Zeiss Jena. Rassbach acknowledged that Fernseh had made impressive progress in design and prototype development, but complained to Kotthaus that no long-term work plan was ever made, that Goldberg's technical talk was difficult to understand, and that Goldberg was extraordinarily difficult to get hold of. He had already suggested to Goldberg that Bosch or Zeiss Ikon should buy out the other investors. In writing to Kotthaus, Rassbach was probably hoping to exert indirect influence on Goldberg, who considered Rassbach a business man of little vision, who failed to understand that heavy, continuing investment in research and development would be needed in such a venture, and that, in an innovative high-technology firm, specific long-term plans were inappropriate. In an effort to educate and impress the Zeiss Ikon's shareholders, Goldberg is said to have addressed a Zeiss Ikon shareholders' meeting using closed-circuit television.

Early popular accounts of television emphasized heroic national rivalries, as in a 1932 book by *New York Times* Radio Correspondent Orrin Dunlap:

GALLOPING AFTER THE IMAGES–APRIL 25, 1926

> More than a dozen inventors teamed with a corps of expert assistants, many of them specialists in radio, electricity, chemistry and optics, have entered the race which will award the winners fame and possibly fortune in television. Alexanderson, a Norwegian by birth, but now an American citizen, represents the United States along with Zworykin, Jenkins, Farnsworth, Sanabria and Hollis Baird. Dr. Alexandre Dauvellier, Belin, and Hollweck carry the colors of France, while Denys von Milhaly is in the contest for Austria. Baron Manfred von Ardenne, Karolus and the house of Zeiss Ikon are doing their bit for Germany. John Baird is in the race for the Union Jack.

But Dunlap's account was a misleading simplification. There was extensive international collaboration and foreign investment in German television until 1935, when Hitler began to insist on German ownership of German companies.

Intermediate Technology

A photographic film absorbs light from the object being photographed, but early photoelectric cells were too weak to operate on indirect, reflected light. Consequently, television cameras could not work out of doors, let alone be used for mobile news coverage. In experiments, the intensity of light reaching the photoelectric cell was commonly increased by using direct light, with a film image of whatever was to be transmitted projected directly into the television equipment. As was appropriate for a firm affiliated with Zeiss Ikon, Fernseh AG developed "intermediate" systems that deployed movie technology to augment television equipment for sending and for receiving.

Working in collaboration with Daimler-Benz, an ordinary movie camera was mounted on a truck and took a conventional photographic film and a sound recording of whatever was to be transmitted. (See Figure 12.2.)

The exposed but unprocessed film went immediately down a light-tight tube into a development tank (E), on into a fixing tank (F), through a washing

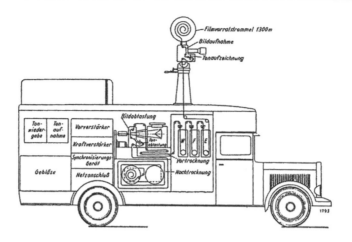

Figure 12.2. Fernseh AG's "Intermediate-film" Mobile Television Camera.

tank (W) and a preliminary drying process *(Vortrocknung)*. The images on it were then projected on to a television camera that scanned the image *(Bildabtastung)* and had a sensor to read the soundtrack *(Tonabtastung)*. The used film was then given additional drying *(Nachtrocknung)* and wound on to a take-up spool. Electronic equipment transmitted the image and sound signals within 60 seconds of filming.

Film, however, was expensive; so, in another version, the movie camera used a loop of film that was exposed, processed, copied, cleaned, resensitized, and reused continuously. By 1937, the time interval for the film loop cycle from movie camera exposure through development, fixing, television camera copying, clearing, resensitizing, and reexposure was down to 90 seconds. At the receiving end, the process was reversed. The television receiver projected the image via a Nipkow disk on to frames of sensitized 35 mm film that were immediately developed and, within 15 seconds, projected, while still wet, on to a large screen. This technique was demonstrated publicly in 1933. Leni Riefenstahl's famous documentary film of the 1936 Olympic Games required a year and a half of editing, but Fernseh AG's "intermediate technology" provided live television coverage of the same games with only seconds of delay.

Fernseh AG publicity pointed out that phonographs and radio coexisted and so could film and television. Making a film copy as part of the process derived some additional validity from the problem that there was then no way to store television images electronically. Undated lecture notes of Goldberg contain the observation that the inability to store electronic images assured the future of film.

As all-electronic technology improved, Nipkow disks and rotating mirrors were abandoned. By 1934, both the Baird company and Fernseh AG adopted the all-electronic technology developed in San Francisco by Philo Farnsworth and at RCA by Vladimir Zworykin. The "intermediate technology" was an immensely difficult technical challenge, especially the high speed processing of the film and, in the continuous loop version, adding a new coating. Zeiss Ikon developed a thin, high-contrast film and a special developing solution, and the optimal temperature for each process was determined. Nevertheless, reliable performance proved difficult, and by 1938, the intermediate technology had been replaced by fully electronic devices for ordinary, domestic television. Some use of intermediate technology continued through the 1940s for the archival recording of television programs and for the presentation of television programs on large screens in movie theaters.

Siegmund Loewe had befriended a largely self-taught, 15-year-old boy, Manfred von Ardenne, and allowed him to spend time in the Loewe Radio company's laboratory. Ardenne became famous in 1931 when he was one of the first to demonstrate an all-electronic television system. Recognizing a promising development, Siegmund Loewe saw an opportunity to repeat with television receivers his commercial success in the retail radio receiver market, so he proposed that Fernseh AG should agree not to compete with Radio Loewe on all-electronic television receivers for the home market. Predictably, this idea was unacceptable to the rest of the Fernseh partners, and Goldberg was strongly opposed. As a compromise, it was agreed that Fernseh AG would concentrate on television cameras and broadcasting equipment, but without renouncing work on all-electronic television receivers.

Goldberg's interest in television was more than that of an industrialist investor. In addition to his Nipkow disk patent, he participated, along with John Logie Baird, Siegmund Loewe, Denes von Mihály, and others in the conference that defined the first German technical standard for television, adopted July 20, 1929: 30 lines, horizontally scanned, 12.5 pictures per second, with a vertical / horizontal aspect ratio of 3 : 4.

With hindsight, one can see in Fernseh AG the combination of powerful corporations, high technology, active government policy making, electronics, and telecommunications that are now characteristic of the modern information society.

13

The 1931 Congress

At the end of the evening in the restaurant roof garden there was a performance in the style of a traditional German puppet play, in which the personalities, events, and outcomes of the day were light heartedly satirized in a drama, Sensitometrica Diabolica; or, Punch on the Standards Committee, written by "Dr. Auromontanus."

—Report on the 1931 Congress

Seven international congresses of photography had been held, the first in Paris in 1889. The eighth, in 1931, was the first to be held in Germany and the photographic world came to Dresden. It was a new peak in Goldberg's career. Goldberg, his friend John Eggert, head of research at the Agfa plant in Wolfen, near Leipzig, and Robert Luther played the major roles in organizing the congress. Their wives prepared a program for the many wives who accompanied the 400 congress participants. A report on the congress noted "the gracious kindness and inexhaustible efforts of Mrs Luther, Mrs Goldberg, and Mrs Eggert, who had prepared for them a program full of receptions, visits, and amusements, made their stay as interesting as it was agreeable." On August 3, 1931, when the congress opened, the weather was excellent, warm, sunny, and calm. In addition to the formal sessions, there were exhibits and a concert in the former royal palace.

Standard Film Speeds

The technical sessions, held in lecture halls at the Technical University, ranged broadly over photography and cinematography. The center of

141

attention, however, was a proposal for a standard measure for the sensitivity (the "speed") of photographic films and plates, which were still used by professionals and serious amateurs. German manufacturers had been measuring and publishing the speed of their products in Scheiner degrees, but this method allowed the manufacturer considerable latitude, resulting in exaggerated and, therefore, unreliable values. In the absence of a dependable common standard, it was only by trial and error that a photographer would know the correct exposure. Good photography requires both standards for the sensitivity of films and reliable measurement techniques. But how should sensitivity be defined and how should it be measured?

Goldberg and Luther were actively involved in standards development. Already in 1920, Goldberg had become chairman of the German National Committee on Standards for Photographic Technology *(Ausschuss für Phototechnik)*. The German Society for Photographic Research had a Committee on Sensitometry, chaired by Luther, which had developed a proposed standard for film speeds that he and Goldberg jointly presented at the congress. They wanted a standard simple enough that even small manufacturers with limited resources could test their own films. The proposal combined a standard light source, an exposure of 1/25th of a second, and a step filter that would progressively attenuate (reduce) the amount of light reaching different parts of the sample to be tested.

The measurement of film speed had been a source of controversy for more than 50 years. The disagreements, mostly between Germans and Americans, centered on four problems: The type of light source; the kind of attenuation generating the Log Exposure scale; the specification for the development of the film; and, last but not least, how to condense the Characteristic Curve with a single number.

1. *Light Source.* The Germans accepted an American light source developed by the U.S. National Bureau of Standards to simulate "average daylight." It consisted of a calibrated, low temperature incandescent lamp, which emitted a reddish but stable light, corrected by an aqueous blue filter that could be manufactured easily.

2. *Exposure Attenuation.* For exposure attenuation, the Germans proposed the Goldberg Wedge, but the Kodak representatives questioned the reliability of gelatin wedges and proposed to modulate exposure *time* rather than light *intensity.* They preferred a fixed light source and a variable length of exposure, an approach based on the Reciprocity Principle by which there is a perfect trade-off between the intensity of light and the length of exposure. The Germans disagreed, believing that the American testing equipment, a rotating drum that would require slits varying from 1 to 1,000 in size to provide an adequate range, was too cumbersome.

More important, they thought that the measurement procedure should be based on ordinary photography in which pictures were taken using a single, short exposure. Further, the Reciprocity Law is a theoretical ideal not achieved in physical reality. Very short time intervals may not register any photochemical effect and very long exposure leads to a reversal of the effect, known as "reciprocity failure," and the American Standards Association's variable length proposals, championed by Kodak, were eventually abandoned as invalid.

3. *Development.* There were prolonged discussions on how to specify the process for developing the film. The proposal by Goldberg and Luther assumed standard commercial film processing and so did not specify how the exposed film should developed, which would allow manipulation by film manufacturers who could claim that their film was faster than it really was. The resulting underexposure could then be compensated for by overdeveloping the underexposed film, but this method would not yield optimal image quality. Goldberg's view was that this was a self-correcting problem because the marketplace would provide an adequate corrective in practice. A manufacturer that used abnormal developing to claim an exaggerated film speed would lose market share because buyers of the film would have their films processed in the conventional way, find that their pictures would be consistently underexposed, and switch to some other, more reliable brand.

4. *Single Number Measurement.* When it came to choosing a single number to represent the lowest exposure (or log exposure) that would produce a useful negative, there were two schools of thought. The American position followed the ideas of Lloyd Jones of Kodak, in which film speed was set at the point at which the slope of the Characteristic Curve reached one-third of the maximum slope. The Germans followed Goldberg's position, described in *Der Aufbau,* in which the sensitivity of the film was defined by the point at which the film recorded a Density 0.1 above the background "fog," which results from the film material itself not being totally transparent. In the end, Goldberg's proposal became the German standard, and Jones's proposal was adopted by the American Standards Association.

Although step filters were considered problematic, U.S. proposals were seen as too sophisticated for industry adoption. Delegates wanted a system easy enough for small film-manufacturing firms to use, not just the laboratories of national standards bureaus. Goldberg considered the German proposal to be a reasonable compromise between industrial and scientific needs.

The congress had no legislative authority, but at the final session, chaired by Luther, there was agreement on recommendations prepared by a small coordinating committee. The specification of a light source combined U.S. and German recommendations: A 40 Watt incandescent lamp (proposed by the United States) with a step-wedge filter (proposed by the Germans) with 30 steps of increased Density (from $D = 0.1$ to 3.0). Exposure was to be for 1/20th of a second, using a drop-shutter. The developer to be used was specified (p-Aminophenol). The development time was not specified but should be whatever would achieve optimal rendering of the lower densities on the film being tested. The sensitivity of the film was defined, following Goldberg, by the step at which the film recorded a Density 0.1 above the background "fog"; this value was multiplied by 10 to produce the film speed rating. Density is a logarithmic measurement and an increase of 3 points in the rating corresponds to a doubling of the film's sensitivity. The national standards committees of France, Germany, Great Britain, the United States, and the U.S.S.R. would, within six months, consider adopting this proposed standard for industrial and commercial purposes.

The German Standards Institute *(Deutsches Institut für Normung)* adopted the congress' proposed standard in January 1934 as DIN 4512. Zeiss Ikon marketed test equipment. Manufacturers collaborated in the testing of films, and the procedures proved reliable. It helped that the Physikalisch-Technische Reichsanstalt, a major German national laboratory, agreed to certify the accuracy of Goldberg Wedges. By 1936, most of the film sold commercially in Germany was marketed with a DIN number and customers' complaints about incorrect exposure were greatly reduced. DIN 4512 was the first national film speed standard and was the origin of the DIN numbers printed, for the next several decades, on boxes of film sold worldwide. Over time, the standard was revised, with a move toward measurement of the Characteristic Curve rather than the point of initial sensitivity, and acceptance in the United States of the Goldberg Wedge.

Dr. Auromontanus

The congress proceedings were heavily technical. However, a special session of a more popular nature was scheduled for the general public at which Goldberg dazzled his audience. "Dr E. Goldberg ... gave an extremely well illustrated popular lecture on 'Fundamentals of Talking Films'" reported the *Journal of the Society of Motion Picture Engineers.* Other reports commented on how "Prof. Goldberg explained with amazingly simple experiments." In his lecture, Goldberg demonstrated how the vibrations from a needle playing a phonograph recording of the Egmont Overture, one of his personal favorites, could be converted into an electric current that produced patterns on an oscillograph, and also fluctuations in a rotating glow lamp that were then converted, by means of a photoelectric cell, from light back to electric current and fed into a loudspeaker to reproduce the music recorded on the phonograph record.

On the second evening a traditional Punch and Judy show presented a lighthearted satire on the personalities and events of the congress. The show was entitled *Diabolical Sensitiometry: or, Punch in the Standards Committee.* One guest noted that it "was more or less a burlesque on the day's proceedings. It was rumoured that Dr. Goldberg had a hand in it—if true he should certainly be congratulated." Authorship was attributed to a "Dr. Auromontanus," which is a Latin form of "Dr. Goldberg" (Figure 13.1).

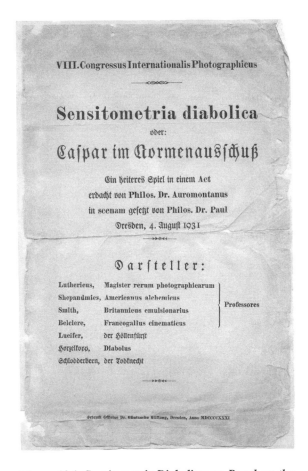

Figure 13.1. *Sensitometria Diabolica; or, Punch on the Standards Committee.* **Leaflet for a satirical puppet show by "Dr. Auromontanus" at the Eighth International Congress on Scientific and Applied Photography, Dresden, 1931.**

At the congress banquet in the city hall, Professor Leopold Lobel, on behalf of the French Society for Photography and Cinematography, bestowed its prestigious Peligot Medal on Goldberg. It was the first time that this honor had been conferred on someone who was not French. In his acceptance speech, Goldberg responded graciously that the award should be regarded as a sign of the friendship that reigned between French and German scientists. A documentary using color film, made during the congress, mostly of the participants socializing, aroused considerable enthusiasm when it was screened during the final session. The congress was a great success, so much so that an additional technical presentation by Goldberg received less attention than it might otherwise have.

14

The Statistical Machine

He was telling us that he was the only person in the world as far as he knew who had on his desk a document retrieval capability where he would dial a number or something like that and push a button and a document would be projected on a screen right on his desk.

—George Lowy, 1997

Machines for Amsterdam

Making very small photographs of objects, microphotography, had been performed early in the history of photography but had served primarily as a curiosity. However, by the early twentieth century, large bureaucratic organizations generating ever-increasing quantities of paper documents became interested in microphotographing texts on to film. In the 1920s, the practice of microfilming business records was becoming common. Banks, for example, found that they could reduce fraud by microfilming the checks they handled before returning the canceled originals to their customers. In 1926, George McCarthy, vice president of a New York bank, invented a rotary microfilm camera for copying bank checks automatically. Soon thereafter, McCarthy assigned his patent rights to the Eastman Kodak Company and became president of Recordak, a new Kodak division created to manufacture and market technology able to record large volumes of documents very rapidly. Microfilm was quickly adopted in the 1930s by businesses, industries, and government agencies, resulting in the creation of a microfilm industry to supply a virtual "machine tool of management."

Libraries, anxious to expand access to resources required by a growing research community, also adopted microfilm. Compared with paper documents, microfilm had some important advantages. Microfilming could easily reduce space requirements by 95 percent, and high-quality copies could be made and transported inexpensively. Academic enthusiasts predicted that microfilm would revolutionize scholarship, although the limitations of microfilm reading machines proved a disincentive. The literature on documentation in the 1930s was as preoccupied with microfilm technology as it is now with computer technology, and for the same reason: It was the most promising information management technology of its time.

Zeiss Ikon approached the mechanization of business records with characteristic sophistication. A check-handling system was developed for the Giro money transfer system in Amsterdam. A workstation using suction to speed the movement of individual checks could microfilm both sides of 2,000 checks in an hour. Ordinarily, finding an individual check on a long roll of microfilm would be intolerably slow, so in this design the checks were presorted and a visually prominent mark was filmed next to each check. This "code-line" mark was gradually moved vertically as checks were filmed. In a microfilm reader, as the film was scrolled at 3,000 checks per minute, the slow vertical movement of the marks provided a visual indication of where one was relative to the sequence of checks. Other equipment allowed the image of a check to be projected on to a screen. This machinery was widely publicized and sold in Germany and other countries.

Another Zeiss Ikon data processing innovation was a microfilm application that reduced labor costs and clerical errors in preparing telephone subscribers' monthly invoices. The Amsterdam city telephone system had a wall-sized array of sets of dials, resembling automobile odometers, one set for each subscriber, counting the number of calls made. Billing was cumbersome and unreliable. Once a month, a clerk would call out each subscriber's number to a second clerk, who wrote down the number, deducted the previous month's number, and used the difference to calculate that subscriber's telephone bill. There were many errors in the recording and in the arithmetic. The Zeiss Ikon solution was to mechanize the process. A Kinamo camera, with two lamps, moved mechanically, and, operating as a still camera, systematically photographed the dials. Each frame copied the dials of about 100 subscribers. A carefully designed workstation displayed two microfilms, the current and the previous months' filming, so that a clerk could easily read and transcribe the subscriber's number, then enter the current month's count, then the prior month's count, into an adding machine. A single motion then performed the arithmetic, generated the bill, and advanced both films to the next subscriber. Labor was reduced by more than 80 percent and errors by more than 98 percent.

The Development of Workstations

Workstations—in the sense of a device on, or built into, a desk that provides a more-or-less organized collection of records and supports the performance of intellectual work—were under development from the 1890s onward. Many used microfilm because of its compactness, flexibility, and reproducibility.

For example, Alexander Rudolph, a former Austrian Army officer, developed library catalog workstations in San Francisco in the 1890s. A chain of cards containing catalog records was wound past a small window. (See Figure 14.1.)

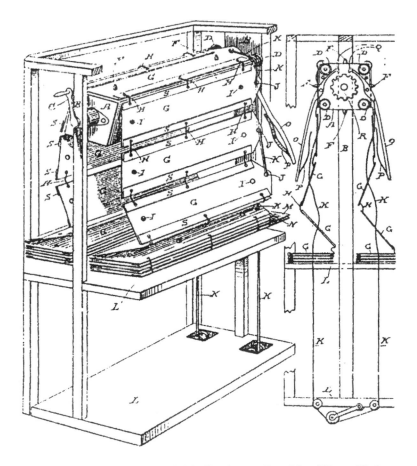

Figure 14.1. Alexander Rudolph's Continuous Revolving File and Index, 1892. U.S. Patent 473,348.

However, neither this invention nor similar designs succeeded, and he committed suicide in Chicago, a ruined man.

Brooks B. Harding was enthusiastic about the possibilities of his "Cataloguing Device," which could display the images of six spools of microfilm (Figure 14.2).

He suggested that movie moguls could use it to browse microfilmed stills of starlets when making casting decisions. Because this was a rather limited market, he also suggested that his equipment would be "particularly useful when employed to assist in the identification of suspected persons. When used for this purpose, the films carry photographs of known criminals." It could also be used to project each portrait on to a screen. It was a relatively low-technology device, using a hand-powered crank. The index, on cards, was housed in a built-in tray.

In the late 1920s, the French architect Georges Sebille attracted attention with his "Apparatus for Reading Books and the Like." It housed 12 rolls of microfilm, each 18 meters long, 330 mm wide, and 25 frames across. The self-loading rolls were searched visually using a movie gate on a numeric or alphabetic index; or addresses could be located electromechanically by sensing holes on the film. Images were projected on to a screen for viewing or copying. Because the film was unusually wide, the machine had a large storage capacity. Sebille claimed that it could hold as

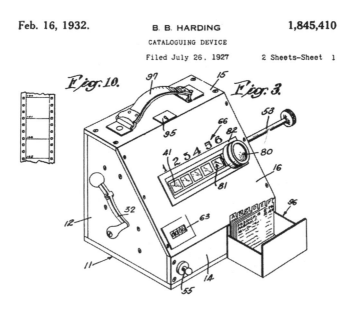

Feb. 16, 1932.   B. B. HARDING   1,845,410

CATALOGUING DEVICE

Filed July 26, 1927   2 Sheets—Sheet 1

Fig. 10.   *Fig. 3.*

Figure 14.2. Brooks B. Harding's Cataloguing Device, 1932. Diagram from U.S. Patent 1,845,410.

many pages as 1,200 books, even without replacing any of the rolls of microfilm (Figure 14.3).

Leonard G. Townsend developed something recognizably closer to a modern workstation, which had an addressing mechanism for locating individual records. Like Sebille's machine, it projected images on to a desktop screen. (See Figure 10.3.)

Some of these microfilm reader devices could *locate* records, but they could not *search* for them. If the user already knew, and entered, the location (address) of a particular record, the equipment would find it and display it. But if the user wanted a particular record or kind of record but did not know its location, the machine was not capable of searching for them. The next big technical challenge was to build a microfilm reader that could *search and select* records.

Microfilm was recognized as an information technology of enormous promise. Another line of technology under active development was the use of punch cards and edge-notched cards, which were used for sorting and searching. A third emerging technology, the use of photoelectric cells, generated great interest from the 1920s onward for a wide range of applications involving sensing and sorting.

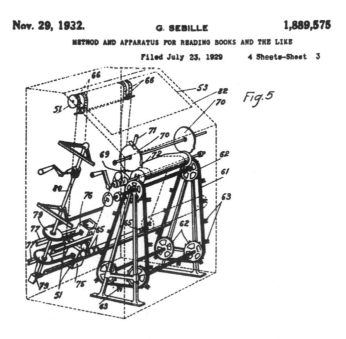

Figure 14.3. Georges Sebille's Apparatus for Reading Books and the Like, 1932. Diagram from U.S. Patent 1,889,575, 1932.

Paul Otlet on Workstations

Among the most thoughtful of the people interested in workstations was Paul Otlet in Brussels. His path had connected with Goldberg's in 1910, when Otlet had been one of the organizers of the Fifth International Congress of Photography at which Goldberg had presented his wedge and his densograph.

In 1895, Otlet and his colleague, Henri La Fontaine, planned an index to all known documents in the world, a Universal Bibliographic Repertory, and they specified the following basic functional requirements:

1. The overall coverage should be as complete as possible in providing access to the whole of human knowledge.

2. Multiple access points should be provided, minimally by subject as well as by author.

3. It should be a distributed system in that everyone should be able to have access to it and, for efficiency, it should be possible for files to be partitioned and copied.

4. Bibliographic records should be correct, concise, correctable, and expandable.

5. The bibliographic universe should be built up piecemeal from existing resources.

6. Bibliographic records should state where copies of documents are located.

7. The bibliographic records should provide a basis for quantitative studies of publication patterns ("bibliometrics").

8. The bibliographic system should help to protect intellectual property.

For decades, Otlet speculated about how new technology might be used. Toward the end of a long life dedicated to two goals that he regarded as related—solving the world's information problems and the advancement of international peace—he published a book on each, summarizing his ideas, in his massive *Traité de documentation* ("Treatise on Documentation") of 1934 and *Monde: Essai d'universalisme* ("The World: Essay on Universalism") in 1935. In these books, among many other topics, he enumerates inventions, such as machine translation, that were needed for information processing and information retrieval. After stressing the importance of telecommunications and the need for technical standards, Otlet provides a concise outline of a personal hypertextual information system:

> We should have a complex of associated machines which would achieve simultaneously or sequentially the following operations: 1. Conversion of sound into text; 2. Copying that text as many times as is useful; 3. Setting up documents in such a way that each item of information would have its own identity and relationships with all the others in the collection and can be retrieved to wherever it is needed; 4. Assignment of a classification code to each piece of information; division of the document, with corresponding classification codes; 5. Automatic document classification and filing; 6. Automatic document retrieval and delivery, either for inspection or to a machine for making additional notes; 7. Mechanized manipulation at will of all the recorded data in order to derive new combinations of facts, new relationships between ideas, and new symbolic operations.
>
> The machinery which would achieve these seven requirements would be a veritable *mechanical and collective brain* ...

Elsewhere, Otlet picked up on Ostwald's notion that a dynamic, hypertextual encyclopedia would be, in effect, an artificial extension of the brain, and he speculated:

> ... that all knowledge, all information could be so condensed that it could even be contained in a limited number of works placed on a desk, and so within hand's reach, and indexed in such a way as to make consultation very easy. In this way the World described in the entirety of the books would really be within everyone's grasp. The Universal Book created from all the books would become very approximately an annex to the brain, a support for memory, an external mechanism and instrument of the mind, but so close to it, and so suited to its use that it would be truly be a sort of added organ, an attachment outside the skin.... The organ would have the function of rendering our Being in all places and all times.

Inspiring as these lyrical passages were, not all of the necessary technology was available. Paper, card, and microfilm provided solid foundations for storage; and Melvil Dewey, Paul Otlet, and Wilhelm Ostwald had promoted standards for paper and card. In 1906, Otlet and his friend Robert B. Goldschmidt, an adventurous Belgian inventor, proposed "a new form of the book," using microimages of pages on rectangular sheets of film known as microfiche. And in 1925, they produced a portable "microphotic" library: a box of reels of microfilm holding as many pages as 18,750 books on 468 meters of shelving, and a viewer. Radio, facsimile, and television added tools for communication. Already by 1925, Otlet had recognized the potential of television for enabling remote access to texts. Library books could be placed in front of television cameras, and the image of the text broadcast, allowing people to sit at home and read from screens. "What possibilities emerge now that television has been invented!" he declared. Otlet and LaFontaine developed the Universal Decimal Classification to provide topical access to all these documents. It was a very powerful and indefinitely extensible tool, capable of expressing very detailed nuances of meaning both for encoding individual documents and also, through its notation, for expressing the relationships between categories.

What was lacking was a machine capable of searching for documents that had been assigned any particular code. The best that could be done was to have presorted entries filed in a single linear sequence on cards or on film on the basis of just one feature, such as the classification number, or the author, or the title. Adding another sequence, for example, by author as well as by classification number, required either the duplication of every document and filing the second copies differently, or creation of an author index, which would lead indirectly to the documents. These approaches, the basis of library catalogs, were laborious, inflexible, and did not scale well. What was needed was the ability to specify any value of any feature and then to delegate the actual search to a machine, which could then display the text of any documents found. To be fast enough with a sizable collection, the machine would probably have to be electronic.

The Statistical Machine

On August 5, 1931, at the Eighth International Congress of Photography, in one of the technical sessions, Goldberg gave a talk about a document search engine. This talk might have received more attention if the delegates had not been preoccupied by the proposal presented by Goldberg and Luther for an international standard for film speeds and, indeed, by Goldberg's widely reported demonstration of sound movie technology the previous evening. His talk was entitled "New Methods of Photographic Indexing" *(Neue Wege der photographischen Registertechnik)*, and it appeared in the published congress proceedings under the revised title "The retrieval problem in photography" *(Das Registrierproblem in der Photographie)*. In it he revealed his solution to the unsolved problem of searching microfilmed business records: how to find and inspect particular records, promptly, when needed, from long spools of film storing images of thousands of records in no particular order. Creating indexes to the microfilmed images manually would be tedious, time-consuming, and only yield an address for the record, not the record itself.

Goldberg's clear and concise paper describes the design of a machine for searching for, locating, and displaying any and all documents having specified characteristics regardless of the order in which they were stored on the film. It was a revolutionary document search and display system using microfilm for document storage, a photoelectric cell for sensing index codes, and digital circuits for pattern recognition, and he demonstrated a working prototype. The *British Journal of Photography* recognized the significance of this invention and took the extraordinary step of republishing Goldberg's paper in English, with the title translated literally, but unhelpfully, as "Method of photographic registration."

The principal application was expected to be retrieving accounting and sales data, so the new device was called a "Statistical Machine." In effect, Goldberg had taken the Zeiss Ikon bank-check equipment two large steps further. First, instead of a single mark to indicate the relative position on the film, detailed codes ("metadata") were used on the film, adjacent to the image of the original document to represent key aspects such as a product code, sales region, or amount paid. Second, he mechanized the process of searching through the codes by using pattern recognition. Movie projector technology was used to handle the microfilm and a photoelectric cell to identify the records that matched the search. Goldberg was interested in electronics for radio and television, and photoelectric cells were already of great importance for Zeiss Ikon for reading movie sound tracks and for light meters. The central idea is shown in Figure 14.4.

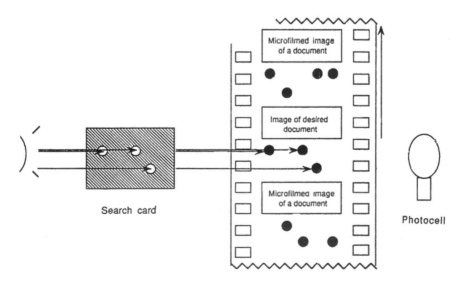

Figure 14.4. The Statistical Machine's sensing mechanism. Rays from the light are blocked by the search card except for holes for the code being sought. Only when the opaque coding on the film corresponds to the holes on the search card is all light momentarily blocked from reaching the photocell, indicating a hit.

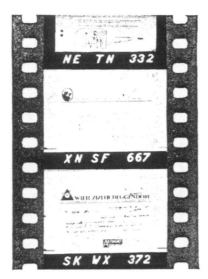

Figure 14.5. Microfilmed documents with associated index codes. Letters and numbers on left and dots on the right.

When the documents are microfilmed, they are also indexed. Each feature likely to be used for retrieval (e.g., amount paid, account number, and sales area) is represented by a code. One could use letters or numbers, but patterns of opaque dots were more easily machine-readable. The index codes for each document would be photographed alongside each image of the document, either to one side of the image, as in a movie soundtrack, or underneath, as in Figure 14.5.

In Goldberg's basic design, a "search card" is created by encoding the search query as holes in a punch card placed between a light source and the film. The search card blocks all light from the light source except for the pattern of very small beams coming through the punched holes defining the code to be sought. On the other side of the film is a photocell. As the film containing images of documents moves through the machine, some of the light that passes through the search card also passes through the film and reaches the photocell where it generates a weak electrical current. But when, and only when, opaque dots on the film coincide exactly with the pattern of light beams defined by the search card, all the light beams are blocked and no light reaches the photocell. And when no light reaches the photocell and the flow of electrical current falters, circuitry detects the loss of current and signals that a desired document has been found.

A modified commercial movie projector was used, with suitable optics to focus the beams of light on to the film, as shown in the lower half

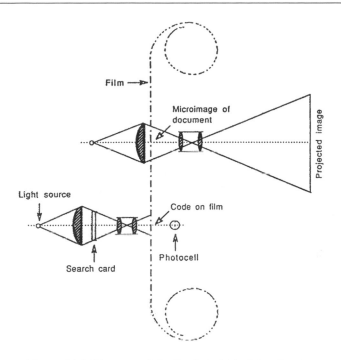

Figure 14.6. Diagram of the Statistical Machine showing the sensing mechanism and, above it, projection of the image of a document.

of Figure 14.6. Another mechanism was needed to project the image of the selected document for viewing or copying as shown in the upper half.

On October 27, 1931, Goldberg finally gave the Traill Taylor Lecture at the Royal Photographic Society in London that he had been invited to give in 1914. He demonstrated the Statistical Machine as part of his lecture titled "The Photocell in Photography" and received "prolonged acclamation." After London, he gave similar presentations in Paris and in Berlin.

Refinements

The initial German patent application was submitted on April 13, 1927, and eventually issued December 22, 1938, as No. 670,190. Patents were also applied for in Britain, France, Italy, and the United States, and three supplementary patent applications were filed in Germany:

Application Z 22,401, submitted on March 20, 1928, became German patent 691,162 *Statistische Machine. Zusatz zum Patent 670,190*

(Statistical Machine. Supplement to Patent 670,190), eventually issued on April 4, 1940.

Application Z 19,459, submitted on August 2, 1931, became German patent 697, 265 *Vorrichtung zum Aussuchen statistischer Angaben* (Apparatus for searching for statistical data), issued September 12, 1940; and

Application Z 19,461, submitted August 3, 1931, was for *Vorrichtung zum Aussuchen statistischer und buchhalterischer Angaben* (Apparatus for searching for statistical and bookkeeping data). No known patent resulted and no copy of the application has been found. The German Patent Office files relating to it no longer exist.

These supplementary patent applications in Germany and elsewhere show that Goldberg's ideas developed rapidly to include, by the summer of 1931:

(i) Clear recognition of how searches for combinations of codes, now called Boolean searches, could be specified;

(ii) Clever use of optics to enable a record on the film to be copied automatically as soon as it is found. (See Figure 14.7.);

(iii) Equipment to count the number of "hits" encountered during a search. (See counter [12] in Figure 14.7.);

(iv) Recognition that what mattered was the ability to specify a search as a pattern of light beams. Light from a lamp being selectively filtered through holes punched in a search card was only one method. The same effect could also be achieved by using an array of small light bulbs that could be individually lit to form any desired pattern as in Figures 14.8 and 14.9.

(v) Use of a telephone dial as a data entry device to specify a search by turning on any desired pattern of light bulbs. One would, in effect, be dialing a document search instead of a dialing a telephone number. This seems to be an exceptionally early use of a telephone handset as a data entry device.

(vi) In addition to detecting the presence or absence of light, the wavelength could also be used as a variable. For example, Goldberg explained, a data field for gender could be coded male or female by transmitting either red or green parts of the spectrum, respectively. The apparatus could be made to recognize red or green, and, potentially other wavelengths, thereby increasing the selecting power of each coding point beyond the limitations of a binary presence or absence of dots or holes.

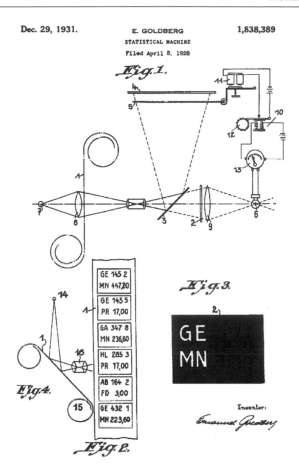

Dec. 29, 1931.

E. GOLDBERG

STATISTICAL MACHINE

Filed April 5, 1928

1,838,389

Figure 14.7. Diagram of the Statistical Machine from U.S. Patent 1,838,389. In this design, the filmed codes are projected on to the search card (2) and a mirror (3) projects the film image of the document upward toward an unexposed film (4). When the photocell (6) registers a "hit," it triggers the shutter (5) to make a copy of the document and advances a counter (12).

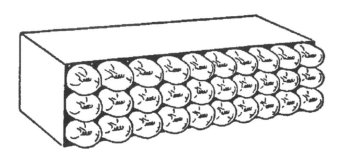

Figure 14.8. Array of light bulbs for specifying a search.

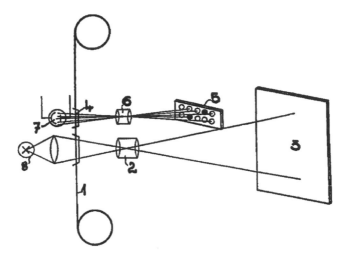

**Figure 14.9. Diagram of the Statistical Machine showing use of
light bulbs to express the search query. From supplementary
German patent 697,265, applied for on August 2, 1931.**

(vii) The selection decision itself need not be a simple binary one
because the *intensity* of the light could also be used as a variable.
The numerical value of a data point could be expressed by the
amount of light transmitted. Drawing on his experience in sensitometry, Goldberg points out that the amount of light transmitted
could, under suitably controlled conditions, be measured by its
effect on a light-sensitive emulsion. The cumulative effect of the
amount of light transmitted by successive records would increase
the total exposure, which could then be measured. It moved the
technology from a simple digital (on/off) basis to a more complex
analog approach based on measurement of values. Within limits,
this measurement would provide a means of *adding* the numerical
values of multiple records. This idea might seem farfetched were it
not that Goldberg had at his disposal at Zeiss Ikon the highest levels
of expertise and precision engineering in the world at that time.

(viii) The light could be reflected off the surface of a roll of records
instead of through it. (See Figure 14.7, lower left.)

Generalizing further, Goldberg explained that such a machine was, in
principle, no different from the visual optical coincidence punch card
selection systems that were already well known, often referred to in English
as "peek-a-boo" systems. But, he observed, because human perception
and reaction times do not allow the inspection of more than five examples

a second, mechanizing the process as in his Statistical Machine would be much faster as well as more convenient.

The increased sophistication of Goldberg's thinking and design is reflected in the difference between the original German patent of April 1927, "Equipment for searching for statistical and accounting data" *(Vorrichtung zum Aussuchen statistischer und Buchhalterischer Angaben),* in which the diagram resembled Figure 14.6, and the British and U.S. patents applied for almost a year later in April 1928, which have more of the feel of a description of an optical computer. The British patent was entitled *Improvements in or relating to Adding, Sorting, Statistical and like Machines;* the U.S. patent (Figure 14.7) is simply entitled *Statistical Machine.*

Both German and U.S. patent applications were challenged but were eventually approved. The Statistical Machine was also patented in France and Italy. IBM promptly acquired rights to the U.S. patent, after Goldberg assigned his U.S. rights to Zeiss Ikon for $2.00. At IBM, the chief scientist, James W. Bryce, was building a substantial patent position for electronic devices during the 1930s, years before IBM had any electronic products. Bryce himself obtained U.S. patents for elaborations of Goldberg's Statistical Machine.

Two different prototypes are said to have been built. A third was built into a desk in his office at Zeiss Ikon and used operationally for his business correspondence. George Lowy remembers Goldberg saying that, so far as he knew, he was the only person ever to have had such a machine:

> He was telling us that he was the only person in the world as far as he knew who had on his desk a document retrieval capability where he would dial a number or something like that and push a button and a document would be projected on a screen right on his desk. So, he could retrieve information from microfilm, right there while he was talking to a customer or colleague. He could project it. That was the only one in existence.... He would dial a number, would press a button and after three seconds the document would be projected. It was not the original but [a microfilmed copy] projected on a screen.

Goldberg's approach was, of course, a form of pattern recognition, using optical means, as has been recognized in a history of Optical Character Recognition:

> Goldberg ... suggested in the late 1920's that statistical equipment could productively apply optical scanning technology for a form of "data entry." He proposed photographing data records for reading and that the resultant photographic-record transparencies could then be matched against a negative "template" or "search plate" containing the desired identification pattern. He further hypothesized that once a match was located, the coincidence of pattern would cause a

light source to be completely blocked from a detection device, more specifically, a photographic [*sic,* photoelectric] cell. Goldberg's 1931 patent was for such a device. . . .

Because of the methodologies employed by [Paul W.] Handel and Goldberg, the critical technique of "template matching" was born. Ultimately, this principle proved to be the basic technique applied to the first, actual-working character readers which were to appear in the early 1950's.

For once in his life, Goldberg received more than his fair share of credit, because two inventive Goldbergs working on pattern recognition devices have not been adequately distinguished. The other Goldberg was Hymen Eli Goldberg of Chicago, who was associated with the Goldberg Calculating Machine Company and changed his name to Hymen Eli Golber. Golber obtained numerous U.S. and German patents, most of them in the years 1907 to 1914 and 1930, for innovations in calculating and printing machinery. One of his techniques was to print characters in electrically conducting ink on a nonconducting surface. A sensor would then test whether surface points were conductive or not, thereby detecting the location and shape of printed characters. Paul W. Handel developed and patented a similar technique for recognizing characters using a photoelectric cell to detect when the silhouette of light reflected from the outline of a printed character coincided with a template for that character.

The Convergence of Electronics and Photography

The design of the Statistical Machine brought together multiple technologies in a creative way: microfilm, for document storage; punch cards, for specifying searches; electronics, for pattern recognition; optics; cinematography for the moving parts; and telephony for data input. It was a pioneering achievement. It appears to be the first workstation to use electronics and the first document retrieval system to go beyond locating documents with known addresses to the far more difficult task of searching, selecting, and displaying any and all documents meeting search criteria.

Goldberg clearly attached great significance to the Statistical Machine. At that time, under German patent law, a patent was granted to the employer, not to the individual inventor, unless some other arrangement had been made. In this case, Goldberg had negotiated a special arrangement with Zeiss Ikon. The German patent, applied for in 1927, was to be issued jointly to Zeiss Ikon and himself and, for this one invention, he would receive half of the royalties.

The Statistical Machine and the development of television technology were both initiatives advancing electronics into areas formerly dominated by photography. The potential was much greater. Goldberg's personal technical expertise, his academic connections, his inventive temperament, and his power as head of a large and dominant high-technology firm positioned him exceptionally well for leadership in this convergence of technologies. How would it work out?

15

Ludwig, Killinger, and Mutschmann

The Workers' Council is not concerned with "Prof. Dr. Goldberg, the scientist and human being," but merely sees in him "the businessman, the Jew."

—Herr Zobler, April 24, 1933

Goldberg's Political Views

In March 1932, Goldberg was awarded the Oskar Messter Memorial Medal by the Deutsche Kinotechnische Gesellschaft. It was in the depths of the Depression. There was widespread belief that Germany had lost the Great War through betrayal by politicians. Germany's victorious enemies had imposed crippling restraints through the Treaty of Versailles. In Germany, the Weimar Republic was unsuccessful, economically and politically, industry was suffering from foreign competition, and the Depression was causing great hardship. As its name indicated, the National Socialist Party offered, a distinctively German alternative to Bolshevik socialism. It was nationalist in putting Germany's needs first, and it was "socialist" in its emphasis on addressing social problems.

Engineers ordinarily consider themselves to be rational, reasonable individuals, who base their work on calculations. But in Germany this stance had become socially unacceptable. Some forms of German nationalism, especially Nazism, depended on a rejection of the rationalism of the Enlightenment. *European civilization* had to be resisted and replaced by an insistence on adhering to true *German culture*. Right-wing intellectuals, including engineers, claimed to be in touch with "life" or with "experience," empowering them to rise above and beyond mere rationality. Engineers were

165

hungry for social status. Many believed that engineering achievements had to be seen as a heroic, cultural performances, or else, like avant-garde art and music, rejected as decadent and unacceptably non-German. Nazi ideology viewed engineering as "cultural," thereby finding a way to accept, even emphasize, the benefits of German engineering without acknowledging any underlying rationality. This aesthetic, "reactionary modernism" was in opposition to the cosmopolitan, technological modernism of Goldberg.

Like other young, educated Russians, Goldberg had initially welcomed the Russian Revolution because of the great need for reform, but, otherwise, he seems to have had little interest in politics. Other practical idealists at that time, such as the architect Le Corbusier, the Bauhaus designer Walter Gropius, and the documentalist Paul Otlet, also appear to have had little taste for partisan politics, preferring to stay detached, hoping that honest men would eventually achieve elevated leadership. Goldberg seems to have thought the same way. The only explicitly political statement found is his acceptance speech on March 16, 1932, when he received the Messter Medal for contributions to cinematography. Entitled "One Path to Cinematography" *(Ein Weg zur Kinematographie),* his speech was remarkable because it was autobiographical and because he addressed three controversial social issues: economic policy, political developments, and the role of engineers. The only surviving account of this speech found is a brief summary printed in the society's journal and reprinted here as Appendix A.3. After talking about the development of cinematography, he demonstrated the Statistical Machine as an example of the potential of cinematographic technology. Finally, commenting on the political and economic situation in Germany, with a powerful allusion to the Western Front in the World War I, Goldberg declared forcefully that technically competent people should be in charge:

> In conclusion, Professor Goldberg noted that in recent times engineers had completely failed, in that they tolerated attacks on machines again, as a hundred years earlier. Examples in great number can be quoted of calls in newspaper articles for reduced production, because of the prospect of "overproduction." In effect that means only that some number of machines are idle and a corresponding number of people are made unemployed. The concept of overproduction would hold only in certain cases. But when it could be said that the machine takes work away, it means nothing less than that we engineers lost control. It is monstrous that hundreds of thousands in Germany are freezing when we have coal in abundance; that our agriculture is on the brink of disaster for lack of fertilizer when Germany has the largest nitrogen industry in the world. With the call "Engineers to the Front!" Professor Goldberg concluded his remarks, which received a storm of applause from the meeting.

Goldberg felt that economists did not really understand the realities of life. He believed that it was better to sustain employment with reduced hours of work than to increase the number of unemployed. However, a year later, as industrial unrest increased, he conceded to his son, Herbert, that it would probably have been better to have taken the advice of his colleagues to lay off more people rather than to reduce the working hours; that way, the laid-off employees would be gone, and the remaining employees would not complaining about reduced wages.

Political Developments in 1933

Field Marshal Paul von Hindenburg failed to get an absolute majority in the presidential election in March 1932. He won in a second ballot in which Adolf Hitler received 40 percent of the votes. Hitler's National Socialist Party won a substantial minority of the seats in the Reichstag, the German parliament, in the elections of July 1932 and again in November 1932. In January 1933, Franz von Papen organized a coalition government that included the Nazi Party and commanded a majority in the parliament *(Reichstag)*. The Nazis held few posts in this coalition, but Hitler himself was appointed Chancellor *(Reichskanzler)* on January 30, with Papen as Vice Chancellor. The government, now led by Hitler, assumed emergency powers after a fire at the Reichstag building on February 27, and justified this move by claiming that there had been a Communist plot to seize power. In new elections on March 5, 1933, the Nazis won 288 seats. An alliance with the Nationalist Party, which had 52 seats, gave them a narrow majority in the 647-seat parliament. On March 23, 1933, an Enabling Act was passed, giving the government powers to issue decrees independently of both the Reichstag and the President. This act provided the legal basis for Hitler's dictatorship.

As the Nazis came to power, they engineered a systematic takeover of political, cultural, and social institutions, and a variety of attacks on Jews. Goldberg saw what was happening, and his daughter, Renate, then 10 years old, remembers him saying to Sophie, "We should leave now." But they had much to lose and they did not leave.

By 1925, Dresden had become the fourth-largest industrial city in Germany, after Berlin, Hamburg, and Leipzig. With the Fusion of 1926, Zeiss Ikon was the most important firm in the Dresden area, and Goldberg, as head of Zeiss Ikon, was a significant public figure. The 5,120 Jews living in Dresden in 1932 constituted only about 1 percent of the local population, as they did for Germany as a whole.

Fritz Busch, the outspoken, anti-Nazi director of Dresden's famous opera house, the *Semperoper*, recalls in his memoirs how he and his friend, the conductor Otto Klemperer traveled together on the train from Berlin to Dresden on March 6. They ate together in the dining car and discussed the

Nazi movement, the success of Hitler, and the future of Germany in loud and disparaging terms. On arrival in Dresden, Busch learned that a stout Nazi officer in a splendid uniform, sitting opposite them at the same dining car table, was Manfred von Killinger, a naval war hero who had just been appointed Governor *(Ministerpräsident)* of Saxony. The next evening, at the opera house, a performance of *Rigoletto* was disrupted by Nazi agitators because Busch had refused demands that Jewish performers be dismissed. The agitators demanded that Busch himself be dismissed. Denounced as a friend of Jews *(Judenfreund),* Busch was forced from his position and the Jewish performers were then fired. Remembering that he had had an invitation to go to Buenos Aires, Busch left Germany.

The next day, on March 8, Nazis occupied the premises of the *Dresdner Volkszeitung,* a socialist newspaper, seized equipment, and publicly burned records and other materials. It ceased publication. The local police were powerless because the central government had forbidden police interference with the Nazi paramilitary force known as the *Sturmabteilung,* or "SA" for short.

On March 14, "on the basis of the order from the Reichspresident for the protection of the people and of the State," the Mayor of Dresden and two of his allies were forced out of their roles. The Mayor, Dr. Wilhelm Külz, was placed on administrative leave *(beurlaubt),* City Councilor Friedrichs was expelled *(des Hauses verwiesen),* and his Social Democratic colleague Councilor Kirchhoff was placed in "protective custody."

The March 15 issue of the official daily of the Nazi Party in Saxony, *Der Freiheitskampf,* reported the dismissal of Mayor Külz and announced new measures to preserve law and order and to support the economy. During March, Communists and other suspects were being arrested by the police, by the Nazi SA, and by the Nazi SS *(Schutzstaffel,* "Protective Detachment"), and imprisoned in improvised prisons in nearby castles such as Colditz and Hohnstein. These illegal arrests led to protests to Governor Killinger, who allowed the arrests in some cases, ordered release in others, and complained of being in an "impossible situation" *("Es ist ein unmöglicher Zustand").*

On Saturday, April 1, SA and SS Nazis paraded in front of Jewish businesses in Dresden urging a one-day boycott. The same day, around 12:50 P.M., Goldberg received a telephone call from a colleague named Reichenbach at Zeiss Ikon's Goerz factory in Zehlendorf, Berlin. Reichenbach told Goldberg that at 10:00 A.M. that morning the Workers' Council *(Betriebsrat)* had made four demands:

1. Immediate dismissal of Dr. Bondi and all Jewish employees in the factory on the grounds of the government's decree that all Jews in leading positions are to be dismissed without delay, including Jews who had adopted another religion since membership of the Jewish race is the sole criterion.

2. Professor Goldberg must resign immediately as managing director, so that the Jewish influence will no longer spread at the film factory.
3. Removal of all Jewish Supervisory Board members.
4. The National Socialist shop stewards and the Workers' Council demand management confirmation by 1:00 P.M. that all of the demands have been implemented completely.

[Signed:] The Workers' Council.

Being a Saturday afternoon, the Ica works was closed, but a few senior staff were still there: Goldberg, Heyne, Schaper, and Steinmetz, a production manager. The next morning, Sunday, April 2, the Zeiss Ikon managers were summoned by telephone to a meeting at Ernemann's house to discuss the situation: Goldberg, Ernemann, Simader (the commercial manager), Schaper (who handled relations with the government and other organizations), Joachim, and Heyne. They had been unable to reach Wohlfahrt (marketing). The Workers' Council's demands were considered unacceptable and the Carl Zeiss Stiftung management in Jena was informed. Meanwhile, in Berlin, Dr Bondi had been taken for questioning by the police but then released.

On Monday, April 3, the Zeiss Ikon managers discussed the situation again. Around noon, an employee, Weberpals, who had been granted a month's leave to work full-time for the Nazi Party during March, arrived in Nazi uniform to request that his leave be extended. About the same time, Nazi members of the Zeiss Ikon Workers' Council *(Betriebsrats-Vertreter)* from Berlin (Heinrich) and Dresden (Ludwig and Henke) distributed leaflets summoning a mass meeting of Zeiss Ikon employees at 4:30 P.M., after the end of the workday. The leaflets, printed in large black letters on bright orange-red paper, alleged that 220 employees were about to be laid off and that the board of managers had received a quarter of a million Marks in the previous year.

120 hourly workers [and]
100 monthly employees will be laid off!
But one quarter of a million marks was swallowed by the gentlemen of the board in 1932/33. That's what the Jewish dictatorship at Zeiss Ikon looks like!

Work comrades! Turn out to protest!
This evening at 4:30 p.m.

Staff meeting in the Community Center on Schandauer Strasse.
Speakers:

Colleague Heinrich—Filmwerk Berlin
Colleague Ludwig—Dresden

In addition colleagues from Stuttgart and Jena.
Come in numbers! It's a matter of your job, of your future.
Ludwig—Henke—Heinrich
The Works Council.

Goldberg's son, Herbert, had just completed high school. During the interval between high school and university, he was working without pay at Zeiss Ikon for Paul Görlich, Zeiss Ikon's photoelectric cell specialist. Herbert stopped by his father's office on his way home, thinking that he and his father could go home together. Goldberg wanted to stay at the office and suggested that Herbert go on home by himself and tell his mother that he would be home in time for dinner.

Martin Ludwig and Comrades

The mass meeting scheduled for 4:30 P.M. was cancelled, apparently as a result of pressure from city officials. The Zeiss Ikon managers were ready to go home at 6:00 P.M. They urged Goldberg to leave when they did, but he lingered on for a short conversation with Simader in Simader's office. Heyne and Schaper were also present. At 6:15 P.M. a group of Nazi SA from the 14th Company of the 117th Stormtroopers' Regiment *(Standarte 117, Sturm 14),* led by Ludwig, Henke, and a third leader, entered the management offices. Threatening Goldberg's secretary, Gertrud Schubert, with revolvers and rubber truncheons, they asked where Goldberg was and went into his office. As he was not there, they also looked in the laboratory *(Versuchsraum)* adjacent to Goldberg's office, staffed by Eduard Grentz and a young assistant, Walter Riedel.

Simader's door was suddenly opened and those inside saw four Nazis, one of whom—their own employee Martin Ludwig—immediately shouted, "Professor Goldberg is the one sitting by the telephone." With pistols pointed at them, Goldberg was told to go out into the corridor. A demand to be shown an arrest warrant was answered derisively by pointed revolvers. Goldberg was rudely told to stand against the wall and threatened: "Don't laugh so sneeringly, else you'll get it!" *("Lache nicht noch so höhnisch, sonst gibt es [et]was.")*

In the laboratory, they had already arrested Eduard Grentz, who was half-Jewish, but they missed Grentz's young assistant, Walter Riedel, who, on hearing the disturbance, had prudently hidden in the darkroom and closed the door behind him.

It was raining heavily outside, but Goldberg and Grentz were not allowed to take their coats and hats as they were led outside.

Those left behind tried unsuccessfully to contact Governor Killinger by telephone. Impatient, Simader and Heyne took a company car, and drove to Killinger's private residence, Marschnerstrasse 6. Killinger was about to leave, but they were insistent that they see him. He stayed to listen to them, and they explained what had happened to Goldberg. Killinger sharply criticized this unlawful action and telephoned the police headquarters *(Polizeipräsidium)*, demanding to speak to the Commissioner of Police *(Polizeipräsident)* in person. The commissioner was not available, so Killinger had to settle for the Deputy Commissioner, Oberregierungsrat Pfotenhauer, whom he ordered to find and to free Professor Goldberg, telling him that he would hold Pfotenhauer personally responsible for ensuring that Goldberg came to no harm.

Manfred von Killinger was a war hero, a famous submarine captain in World War I. He had joined a postwar military adventure in Silesia and had been jailed for involvement in the murder of Matthias Erzberger, who had signed the armistice on November 11, 1918, and who, as a result, had been regarded by the right wing as a traitor to Germany. A Nazi since 1927, Killinger had been elected to the German parliament *(Reichstag)* in 1932. He was the author of two positive books about the SA, of which he was a senior officer. At the time of Goldberg's so-called arrest, Hitler was about to name a deputy to represent the central government *(Reichsstatthalter)* in Saxony. Killinger was the obvious candidate, but Martin Mutschmann, the head of the Nazi Party in Saxony, also wanted to be *Reichsstatthalter,* and so there was a rivalry between them. The unauthorized kidnapping of Goldberg by a small group of SA members was an embarrassment for Killinger.

Simader and Heyne became hopeful that the problem would be resolved quickly. They drove on to Simader's apartment. It was time to tell Mrs. Goldberg what had happened. It was agreed that Mrs. Simader would break the news to her, and Simader and Heyne set off again to take Mrs. Simader to the Goldberg home on Oeserstrasse.

On the way, as they passed the Ernemann works, Steinmetz and Heyne's son, Werner Heyne, saw their car, waved at them to stop, and told them that Goldberg and Grentz had been taken away. Goldberg, along with Grentz, had initially been taken to a nearby bar, where he had to stand to attention before the Swastika and endure very degrading treatment.

The kidnappers had decided to make their getaway by commandeering the Zeiss Ikon company car that was used to drive the directors to their homes at the end of each workday. But the chauffeur, Hamisch, refused, despite their threats, to do as they ordered, so they took Goldberg's own car, a red Mercedes convertible instead. They filled up its gas tank at the Ica works, then they drove away with their captives in Goldberg's car and a six-seat limousine *(Elitewagen).*

Simader, Heyne, and Mrs. Simader drove on to Loschwitz to break the news to Sophie.

During the evening and into the night, Schaper, Simader, and Heyne repeatedly telephoned the police headquarters, Deputy Commissioner of Police Pfotenhauer, and each other. Pfotenhauer confirmed to Heyne that he had ordered the immediate release of Goldberg and Grentz as soon as he had heard the news of the abduction, but they could not be found at any of the places to which arrested people were normally taken.

Next morning, Tuesday, April 4th, word of the abduction caused a furor among the leading figures of Dresden. The Nazi Party held power through a coalition with the Conservative Party, and a small group of conservative leaders, outraged by what had happened, is said to have taken the train to Berlin to bring pressure at the highest level through the conservative party leadership.

At 8 A.M. Killinger telephoned Heyne, asking him for another description of the kidnappers, and assuring him that he had the matter in hand. Around 10 A.M. Ernemann, Simader, and another manager who arrived in Dresden that morning, probably August Kotthaus from Jena, went to see Killinger. Kotthaus pointed out Goldberg's importance and also the negative publicity that would be created abroad when it became known that a director of Zeiss Ikon had been kidnapped. Killinger agreed that it was a catastrophe and said that he would squeeze information out of Ludwig under duress if necessary.

The police *(Beamte der politischen Polizei)* had already taken the two Zeiss Ikon employees Ludwig and Henke from their workplaces for questioning at 9 A.M. but could get nothing out of either. Henke was soon released. Ludwig was kept under arrest until the next day, Wednesday, in the hopes of a confession, but he continued to refuse to make any statement. He showed up briefly at work on Thursday, April 6th.

The Zeiss Ikon managers made repeated telephone calls to the civil authorities and to the police and were told that everything was being done to find out where Goldberg was being held. It appears that the Nazi Party leaders told the police that they knew that Professor Goldberg had been abducted by their people and that he would not be harmed. The Zeiss Ikon managers concluded that the civil authorities were unable to solve the problem.

Goldberg had been taken into a forest where he was tied to a tree. The next day, Tuesday, April 4th, he was given a pencil and forced to draft and then write a two-page letter resigning from his position at Zeiss Ikon and excusing his captors. (See Figure 15.1.)

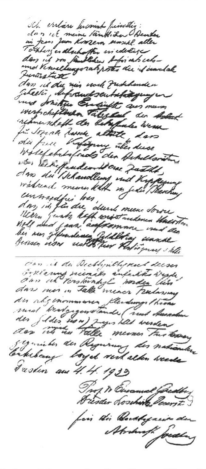

Figure 15.1. Goldberg's forced letter of resignation written while kidnapped, April 4, 1933. A transcript can be found in the notes.

I hereby declare that I voluntarily resign all my positions in the Zeiss-Ikon company, including all subsidiaries; that I withdraw from all advisory and administrative posts I hold; that I relinquish all salaries due me, compensation for work, and other income from my scientific business activities for social needs of the workers; that the unrestricted dispensing of this welfare fund is vested in the workers of these firms; that the treatment and food during my detention were without reproach in every way; that I will be fully and completely responsible for my own as well as Herr Grentz' costs during our detention; and that I give up money found on me, including securities, etc; that I will never contest the legality of this statement; that

I fully understand that in the event of my release, the clothes and valuables (with the exception of money, etc.) taken will be returned; that I will, in the event of my release, remain loyal to the National Socialist assumption of power.

The weather remained cool, cloudy, and rainy. Goldberg overheard his captors discussing what to do with him now that they had him. One suggestion was to drown him in the Elbe. A young man, who had been a student of Goldberg's at Luther's Institute for Scientific Photography, recognized who the captive was, and, aware of Goldberg's inability to digest fat, obtained some bread and jam for him to eat. Goldberg believed that it was this former student who finally informed the authorities about where he was being held.

Around 3 A.M. on Thursday morning, April 6, Goldberg was released. He arrived home, shaken, but alive. At 8 A.M. he telephoned his colleagues to let them know that he was free.

Cryptic News

In ordinary times, the kidnapping of a top industrialist would generate sensational coverage in the newspapers, but circumstances in Germany were far from normal. The *Dresdner Neueste Nachrichten* was one of the leading newspapers in town and, the previous month, had moved its editorial position into solid support of Hitler's "national revolution." It declared that Hitler's election victory was the "proud and self-confident mobilizing of a nation that had decided to free itself from the right and left wing corruption." It challenged anyone who disagreed: "The following question must be submitted with special seriousness to critics of the national revolution: Have you already forgotten what would have happened if the national revolution had not achieved fundamental change?—Not only understanding but also deep gratitude should be expected of every good German for national revolution having staved off Bolshevism at the last minute."

And what was there to say about Goldberg's kidnapping other than reporting that members of the party that was the savior of the nation had, in blatant disregard of the law, attacked an innocent person without provocation? Even if an editor had wanted to report the crime, the vivid memory of the violent destruction of the *Dresdner Volkszeitung* newspaper a month earlier would be a strong disincentive. It is unlikely any newspaper would have dared to report anything. The main news story in the *Dresdner Neueste Nachrichten* that week was the progress of the national boycott of "non-German" firms, which meant any firm in Germany owned or operated by Jews, Marxists, or foreigners. Two other major topics were concern that foreign countries might boycott German goods and the crash, with much loss of life, of the U.S. Navy dirigible *Akron*. Small news items included the dismissal of all Jews employed by the City of Dresden, the conversion of a local castle into a jail for political prisoners, and moves to purge the legal system of Jews. Goldberg is mentioned in the business section in a brief report on the Zeiss Ikon Annual General Meeting, but there was no mention of his kidnapping in any of the Dresden newspapers or in a leading Leipzig newspaper, the *Leipziger Neueste Nachrichten.*

On Saturday, April 8, the *Dresdner Neueste Nachrichten* printed two official statements that had been issued after Goldberg's release on the previous Thursday. These two cryptic statements seem to refer indirectly to the kidnapping. The first was issued by Georg von Detten, whom Killinger had put in charge of all police forces in Saxony:

Irresponsible Elements

The Information Office of the State Chancellery announces:

On Thursday several officials were arrested in Dresden. The newly appointed Oberpräsident for Police in Saxony, von Detten, states emphatically in this matter, that these arrests were not ordered by the administration of the Commissioner for Saxony or by any agency under it, or by the SA leadership or by the political directorate of the National Socialist Party. *Totally irresponsible elements* have taken advantage of the good reputation of the SA membership. Those arrested were released again after a short time. All measures have been taken to prevent a repetition of this kind of incident.

The second statement issued was by Martin Mutschmann, the Nazi Party leader *(Gauleiter)* for Saxony, and was printed in the *Freiheitskampf,* the Nazi Party newspaper in Saxony:

Ban on Individual Actions

An official order by Gauleiter Mutschmann

The National Socialist Party Gauleiter for Saxony has issued the following order to the membership in the "Freiheitskampf":

"In the course of the coordination of public life desired by the leaders of the Reich, I am continually being informed of cases in which party members usurp official responsibilities through their personal actions. Such behavior is inconsistent with the conduct with which, according to the express wishes of the Führer, the national revolution is to be achieved.

Dr Goebbels, in his radio speech yesterday, stated that the revolution is not yet complete, using the following words: 'The revolution will not come to a standstill until it has engulfed all social life and until the last fiber is steeped in it.'

This end will, however, be completed henceforth only through the systematic taking of control from above. I hereby once again order that *any separate individual action is absolutely forbidden.* Whoever nevertheless contravenes this ban, immediately excludes himself from the ranks of the Party. [Emphasis in original.]

Nevertheless, Goldberg and others thought that Mutschmann was behind the kidnapping, with the embarrassment of Killinger as part of the motivation. Already in a speech in 1926, Hitler had praised Mutschmann's ruthless effectiveness: "Mutschmann, as leader, has quickly taken Saxony in hand, moved it completely into the National Socialist Party, held it perfectly in his hand, so that no opposition can arise." Goebbels's diaries refer repeatedly, with grudging respect, to the brutality and "gangster methods" of the dictatorial Mutschmann, "a real old Gauleiter of the good old type." For Mutschmann, the kidnapping of Goldberg was an attractive opportunity to embarrass Killinger as well as an opportunity to get rid of another highly placed Jew. Most of the acts of violence against Jews during the spring of 1933 were carried out by the SA and politically motivated.

The rivalry at this time between Mutschmann and Killinger for the new administrative post of Reichsstatthalter, in effect Hitler's deputy in Saxony, was openly discussed. It was reflected, with surprising openness, in statements by Killinger printed in the official gazette, the *Sächsisches Verwaltungsblatt.* In a statement dated March 9, Killinger announced his appointment, thanked the SS and the SA for their efforts, and stated that they must now follow his orders. In a later statement, on March 28, Killinger denounced the SA and SS for improper activities, especially illegal arrests of innocent individuals, and bluntly asserted that all decisions must be made by himself and his appointees. On April 7, the day that Goldberg was released, the exasperated Killinger issued yet another decree insisting that officials must follow and not criticize his orders. He ordered a policeman to be placed in front of Goldberg's house to make sure that he would not be kidnapped again.

The kidnapping was organized, at least in part, by Zeiss Ikon employees. Two years later, a young woman, Anna Schütz, told Simader that one of the kidnapers, named Ebert, who worked for Zeiss Ikon in Berlin, had induced her to lend him money, making various promises and saying that he would soon be receiving a reward for the kidnapping, which was done on Mutschmann's orders. She had not been repaid and, in the meanwhile, Ebert had been dismissed for embezzlement.

Flight

On the first day after the abduction, Ingeborg Mengel, the 23-year-old daughter of Guido Mengel, the man of steel who had been Goldberg's superior at Ica, came round to the Goldberg residence. She said that she would take out a bank safe deposit box in her own name so that the Goldbergs could put their valuables there, where they would not be found.

Goldberg did not go back to his office at Zeiss Ikon, even though his senior colleagues urged him to do so. Instead, he and the family went immediately to Jena, where they stayed for several weeks until Zeiss could obtain exit visas for them to leave Germany. Traumatized, for several days he would not stay in the same place on two consecutive nights. The Goldbergs had dinner at the Kotthauses' and the Henrichs' and lunch with Straubel and his son, Herald, who was a Jena University student and showed Herbert his solar heating project there. Sundays were spent with the Wanderslebs, who had six children. On Sunday mornings, Wandersleb required the children to sit quietly through lengthy concerts, sometimes followed by a picnic lunch outside Jena where Wandersleb owned some land.

It was clear that Goldberg could not continue at Zeiss Ikon, even though the Nazi-controlled Workers' Council carefully explained that they were not, in fact, opposed to Goldberg himself as a person. "The Worker's Council is not concerned with 'Prof. Dr. Goldberg, the scientist and human being,' but merely sees in him 'the businessman, the Jew.'" A Jewish manager was now simply unacceptable. In late April, Goldberg and Sophie went to Italy, ostensibly on a business trip, after giving power of attorney to Goldberg's secretary, Frau Schubert, and to Eberhard Falkenstein, the lawyer. The children, Herbert and Renate, returned to their home in Dresden where the maid, Olga Krumbiegel, stayed on with them. The Simaders and especially Frau Schubert were available for advice.

Herbert had registered at Dresden's Technical University for the summer semester, which started at that time. He remained in constant touch with his friends, most of them not Jewish, and life went on. On Sundays, he and Renate were often invited for brunch by the Simaders or other colleagues and friends of Goldberg. At the time, such people thought that somehow normalcy would return. After Herbert received his emigration visa, he took the excursion steamboat up the Elbe River to the first stop in Czechoslovakia to meet his parents. When they asked him whether he wanted to stay in Germany and continue at the Technical University, he opted to be with his parents outside Germany. He then returned to Dresden to make arrangements for the move.

News of Goldberg's difficulties reached Mees in Rochester. On May 11, not knowing Goldberg's whereabouts, he wrote on his personal stationery to "Dr. E. Goldberg, Holland":

> I was very sorry to hear that the change of government had involved difficulty for you and that you are no longer able to retain your position in the German photographic industry, in which you have served with so much distinction for so many years.

If there is anything I can do to assist you in any way, please do not hesitate to let me know. It occurred to me that the change may have involved you in some immediate financial difficulty. If this is so, I am always glad to help a friend for whom I have so much regard as I have for you.

Mees's letter eventually reached Goldberg through Kodak's British operation. A cover letter from W. G. Bent, at Kodak, Wealdstone, Middlesex, U.K., to Goldberg, May 22, 1933, enclosing the letter from Mees, stated: "... if you are in any of the countries where we have a Kodak house—and this means most of Europe—I hope that you will not hesitate to call on any of our Managers if you need any help, and you can use this letter as a means of getting it."

Goldberg's authority to represent Zeiss Ikon was formally rescinded. A memorandum dated September 18, 1933, signed by Martin Mutschmann, now Hitler's deputy *(Reichsstatthalter)* for Saxony, announced the dismissal of Goldberg from his position as adjunct professor at the Dresden Technical University, and another memo, dated September 25, 1933, from the Saxony Ministry of Education revoked his right to teach there. Both cited the April 7, 1933 law on repurification *(Wiederherstellung)* of the civil service.

The 25th anniversary of the founding of the Institute for Scientific Photography was celebrated shortly after the kidnapping. In an auditorium with numerous uniformed Nazis in the front rows, Robert Luther had the courage to acknowledge warmly the decisive contribution that Goldberg had made to the lectures and exercises in the institute. After a moment of silence, the Nazi officials were stunned by the thunderous applause of the students, expressing their appreciation for Goldberg. A year later, in a report to the Ministry of Education on the importance and activities of the Institute for Scientific Photography, Luther drew attention to the pressing need to replace "the very successful and well-attended lectures of Prof. Dr. E. Goldberg on Cinematography and Sound film."

16

Paris

Étape ... stop, stage, leg (of a journey).

Ikonta and Optica

From Italy, Goldberg reported to the Carl Zeiss Stiftung on Zeiss interests in Italy and speculated on what he could do for Zeiss in France, Italy, or Switzerland. He concluded with a plea from his heart, "I only want one thing, and this as soon as possible: a place to work where I have a goal in sight which depends on *my* abilities alone. I know that I still have my former energy and initiative."

Goldberg and Sophie traveled around Austria to Czechoslovakia and came to Cinovec (in German, Zinnwald), a small border town in the Sudeten Mountains only about 20 miles from Dresden. The main street was the border. One side of the street, Zinnwald, was German territory; the other was in Czechoslovakia. At this time, Renate was on vacation with the Simaders in the Erzgebirge, near Zinnwald. Simader had only to cross the street to meet with Goldberg and to discuss what to do. Goldberg still had an employment contract with Zeiss, yet it was clear that he could not go back to Germany. Meanwhile, the children were not allowed exit visas. They were, in effect, being held hostage because of official concern that Goldberg might go to work for a foreign competitor. Herbert was now 18 and Renate was 10.

The negotiations at Cinovec resulted in an agreement in July. His existing 10-year employment contract through April 8, 1937, would remain valid, but the terms were amended and made enforceable under Swiss law, which would presumably gave Goldberg better protection. Goldberg would not be required to return to Germany. He would go to Paris, where he would work with the two Zeiss subsidiaries in France: Ikonta, the French

179

subsidiary of Zeiss Ikon, and Optica, the French subsidiary of Carl Zeiss Jena. He was appointed technical director of Ikonta and of Optica and agreed to accept a salary equal to that of the head of Zeiss operations in Paris, a good salary, but, for Goldberg, a very significant reduction. The agreement was conditional upon a waiver of the tax of up to 70 percent being imposed on all Jews leaving Germany *(Reichsfluchtsteuer)*, exit permits for the children, an intellectual property agreement, and full relocation expenses. The noncompetition provisions were strengthened. If and when he ended employment with Ikonta, he could not undertake any business activity in any way related to Zeiss Ikon's interests within a year, or he would be liable to pay Zeiss Ikon 250,000 Reichmark, and potentially more, in consequential damages. In addition, he could not under any circumstances reveal to anyone anything he knew about Zeiss Ikon's business practices, including his activities with Zeiss prior to his appointment in Dresden. If any such information were revealed by him, or by a member of his family, all benefits due to him from Zeiss Ikon would be forfeited.

The Zeiss managers in Jena must have been very pleased with the outcome: Goldberg was safely outside of Germany, his employment contract with Zeiss could be honored, and, because he was working for a German firm, not a foreign competitor, the German government was willing to allow the two children to leave. It was his task to think about new products, new equipment, new production processes, and also to extend and improve existing ones.

In Dresden, Herbert and Simader made arrangements as best they could. Simader arranged to rent the Goldberg home after the children left in order to ensure that it would be looked after. Herbert modified the electrical mechanism of the massive moving window so that it could be raised or lowered by hand, by turning a crank. Simader asked Herbert to estimate how much coal was left. Herbert replied, "Well, never mind how much coal is there, just make a line on the wall, and, when we come back, you just fill it up to that line."

The Mercedes convertible in Dresden was exchanged for a new Citroen in Paris. Sophie's magnificent Blüthner grand piano was exchanged for Frau Schubert's upright, which was shipped to France, along with the Lorch lathe and the rest of Goldberg's workshop tools. In September of 1933, six months after the kidnapping, the family was reunited in Paris. The relocation agreement that everything in his house would be transported to Paris was interpreted literally. Everything was sent, including door handles, fittings, old bent nails found in the workshop, and a huge roll of unused packing paper.

Goldberg's French acquaintances were very friendly and helpful, and he built up a social circle among Russians in Paris, some of whom he had known in the distant past. Regular dinner guests were two poor art students, the son and daughter of Sophie's cousin Boris Schatz, founder of the

Bezalel art school in Palestine. The Goldberg children adapted. Herbert attended the Institut d'Optique and the Ecole Superieure d'Electricité, studying mathematics, physics, and optics, and then electronics. Many Sorbonne courses required only passing the final examination, not actual class attendance, so he managed to complete all course requirements for a doctorate, which came in handy 30 years later when he returned and did complete a doctorate. The Ecole Superieure d'Electricité, one of the elite "Grandes Ecoles" that admitted students by competitive examination, had recently started a "Radio Electricity" division. When Herbert opted for "radio electricity" in 1935, his father's friends warned that it would be a grave error to sacrifice a respected diploma for an upstart program. When Goldberg told them he thought that, with the invention of the photocell and the amplifier tube, the combination of optics with "radio electricity" had a great future, they shook their heads in doubt.

But Goldberg himself was very unhappy. He had no factory, no laboratory, no staff, and no real responsibilities. The founding head of Zeiss Ikon was not about to become a mere salesman. The appointment had been an administrative convenience, and there was really nothing for him to do. He was paid, but there was no job to be done, and little he could do about it. He was, he said, in a golden cage. If only he had the capital, he confided to Herbert, he would move into vacuum technology, the techniques for adding fine layers of materials that later became so important in high technology.

The Goldbergs lived in an apartment at 1ter Rue Mornay in Paris, near the Place de la Bastille, and Goldberg installed his workshop in a basement that had rough boulder walls, no windows, and no outside air or light. He built a small summer house at Chenevières, near La Varennes on the river Marne, east of Paris, about 20 minutes by train from the Gare de Lyon. The location was rather similar to that of his house on Oeserstrasse in Loschwitz overlooking Dresden. He had to walk down a hill to reach it. The hill was not as high as at Loschwitz and the river was not as large as the Elbe, but the view that he had had of Dresden was replaced by a fine view of Paris as part of a broad panorama. It was a lovely place. He did much of the work himself. It gave him something to think about and he worked there on weekends.

It was a primitive building, a long way from the street, the Chemin de Moulins, and it had no electricity. It did not have a sewer or even a proper septic tank. In the summer, the family lived there. He called the house "Une Étape," which means a place to rest on a journey, because he knew it was only temporary. But how long would he rest there, and where would he go on the next stage of his journey?

After about a year, Goldberg felt he just could not stand being in the Ikonta office every day with little to do, and nothing that interested him. He proposed to Zeiss that he reduce his time in the office to three days a week, with a corresponding salary cut. The Zeiss managers in Jena were very happy to agree. They were being subjected to sustained criticism for treating a Jew with excessive generosity; they would save money; and Goldberg was still bound by a noncompetition clause. The reduced income meant some changes. The Citroen car was sold. The maid, Olga Krumbiegel, was sent back to Germany, but, before she went, she was given several months of training in millinery and some capital, so she could start her own business in her hometown and would not have to work as a maid anymore. Goldberg now had time to design and build a specialized camera for copying documents in libraries.

A Copying Camera

For centuries, the only mechanical method for copying documents was the letterpress technique in which a thin, moist sheet of paper was pressed against the original in the hope that enough of the ink on the original would transfer to and through the moistened sheet to create a legible copy. However, from the late nineteenth century until the present-day dominance of electrostatic photocopying (so-called Xeroxing), a wide variety of techniques were tried in efforts to develop mechanical copiers and duplicating devices for which there was a very large potential market. As a specialist in reprographics, photochemistry, and printing, Goldberg would have been very familiar with these processes: mimeographs, cyclostyles, hectographs, zincographs, multigraphs, and the many other processes. In the particular case of copying printed documents, the photostatic copying machine became dominant from 1911 onward.

The photostat machine was a large camera on a stand that made a photograph directly on to photographic paper instead of on to a negative emulsion. But there were disadvantages. The machines were large and expensive, and only large libraries and other institutions had such equipment. The initial image was ordinarily white letters on a black background. The images needed to be developed and fixed promptly. Movie cameras and 35 mm cameras, such as the Leica and the Contax, were used, but neither type of camera was convenient for the rapid copying of only a few pages.

Goldberg's specialized camera for copying documents would be more convenient, more portable, and more flexible. A central problem is that the amount of film required for copying is unpredictable. One might want to copy many pages, a few, or just one, so any standard length of film would almost always be unsuitable, too short for large copying tasks or too long for small ones. If only a few pages were copied, there would either be an indefinite delay until the rest of the film was used up; or, if the copies were made promptly, most of the film would be wasted. His solution was to modify a 35 mm camera in several ways:

1. Two formats could be used, either a standard movie frame, 18 × 24 mm, or the double frame used for still photography, 24 × 36 mm. The choice could be changed from one exposure to another;

2. The film cassettes were large enough for 200 exposures, if all were in 24 × 36 mm format, or 400 exposures if 18 × 24 mm, and the camera could be built with even larger film cassettes;

3. A small knife blade (marked 8 in Figure 16.1a) was built into the camera back. When pressed, it would cut off the exposed portion of film so that it could be removed for immediate processing, leaving the unexposed film intact;

4. The take-up spool was contained in a lightproof cassette (marked 9 in Figure 16.1a) that could be removed conveniently at any time without opening the back of the camera;

5. A special take-up cassette, holding up to 24 double frame exposures could be used as a developing tank, so the exposed film could be developed without being removed from the cassette. As a result, there was no need for a darkroom, and microfilm copies of documents could be made and processed immediately, anywhere.

6. An automatic self-loading mechanism contained hooks on the rotating take-up spool that would reach out and grab the sprocket holes of the exposed film as it entered the take-up cassette and ensure that the film was wound properly on to the take-up spool. (See 10 in Figure 16.1a; details in 16.1b–d.)

The ability to make and to process a few exposures immediately, anywhere, without a darkroom, had multiple benefits. Small runs of microfilm could be produced without delay. The copying could be done anywhere. A few test copies could be made, processed, and inspected, whenever lighting conditions were difficult, in order to determine that the shutter and aperture settings were satisfactory. In a way, this approach anticipated the immediacy of the Land Polaroid system.

The World Congress of Universal Documentation, held in Paris in the summer of 1937, was attended by H. G. Wells, Watson Davis, Paul Otlet, Suzanne Briet, and other luminaries of what would now be called Information Science, but was then called Documentation. Paul Otlet and H. G. Wells, both now old and famous men, met and speculated on the idea of a World Brain, by which they meant a continuously updated hypertext encyclopedia based on the monographic principle advanced 25 years earlier by Wilhelm Ostwald and his partners.

Goldberg presented a paper on a "special camera," his copying camera. He had applied for a patent for it in Luxemburg in October 1936, and then, the following October, in Germany and in the United States, where it was entitled *Photographic camera for flexible materials sensitive to light.* Initial filing in Luxemburg was convenient because applications written in German were accepted. Also, under the rules of international

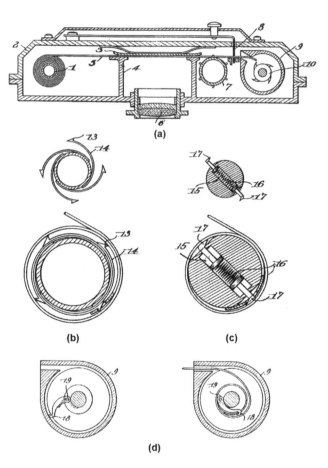

Figure 16.1 (a)–(d). Copying camera with an automatic take-up spool in a removable cassette. Pressing a knob at the back of the camera (a) causes a knife (8) to cut off exposed film in the take-up spool (10) in a cassette (9). After cutting, the film advance mechanism (7) causes the end of the film to enter an empty take-up cassette. In (b) the spindle of the take-up spool has hooks (13) on thin springs (14); in (c) the hooks (17) are on rods extended by springs (16), and in (d) the hook (18) is on a hinged arm pushed out by a spring (19). In all cases, in an empty cassette the springs induce the hooks to reach out and catch the perforations in film inserted into the cassette by rotating faster than the film. The lower figures in (b) and (c) and the figure on the right in (d) show how, as the film is wound on to the spindle, the hooks are retracted.

patent law, as Luxemburg was part of the same "patent family" as Germany, the United States, and other important countries, protection was established in these other countries too if a patent application filed in Luxemburg was subsequently filed in them within one year. Automatic film take-up mechanisms are now a standard feature of 35 mm cameras.

Goldberg continued to work for years on his photographic copying apparatus, until it reached the form shown in Figure 16.2. The size of an attaché case when not in use, it unfolded to become a portable copying station. Pages to be photographed would be placed under a sheet of glass. Four electric lights provided illumination. The "copying camera," housed in a box next to the glass plate, photographed the reflected image of the page. It was so highly automated that merely raising the hinged sheet of glass to insert the page to be copied, then lowering it, caused the lights to be turned on, the photograph to be taken, the exposure counter to be advanced, the film to be moved forward for the next exposure, and the shutter to be reset, so that the copier was immediately ready to copy the

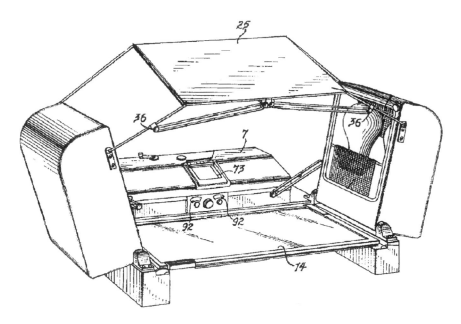

Figure 16.2. Photographic copying apparatus. A horizontally mounted 35 mm camera in the housing (7) takes a photograph of pages under the glass sheet (14), illuminated by four electric lights. The image is reflected downward by a reflecting sheet (25), then sideways through a prism (73). Raising, then lowering, the hinged glass sheet to insert pages to be copied automatically operated the electric lights, took the photograph, advanced the film, and moved the exposure counter (92).

next page. This remarkable convenience in use, however, required very complex mechanical components.

More Negotiations

Building a summer house and developing his copying camera provided some distraction, but it was not enough. Goldberg was deeply dissatisfied with the lack of meaningful work to do. He tried, without success, to interest a doctor in the design of a camera capable of photographing the inner ear. Predicting another war between France and Germany, he urged the French Army to develop factories to manufacture their own military optical equipment independently. They replied that they did not need factories, because they could buy what they needed from Zeiss in Germany. Goldberg was still being paid, but he was trapped in an unsatisfying, unproductive existence, and he began, probably in 1935, long and difficult negotiations to terminate his relationship with Zeiss.

Negotiating termination proved hard and emotionally distressing. Zeiss was willing to allow Goldberg to retire, to pay him his pension with provisions for inflation adjustments, and to waive restrictions on purely academic work. But they wanted to extend the noncompetition clause in his existing contract from one year to five years, so that if he retired when his 10-year contract expired in April 1937, he could engage in no business activity until April 1942. Worse, Zeiss wanted him to agree to a lifetime ban on work on specified instruments and processes and sent him an eight-page list, which included just about everything that he had ever been interested in. He annotated a copy of the list with pointed remarks, denouncing some items, for example, types of emulsions, as overly broad, and others as too vague. "It cannot be expected that I agree to renounce all activity with light-sensitive material. Under such a ban Z[eiss] I[kon] would take every technique for reprographics (printing), and thereby areas lying completely outside of Z. I." The Statistical Machine, he noted, should not be on the list because he owned the intellectual property rights jointly with Zeiss Ikon. Under Sensitometer and Photometer, he noted that these were for the most part his own personal scientific work, published before he joined Zeiss Ikon. He was not even to be allowed to work on the Goldberg Wedge, listed as Neutral Wedge, next to which he added tartly, "Why not call it, as the rest of the world does, 'Goldberg Wedge.'" Crossing out a long list of television equipment, he asks, "What has Zeiss Ikon actually done with these?" Repeatedly he wrote next to forbidden items, "Please release me" *(Bitte um Freigabe),* adding, next to Photocells and Loudspeakers, "This is intolerable for me."

He was corresponding with managers who were friends and former colleagues, but, in reality, he was dealing, indirectly, with lawyers whose job it was to protect Zeiss corporate interests. Zeiss would not agree to any activity that could possibly be in competition with its business interests, and most of the things that he wanted to do would be potentially in competition with Zeiss's wide-ranging interests. He did not know that Straubel, Wandersleb, and others had been forced to resign. Nor did he understand how much the situation had changed inside Germany or the acute pressures on the Zeiss managers, who were subjected to sustained Nazi criticism for treating him, a Jew, with excessive generosity. They could not help him.

Carl Zeiss and Zeiss Ikon had an extensive network of foreign subsidiaries and partners. An organizational chart of 98 Zeiss subsidiaries dated 1941 shows Zeiss factories in Czechoslovakia, Hungary, the Netherlands, and Poland. At the outbreak of World War I, Zeiss had been the world's leading supplier of military optics (binoculars, rangefinders, gunsights, etc.), but, under the punitive terms imposed on Germany by the Treaty of Versailles in 1919, German manufacture of military equipment was essentially prohibited and an Inter-Allied Control Commission established to enforce the ban. In fact, the prohibition was systematically evaded by companies' covert activities inside Germany and by the movement of prohibited activities to its foreign subsidiaries or affiliated companies in, for example, the Netherlands (Fokker aircraft) or Sweden (Krupp guns). Whether or not Zeiss did engage in covert or offshore manufacture of military optics, its public stance had been compliance with the treaty prohibition on military manufactures. However, on March 16, 1935, Hitler unilaterally abrogated the Treaty of Versailles, and the Zeiss documents in Goldberg's negotiations reveal Zeiss's interest in military equipment clearly.

Finally an agreement was reached in May 1937, with elaborate procedures to index Goldberg's pension to salaries paid by Ikonta. That summer Herbert and some friends went on a long hike through southern France. At Sophie's suggestion, Renate, now 15, also went. Meanwhile, in February of 1937, Goldberg had himself taken a trip and had decided on the next stage of his life's journey.

17

Palestine

It is my intention to place my experience in the areas of instrumentation, optics and practical precision engineering at the disposal of Palestinian science and technology.

—Emanuel Goldberg, October 23, 1937

Goldberg's trip in February 1937 had been to Palestine, where he met and talked with the Zionist leader, Chaim Weizmann. Goldberg and Weizmann had much in common. They were both cosmopolitan Russian Jews who had studied chemistry in German universities. Goldberg would have appreciated Weizmann's views on the need to link scholarship with a national renaissance, and the Sieff Institute founded by Weizmann in Rehovot put these aspirations into practice. Weizmann's biographer, Norman Rose, wrote: "The Institute personified his conception of the role Zionism could play as a force in Israel and in the modern world: erudition and vision combined with practicality and purpose, learning harnessed to the needs of society. 'Israel is a small country,' he once observed, 'but it can be like Switzerland—a small one but a highly civilized one, a force for enlightenment and progress out of all proportion to its size.'" The charismatic Weizmann was just the person to inspire Goldberg, who bought a plot of land in Rehovot where he would be able to collaborate with Weizmann and his institute. He then returned to Paris to tell Sophie, Herbert, and Renate that they were moving to Palestine. The move was the more feasible because Sophie's father had died in 1931 and her mother, who had been living with them in Paris, died in the summer of 1937.

Herbert, however, preferred to go to the United States, and Sophie quietly encouraged him. He was 22 years old and had completed his university studies. He wanted to make his own way, independently of his father, and the United States seemed to offer many more opportunities than Palestine. Goldberg wrote to his old friend Mees of the move to Palestine, "Some time ago I succeeded in breaking the chain which, contrary to my wishes, connected me to the Zeiss Company. I plan now to leave Old Europe in some months and go to Palestine. On my recent visit there, I found an extraordinary building up work in progress, and I hope to find there a possibility to apply my remaining force and knowledge." He asked Mees, who had so often offered assistance, if he would help Herbert to obtain an American immigration visa and to find employment. Mees obliged, and Herbert went to work in Rochester at the Kodak Research Laboratory.

Sophie, fond of the frozen north, had no desire to go to Palestine, but, a dutiful wife, she went. Goldberg, Sophie, and Renate went by boat to Haifa where they arrived on October 11, 1937, and then traveled on to Tel Aviv by taxi. The road from Haifa to Tel Aviv was not yet properly paved, and their taxi got stuck in the sand on the way. Sophie was very upset.

Tel Aviv was a rapidly expanding Jewish community, with an ambitious municipal council, growing out into the sand dunes north of the ancient port of Jaffa. A British government report describing Tel Aviv in 1937 commented: "It has grown too fast for orderly town-planning; its frontage to the sea has so far been neglected; and it has not yet acquired public buildings worthy of it, but its main boulevard and some of its residential quarters, its shops and cafes and cinemas, above all the busy, active people in the street, already reproduce the atmosphere of the older Mediterranean sea-side towns of Europe. But it is essentially European." At that time, Tel Aviv was still primarily a Russian Jewish community and knowing Russian was an advantage. During the 1930s, immigration from Germany increased sharply and the German immigrants had soon had a disproportionately large influence. As a Russian and as a man of achievement, Goldberg could fit right in immediately. One of his cousins, Lowa Goldberg, was already living there. Lowa Goldberg had studied medicine in Paris and set up a clinic in Palestine. During World War I, he served as a major in the Ottoman army medical corps and, in a bold move, Marousia, his wife, interceded in person with Jemal Pasha, the local governor, commander-in-chief, and one of the leaders in the Young Turk movement, to protect the clinic from destruction. Lowa Goldberg had visited Paris in 1937, not knowing that his cousin, Emanuel, was there. Buying a camera, he had mentioned to the salesman that he had a cousin, with whom he had lost contact, working for Zeiss in Germany. In this way, acquaintance was renewed and, when they arrived in Palestine, Lowa introduced Goldberg and Sophie to the intellectual and professional elite.

Another renewed friendship was with Max and Sima Koppelmann, whose wedding had also been one of the three related weddings in Warsaw in June 1907 noted in Chapter 4. Max and Sima were both cousins of Sophie, and Max's sister Sonja Koppelmann had married Sophie's brother

George. In 1936, Max and Sima Koppelmann had moved from Germany to Palestine where he became postmaster in Kfar Shmarjahu. Another long-established friendship was with the family of Sophie's cousin Boris Schatz, founder of the Bezalel School of Arts and Crafts.

Goldberg could easily have gone to the United States or elsewhere. His explanation for why he did not was that he had already been the victim of anti-Semitic discrimination in two countries, in Russia, as a student, and in Germany, as an adult. It could happen again in any other country, except Palestine. There was only one country where he thought that he should be. By the time he arrived in Palestine, he was 56 years old and he had already had a very full and successful career both as an academic and in industry. He was not interested in starting a business, and he was too energetic to consider retirement. He wanted to do what he most enjoyed, applied research and development in his own laboratory. He also wanted to play his part in building a country where Jews could live.

> My aim now is to lay the foundation of an optical-mechanical indus-
> try in Palestine. We shall proceed along similar lines as in Germany,
> to establish in the first place the closest possible connection between
> the manual and the scientific processes, and, in the second, to train
> a nucleus of specialists to pass on our methods.

Goldberg was in an excellent position for this goal. He had the requisite technical expertise, he had long experience with technical education, he was respected in the community, and he was financially independent. He had brought some capital, and he was receiving his pension from Ikonta.

The Laboratory

The idea of a laboratory of his own was powerfully attractive after the trauma of his experience in Dresden. "Whatever I do," he said, "I do for my own pleasure, because I like to work. I like to invent. I will stop the moment I have no pleasure." Goldberg expected to work with Weizmann in Rehovot, but, when the time came, Weizmann was abroad and, in any case, was far too preoccupied with politics to be able to collaborate effectively in scientific research and development. Frustrated, Goldberg accepted an invitation to set up his laboratory in partnership with the Association of Engineers and Architects at their property at 200 Dizengoff Street in central Tel Aviv. With the help of his friend Joseph Brawermann, also Russian, an arrangement was made with the Founding Director of the Standards Institute of Israel, Moshe Arnstein (later Arnan), to build an extra floor, with three rooms, on the roof of the Engineers and Architects building. The arrangement was that Goldberg would fund the cost of construction as a loan, repayable as prepaid rent. The ground floor, at

Goldberg's urging, became a Standards Institute. Goldberg had originally wanted to call his enterprise an Institute for Applied Optics, but instead he chose Professor Goldberg's Laboratory for Precision Instruments. The Lab opened officially on March 1, 1938, and each subsequent March 1 was celebrated as an anniversary.

Early in 1947, a Dutchman named Bernhard van Leer, visited Goldberg's Laboratory. Weizmann had encouraged Goldberg to seek financial help from van Leer to expand the educational role of the Lab, and, at the same time, to finance his research. Van Leer was a philanthropic entrepreneur who had made a large fortune manufacturing steel barrels for petroleum and other products. Over dinner, van Leer said, "Look, I see you are doing a great job. Here, I give you a cheque for 5,000 British pounds. Take this money and do with it as you feel. Should you ever think about setting up a company, give me some shares in your company." Goldberg asked him, "Look, do you do it out of altruism, or Zionism, or why do you do it?" Van Leer laughed and told him, "I have a son. He is also a fool like you. He is in Physics instead of in business. Maybe at some point he will be interested."

Later in 1947, with the aid of some investors, Goldberg did form a company, which was called Goldberg Instruments Ltd, with Goldberg as General Manager. The word *Instruments* was less than ideal, because, although its meaning is clear in English, in Hebrew it was ambiguous. It might be taken to mean "utensils," such as kitchen appliances. Goldberg's investors were very varied, brought in through the Palestine Corporation, a British ancestor of the Bank Leumi. The purpose of the Palestine Corporation and of the similar American company, the Palestine Economic Corporation, was to build up the country. Both were shareholders in Goldberg Instruments. The Palestine Corporation arranged for additional investments by sympathetic British Jews, including Sir Simon Marks and the Sieff family. Marks, of the Marks and Spencer retail chain in England, and several of his children gave money to Goldberg. These investors may have had little idea what Goldberg's company actually did, but they were willing to support his work and to support Palestine through him. They saw it as an investment in the development of a Jewish country. It was a philanthropic act as much as a financial investment.

The manufacture of precision instruments requires a high ratio of skilled labor to raw materials and developing a precision instruments industry was a shrewd move because it would be minimally dependant on natural resources unavailable in Palestine. Goldberg wrote, "Such an industry seems to be eminently suitable for a country, which like Palestine, has no sources of raw material (Dead Sea chemicals excepted) but which is full of men wishing to work." Although some industry already existed in Palestine, it was not high tech. Chemicals and some other materials were available, often not the right ones for his needs, but Goldberg had a talent for adapting what was at hand. What was new was that he had precision tools, and he knew how to use them. He brought with him the first micrometer in Palestine; until then, the nearest one was said to be in Budapest.

Goldberg's Laboratory was badly needed. Until then, when a precision instrument needed repair, it usually had to be sent to Europe, a long and expensive process, or else discarded. Goldberg's Laboratory, apparently the only one in the eastern Mediterranean, provided a welcome alternative. The *Davar* newspaper wrote about Goldberg's Laboratory in 1940:

> Most of the work today is repair of expensive microscopes, cystoscope, film mechanism, optical engineering instruments and expensive objects of photography. They are not lost anymore even if they are severely damaged. You need not send them to Germany or Holland anymore and wait months for their repair. It is done in this lab. The Hebrew University, the Technion, Government, Kopat Holim [the General Federation of Labor's health organization], Tel Aviv's municipality, and others use this lab. Prof Goldberg said that he is overwhelmed with this work but he recognizes its importance for the continuing work of these institutions even though it takes his time from producing new instruments. He could have enlarged his lab faster (today there are only one academic assistant and a helper there) but there are no experts for the job and to train them would take time.... Torah and craftsmanship [i.e theory and practice] are merged in him. In a blue working coat he is working with oily and dusty hands in addition to his brains.

Apprentices

To resolve the lack of qualified technical labor, Goldberg reached back to his days at the Academy of Graphic Arts in Leipzig and initiated a traditional German apprenticeship scheme. The need to train the next generation was very much on his mind, and, ever the teacher, his idea was to use his Laboratory to provide technical education for young people. The apprentices were usually 18 to 22 years old. They had very good intentions, but little technical background.

Goldberg was very selective about his apprentices, and he interviewed them carefully. One whom Goldberg rejected later told Renate, "I have to thank your father for not taking me on. He said he thought I would not be so good at the technical side. He thought I should get into the theoretical side." One of Goldberg's conditions was that he would take an apprentice only if his science teacher or one of his other high school teachers would come in person to recommend him. Although he said that women didn't need education, he did take on some female apprentices. It was a four-year program that started with simple tasks in the first year and moved on to progressively more complex assignments. The hours were not fixed. They started early, took a break for lunch, and then continued, with homework in the evening sometimes. "It was very nice to be there," recalled Jakob Beutler, "I learned a lot." Then, at the end of the fourth year, Goldberg issued a certificate.

The Lab began to fill up with his daughter's high school friends and other teenagers. Goldberg had a good relationship with the young people. They had parties and outings, including a longer annual excursion lasting a few days and going as far as present-day Jordan. Aviva Kelton recalls,

> He was part of it. Let's say he had a sense of humor. Across the street, across Dizengoff, there lived two girls who every morning were doing gymnastics or whatever near the window, not dressed. Well, all the sniper's scopes were being used. And he came in. It didn't bother him. It was his window that was looking across. He laughed at it. Then we had the party and they had invented all sorts of things to make sandwiches. French bread was cut on the bench saw, length-wise, or we whipped cream on the drill press. One time it went too fast and it became butter. We had to buy new. He let us. He was in on the fun. We had a wonderful time, really wonderful.

The staff wrote verse about the Lab and drew cartoons of Goldberg inventing, similar to Rube Goldberg cartoons, which Goldberg enjoyed. One was "Professor Goldberg's Greatest Invention," a picture of a chain with one link much thicker than the others, with an explanation: "The Professor knew that the strength of a chain depended on the strength of its weakest link, so he made the weakest link twice as strong as the others."

Despite the informality, Goldberg could be quite sensitive if he thought that his status seemed in any way challenged. In 1950, Moshe Arad was told, "Professor Goldberg needs a personal assistant. It will be very hard because you have your own ideas and the Professor doesn't like that." Jakob Beutler recalled his first meeting with the Professor.

> I was supposed to come at 10:00 or something to make my credentials. My physics teacher knew how to speak in Russian. He arranged this for me. Ten o'clock, and I came at 10 o'clock. 11 o'clock, no Professor. 11:30. Finally I heard that he was coming in and I made the mistake—later on I thought it was a mistake—I made a remark. I was 18 years old. I made a remark that it seems to me that I have been invited for 10:00 o'clock. It was now 11:30 and I hoped to be—whatever. And he understood this as kind of criticism, you know, and he started to shout at me, "Forget about it!" And a month later I got a letter from his office that I can present myself again. I came and he was shining and said, "Please, don't get the wrong impression. If I accept you, it is with all my heart. It was only to teach you a lesson."

Despite the strong pressure in the Jewish community to adopt Hebrew, the language of the Lab remained German. Anyone who did not speak German felt isolated. Goldberg, who in his youth had learned seven languages, never did learn Hebrew.

The Lab originally had no air conditioning and no dust-free "clean chamber." Ice was used, when necessary, to cool materials. The Lab had almost no technical journals on engineering, physics, or chemistry. Books used by the apprentices included *Bauelemente der Feinmechanik*, by Otto Richter; *Machinery's Handbook for machine shop and drafting-room; a reference book on machine design and shop practice for the mechanical engineer, draftsman, toolmaker and machinist,* by Erik Oberg and F. D. Jones; *Klingelnberg Technisches Hilfsbuch; General Engineering Workshop Practice;* and Grimsehl's *Chemie,* a basic manual for the workbench chemist.

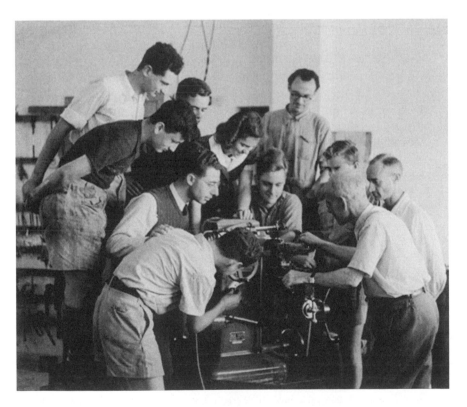

Figure 17.1. Goldberg instructs his staff in the Laboratory, probably 1941. His daughter, Renate (Chava), is upper center and Dr. Otto Gold at extreme right. At left, top to bottom: Michael Spiegel, Yona Meyerowitz, Wolfgang Zeev Plaot, Zwi Reiser, Zwi Adam. Center, sitting: Ludwig Michael Plaot. The other two men, center standing, and beyond Goldberg, are unidentified.

Goldberg had brought everything that he had had in his well-equipped workshop at Oeserstrasse in Dresden: carpentry tools, including a band saw, a circular saw, a press, a shaping machine, many smaller pieces, and the Lorch lathe. New machines were built as needed, including an engraving machine, a dividing machine, grinding machines, a pantograph, a hobbing machine to cut worm-wheels and spiral gears, even a furnace for melting brass and aluminum. Another instrument was built to measure the angles of prisms. For the Standards Institute, on the ground floor, a machine for testing the tearing strength of fibers was built. Among the high-tech work was the making of reticles with etched lines, as little as a hundredth of a millimeter apart, along with a lot of work in high vacuum technology, depositing coatings on to glass surfaces. Goldberg would carefully instruct the apprentices in the use of each machine. (See Figure 17.1.)

Life in Tel Aviv

Goldberg and Sophie lived very simply and frugally in Tel Aviv in an apartment at 128 Rothschild Boulevard, a spacious street with fine art deco houses. Although Sophie had well-rounded interests and her own intellectual life, she gave complete priority to her husband's needs. She had become stout. Walking was a strain in the heat of Tel Aviv, and for years they did not have a car. She did not enjoy public events and was not directly involved in the Lab, which she visited only for its parties. Starting in 1954, she received an Israeli state pension and commented that it was the first money she had ever received from anyone other than her husband. Their daughter, Renate Eva Goldberg, adopted the name Chava, the Hebrew form of Eva, and, after completing high school, she became her father's assistant in the Laboratory. In 1948, she married Mordechai Gichon, previously Gichermann, another immigrant from Germany, whose father published a newspaper in Palestine. At this point, the plot of land in Rehovot, that Goldberg had bought during his spring visit in 1937 to be near Weizmann, was sold and the proceeds enabled the newly-weds to buy a house.

Goldberg became a naturalized Palestinian on December 20, 1939. A passport, issued a few months later, notes gray eyes, gray hair, and a height of 166 cm (5 ft 4 in). In 1946, Goldberg wrote,

> I feel very well and my energy is maintained. I have not become rich. We live modestly, but do not go hungry. The only thing I miss is open country, mountains, snow, etc. At home everything is OK. My wife has to work hard because everything is hard to come by and paid help can't be found. She has not become younger (nor, unfortunately, slimmer) and she does not tolerate the climate as well as I do.

Comfortable Housing

In one of their first undertakings, Goldberg and Renate went through the Jordan Valley and other hot areas to gather empirical data on building practices that would make the inside of the houses cooler and more comfortable. They placed thermocouples inside and outside, using the difference in voltage differences in temperature, which were then correlated with the roofing materials. They found that asphalt, then widely used, was the worst choice for roof covering because it absorbed so much heat. A coating of silvery, aluminum paint did not reflect much heat, and a coating of chalk was much better. The best technique was to provide a ventilated cover so that air could circulate between the house and the roof.

They also looked at day and night differences and used a katathermometer, which measures both humidity and temperature, to develop and measure a Comfort Factor based on a combination of humidity and temperature. They found that it was best to build houses facing south because in summer the sun was high in the sky and little sunshine came in through windows. In winter, however, when the sun was at a lower angle, it would provide warmth by shining through the windows. It was then common practice to build houses facing west because the wind came from the west, but west-facing windows let in the hot afternoon sun in the summer.

In 1958, H. Tabor of the Israeli National Physical Laboratory asked permission to develop some of Goldberg's ideas on dehumidification. Goldberg replied: "I have no aspirations regarding patents, having (according to long previous experience) no hope to live until monetary results are obtained. If (what I do not hope) I will live up to 120 years you will surely be so generous as to let me have a small part of the fortune obtained."

Commercial Products

The range of work undertaken by the Lab was remarkable. One of the first tasks on arrival was to build a periscope for the harbor master of Jaffa, so that he could see the harbor from his office. In a way, this example reflects the fact that Goldberg was more interested in innovation than in business. The few surviving documents provide only occasional hints of his very varied activities. For example, a receipt from the Meteorological Officer at Lydda Airport, dated July 17, 1940, acknowledged delivery of five actinographs (instruments for recording variations in solar rays), two air thermometers, two other thermometers, an aspirator, and a screen. Nevertheless, the Lab had to pay its way and with the end of World War II, there had to be a serious effort to develop civilian commercial products. Among the new devices for peacetime use were a pyrometer (an instrument for measuring the temperature of a body based on the wavelength of radiated light), a colorimeter (for measuring color), and, more profitably, refractometers.

Goldberg's friend Brawermann worked in the citrus fruit industry, a growing industry that was very important for Israel, and it was an improved refractometer, an optical device for measuring the sugar content of juices, that made Goldberg Instruments well known, even outside Israel. A refractometer uses differences in the refractive index of transparent or semitransparent materials in order to get some information about the material. The denser the material, the more it refracts ("bends") light. In a refractometer, light travels through a sample of juice, is refracted, and hits a scale that shows the degree of refraction, indicating how dense the material is, and, thereby, the sugar content. So, using a refractometer is an easy way to find out if an orange is ripe. Also, in the process of making concentrates or jams, water is boiled away until the sugar content reaches 70 percent, at which point the concentrate keeps well without refrigeration. Because any further processing is unnecessary and reduces profit, accurate measurement of the sugar content is essential for profitability. In the wine industry also, payments to farmers for grapes depended on measurement by refractometer.

Herbert became a specialist in refractometers and eventually completed a doctorate with a dissertation on refractometer design. Goldberg and, more especially, Herbert continued to develop improved designs. One early improvement was to coat internal surfaces with black to minimize internal reflections, a topic that Goldberg had investigated many years before in his studies of the optical performance of camera lenses. Because temperature affected refractometer readings, Herbert developed a bimetallic element that would correct the readings for changes in temperature. Hundreds of "Goldberg Refractometers" were sold, many of them exported to other Middle Eastern countries and elsewhere. (See Figure 17.2.)

After the State of Israel was founded, Goldberg refractometers were marketed to Arab countries through Cyprus under a non-Israeli name. Later

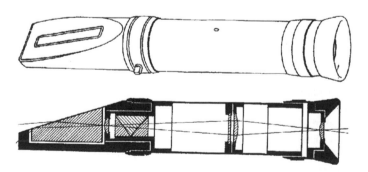

Figure 17.2. Goldberg refractometer, used for measuring the sugar content of juices.

on, "boiler refractometers" were developed, which could be permanently installed on the side of boilers and provide continuous readings, accurate to 1/4 of 1 percent, without any need to open the boiler to take a sample. They had a built-in light source and measured reflected light, thereby solving the problem of dark concentrates, and they could be adjusted to allow for the effect of temperature. (An example and a drawing can be seen on the left in Figure 17.3.) Herbert Goldberg later worked for the American Optical Company, which also manufactured and marketed Goldberg refractometers.

Goldberg had continued to develop the portable copying camera with its automatic film take-up spool that he had described at the World Congress for Universal Documentation in Paris in 1937. He added a stand, with its own lamps to provide illumination. The entire device folded neatly into a carrying case the size of a small attaché case and was self-contained. One could go to a library, open it up, connect the electrical lead to a power outlet, and start to make copy pages of books.

In 1949, Bell & Howell provided an advance of $10,000 for further development of the copying camera, and the following year, at Goldberg's

Figure 17.3. Goldberg at his desk, with boiler refractometer in box at left.

request, Herbert came out to Israel, with his American wife, Frances, and son, Dwight, to help his father work on it. After three years, Herbert, Frances, and Dwight returned to the United States, where he had a career at the American Optical Company.

An additional U.S. patent was received in 1953 for a *Photographic copying apparatus,* and in 1958, Goldberg was working on a more compact version using 16 mm film, but neither Kodak nor Zeiss were interested in the copying camera as a product. Although Goldberg knew about marketing and advertising, he probably underestimated what it would take to make such a specialized item into a profitable product. He had a lively interest in developing new products, but he had probably never needed to concern himself much with details of the marketing process. At Zeiss Ikon, there had been a department to take care of marketing. Eventually, his copying camera became obsolete when xerographic copying machines became available. In related work, the Lab provided servicing and training for the Kodak Recordak bank microfilming equipment, and several hundred overhead projectors, that also folded into a suitcase-sized carrying case, were built and sold.

The manufacture and repair of leveling and surveying instruments with small glass tubes containing liquid and a bubble provided a small but steady income, along with manufacturing prisms used by builders to establish the squareness of plot lines and buildings. A microtome, an instrument for cutting very thin slices, was developed. Another specialized instrument was an optical comparator for microscopic objects *(Messmikroskop),* essentially a microscopic projector that allowed one to project the outline of a miniature part that is being shaped in such a way that it could be compared with a line drawing. When Herbert showed how his father's design could be improved upon, making it easier to use, Goldberg reacted without enthusiasm or appreciation.

In the mid-1950s, Goldberg drew on his theories of visual perception in an attempt to reduce the driving hazard of being dazzled by the headlights of oncoming automobiles. "As an old driver I try to help myself," he said. It was an acrylic panel coated with celluloid-based lacquer to be positioned on the windscreen and intended to transmit only 3 percent of the light from the headlights of approaching automobiles. He called this anti-glare device "aglar."

Improvisation

An article entitled "Bricks without straw" commented in 1945 on Professor Goldberg's Laboratory "as an example of masterly extemporization":

> The difficulties presented by the making of [high-class] pressure gauges (two per day by four men) must have been of considerable

magnitude, since they involved the construction of an optical comparator, small dividing head, minute gear cutters, measuring instruments, etc. The comparator was made from lenses from a damaged microscope and binoculars, a Quaker-oats tin and a few lengths of wire and string.

This example seems to be journalistic exaggeration, but Goldberg's talent for creative improvisation was real. Optical glass, for example, was unobtainable during World War II, so suitable glass was obtained wherever it could be found, and lens designs adapted accordingly. On the battlefield, the special glass used in tank windows was salvaged when possible. After disturbances in Tel Aviv, the apprentices went out on bicycles to collect shards of glass from broken shop windows. Even the glass of a Belgian wardrobe mirror was used. For some instruments, gemstones were needed, so gems in broaches or bracelets were recycled. The wing of a downed airplane provided a supply of aluminum that lasted throughout the war. Other materials were obtained through clandestine exchanges with Germany through Turkish intermediaries.

In photoengraving, the glass plate or other object to be engraved is covered with a light-sensitive coating, and the image to be engraved is projected on to it. Those areas receiving light are developed and remain on the surface. The emulsion in areas not receiving light is washed away, leaving the surface exposed. The entire surface is then treated with acid that eats away the unprotected areas of exposed glass, and these etched areas could then be filled with paint or powder to make them more visible. The acid could not etch the other areas because their surface was protected by the remaining coating, known as the "resist." Goldberg knew that Niepce, whose portrait was in the microdots he had handed out at the International Congress of Photography in Paris in 1925, had used a naturally occurring substance, Syrian asphalt, as a resist in photoengraving early in the nineteenth century. Syrian asphalt, also known as bitumen of Judea, floats to the surface when storms disturb the Dead Sea. Refined, first with ether, and then with alcohol, powdered Syrian asphalt becomes "washed bitumen," which, when mixed with benzene, becomes a light-sensitive film suitable for exceptionally precise photoengraving. Because of the high costs of transportation and refining, Syrian asphalt had been abandoned in Europe and elsewhere, but, for once, Goldberg could make good use of a Palestinian resource. The Lab made thousands of engraved lines using emulsion made from highly purified asphalt from the Dead Sea.

Vera Salomons

Goldberg's pension, paid by Ikonta, provided financial security, but with the outbreak of World War II, his pension payments stopped arriving and he faced a financial crisis. He was rescued by an English philanthropist, Vera Salomons. Her father, Sir David Salomons, was an inventor and the first Jewish Lord Mayor of London. Vera Salomons had visited Palestine in 1925, been charmed by the vitality of what she found, returned repeatedly, and became a philanthropist. As she later explained, "In Jerusalem, among other places we went to the Wailing Wall. The manner in which Arabs pushed pack donkeys through Jews praying at the Wall, disgusted me. It was in order to reach the surrounding houses facing the Wall that the animals came by with their loads. I decided to try to buy these houses." She raised £100,000, which she offered to Lord Reading, the Mandate High Commissioner, so that the houses could be bought. The offer was not accepted, so, instead, she established a fund named David Salomons' Charity and used her considerable wealth to support both Arabs and Jews, especially through aid for the blind and education for immigrant children. Through these activities, she learned of Goldberg's apprenticeship program. They met and planned a project together. Although the project did not work out, she valued his apprenticeship program and gave him money to support his work.

After a while, Vera Salomons's contributions no longer came, and he was again worried about money. Soon after, at the end of 1940, he went to India. He was part of the Palestinian delegation to the Eastern Group Conference in New Delhi, a meeting on how India, Australia, and other British dominions and dependencies in the East could best contribute to the war effort, and he also advised on the manufacture of optical equipment in India. After a three-day journey by seaplane, when he finally reached his hotel in New Delhi, he saw Vera Salomons, sitting in the lounge. Her enthusiasm for Goldberg and his apprenticeship program returned and she gave more money, enabling him to sustain the Laboratory until work performed for the British Army brought financial stability.

Advisory Services

Because of his expertise and status, Goldberg was constantly being asked for advice on a wide range of topics. Already on February 3, 1938, Chaim Weizmann appointed him Honorary Technical Advisor of the Daniel Sieff Institute, now called the Weizmann Institute, in Rehovot. In the 1950s and 1960s, he served on committees of the Hebrew University in Jerusalem, and the Technion, the technical university in Haifa. He helped an unsuccessful effort to establish a science museum and gave some material to a museum in Haifa. He was consulted concerning the approval of import licenses, being asked to advise on whether the request would be good use of scarce hard currency. He eventually had official status in the government agency responsible for issuing permits to import optical and photographic materials.

In 1943, a Mrs. Jacobs of New York had announced funding for a "Freedom Village," a youth settlement with vocational training. Goldberg joined the planning committee. The minutes of the committee reveal his thinking: He was in favor of an industrial rather than an agricultural emphasis. He thought it should be a closed cooperative *(gebundene Kooperative)* in which persons leaving had no right to sell their shares.

> Prof. Goldberg, who has had many years of pedagogical experience with apprentices, joined Dr. Scheeman in complaining of the failure of the youths to stick to one place. He is of the opinion that an improved training could be achieved if the young people commence to work in the workshops from the very first day. . . . Prof. Goldberg described his own methods of picking candidates from various circles. Teachers of vocational schools approach him, recommending gifted pupils, as do the Heads of "Kibbutz"-workshops or parents who wish their children to become apprentices in his workshop. Mrs. Jacobs had suggested the grinding of eye glasses as an activity. Goldberg observed that there was insufficient demand for eye glass grinding and steered the group towards precision instruments: "The proper thing is skilled mechanical work which includes optics. As a basis, a workshop for general metal work should be established to afford the young people a proper training in quality production. The ultimate aim should be precision instruments (Fein Mechanik). A group for this type of qualitative [*sic*, quality] production is already in existence. He (Prof. Goldberg) employs a staff of 2–5 instructors and 15 apprentices, each group learning from the other. Jewish youth has proved to be very intelligent; they can easily be trained and have a natural feeling for quality in work. He is rather optimistic as far as the human material is concerned. The main problem is that of marketing which will have its bearing on the budget. At the moment there does not exist a marketing problem. However, as everywhere else in the world, prospects for the future are doubtful. A turn of the tide is certain. It is inadvisable for a new undertaking to rely on army orders.

The Freedom Village plan did not work out. At one point Goldberg wanted to go and live in a kibbutz and to establish a workshop there. Sophie did not want to go, although she would have gone with him.

A Visit to the United States

Goldberg visited the United States for the first time in 1946. In addition to business reasons, he was eager to see his son, Herbert, daughter-in-law Frances, and his first grandson, Dwight. He traveled on an Israeli diplomatic passport, and he enjoyed the VIP status that resulted. In July 1946, he finally went to see Mees at Kodak Park in Rochester. The Kodak in-house newsletter, *Kodakery,* featured the visit with a photograph and brief article, "Noted scientist visits son at Park; Renews friendship with Dr. Mees." T.H. James later recalled the visit:

> Professor Goldberg visited Rochester about 23 years ago. He was one of the youngest old men I have ever met. He told me he couldn't understand the American scientists. He had visited several who were about his own age, and the things that seemed uppermost in their minds were their plans for retirement. He was 65, and said he expected it would take him 15 years just to complete work on the ideas he already had. And during those years he fully expected to get other ideas.

Herbert introduced his father to his baby grandson, Dwight, but also showed him a magnetic tape recorder:

> One visit was in 1946 and Kodak had had some scouts in Germany after the war, like other companies, and they came back with magnetic tape.... It wasn't just the tape. It was also the electronic procedures and so on. Anyway, they came back with some tape heads, recording heads, and I got hold of one and I built myself a tape recorder. It was running with the then speed of 7.5 inches a second and it had reels, 400 foot, 800 foot reels. I showed it to Father. It was good music. "Ah!" he says, "What a thing! If it could record sound, you also can record pictures." "Oh," I said, "Dad, forget about it. Forget about it. This thing has a bandwidth of 5,000 to 10,000 Hertz. You know, what you need for pictures. You need millions of Hertz. Instead of going 7 inches a second, we'll go 7,000 inches a second. It may go many miles. It will go, I don't know, 300 miles an hour, and there isn't enough tape in the world to record anything." So he said to me, "You know, you have to consider the difference between a newborn baby and a grown adult. Now here is this newborn baby. It is not good for anything, but you just wait forty years and it will be a person and you don't know what is really accomplished. Same thing here. What you are showing me is a newborn baby. You just wait forty years. I think there will be pictures on tape.

Goldberg was exactly right. Forty years later, 32 million households in the United States owned a videocassette recorder.

Goldberg received a friendly postcard from Luther, Eggert, and several other participants at a conference on sensitometry in Munich in 1938, and in 1949, he received a letter signed by Eggert and 50 other participants at a photographic conference in Zurich expressing regret that Goldberg could not attend. Even though much of the work was practical, Goldberg was well aware that technology was changing. "Optics is finished. It's electronics now," he told Harry Tabor around 1951. The reality was, however, that through isolation and changed circumstance, his career as a scientist was over.

18

Military Needs

The small Hebrew seal on the new precision instruments is my answer to Hitler.

—Emanuel Goldberg, 1940

There were also, of course, military needs. The lack of manufacturing or repair facilities in the Middle East for military instruments became more serious when World War II disrupted European and Mediterranean transportation routes. Goldberg's experience during World War I, helping Luther on the Western Front and working with Carl Zeiss Jena, had given him valuable expertise in military optics. He and his Lab were badly needed. He worked very intensively for the Allies. The Lab's logo was composed of two Hebrew characters, *ayin* and *gimal*, in cursive script, for Emanuel Goldberg. Referring to it, he liked to say, "The small Hebrew seal on the new precision instruments is my answer to Hitler." The British Army, the U.S. Army, and the underground Jewish Defense Force, the Haganah, all come to him for help, and additional work was done for the Czech and French forces.

He served as an advisor and prepared a report on the capacity of the Jewish community in Palestine to contribute to the war effort. In December 1940, he went to Delhi, where he encountered Vera Salomons again, and advised on the production of optical equipment in India.

Goldberg had very cordial personal relations with the British military authorities and in 1941 began engineering work for the British Army. His experience with military technology facilitated his dealings with the Royal Electrical and Mechanical Engineers and the Royal Army Ordnance Corps, and there was a friendly relationship between the British military officers and the Lab staff. The contractual arrangement is reflected in a May 13, 1943, agreement with the Directorate of War Production of the Government of Palestine. The Directorate agreed to pay a minimum of 800 Palestinian pounds, to lend machine tools, and to supply raw material free of cost. Ten percent of the time paid for was to be reserved for Goldberg's scientific work. There would be an increase in employees, and the agreement was to continue for the duration of the war.

Later, the U.S. Army wanted Goldberg to work for them in Egypt. He visited, but insisted that he would work only in Palestine. There was an amicable relationship through Major Henry N. Sachs, Acting Ordnance Officer for Palestine and Syria, and a contract with Head Quarters, U.S. Army Levant Service Command, U.S. Army Forces in the Middle East, dated October 9, 1942. The U.S. Army built a substantial addition to the building at 200 Dizengoff for Goldberg to use. Legally and technically, it was not an addition, because U.S. regulations allowed only the construction of separate, detached buildings. But by building it with a separation of just one inch, with aligned doorways and the one-inch gap covered, it functioned as an addition. Because the United States did not have military forces in Palestine, little work was brought for him to do. The building was not reclaimed after the war and ownership was eventually assumed by the City of Tel Aviv, which owned the land it was on.

But if the U.S. Army was absent, the underground Jewish Defence Force, the Haganah, was very much present. The Haganah had plenty of work for him, which was done secretly when the British Mandatory Authorities were not looking. A whistled tune was used to signal the arrival of British visitors to the Lab. Aviva Kelton recalled, "We had a special signal. So when the English came to visit or to inspect, everything was in the drawer. We took out the work we were supposed to do for them, which we didn't do very much because we were working for the Haganah the whole time. And actually it was dangerous because there were arms." Once when Goldberg's daughter Renate, now Chava, was engaged on some Haganah work, a bullet went through her hair, grazing her head. A sniper, firing from Jaffa, missed killing her by an inch. Occasionally, British military would be in one room in the Lab while Haganah people were in another room.

The tension between underground Jewish activists and the Mandate Authorities was a central feature of the political situation. One apprentice, Martin Strauss, was born in Leipzig. His family fled to Palestine in 1939, and he worked in Goldberg's Lab for "seven glorious years." After hours, however, he was engaged in smuggling Jewish refugees into Palestine illegally. In 1947, the British Mandate forces arrested him and gave him a choice between jail or voluntary emigration to some other country. He remembered that he had an uncle in New York, opted to go the United States, and, in 1949, set up Strauss Photo-Technical Service in Washington, D.C., with a workshop inspired by Goldberg's Lab, which Goldberg later visited and rightly admired.

With the establishment of the State of Israel, the Lab acquired a protected status as a military asset. This meant that employees were not entirely free to move to other jobs and, in 1948, when young people had to go into the army, those working in the Lab were liable to be required to continue working there as their military service.

Compasses

One of the biggest and most successful tasks at the Lab was the manufacture of prismatic compasses. They were called "prismatic" because if one looked across the top of the compass at a distant object, the compass reading would be visible through an angled prism. It was a copy of a British Army compass, with fluorescent paint markings on the dial for nighttime use. Its most impressive feature was the rotating compass dial made of mother-of-pearl cut from large seashells acquired from the Dead Sea, Australia, Saudi Arabia, local markets, and other places. A circular disk was cut out of the central, flatter part of the shell and ground down until it was very thin, 2 or 3 tenths of a millimeter, yet very strong. The orientation markings were then added using photoengraving, with fluorescent paint markings added. A pantograph and a dividing machine were built, and chemical etching procedures were developed specially for this purpose. Old gramophone needles were used as pins to support the rotating disks.

Aerial Photography

The British asked for help because the cameras being used for aerial reconnaissance were malfunctioning in cold temperatures. Heating elements were removed from domestic laundry irons, adapted for the voltage available in the aircraft, and mounted alongside the cameras, following experiments using the cameras inside a refrigerator for lack of a better facility.

Photogrammetry, the precise analysis of aerial photographs, is very difficult unless the camera is pointing exactly vertically downward. However, airplanes are nearly always at some kind of angle or tilt, resulting is distorted perspectives. An English officer in Egypt requested a rectifier, a copying device, which reconstructs and reverses the effects of any angles in the photograph to produce a "rectified" image. Six "Goldberg Rectifiers" were built, five for 5-in images and one, a very large and complex piece of equipment, for 9-in images. (See Figure 18.1.)

The first Jewish military airplanes were brought in clandestinely in the mid-1940s, after the World War II, and there was almost no aerial photography in the region at that time. When the State of Israeli was established,

Figure 18.1. Aerial photo rectifier built during World War II.

the new government acquired American air force surplus handheld cameras for aerial photography. The Lab serviced these cameras and, when an air force was established, assisted in installing them in the airplanes. In a small airplane, a large camera could only be installed horizontally, so the Lab designed and built an optical system to deflect the view downward toward the ground.

Clinometers

In the fighting that followed the declaration of the State of Israel, the Jewish artillery forces could not fire accurately for lack of instruments to measure the elevation of the target. They knew the ballistics of the projectiles and they had rangefinders to measure the distance, but for accurate aiming, they also needed clinometers to show if the target is higher or lower than the gun and by how much. Israel Tal, later General Tal, appealed personally to Goldberg. Goldberg said that he lacked the resources to make what was needed, but that he would think about it. Forty-eight hours later, he telephoned Tal and invited him to try out a device he had improvised, by reverse engineering a British military clinometer. Tal found it to be satisfactory, so the apprentices worked around the clock to produce, within two weeks, all the clinometers the Israeli Army needed. Tal became famous for his work developing tanks and widely known by the nickname "Talic"; he stayed on at the Ministry of Defence, where he kept one of the Goldberg clinometers on his desk. Interviewed in 1995, nearly 50 years after the event, he was eager to sing the praise of Professor Goldberg. "I tell my staff," he declared dramatically, "that if they are good enough to reach the stature of Professor Goldberg's ankles, I will call them geniuses!"

Sniper Sights

Before it was disbanded, members of the Jewish Brigade that fought with Allied forces during World War II stole considerable quantities of weapons that were smuggled into Palestine. Among them were a few sniper rifles with telescopic sights, but not nearly enough. The commander of the sniper squad of the 1st Battalion of the British Army Jewish Brigade, Sniper Sergeant Alex Eliraz, had become head of the training program for the Haganah. Early in 1946, Eliraz took a British Enfield rifle with a telescopic sight to Goldberg and asked if he could make more sights. The Lab had not previously made telescopes and Goldberg replied that, lacking the proper optical glass, he could not copy it. However, in view of the compelling need, he decided that he could substitute heavy glass from broken shop windows. This had a different refractive index than the glass in the Enfield sight, so he had to calculate new curvatures for the lenses and grind to different specifications. This reverse engineering was successful; some 30 or 40 were built and were used by the Israeli forces for the next two decades. One of the Goldberg Instruments rifle sights is displayed in the Collection Sheds Defense Museum in Jaffa. Several years later, when the Lab had moved to Rehovot, it established a subsidiary plant at Sderot, following a government appeal to move industries into settlements inhabited by new immigrants that had high unemployment and social problems. At the inauguration of the Sderot plant, Alex Eliraz, now the venerated "Father of Marksmanship," wrote a commemorative poem in Hebrew entitled *Am I really from Sderot?* His English translation of it reads:

> The Goldberg Instruments at 200 Dizengoff Street,
> Spread wings to El Op Rehovot,
> By the pupils of the wise "Yeke" professor.
> They are also retired by now.
> Boys and girls from Sderot
> Are filling work halls.
> I will use the famous saying
> "If you wish this is not a legend."
> A telescope, that I and my comrades have stolen from the British,
> When returning the sniper rifles at the dissolution of the "Brigade,"

By reverse engineering
At "El Op" converted into number 32 telescope,
Participated in the war of
Independence, and fought till the "Six Days War."
All the Jerusalem snipers remember.

"Yeke," more fully "Yehodi Ksehe Havana," means "a Jew who hardly understands," and was used to refer to immigrant Jews from Germany whose knowledge of Hebrew was limited, as Goldberg's was.

The Ktina

Goldberg resumed his interest in extreme resolution photography. He used his Goldberg emulsion to show the staff what could be done. "He did something just to show us. He made a map of Israel that was the size of a dot and the resolution was wonderful," recalled Aviva Kelton.

In 1940 high-resolution photographic plates became commercially available and, in 1956, a microdot portrait of Goldberg on a Kodak Maximum Resolution Plate was sent to Kodak Museum in Harrow, England. About this time, Goldberg designed a spy camera disguised as a fountain pen and known by the Hebrew name *Ktina*, meaning "the tiny one." At least six different pen cameras were made, probably for copying documents. They were identical in design but the shape and color were varied. The main part of the camera body was made of plastic. The cap was metal. A small square of about 3×3 mm was cut from a high-resolution glass plate and mounted so that it could rotate, allowing a circle of six exposures on the same small square. A microscope objective was used as a lens, and, with an adaptor, the camera could also be used in reverse as a reader for exposed and processed images. The camera lacked the internal sac of ink usually found in fountain pens, but it could be used as a pen if the nib was dipped in ink. Jakob Beutler recalled,

> So we built for the Secret Service. We built a camera to make these images. The material was Ilford maximum resolution plates. Maximum resolution plates are not sensitive. The sensitivity is not very high, but very high definition. An ingenious cartridge for these small 3 by 3 millimeter [pieces] ... and by doing a certain clever motion it would make six images. One two three—click, click, click—until now you do this, like this, you know, and whatever you wanted to make image of, you click and click and click. I don't know if somebody did any real spying job with it, but I made, I think, six or ten of these. And every one was different, wasn't the same fountain pen. Later on there was another cover for it and you could read it.

In June 1958, Dan Barli, Lieutenant-Colonel, Israel Defence Force, wrote, "Let me convey to you my sincere appreciation of the development efforts and production of the ktina instrument. Our laboratory experiments on the equipment you developed and built, persuaded us of the operational significance of the ktina. It won't be long before the equipment will be put into efficient use."

Other work for military purposes included the use of diamonds for testing the hardness of steel, bubble levels for the PIAT Personal Infantry Anti-Tank rocket launcher, and mortar sights. Glass tubes for the bubble levels were obtained by getting permission from the British authorities to import glass ampules as medical supplies. To economize on optical glass and grinding, the lenses for the mortar sights were cut in half, because a mortar sight could be used with only half a lens.

Advisory Services

Much of Goldberg's advisory work was with military and intelligence agencies and was quite informal. In that small, close-knit community, whenever anyone raised a technical question, the answer was likely to be, "Call Professor Goldberg." He worked especially with his friend Grisha Schapiro, an immigrant from Memel in Prussia, who ran a small, secret unit in the Tel Aviv area. George Sorenson, Schapiro's assistant from 1954 to 1960, explained.

> I made my first acquaintance [with Goldberg] when Grisha took me to him at Dizengoff Street 200 and introduced me to him ... I don't think that he ever came to our place. He was a very, very warm personality. He was very—How would you say in English?— "bescheiden" [= unassuming] ... He was a modest man, but he was a genius. No doubt about it. He was a chemist. He was a physicist. I think he also had some fields in arts and he was also interested ... I must say in a way I was overwhelmed by this person, his personality. He did help us a lot ... He helped us whenever we had a problem, Grisha would say, 'I am going to see the Professor' and he came back with 'Look, let's try it this way.' ... We developed things that were good and useful and he helped us in mechanical matters.

Among Goldberg's surviving papers are a few letters from the officers he dealt with. In September 1950, H. Slavin wrote, "With my departure from the Military Industry [an organization] I would like to convey to you my thanks and appreciation of your work and help in laying the foundations for the security of the people and the land." In May 1956, Colonel (later General) Yehoshafat Harkabi, Head of the Intelligence Department of the

Israel Defence Force noted that, "We are very pleased that you accepted our request to take upon yourself to be our scientific consultant ... " Shimon Peres, then General Manager at the Department of Defense, in August 1957 appointed Goldberg "to be responsible for the development of special technical issues for the Department of Defense." Dan Barli, Lieutenant-Colonel, IDF, wrote in December 1958, "I am concluding my mission as the commander of the unit you helped so much. On this occasion I would like to thank you again for your important help and the voluntary spirit in which it was given. I have no doubt that in some fields, we reached excellent achievements, thanks to your theoretical and practical knowledge, interlocked with patience in dealing with our issues. By doing so you have made a vital contribution to the security of the State." The details of what he did are still considered sufficiently vital that they remain classified on the secret files of the Israeli defense and intelligence services. The specific topics probably involved photographic processes, optics, night vision equipment, military optics, and much else.

In May 1949, Goldberg went to the United States on a six-week business trip. Herbert drew his attention to a newspaper account of a new machine that, from the report, seemed to resemble the Statistical Machine Goldberg had designed. Intrigued, Goldberg went to see it.

Appendix: Goldberg Laboratory Products

A list of products of Professor Goldberg's Laboratory for Precision Work, later The Israel Electro-Optical Industry Ltd, up to approximately 1967, prepared by Shmuel Neumann from various sources, March 30, 1995.

Year (approx.)	Product	Market
1942	Reticles for optical devices	Defense
1943	Compass Components (Dials, Bearings etc.)	Defense
1943	Diamond Hardness Tester (Rockwell type)	Defense
1943	Rectifiers for aerial Mapping Photographies	Defense
1943	Spirit Levels (Glass, ground and heat-formed)	Defense/Civilian
1944	Artillery Elevation Meters	Defense
1944	Clinometers for Field Guns	Defense
1945	Hand and Laboratory Refractometers	Civilian
1945	Tensile Strength Measuring Machine	Civilian
1945	Industrial Pyrometers	Civilian
1946	Building Contractor's Prisms	Civilian
1946	Door Spies	Civilian
1946	Microfilm Camera	Civilian
1947	Industrial (Vacuum-Pan) Refractometers	Civilian
1947	Rifle Sights	Civilian
1948	Beer Bottle Inspection Machine	Civilian
1948	Loupes for Watchmakers	Civilian
1950	Bullet Cartridge Inspection Machine	Defense

1950	Field Compasses	Defense
1950	Hinges and Screws for Spectacles	Civilian
1953	Measuring Magnifiers	Civilian
1953	Sex Determination device for Chicks	Civilian
1955	Levelling Device for Contour Ploughing	Civilian
1955	Open sights for AA guns	Defense
1955	Telescopic Spectacles for visually handicap.	Civilian
1955	Collimators for Mortars	Defense
1957	Missile Components (optical, quartz)	Defense
1958	Choppers for electrooptical devices	Defense
1958	Collapsible Tripods for Theodolites	Defense/Civilian
1958	Microscope Eyepiece and Objective Lenses	Civilian
1958	Missile components (electrooptical)	Defense
1959	Missile components (mechanical)	Defense
1960	Infra Red Glass filters	Defense
1961	Mortar Aiming Sights	Defense
1962	Overhead Projectors	Civilian
1962	Technical Drawing Devices (for crosshatching)	Civilian
1965	Infra Red Foil filters	Defense
1965	Optical Components for Night Vision Devices	Defense
1965	Reflex sights for AA guns	Defense
1965	Typewriter for the Blind	Civilian
1965	Active (IR) Night Binoculars	Defense
1965	Microtomes	Civilian
196?	Aiming Periscopes for Tank Guns	Defense
1966	Active (IR) Night Aiming Sights	Defense
1966	Artillery Flashspotters	Defense
1967	Active (IR) Night Tank Periscopes	Defense
1967	Text Reader for the Blind	Civilian

19

The Microfilm Rapid Selector

A Top U.S. Scientist Foresees a Possible Future World In Which Man-Made Machine Will Start To Think.

—Heading in *Life* magazine, 1945

Zeiss Ikon and the Statistical Machine

Goldberg's work on microdots had been continued in Dresden by Hellmut Frieser, who succeeded Robert Luther as Head of the Institute for Scientific Photography at the Technical University. In 1941, Frieser published a paper on the use of microphotography for government purposes. He calculated that a government archive containing one standard A4-size sheet of paper for each inhabitant of Germany would occupy 500 cubic meters, enough to fill a small house. However, the same archive would occupy only 0.08 cu m if it were photographically reduced so that 10,000 sheets were recorded on a photographic plate 9 × 12 cm, about the size of a standard library catalog card. If the 9 × 12 cm sheets were filed in trays, the trays could be laid out on an average-sized table, requiring an area of about 9,000 sq cm, less than 3 ft × 4 ft. A microfilm archive would have the additional advantage that copies could be made available at additional locations. Frieser's paper includes examples of text and of a halftone picture enlarged from this size, but there is no mention of a search mechanism.

The German patent for the Statistical Machine was finally approved in December 1938 and in 1939, Goldberg wrote to Zeiss Ikon asking what they intended to do with it. Simader and Küppenbender replied in a letter dated February 3, 1940, that they had no definite plans. They explained how they would calculate the amount that would be payable to Goldberg under his right to half of any patent royalties. Interpreting the patent's scope narrowly,

217

they argued that it applied only to the search component *(Sucheinrichtung)*. Assuming that the price of this component were 2,000 Reichmarks and a total patent royalty of 5 percent, they concluded that Goldberg's half of the royalty would be a mere 50 Reichmarks per machine built.

No evidence of interest in developing the Statistical Machine has been found. If there had been interest, the evidence might be hard to find. In 1940, Germany was a totalitarian state at war and any development of the Statistical Machine would probably have done secretly for the central government or for military purposes, and Zeiss Ikon's corporate records no longer exist. Most likely, there was no interest. In the 1950s, Carl Zeiss Jena was marketing, for "modern documentation," the Zeiss-Dokumator-System, composed of conventional equipment for microfilming documents and for storing and reading microfilm, without the search capability that Goldberg had developed.

Ralph Shaw

In 1949, when Goldberg went to the United States on business, his son, Herbert, drew his attention to reports of a microfilm-based document retrieval machine at the National Agriculture Library. The magazine *Electronics,* for example, carried an article entitled "Photoelectric Librarian," which included a photograph of Ralph Shaw, the Director of the Library, posing proudly in a suit, with bow tie and pipe, next to a complicated-looking machine as tall as he was, called a Rapid Selector. It was a new version of an earlier machine developed from 1938 onward at Massachusetts Institute of Technology by an engineering professor named Vannevar Bush. Goldberg went to the library to see this machine, which Shaw demonstrated to him. Goldberg immediately recognized that this Rapid Selector was a variant of his own Statistical Machine of 20 years before. *Fortune* magazine later reported what happened: "Not long after a public demonstration of the Rapid Selector, Shaw was visited by an engineer named Goldberg, who had worked before the war with the famous German optical firm of Zeiss-Ikon. Goldberg said he was delighted to see that someone had finally found a use for his idea of a microfilm record combined with an index code–essentially the same idea as Bush's."

Shaw, unaware of Goldberg's prior work, was taken by surprise, and startled to be told that his elderly visitor had long held the U.S. patent for the innovative machine that he had been so proudly publicizing. Two patent searches made for Shaw had not found Goldberg's patent. Reportedly, Shaw's searchers neither knew nor discovered that the established technical name for such equipment, already used in several patents, was "Statistical Machine." They must also have failed to determine the proper patent classification number. The vocabulary used to describe Goldberg's machine did not made clear its purpose as a document retrieval device. The English version of his paper had been entitled "Methods of photographic registration" and *Electronics* magazine included Goldberg's U.S. patent in its regular patent listings with the following summary: "Statistical machine. Use of light beam and phototube for adding, sorting and other statistical operations."

Vannevar Bush

Vannevar Bush was a forceful, ambitious professor of engineering at Massachusetts Institute of Technology. In 1938, Bush and some students had started to build a document retrieval machine with financial support from Kodak and National Cash Register. The machine was intended to be fast and so was called the Bush Rapid Selector. Bush also understood a close relationship between information retrieval and cryptanalysis in that both involve searches for the occurrence of codes. Document retrieval systems are designed for the document searcher to find encoded index terms, while, in contrast, with encryption systems, the hope is that a cryptanalyst will not find any recognizable patterns, but the same process of searching for codes can be used for both. This insight led to the secret parallel development, under Bush's supervision, of the Comparator, a statistical machine to help Navy cryptanalysts to break enemy codes.

The Microfilm Rapid Selector machine developed by Bush and his assistants was simpler than the Statistical Machine that Goldberg had demonstrated and publicized in 1931. Goldberg had used a movie gate to advance the film in a controlled manner, rapidly, precisely, but intermittently. In Bush's design, the film flowed continuously, nonstop, past the search card and sensor and then copied images at high speed using a stroboscopic light. But simpler did not prove easier, and Bush's continuous flow design proved troublesome. Bush hoped to scan at 1,000 codes per second, claiming that this would be 40 times faster than a movie gate at the standard speed of 24 frames per second. This claim was an exaggeration. The later improved, ERA Rapid Selector was designed to run at 10,000 frames per minute, and each frame could contain *up to* six codes, so, if every frame had six codes, up to 60,000 codes could be searched per minute, which would be 1,000 codes per second. However, the assignment of index terms is in practice highly skewed, so six codes on every frame is improbable. A speed of 10,000 frames per minute is 167 frames per second, seven times faster than the standard movie gate speed (180 frames per second was reported for Shaw's machine by Engineering Research Associates [ERA], the firm that built it). But movie gates can be run faster than the standard 24 frames per second, and a movie-gate selector could be designed to search for more than one code per frame. In brief, Bush's continuous flow design was faster, but considerably less than 40 times faster.

In practice, Bush and his assistants found that the film itself would distort under this kind of treatment. They never found a way to punch reliably the tiny holes in the search card, and it was difficult to make copies of selected frames without first stopping the film. Bush did not have access to the precision engineering expertise available to Goldberg at Zeiss Ikon both for movie-gate engineering and also for the continuous flow film technology used in its high-speed "time-magnifying" Zeitlupe cameras. The Zeitlupe, originally developed by Ernemann, had initially run at 300 frames per second in 1916 and was steadily made faster. In 1928, Goldberg decided that Zeiss Ikon would develop improved designs. A Zeiss Ikon Zeitlupe running at 1,000 frames per second was used to record photofinishes at the 1936 Olympics, and the amazing speed of 3,000 frames per second was achieved by 1938.

The MIT-designed Microfilm Rapid Selector was adapted for cryptanalysis during World War II, and it was revived after World War II at Engineering Research Associates (ERA) by Bush's former assistants. They obtained $75,000 support through a contract with Ralph Shaw, who had access to funding from the U.S. Department of Commerce. It was an ERA rapid selector that Shaw demonstrated to Goldberg in 1949. Shaw wrote several widely read articles about the Rapid Selector, but he found that his ideas and his claims were subjected to skepticism and criticism by experts in documentation. He himself became more cautious and eventually concluded that the machine was not viable, although a microfilm rapid selector did find a use in the U.S. Navy's Bureau of Ships.

The long, complicated, and obscure story of Bush's 30-year effort to develop his Microfilm Rapid Selector for document retrieval and for cryptanalysis has been painstakingly reconstructed in Colin Burke's book *Information and Secrecy: Vannevar Bush, ULTRA, and the Other Memex.*

The Paradoxical Memex

Bush's work in this area was not particularly early, original, or, even, mechanically successful, but it was Bush, not Goldberg, who became world-famous for it, largely because of an essay Bush wrote speculating on the future use of such a machine. The essay, entitled "As we may think," notes the increasing difficulty of finding relevant documents and argues that advances in photography, circuitry, and the use of photoelectric cells could be combined to create a personal microfilm-based library, with a search capability, built into a desk. A feature emphasized by Bush was that the owner could index documents by arbitrary themes so that any two or more documents considered relevant to each other would be assigned the same indexing term and, thereby, be linked with each other. Bush called these links "trails" and the overall concept a "Memex," from *memory* and ind*ex*. The wording of the essay reveals a lack of familiarity with techniques of document indexing and retrieval. Robert Fairthorne, a knowledgeable and incisive observer, commented:

> Dr. Bush does not seem to have gone deeply enough. In spite of his complaints about "the artificiality of systems of indexing," his system of "associative trails" is logically equivalent to any system that allows for associations of subject-matter. The speed of the device, however high, is not enough to deal with the accumulation of data if one uses one microcopy only of each entry. If one microcopy can be made, so can several, and these can be stored in all conceivable relevant "memories," since storage is no longer a major problem. The fundamental library problem is not touched, for Dr. Bush considers only a device for an individual, who can apply arbitrary criteria of relevance, has all the world's literature stored as a microcopy, and *has already read and classified it....* [A]s a description of what machines can do, as opposed to what they should do, [it] can hardly be bettered.

Drafted in 1939, the essay was published in 1945 in the *Atlantic Monthly* and promptly reprinted in *Life* magazine with drawings and the subtitle "A Top U.S. Scientist Foresees a Possible Future World In Which Man-Made Machine Will Start To Think." The following year it was reprinted in Bush's book *Endless Horizons.* Despite its limitations, the essay was immediately popular. It has been reprinted frequently, and it was cited constantly for two reasons that had little to do with the technology that Bush describes. One reason is that it is well written. It stimulates the reader's imagination to go beyond the technology on which it was based. The mythical Memex became a symbol of what might one day be achieved if only one were inventive enough, an image of potentiality in information retrieval research and development. There is no doubt that Bush's vigorous and imaginative writing was an inspiration for many readers, notably work on hypertext by Douglas Engelbart and Theodore Nelson in the more promising technological context of digital computers.

A second reason why Bush's essay was, for 50 years, the iconic symbol for the application of new technology in an information age is that Bush's personal prestige gave legitimacy to all who invoked his name. Bush had led the scientific effort to win World War II, and he had proposed the National Science Foundation. He was the "the engineer of the twentieth century," the academic inventor who had achieved power in Washington. In a world of "Big Science" in which the largest machines brought the most prestige, there were many who felt a need for legitimacy, either because they were concerned with small machines, such as personal computers, or with "softer" tasks, such as combining components for human-computer interfaces or providing information services. Invoking an association with the towering prestige and slightly folksy image of Bush was compellingly attractive to a wide range of writers. And once the pattern was established, others followed. Authors cited "As we may think" even when it had little or no relevance to what they had to say and, occasionally, in a way that indicated that they had not read it. It is still widely thought to have been about digital computers and even, somehow, related to networks, instead of an isolated, personalized microfilm reader with a search mechanism.

What reveals the widespread invocation of the Memex to have been a cultural and political gesture rather than an ordinary technical acknowledgment is the striking absence of accompanying references by Bush or by those who cite him to any of the many people who had expressed the same or similar ideas before Bush. Some of these were internationally famous: Wilhelm Ostwald, who had used his Nobel prize money to promote hypertext; Paul Otlet, the founder of the International Federation for Documentation, with visionary ideas about workstations; Watson Davis, of Science Service, a tireless advocate of microfilm technology; James Bryce, the Chief Scientist at IBM, who built up IBM's patent holdings in electronics and personally received patents for rapid selector technology; H. G. Wells, who, like Ostwald and Otlet, had championed a vision that was much more ambitious than Bush's under the name "World Brain"; and, of course, Goldberg, industrialist, authority on photography, and the first of the several inventors who worked on rapid selector technology in the late 1920s and 1930s. Citing these and others who anticipated Bush's Memex would have been appropriate historically, technologically, and ethically, but in the late twentieth century, they lacked Bush's cultural appeal and were ignored until they were rediscovered during the 1990s.

Acknowledgment

Bush's Microfilm Rapid Selector may not have been plagiarism. Goldberg's German and English papers on the Statistical Machine had been prominently published, and reference to it and to the microfilm rapid selector of Merle C. Gould can be found in documents that were known to have been distributed to Bush in 1938. However, Bush might not have read them or might not have recognized them for what they were. These ideas were "in the air" at least by 1935 and inventions routinely occur duplicatively when the time is ripe. Russell C. Coile, the only surviving member of Bush's original 1938–40 team at MIT, does not remember any mention of Goldberg at that time.

When Bush came to know of Goldberg's prior invention is not clear. He was definitely informed in September 1949 following Goldberg's visit to Shaw, but it is likely that he had already known for some years. In 1937 and again in 1940, Bush had tried to patent his microfilm rapid selector technology, but his claims were mostly rejected by the Patent Office examiners who cited Goldberg's prior patent as a reason. Goldberg reportedly wrote to Bush, describing his work, in 1940. In 1954, an Advisory Committee on Application of Machines to Patent Office Operations, chaired by Bush, issued its report, which had a useful technical appendix, "Mechanization of patent search: The status of the data handling art," prepared by National Bureau of Standards staff. In the section on microfilm selectors, the Appendix stated: "In 1931, a patent was issued to E. Goldberg ... Practical ideas ... were independently advanced by Bush and a prototype was developed at the Massachusetts Institute of Technology."

At ERA in 1946, the latest version of the comparator was renamed "Goldberg," which has generally been assumed to be, and may well in fact have been, in honor of the inventor Rube Goldberg, rather than the Goldberg whose invention was being developed.

Shaw's actions are difficult to explain. It is not clear why he so completely misjudged the capability of the Rapid Selector. Shaw may have been manipulated by Bush and others because he was in a position to obtain funding from the Department of Commerce to support continued work on the Microfilm Rapid Selector at ERA. He may have been motivated to promote his professional reputation, which it did. Perhaps he had not been paying attention. To his credit, Shaw was very quick to acknowledge Goldberg's priority as soon as he learned of it. At the beginning of a widely read article published soon after Goldberg's visit, Shaw wrote, "The first practical application of electronics to selection of data on film appears to have been made some twenty years ago by Dr. E. Goldberg, who at the time was with Zeiss in Dresden. His invention was protected by United States Patent No. 1,838,389, issued on 29 December 1931." This statement was made in the widely read and highly respected *Journal of Documentation* and, as a result, Goldberg's U.S. patent is, on rare occasions, cited in the later technical literature.

Two exceptionally well-informed authorities on the use of technology for documentation mentioned Goldberg's Statistical Machine at international conferences. The International Institute for Documentation (IID), the institute founded by Paul Otlet, had a committee on technical methods in documentation, chaired by the German librarian, Walter Schürmeyer. In a paper presented to the 1933 conference of the German Librarians Association, Schürmeyer drew attention to the Contax 35 mm camera for library microfilming needs and to the Zeiss Ikon Giro check machine as suitable technology for mechanized, microfilm-based library catalogs. He described what is recognizable as the Goldberg microdot and the Statistical Machine at the IID conference in 1935 and also at another conference of German librarians, but he named no names and cited no sources. Frits Donker Duyvis, a Dutch patent official who succeeded Paul Otlet as the central figure in the Documentation movement, mentioned the Statistical Machine during discussion at an international conference in 1936. He clearly recognized its significance, but apparently did not associate it with Goldberg: "Prof. Joachim (Zeiss Ikon Werke) has realised a device for selecting images from a microfilm with aid of the photoelectic cell." Hermann Joachim, an authority of movie technology, had taken over some of Goldberg's responsibilities at Zeiss Ikon after Goldberg left, and represented Zeiss Ikon at meetings of documentalists. Donker Duyvis commented that various patents existed that were based on the reading and selecting of written texts with the aid of photoelectric devices and added, "There seems to be some indication that in future photoelectric selection will be an important tool for documentary search."

In 1957, Shmuel Neumann, Goldberg's loyal assistant, gave proper credit in his introduction to a special issue of an Israeli technology journal honoring Goldberg's 75th birthday, but he cited no sources, and his comments are unlikely to have been noticed by European or North American information retrieval specialists.

Curiously, although Goldberg's patents were known, nobody seems to have been aware of Goldberg's two papers describing the Statistical Machine, even though they were published fairly prominently, in German in the proceedings of the 1931 Dresden congress, and in English translation in the *British Journal of Photography*. Any competent librarian or scholar who knew of the patent should have been able to find these papers if he or she had looked. Ralph Shaw, for example, whose parents were Austrian, was fluent in German and an expert on bibliography. Perhaps nobody had enough curiosity to look to see if Goldberg had written papers in addition to obtaining a patent. His congress paper was included, without comment or explanation, in a European bibliography in 1937 and in a U.S. bibliography in 1938, but, thereafter, neither paper appears to have been cited anywhere until an early version of this chapter was published in 1992. That Goldberg had actually used a prototype machine operationally for his business correspondence was not reported in print until 2004, so even those who knew of Goldberg's patents had no reason to assume that he had done more than outline a patent-worthy design. If it had been known that any working prototypes had been built, interest would have been greater. As a result, people assumed that the Bush Rapid Selector was the first such machine ever built. Careless writers sometimes credited Shaw himself with its invention. Even in 1975, an otherwise knowledgeable tribute to Shaw and his interest in machines, stated: "The rapid selector, which he invented while working with Vannevar Bush, was the first complex piece of equipment designed for searching recorded information."

Bush continued for the rest of his life to accept adulation for his Memex, to take credit for what he had done, and to write about it, with Goldberg's work arising in private memos on how prior patents could be "worked around." Bush's biographer, G. P. Zachary notes that this was not the only time Bush chose not to acknowledge the prior work of others. Bush caused considerable sums of other people's money to be spent over many years on his rapid selector. The very detailed reconstruction by Colin Burke shows clearly that whole effort was never thought through and that it was poorly managed. Once Bush's work is seen in context, he becomes a curious icon for information science.

A Networked Search Machine

While the engineers at ERA were struggling to make work what was now 20-year-old technology for an isolated retrieval device, Goldberg was designing "Searchphoto," a remotely accessible retrieval system for a networked environment.

Already in 1931, in his paper at the Dresden Congress, Goldberg had explained how the dial of a telephone handset could be used as a data entry device to specify a search query. The sequence of numbers dialed would light up selected bulbs in a two-dimensional array, as shown in Figures 14.8 and 14.9. The pattern of light sources was a convenient alternative to placing a punch card with holes in front of a lamp. If a telephone handset were used to enter a search into a statistical machine, the pulses would be conveyed over wire, and this could be done at a distance limited only by the length of the wires. A telephone network would greatly extend that distance. It was probably in 1949, after his encounter with Ralph Shaw, that Goldberg drafted a patent application for methods for submitting search queries remotely. He sketched a diagram on a sheet of stationery from the Hotel Commodore in New York City (Figure 19.1) with a handwritten text in English:

> The object of the present invention is a device known as "searchphoto" in machines for locating by means of radiation some predefinite [presumably, predefined] design out of a quantity of different designs introduced in such a machine. These machines, based on U.S. 1,838,389 are known as "statistical machines" or "rapid selectors." According to this patent the process of locating some predetermined indications, e.g. carrying adding sorting statistical and like operations consists in exploring such indications by causing radiation energy to actuate a recorder when the exposed indications on the search plate and the record element are identical.
>
> The known machines based on this principle use literally [or liberally?] the elements described and shown in this patent, that is plates bearing punched or photographed indications as holes in the material or transparent places on a sheet produced by means of photography.

This kind of establishing a search element implies that the handling of the rapid selector must be performed by a person present at the place where the machine is located.

According to the present invention the search plate is composed of a [sic] single elements, the situation of which can be governed by remote control, so that the rapid selector can be situated in any place and the person wishing to locate an indication or to perform any other statistical operation is situated in any other place the action being propelled by wire, electronic means, mechanical steering or any other possibility of remote control.

This draft appears not to have been developed into an actual patent application.

The development of photo-optical retrieval machines combining microfilm, pattern-recognition, and photocells continued. Several different rapid selector machines were developed during the 1950s and early 1960s. A Film Library Instantaneous Presentation system was designed to

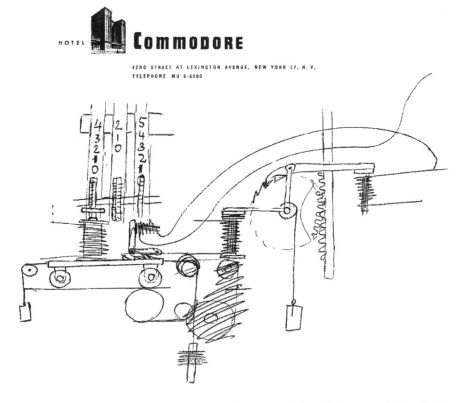

Figure 19.1. Diagram for conducting searches remotely by telephone, probably 1949.

scan up to 72,000 frames on a 1,200 reel at 300–600 frames per second. The FMA File Search system searched 35 mm film with up to 32,000 pages per reel. The latest example found of this technology is a Russian design described in a 1965 publication. The diagrams resemble those in Goldberg's initial German patent application submitted in May 1927. The author, I. I. Kliachkin, when contacted, said that he had never heard of Emanuel Goldberg.

The delay imposed by the necessity for searching the entire length of long rolls of microfilm was a problem inherent in the design. Also, although new records could be added, erasing or correcting records was impractical. In the late 1950s, Goldberg, like others, experimented with the use of smaller, replaceable chips of film to resolve both problems. Shmuel Neumann wrote:

> Now after his 75th birthday, his dream is still as it was thirty years ago: a library consisting of an automatic "record" changer with viewing screen, equipped with discs bearing minute photographic images made according to his process and holding not less than 25,000 books of 250 pages each. With 10 discs such a "library" would contain the equivalent of a quarter of a million books, and would occupy less space than a conventional writing desk.

Eastman Kodak with its Minicard system and IBM with its Walnut machine were taking the same kind of approach. Kodak used metal sticks, each carrying up to 2,000 chips of microfilm. IBM stored small strips of film in small canisters. The engineering requirements for mechanically manipulating, searching, and copying the chips at high speed were extremely demanding, and the development costs were so expensive that only the U.S. military and intelligence agencies could afford them. The first Minicard system, delivered to the Pentagon in 1957 to store and retrieve data on people, technical developments, military forces, and political and economic trends for Air Force intelligence analysts, reportedly cost well over $8 million in mid-1950s dollars.

Even the simpler systems using reels of microfilm were too expensive for libraries and found little acceptance. In the early 1960s, microfilm rapid selector technology was overtaken by digital computers. The first recorded online remote search of a computer database using telephone lines was in California in 1963, 14 years after Goldberg outlined his Searchphoto design.

Goldberg's technology carried over into the development of digital computers. The use of patterns of opaque shapes sensed by photoelectric cells had potential as an input medium for digital computers. In 1947, the use of rows of 10 opaque (or clear) spots 0.01 in $\times$ 0.02 in across the film was reported. This allowed a storage density of 1,000 bits per square inch of film. Each of the 10 positions across the row could be scanned reliably at 100 bits per second. As in the "intermediate" television technology, digit output on to film could also be processed rapidly at up to 6,000 bits per second. "A strip of 35 mm. film 100 feet long will store about 10^7 elements, which is at least an order of magnitude larger than presently contemplated electronic storage.... Photographic film at present appears to be the most useful form in which to store permanent records of both input and output data," claimed a Kodak engineer. Punch cards, punched paper tape, and magnetic tape, however, did not require chemical processing and came to be preferred.

The other component, the microfilm storage of images of documents, has lasted longer. *Giant Brains; or, Machines that Think,* a popular introduction to digital computers, assumed, in 1949, that future "automated library" catalog records (and, eventually, the documents) would be on microfilm and retrieved by a digital computer: "You will be able to dial into the catalogue machine 'making biscuits.' There will be a flutter of movie film in the machine. Soon it will stop, and, in front of you on the screen will be projected the part of the catalogue which shows the names of three or four books containing recipes for biscuits." It was not until the end of the century, nearly 75 years after Goldberg filed his first Statistical Machine patent, that digital storage technology routinely matched microfilm's ability to retrieve, display, and copy entire texts and images.

20

Finale

I must work simply to continue the daily life.

—Emanuel Goldberg at age 86

Difficulties

During the 1950s, sustaining the Laboratory became progressively more difficult. Israeli government agencies recognized Goldberg and his Laboratory as a significant national asset and were consistently supportive. But research and development work tended not to be profitable and long-term development loans increased his obligations. The set-up cost for making instruments was high. The investment required for improved designs or new products was even higher, so only a large production run would yield a profit. Manufacturing precision instruments for the private sector tended to be uneconomical because the production runs were too small. The Laboratory's space was too small for increased production, and, in any case, the Israeli market was limited and exporting was difficult.

A visit by Goldberg to Zeiss resulted in an inflation-related increase in his pension in 1955, with provision for future inflation adjustments. He was also given a lump-sum payment of 67,000 Deutschmark, then worth U.S. $16,000, and, in 1961, had some back taxes paid for him. His personal finances were improved, but financing the Lab remained a problem. Substantial profit or significant additional capital was needed to upgrade the equipment or to acquire larger premises, but investors who could bring in significant new capital would expect a share in the control of the company. Goldberg did not want to cede any control, and he opposed allowing a union to represent the employees.

The salaries he could afford to pay were not competitive and, understandably, good employees left, some to go to university, others to Europe

229

or to the United States. As Israel developed, more employment options became available and new staff became more difficult to recruit. His apprenticeship program, initially so successful, began to break down. He wrote to Herbert, "Training new people is practically impossible. The situation changed in this respect enormously... There are very good professional schools splendidly equipped, so that apprentices as we had in previous years do not come. And the boys leaving the schools or the technical high schools are immediately absorbed by the Government, Army or big concerns." With these new options, apprenticeship to an inventor, now nearly 80 years old, with aging equipment, had become less attractive.

Worse, Goldberg did not find an acceptable successor. His son, Herbert, had the technical expertise, and Goldberg would have liked him to take over. But Herbert's family and career were well established in the United States. Although he had come to Israel with his family to help his father complete the development of the copying camera, Herbert had been careful not to commit to taking over the company. In 1953, Herbert and his American wife, now expecting their second child, returned with Dwight to the United States. Goldberg wrote, later that year, "For us it was quite a shock to have Herbert leave us and, apart from our own personal grief, I do not really know up to now how to fill the gap left by him."

Shmuel Neumann excelled in managing the business and marketing aspects of the Lab, but Goldberg's vision called for a scientific innovator to be in charge. Shmuel believed that the Lab needed to be expanded if it were to become a financially viable company. Goldberg would have preferred a smaller operation focused on research and development. He felt that making products for the private sector interfered with the research mission of the Lab, but he could not afford to stop private sector work. Thousands of compasses and refractometers were made over the years, but production was on too small a scale to be really profitable. The result was that his energies were exhausted dealing with day-to-day training and supervision. "I continue to be at 7 a.m. there, occupy myself with senseless detail work (e.g., how to prevent field lenses and graticules from dust in rooms, where sand blasting is done in the next room and grinding wheels in the room on the other side). After 11 hours work I am coming home and begin to repair something broken in the meanwhile." A year later he writes, "I have to step again in the daily production and to do nothing else than showing some girl how to clean engraving parts or how to grind a line, etc. It is very disappointing because I hoped to step again in my old line, that is modern methods of documentation."

There seemed to be no solution. He poured out his difficulties and frustrations in letter after letter to Herbert, who understood the problems and in whom he could confide. "It is simply impossible to go on in this way," he wrote in 1956, "How to find a solution is another thing. ... I do not want to be a producer of compasses and other similar things until the end of my days and to be in reality a 'supervisor' whose only duty is to fulfill the orders taken and forwarded to me by Shmuel without the smallest personal influence and authority."

At the end of 1955, already 74 years old, he was feeling the effects of age. He wrote, "Aside of all these unpleasant things, my age itself begins to be a burden. If I still work 12 hours a day, it does not mean that I am feeling all right. I am simply doing it because I do not see any other way to live. But I have firmly decided that I have to change the situation.... I am rather unhappy that my personal work is absolutely neglected." Then, in 1958, aged 76, he fell off a ladder while pruning bushes and broke his leg close to the hip joint. Doctors inserted a stainless steel pin to hold the bone in place, but it did not heal. The pin was later thought to have affected a nerve. His leg would swell up daily, and he remained in constant pain. The wound seems to have aggravated circulatory problems and strained his heart. As he needed two crutches to walk and had to use both hands to hold the crutches, he found that running the Lab became ever more burdensome.

El Op

Pressures built to expand the company and Goldberg had no effective alternative to offer. "I am in a real spider web and do not know how to extricate myself," he wrote to Herbert. In 1960, the company was enlarged, still under the name Goldberg Instruments. The Israeli government owned half the shares. Goldberg and his other investors owned the other half. The following year, an American investor, Paul Kapilow, wanted to invest in the company. Goldberg wanted nothing to do with it, but he was under pressure to allow American investment. He wrote afterward,

> Mr. Kapilow suddenly appeared, and like a classic American as described in the book, had just six hours in one day to make two important agreements (one with me and one with the government), and another three hours for a big dinner, disappearing on the third day to New Orleans.
>
> To tell you the truth, the story was too sudden and not enough prepared to make something really elaborate.... If you want to know my personal opinion, the deal was indeed a very difficult one for me, but I did not have the courage to say 'no' to a plan which depended on my consent, and which *possibly* might establish a bigger industry [i.e., company] of the kind I started 24 years ago. But you will understand that it is not easy for a man as you know me to be, to 'retire' as every man is doing at my age and health situation. To be quite open, I do not know whether it is necessary, as

Mr. Kapilow did it, to abolish even my name in the new company, hoping at the same time that the Goldberg spirit will prevail.

Goldberg agreed, unhappily, to give up his role and he allowed Kapilow to acquire his shares at a nominal price. The company became jointly controlled by Kapilow and the Israeli government, and Goldberg withdrew from managing it. The minutes of the meeting of the Board of Directors of Goldberg Instruments held on November 23, 1960, noted: "Prof. Goldberg says that all of the plans under discussion are against his ideas as advisor of the Co[mpany]."

Within less than a year, the company was on the verge of bankruptcy. The Israeli government took control of Kapilow's shares and so owned the company outright. At that time the company was working virtually exclusively for the Ministry of Defence. It was considered to be a company "in the national interest" and the government saw to it that it would not be allowed to close down.

The Ministry of Defence was asked to run the company for a while, then some investors from the Netherlands appeared, led by Oscar Van Leer, the physicist son of Bernhard Van Leer. When the Dutch investors visited, there was a reception at the home of Moshe Kashti, the Director General of the Ministry of Defence. Various individuals, including Goldberg, were encouraged to say a few words. Goldberg said, "I want to tell you, first of all, that I wish you luck and I am glad that I am out of it. But, if you ask me what I have to add, do me a favor and change the name of the company." Someone replied that they did not want to change the name so long as he was associated with it. "On the contrary," replied Goldberg, "you *should* change the name of the company!" Asked what he would propose, Goldberg recommended The Israel Optical Industry, which reflects the Israeli practice of referring to an individual firm as an "industry." Oscar Van Leer said, "No! Let's call it the Israeli Electro-Optical Industry."

The Israeli Electro-Optical Industry Ltd was established in 1965 as the successor to Goldberg Instruments Ltd. The shareholders were the State of Israel 40 percent and Optische Industrie de Oude Delft, Delft, Netherlands, 60 percent. Oscar Van Leer was Chair of the Board and J. V. Weiler was Managing Director. Goldberg was not a member of the Board. It was decided to build a factory in Rehovoth because of the vicinity of the Weizmann Institute. In this way, Goldberg's Lab finally reached, 30 years late, the originally intended location.

By the late 1970s, both the Dutch investors and the Israeli government wanted to divest. The Dutch company had been promised large orders from Arab countries if they divested their investments in Israel. The Israeli government wanted to divest because there was a sentiment that the government should not be an investor in companies like the Israeli Electro-Optical Industry that it controlled.

The company was sold in part to Tadiran, a very large electronics group, interested in branching out into electro-optics. However, because the government did not want the Israeli Electro-Optical industry to be entirely controlled by Tadiran, the Federmann group, owners of the Dan hotels, was asked to step in. Tadiran and Federmann each acquired 50 percent. Tadiran had acquired another, much smaller electro-optical company, Rehovot Industry, founded by a physicist, J. H. Jaffe, and, preferring not to have two subsidiaries with the same speciality, arranged for the Israeli Electro-Optical Industry to buy Rehovot Industry. The combined companies then became Electro-Optical Industries, plural, or, in short, El Op. Arab threats of boycotts against firms that dealt with Israel had made the prefix "Israeli" a hindrance in export markets, and so it was dropped. In 2000, El Op merged with Elbit Systems Ltd.

An Engineer at Last

Goldberg was pleased when, on April 21, 1956, precisely the 50th anniversary of receiving his doctorate, the Faculty of Mathematics and Natural Sciences of the University of Leipzig formally renewed his doctorate as a way of honoring him "for his contributions to the clarification of fundamental questions in the science and application of photography."

In 1957, the Technion, the technical university in Haifa, celebrated the dedication of a new Electrical Engineering Department and the laying of the foundation stone for a new Department of Mechanics, both made possible by many millions of dollars donated by U.S. benefactors. The Technion used the occasion to confer its first honorary doctorates. Three Americans (Dr. F. Julius Fohs, Gerard Swope, and Abraham Tulin) and two Israelis (Emanuel Goldberg and M. Novomeysky) were awarded honorary degrees. Goldberg made a brief acceptance speech in English on behalf of the two Israelis. He concluded with an acknowledgment that he was receiving an honorary degree in engineering:

> Now please allow me a personal reference. At the age of six I was shown by a friend of the family how a lever can be used to lighten work. Since then I have been obsessed by the idea that, by using a tool, life can be made more pleasant. To be an engineer seemed to me the highest goal. It was not easy for a Jewish boy in Czarist Russia to reach this goal. Instead of playing with my tools I had to learn the irregular verbs of Russian, German, French, English, Greek, Latin, Slavonic and not least Hebrew for the Bar-Mitzva. I hated learning languages and so you will understand if not excuse my deplorable state of being illiterate in our country.

To be admitted to the Technical High School of Moscow I had to pass the examinations with the highest marks. But two Jews passed with this mark and only one could be accepted. The winner had to be decided by lot. I drew the black ball, my hope of training as an engineer was destroyed and I became a chemist.

I could never overcome this setback. Now you fulfilled the dream of my childhood. I am an engineer. Thank-you.

Writing to Herbert a few days later, Goldberg wrote: "I made a short speech and had really a big success. . . . so many came up to me afterwards and said: 'You stole the show.' I have only seen that Ben Gurion was very amused by my words. But we were astonished when in two days (in midst of a cabinet crisis and deliberations over the Eisenhower Doctrine) a letter came from Ben Gurion where he writes that he will never forget my address. We were naturally very happy, espec. about this letter." Prime Minister David Ben-Gurion's letter read, in translation:

Jerusalem, May 22, 1957

To Dr. Emanuel Goldberg—Greetings.

I feel an emotional need to convey to you my deepest feelings of gratitude for the wonderful time you bestowed on us with your brief words that glow with the light of wisdom, humor, charm and refreshing youthfulness. I will not forget these few moments of spiritual and aesthetic pleasure. I am sure that all those who attended shared my feeling, and blessing will come on you.

With appreciation

D. Ben-Gurion.

Goldberg wrote back:

Dear Dr. Ben-Gurion,

It is difficult for me to find proper words expressing my gratitude for your kind letter. If, as you mention, the participants have appreciated my address, it was because of an unforgettable scene: a magnificent hall where the new generation will get all the knowledge their grandfathers could never reach, and the creator of our state giving to an old man what racial injustice has withheld from him more than half a century ago. You have made this scene possible and to you our grandchildren will owe their freedom from fear.

In 1968, on the 20th anniversary of its establishment, the State of Israel conferred on Goldberg the Israel Prize, the government's highest honor. Figure 20.1 shows Goldberg during the 1960s.

Figure 20.1. Emanuel Goldberg in the 1960s.

Old Age

In their old age, Goldberg and Sophie lived in Ramat Gan, at 10 Mate Aharon. The hot climate had never suited Sophie. She had put on more weight and had problems with her legs, which discouraged walking. She looked after her husband and worried about his health and strength. She and Goldberg increasingly focused on their children and their children's families. They had close contact with Renate (Chava) and her family, and they both wrote regularly, in English, to Herbert and Frances, using the German terms *Vati* for Papa, and *Mutti* for Mama for each other. In 1959, they went to the United States to visit Herbert and for medical advice concerning Goldberg's injured leg. They returned in 1961 for successful hip replacement surgery.

Sophie would read and reread the classics of Western literature, often in their original language. Goldberg modified a tape recorder so that it could play continuously for two-and-a-half hours. In the evenings, they would sit and listen to the music they had enjoyed in Leipzig. Goldberg continued to derive pleasure from his garden, rising at 5:30 A.M. to tend to it. He gardened every day for an hour or two and continued his personal research in his home workshop. "I *must* work simply to continue the daily life," he wrote to Herbert. Jakob Beutler helped him and, looking back later, commented, "I can only tell you that we were playing around trying things, not really getting any result, but he enjoyed himself."

Hebrew had become the prevailing language. Sophie had learned some, but he knew little. Their old friends were dying and there was now a language barrier to making new friends. "We are now very lonely," wrote Sophie, "Vati regrets now he went to a country not knowing the language." Renate helped them greatly. "We are happy that Renate is coming every day," Goldberg wrote, "and from time to time she is sometimes going with me to Tel Aviv to carry out things I cannot do because not talking Hebrew. Years ago it was not of great importance because the population consisted of immigrants talking some European language." In another letter to Herbert, he wrote, "Very important is, that the young people speak practically only Hebrew language, so that we cannot have even discussions with our grandchildren."

Sophie's health declined, with eye and heart problems. "Well, I know my age," she wrote to Herbert and Frances in September 1967, "but still I hope I am able to look after Vati—and that is all I want." With anemia and failing kidneys, she became less and less active. By the summer of 1968, Goldberg wrote to Herbert and Frances that she had even stopped reading, "Mutti's strength was always to read books, but in the last time she sits in the easy chair and thinks about you, Renate and the past times.... Even her normal occupation besides reading—the knitting of pullovers is stopped." On December 10, 1968, she died.

Goldberg simply stopped working. He moved to Zahala, northeast of Tel Aviv, to live next door to Renate and Mordecai Gichon. Herbert came over to help with the move. Goldberg finally stopped driving his little Fiat Topolino. His health deteriorated.

In May 1970, the American Society of Photographic Scientists and Engineers honored Goldberg with Honorary Membership, conferred only on a person "who has performed eminent service in the advancement of photographic science and engineering." It was just in time. Emanuel Goldberg died on September 13, 1970, nearly 90 years old. "For all of us," Renate wrote to Herbert, "it was the end of an 'age,' there are not many people of his kind left and he represented an era which is gone."

21

After Goldberg

...the famous Professor Zapp, inventor of the micro-dot process, at the Technical High School in Dresden.

—J. Edgar Hoover, 1946

What happened to the individuals and institutions in Goldberg's life after his contact with them?

Russia

Colonel Grigorii Goldberg is thought to have died in 1912. At Zeiss, Goldberg was involved in serious discussions of doing increased business with Russia, but the Zeiss managers decided that the terms wanted by Stalin's government were unfavorable. Under Stalin, it became dangerous for Russians to be in contact with foreigners, and in 1935, Goldberg's mother asked that letters no longer be sent to family members in Russia. Contact was never regained.

Goldberg's younger sister, Tamara Grigorevna Goldberg, became a curator in the State Historical Museum in Moscow. In 1943, she received a diploma from the People's Commissariat in recognition of her work during the Great Patriotic War, as the Russians call World War II. She became an authority on the history of gold and silver jewelry in Russia and authored a number of scholarly publications. She seems to have lived until the early 1960s. Goldberg's older brother, Raphael, also remained in the Soviet Union and is thought to have become a professor of physics, first in Leningrad, later in Moscow.

Several relatives of Goldberg and of Sophie left Russia. One of Sophie's brothers, George Posniak, moved to Paris. Another, Evgeny, became a geochemist at the Carnegie Institution in Washington and a mineral, posnjakite, is named in his honor.

237

Leipzig

In Leipzig, the Academy of Graphic Arts and Bookcraft at which the young Dr. Goldberg had taught was overshadowed for a while by the more famous Bauhaus school of Weimar. The Bauhaus was closed in 1933, but the Leipzig academy still continues as the University for Graphics and Book Art *(Hochschule für Grafik und Buchkunst)* and is still in the same fine building. Two-thirds of the building was destroyed by wartime bombing in 1943, but the academy reopened in 1947. After many years of neglect, the building was carefully restored during the 1990s.

Loewe and Fernseh AG

Siegmund Loewe had been very successful in the German market for domestic radio receivers and wanted to repeat that success in a new market for domestic television receivers. Goldberg and Erich Rassbach wanted to do the same, but it didn't happen, even though Germany was, in 1935, the first country to have regular television broadcasting. One cause was the theory then in vogue concerning mass persuasion that group reception was more likely to result in the intended interpretation of messages than solitary reception. For this reason, influential senior officials in a position to influence the development of television broadcasting, notably Eugen Hadamowsky, National Director of Broadcasting *(Reichssendeleiter),* and Joseph Goebbels, the Minister for Enlightenment and Propaganda, steered television reception to public television halls, like small movie theaters, with 40 to 400 seats. Another reason was that the potential military uses of television for night vision and remote viewing were given a high priority. Despite talk of a "people's television set" *(Volksempfänger),* analogous to the Volkswagen, the people's automobile, it was not until 1939 that Fernseh AG was permitted to build retail television receivers. Then the outbreak of World War II halted nonmilitary television, and there were only about 200 domestic television receivers in all of Germany.

In 1935, the German Post Office reduced its support for Fernseh AG, explaining to Paul Goerz that funding was intended for military applications of television, for which Fernseh AG was unsuitable because its ownership was partly foreign (Baird) and partly Jewish, as the Loewe brothers had a Jewish father. Baird was persuaded to sell his shares to Bosch and to Zeiss Ikon. David Loewe had already left Germany in 1933, but Siegmund Loewe resisted pressure to sell his interest in Fernseh AG until early 1938 when his company, Loewe Radio, was expropriated by the government and he left Germany.

Goldberg's forced departure in April 1933 had ended his role in Fernseh AG. At Zeiss Ikon, responsibility for television was assigned with

movie equipment to the Ernemann works and liaison with Fernseh AG
was assumed by Hermann Joachim, an authority on movie projectors.
Goldberg's successors decided that television was not central to Zeiss
Ikon's corporate interests. They noted that Fernseh AG was not only losing
money, but needed a substantial infusion of capital. They preferred Zeiss
Ikon to be a supplier of specialized parts, without the responsibilities of
ownership of Fernseh AG. In addition, support for television at the Carl
Zeiss Stiftung in Jena had been weakened when Straubel was forced out of
office late in 1933. In 1939, Robert Bosch AG bought out Zeiss Ikon's
interest and achieved Erich Rassbach's goal of sole ownership of Fernseh
AG, just as it finally approached profitability.

Fernseh AG flourished because it was supported by Wilhelm
Ohnesorge, a Post Office official with responsibility for television, who
was interested in its use for a video telephone service. During World War I,
Ohnesorge had served the Fatherland by implementing military use of
radio, and he became determined to serve the Reich through the military
use of television. The German Air Force bombers were having difficulty
hitting specific objects, such as ships at sea. The state-of-the-art technique
was to launch a steerable gliding bomb from the air, and a marksman in the
plane would steer it by remote control using radio signals. The aiming was
visual: The bomb would be on a correct trajectory if it was kept always and
exactly in line of sight between the marksman and the target. This task was
more difficult if the target was moving, or if atmospheric haze reduced
visibility. Flying over the target in a clear sky to maintain visual contact
made the plane vulnerable to antiaircraft fire and was particularly dangerous when enemy airplanes controlled the air space over the target. Even in
the absence of enemy firepower, the bomb became progressively more difficult to see and to steer the closer it got to the target. Ohnesorge's solution
was to develop guided missiles with eyes. Specifically, flying bombs, and,
potentially, rockets and torpedoes, could be directed on to their targets
from a safe distance using radio-controlled steering if they carried miniaturized television cameras and transmitters showing both where they were
headed and where the target was. The marksman would watch the transmitted picture and steer accordingly. The plane that launched the bomb
could hide in clouds or otherwise avoid enemy fire. Developing television
technology suitable for Ohnesorge's "wonder weapon" became Fernseh
AG's top secret mission.

A very early member of the Nazi Party, Ohnesorge became minister
in charge of the Post Office, so he was in a position to provide substantial
funding. Because the government did not coordinate wartime scientific
research, he could act independently. Fernseh AG doubled in size during
the war and, when the Allies started to bomb Berlin, it was moved to
Morgernstern in the Sudentenland, now known as Smrzovka, near Tanvald,
Czechoslovakia. The television camera and transmitter had to be small,

light, require little power, yet be robust and simple. Ohnesorge spent more money on his "Seeing Bomb" *(sehende Bombe)* than was spent on efforts to develop a German atom bomb. After some 70 bombs were used on flight tests at Peenemünde-West, the equipment was deemed ready for military operations and mass production was planned. But then the war ended. The engineers' expertise and their devices (code named Tonne and Seedorf) were quietly absorbed into secret postwar Cold War military development efforts and what they had done remained little known. Erich Rassbach, meanwhile, seems to have had some kind of breakdown. He had become implicated in the opposition to Hitler, but survived the war.

After the war, 120 Fernseh AG employees got together at a Bosch subsidiary, Blaupunkt, in Taufkirchen, Bavaria, and resumed business as Fernseh GmbH. They started out by manufacturing measuring instruments for the radio industry because the Allied Control Council had banned German companies from working on television, which had been so closely associated with the military during the war. As soon as the ban was lifted in 1949, Fernseh GmbH started to produce television receivers. Bosch, however, decided to concentrate television receiver production in its Blaupunkt division, and Fernseh was directed to work on television studio equipment, which it did with success, becoming a major supplier. Fernseh moved to Darmstadt and in 1972 became Fernsehanlagen GmbH. In 1986, in a partnership between Bosch and Philips, Fernsehanlagen GmbH became part of Broadcasting Television Systems GmbH, wholly owned by Philips since 1993.

Siegmund Loewe had moved to New York in 1938 and became President of the Radio Loewe U.S. affiliate Loewe Radio Inc. In 1944, he took U.S. citizenship. His shares in Radio AG D. S. Loewe were confiscated as a "Refugee tax" *(Reichsfluchtsteuer)* and the firm, with its name "Aryanized" first to Radio Löwe, then to Opta Radio, worked on radio and radar under Air Ministry control. In 1949, Loewe regained control of the firm and renamed it Loewe Opta AG. In 1953, he sought Goldberg's help in seeking to recover from Bosch his entitlement to share in the Fernseh AG patents under the original agreement. Loewe Opta is now located in Kronach, in Bavaria, and continues its traditional of successful innovation. If Goldberg's career had not been disrupted, Zeiss Ikon, unlike other photographic firms, would have developed a strong and early position in electronic imaging.

Zeiss and Zeiss Ikon

In 1937, Zeiss Ikon published a corporate history of itself and of the firms involved in the Fusion that had created it, *75 Jahre Photo- und Kinotechnik; Festschrift herausgegeben anlässlich der Feier des 75-jährigen*

Bestehens der Zeiss Ikon AG. und ihrer Vorgängerfirmen 1862–1937 ("75 Years of Photo and Movie Technology: Volume Edited in Honor of the Occasion of the Celebration of 75 Years Existence of Zeiss Ikon AG and Its Predecessor Companies 1862–1937"). It was a Nazi-period publication, and Goldberg, who was Jewish and Russian, is not mentioned, even though he had led Zeiss Ikon for most of its existence.

Eduard Grentz, who had been kidnapped with Goldberg, was also released. He left Dresden, avoided contact with Zeiss Ikon, survived the war, and managed a small factory near Leipzig. Walter Riedel, his young assistant, who had remained hidden in the darkroom until everyone had left, was told, a few days later, by the Nazi leader within Zeiss Ikon, named Riess, that if he had been in the Laboratory, he too would have been arrested. Goldberg and the kidnapping were topics avoided in discussion at the company. Dr. Riedel remained in Dresden, opposed to the Nazis and later to the Communist government. Now more than 90 years old, he runs a small company and was pleased to share his recollections of his hero, Professor Goldberg, 67 years after the kidnapping.

Hermann Joachim, a Zeiss Ikon manager who was an expert on movie technology, seems to have acquired responsibility for television and microfilm-based office products with Goldberg's departure, presumably including the Statistical Machine. He also took over Goldberg's professorship at Luther's Institute. Joachim presented papers on the use of microfilm at conferences on documentation. He seems to have focused on Zeiss Ikon's existing products, not the Statistical Machine. The Dutch documentalist Frits Donker Duyvis, who replaced Paul Otlet as the central figure in the International Institute for Documentation, mentioned the Zeiss Ikon Statistical Machine at a conference in 1938, and thought that it had been developed by Joachim.

Three weeks after Goldberg had been forced out of Zeiss Ikon, Martin Mutschmann was boasting that Zeiss Ikon was hiring more workers because of the success of the Contax. There was unintended irony in this claim, given Goldberg's role in the development of the Contax. New models were produced and, like its rival, the Leica, the Contax camera became a collector's item with its own specialized literature.

In Jena, the head of the Carl Zeiss Stiftung, Rudolph Straubel, was forced by his colleagues to choose between divorcing his Jewish wife or leaving Zeiss. He left Zeiss and was prevented from teaching but was allowed to continue as chairman of the supervisory board of Zeiss Ikon. After he died in 1943, his wife committed suicide to avoid being sent to the Theresienstadt concentration camp. August Kotthaus, who succeeded Straubel, was killed in car accident in 1941. These losses provided an opening for Heinz Küppenbender, who acquired considerable power within the Third Reich. He became the head of the Carl Zeiss Stiftung and was made responsible for the national allocation of raw materials for the optical industry. Küppenbender advocated the deportation of workers from German-occupied countries, especially women from Eastern Europe, to provide forced labor inside Germany. These importees were not protected by German labor laws and, under Küppenbender, nearly 4,000 were working in the Zeiss works in Jena by 1945.

Ernst Wandersleb, who had originally invited Goldberg to work for Zeiss, was dismissed because his wife was Jewish but was supported privately by Zeiss managers. His wife was sent to the Theresienstadt concentration camp, but was freed by American troops after a few months. Wandersleb resumed working for Zeiss after the war. He retired aged 78 in 1957, and died in 1963.

After the war, the Iron Curtain divided both Carl Zeiss, Jena and Zeiss Ikon into two parts. The eastern and western parts both claimed to be the original company, and years of litigation followed. The Soviet occupying forces removed what little was left of the Ica factory in Dresden as reparations. Three production lines for manufacturing the Contax camera were created at Carl Zeiss Jena, then taken to Ukraine, where Contax clones were marketed with the brand name "Kiev" until 1986. The East German Zeiss Ikon company struggled on in Dresden under difficult circumstances. It was eventually forced to abandon the Zeiss Ikon trademark but continued to manufacture cameras under the trade names Ikonta and Penta until the collapse of the German Democratic Republic.

When the war ended, Heinz Küppenbender was arrested at the insistence of those who had been in forced labor under him. But, after a brief de-Nazification, he was released and allowed to assume leadership of the West German Zeiss Ikon, which resumed manufacturing in Oberkochen and benefited from the high demand for cameras in the years immediately after the war. Küppenbender cultivated an expansive account of his own contributions, taking credit for the rationalizing of the Zeiss Ikon product line after the Fusion and for the innovative design of the Contax. In this account, Goldberg was dismissed as incompetent. "He was a player. He didn't know engineering. He couldn't calculate a spring!" declared Küppenbender. In 1951, on the 25th anniversary of the founding of the firm, another corporate history of Zeiss Ikon was published as a special issue of *Die Leistung,* a business magazine. This second corporate history showcased Küppenbender and the other current managers, and it, too, made no mention of Goldberg.

The Küppenbender-centric narrative was amplified in corporate publicity. In 1981, when he was 80 years old, Küppenbender was interviewed by Fridolin Berthel of the Zeiss Ikon public relations staff and reminisced about his involvement with Goldberg and the Contax 50 years prior. In this account, Goldberg not only receives no credit in the development of the Contax, but treated Küppenbender badly and was jealous and resentful: "Professor Goldberg ... was jealous, that a young man had been sent [from Jena] as an expert and to keep an eye on him." A summary of the interview was published in Zeiss Ikon's in-house magazine *Im Bild* and, later, in English, with the title "Heinz Küppenbender's role in Contax history," in *Zeiss Historica*, the principal journal on the history of the Zeiss companies. In 1989, Armin Hermann, an author of popular books on the history of science and technology, published a book about the history of the Zeiss companies, *Nur der Name war geblieben: die abenteuerliche Geschichte der Firma Carl Zeiss* ("Only the name remained: The adventure-filled history of the Carl Zeiss company"). Hermann was a personal friend of Küppenbender and dedicated the book to him. Unfortunately, in the book, Hermann's account of Goldberg and the Contax is limited to an uncritical repetition of what he found in the transcript of Küppenbender's 1981 interview. Herbert Goldberg, who, unlike Hermann, had been in a position to observe the original events, calls Hermann's account "fanciful nonsense." However, subsequent authors have assumed that these recently published accounts were historically reliable and so Küppenbender's account continues to be repeated without question in writings about Zeiss Ikon.

The erasure of Goldberg is almost total in a three-volume corporate history of the Zeiss companies. The second volume, *Zeiss 1905–1945*, published in 2000, has entries for two Goldbergs in its index. An entry for "Emanuel Goldberg" leads only to a note stating that, in 1933, Goldberg was the highest-ranking of Zeiss' Jewish employees. A separate entry for "Goldberg" leads to the erroneous statement that a Jew, a Professor Dr. Goldberg, was employed in Paris "until 1933." That these two Goldbergs were the same person went unnoticed.

Although Küppenbender took credit for the product rationalization and innovative engineering under Goldberg, he failed to achieve either in the postwar Zeiss Ikon when he was in charge. He emphasized rangefinder cameras and leaf shutters, near the lens, while competitors' single-lens reflex cameras with focal plane shutters captured the market. With a lack of responsiveness in a competitive marketplace, outdated production methods, and too many of the wrong kinds of products, Zeiss Ikon went into a steady decline, losing money and market share year after year until it had to abandon camera production in the early 1970s. The Zeiss Ikon subsidiary in France, Ikonta, was liquidated. Küppenbender died following a horse-riding accident in 1989.

Zeiss Ikon had always had nonphotographic products. By 1989, with 1,150 employees in three factories, its principal business activity was making door locks, along with slide projectors and dies for die-casting *(Druckgussteile)*. That year Carl Zeiss sold its controlling 93.8 percent holding of Zeiss Ikon AG shares to the Finnish group Oy Wärtsilä of Helsinki, whose manufacturing interests included locks. With its separation from Zeiss, the name became, simply, Ikon AG, retaining the part of the name that Goldberg had contributed. In 2003, it became Ikon GmbH Präzisionstechnik.

The Contax brand name still had market appeal, however, so Carl Zeiss used it to market its camera lenses. Yashica, in Japan, which merged with Kyocera, was licensed to manufacture and market expensive range-finder 35 mm cameras with Carl Zeiss lenses, using the brand name Contax decades after rangefinders were replaced by single-lens reflex cameras. In this way, Zeiss continued to benefit from the Contax, but in old-fashioned designs that contradicted the magic of the original Contax, so original and advanced in its design that it was a triumph of innovative engineering.

Saxony

Martin Mutschmann, the Nazi Gauleiter, not Manfred von Killinger, became the Reichstatthalter of Saxony. Nicknamed "King Mu," he maintained an extravagant lifestyle paid for by "voluntary" donations from industry and became notorious for particularly brutal measures in the persecution of Jews. Goebbels wrote in his diaries, "I would not want to work in Saxony as a private man. One is not even sure of one's freedom and life. At some point the Führer must interfere." He scorned Mutschmann's humorless efforts to persuade Goebbels and Hitler to ban jokes about Saxons and the Saxon dialect. At the very end of the war, Mutschmann tried to flee west but was captured by Soviet troops. He is assumed to have died in a Soviet jail after a trial in 1948.

Killinger continued his stormy career. He was briefly Premier of Saxony, jailed, and then joined the German Foreign Service. The *New York Times* reported his appointment as the German Consul General in San Francisco in 1937 with the headline "Fiery Nazi Named Consul on Coast." Killinger later became the German ambassador to Roumania, a German ally. In 1944, as the Red Army fought its way into Bucharest, the Roumanian government changed sides, reportedly with the connivance of local German generals and embassy staff. Shouting "We must all die for the Führer!" Killinger started to shoot his own staff with a machine gun, then committed suicide in front of a portrait of Hitler.

In November 1942, most of the Jews remaining in Dresden were rounded up and forced to live in Hellerberg, a camp created for this purpose at the edge of the town. Some were allowed to continue working for Zeiss Ikon, others would be sent on to Buchenwald or Theresienstadt. The roundup was filmed and a copy of the film survives. Hellerberg was built and operated by Zeiss Ikon, which also used forced labor from other camps. Küppenbender was at least complicit in these developments because Zeiss Ikon was in effect controlled by the Carl Zeiss Stiftung, then under his leadership.

Dresden itself was devastated by the appalling, repeated Anglo-American bombing of February 13–14 1945. There has been little explanation of why Dresden was bombed; full of refugees, it had no military strategic significance and was about to be occupied by the Red Army. The main Zeiss Ikon factory on the Schandauerstrasse, the old Ica works, was largely destroyed. For lack of any other evidence to the contrary, we assume that the three prototype Statistical Machines and associated documentation were destroyed at that time. The Ernemann works, although nearer the city center, sustained less damage. The Ernemann business records are now preserved in the State Archives in Dresden, among them some Zeiss Ikon records, including those documenting its involvement with Fernseh AG. The Ernemann building itself now houses the Technische Sammlungen der Stadt Dresden, a technology museum with a special interest in Dresden as the past center of the German photographic industry.

When the Red Army occupied Dresden, the kindly Alfred Simader was arrested. After a decade of forced labor in a camp in Siberia, he returned to West Germany in early 1955 and worked again for Zeiss Ikon. Goldberg's secretary, Frau Schubert, visited the Goldbergs in Israel in 1966 and died soon after.

Microdots

In 1946, 20 years after the publication of Goldberg's classic paper on microdot technology, the *Reader's Digest* published a boastful article about espionage and microdots by J. Edgar Hoover, Director of the U.S. Federal Bureau of Investigation. Goldberg's name is changed to Zapp when Hoover writes of "the famous Professor Zapp, inventor of the microdot process, at the Technical High School in Dresden." An erroneous description of microdot production follows. Goldberg's work on microdots had been published prominently in the technical literature and cited by others. Anyone at all familiar with the use of photography in espionage should have recognized that Hoover's statement was wrong.

British Intelligence had intercepted microdots sent by back to Germany by German agents in South America and had arranged for one to be given to Hoover by double-agent Dusko Popov in August 1941. On September 3, Hoover sent over to the White House an account of the FBI's achievement in obtaining German microdots, along with a translation of part of the text, but he did not tell the White House or other intelligence agencies that fully one-third of the text of the microdot was concerned with army bases and airfields on the Hawaiian island of Oahu and with the defenses of Pearl Harbor. Historians have asked why the attack on Pearl Harbor was a surprise three months after the FBI had become very well aware of this interest, and why Hoover had shared the fact that a microdot had been intercepted but did not share the full text with the White House or with other intelligence agencies. Meanwhile, the mythic "Professor Zapp" lives on, unquestioned as the inventor of microdots, in book after book in the literature on espionage, all citing Hoover's widely reprinted article as an authoritative source.

Because there never has been a Professor Zapp at the "Technical High School" (*Technische Hochschule,* i.e., Technical University) in Dresden and nobody called Zapp was living in Dresden at the time, the discrepancy has been attributed to a confusion, deliberate or otherwise, between Goldberg and Walter Zapp, inventor of the Minox subminiature camera, a small conventional camera, the size of a cigarette lighter. The Minox was well known from 1936 onward and was used in espionage but is incapable of producing microdots.

William White, an authority on microdots, wrote of Hoover's article: "It was, to say the least, a concoction of semitruths and overt disinformation" and he denounced other writers for perpetuating the Zapp myth. White was unaware of the probable source of Hoover's "Professor" Zapp. In January 1946, FBI agents summarized in a secret report their debriefing of a German intelligence agent, Johannes Rudolf Christian Zuehlensdorf, who told them that he had been trained in the making of microdots by a microdot camera developer named Kurt Zapp. According to Zuehlensdorf, this Zapp was a resident of Leipzig but worked on the development of microdot cameras in Dresden, where he received technical assistance.

There was, in fact, an active military research program at the Technical University in Dresden during the war, and Hellmut Frieser, Luther's successor, was openly engaged in research on extreme reduction microphotography. A government security agency assigned Kurt Zapp the task of adapting Goldberg's techniques for use by secret service agents and he did this work at the Institute for Scientific Photography, where two laboratory assistants were assigned to help him. Even so, working on microdot cameras and using Goldberg's emulsion did not make Zapp a Professor or "the inventor of the micro-dot process," as the FBI technical experts should have known.

For agents in the field, possession of a specialized microdot camera was a major liability because it would be highly incriminating evidence if they were arrested. During the Cold War, Russian spies changed to the use of regular 35 mm cameras, sometimes using a special close-up lens, in a two-stage process. First, the document was photographed; then the negative, with light shining through it from a lamp behind it, was photographed, yielding a positive image on high-resolution emulsion. Reduction as small as 700 : 1 could be achieved, but less than 400 : 1 was more reliable. Whether they knew it or not, this was a return to the method developed by Goldberg during World War I.

Goldberg's Vision for Israel

Goldberg had set out to develop a precision instruments industry in the Jewish community in Palestine. In 1949, he told the *New York Times,* "Twelve years ago the only precision men we had were the blacksmiths. And during the recent fighting, in the first months of the air bombardment, we did not have a single anti-aircraft gun." By 1949, Goldberg Instruments, with 30 employees, was a relatively large enterprise for Israel, and it had an even larger impact. His basic work in making reticles enabled El-Op to become the nucleus of the Israeli optical industry, including laser rangefinders, bomb sights, and airplane cockpit control displays. Alex Eliraz, marksman and poet, continued to work with the Lab and its successors, El Op and a subsidiary, Orthek.

The growth of Israel's high-tech industrial base has been attributed to U.S. military aid, but the foundations of the Israeli military-industrial complex were laid much earlier, in the 1940s, before there was a State of Israel, and long before significant U.S. aid was received. It was in those formative years that Goldberg with his expertise in military optics, his past experience with Zeiss in supplying the military, and his strong belief in the need to couple research with industry was an active and significant contributor.

During the 1980s, Israeli high-tech companies, strong in research and development, but lacking adequate markets, adopted a "two-legged" binational policy through which they partnered with larger American companies whose marketing and distribution capacity outstripped their research and development capabilities. Nearly every large American high-tech firm now has some sort of research and development center in Israel, attracted by the high-quality technical labor force and by a desire to tap into what is seen as an important source of technological innovation. Israeli companies gained access to export markets and close ties were developed between Israeli firms and the two main centers of technology innovation in the United States, around Boston and in Silicon Valley.

A study of the development of the high-tech industries in Israel and of their influence on California's Silicon Valley concluded, "El-Op, through its work on missile guidance systems, detection systems, night vision, etc., has contributed to the development of at least three broad areas of expertise which have been applied to semiconductor inspection and testing: precision mechanics and related optics, lasers, and image processing and recognition. El-Op's strength in precision mechanics and optics stems from the original tradition brought by Goldberg from Germany, and more specifically from Zeiss Ikon and the associated Carl Zeiss companies...Goldberg instituted a German-style apprenticeship program which was instrumental in transmitting this tradition to the pool of workers in Palestine and Israel. The firm's expertise in lasers and image processing/recognition, meanwhile, is primarily the result of government investments in the development of military systems. These skills have been transferred into the civilian sector by the movement of personnel and the maintenance of close ties between El-Op and other firms."

From a very small beginning addressing local urgent needs for defense and security, the electro-optical industry in Israel has developed into a large export industry. Israel takes an important place on the world map of electrooptical engineering. About 100 different factories in this field in Israel produce about two billion dollars of goods per year, 70 percent of it for export. Most of the optical industry in Israel has, or had, key personnel trained by Goldberg or at El Op. Goldberg's vision became reality.

22

Goldberg in Retrospect

I have no trust in memory or reminiscences. I was always a bad history student and my experiences of life have taught me that it always comes out differently than one might have expected on the basis of the past.

—Emanuel Goldberg, 1955

Memory and Method

Goldberg liked to describe himself as "a chemist by learning, physicist by calling, and a mechanic by birth." His employees commented on his very wide repertoire of skills, including woodworking, metal work, lens grinding, photoengraving, and diamond-cutting. "He was certainly the best craftsmen I ever met," said Benno Erteshik. "He was a perfect turner or any skill you need." Shmuel Neumann commented that Goldberg had "the unique capability of being a scientist [and] an engineer, together, who also had two right hands." And these "two right hands" had unusually nimble fingers. He could assemble a Contax camera without a pair of tweezers.

In the early years of the twentieth century, there was great interest in efficiency through scientific management, popularized by F. W. Taylor and the Gilbreths. Goldberg shared their interest in reducing the effort required for repetitive tasks. Goldberg liked to boast that he was one of the world's laziest men. "I could say that I am so lazy that I am prepared to spend initially a dreadful amount of work to save subsequently a very small amount." For working on his antiglare device, pieces of wood needed to be sanded. He gathered his staff around the sanding machine and offered 10 Palestinian pounds to anyone who could halve the machining time. He then showed them how to sand two pieces at a time. "He was like Gilbreth," commented Moshe Arad, referring to Lillian Gilbreth, who, with her husband, Frank, pioneered the use of time and motion studies to improve efficiency. Goldberg's interest in efficiency was also reflected in his enthusiasm for miniaturization, as in the Kinamo. He enjoyed rebuilding and modifying radio sets, making them more compact.

It was more than a simple pursuit of efficiency, however. Goldberg shared the passion for improved design of practical objects that flowered in Germany with the Werkbund and the Bauhaus. He was a designer as much as an inventor. Good design for practical purposes requires an understanding of the relationship between human and machine. It is significant that, when he expressed his appreciation to the University of Leipzig for renewing his doctorate, he paid homage not only to Wilhelm Ostwald, but also to Wilhelm Wundt, who studied the physiology of perception and relationships between the physical senses and the mind, with a strict adherence to measurement in experimental psychology. Goldberg himself published papers on human visual perception. He noted the different effects of different colors in his moiré investigations, and he established experimentally the difference between aesthetically pleasing and scientifically optimal tonal gradations. The Kinamo movie camera and the Contax camera were both good examples of ergonomic design. He wrote to his grandson Brett, "Pure mathematics did not attract myself as physics [did] and especially the laws of physics applied to the human body." In another letter, he wrote, "I always considered the use of the computer to replace the brain function as the most important advance in the coming [years]."

Goldberg had a vast general knowledge across a wide range of subjects, including geology and zoology. "He knew everything," said one employee. In this sense, Goldberg must have had a good memory, despite his statements to the contrary. Nevertheless, he repeatedly said that he had always had difficulty with memorizing, for example, lists of irregular verbs in a foreign language. "I learned to speak very late and the grammar (of the many languages) was always a torture." He adapted to this handicap by developing, and depending on, an enhanced ability to use intuition and reason to work out what he could not remember. "I had bad memory even as a child and made my way through logical thinking," he wrote. He thought and worked constantly, with a part of his mind thinking consciously or subconsciously about designs and improvements, even when not in his workshop. He seemed to have unlimited energy and willpower. He would often came to work in the morning with new ideas to replace what had already been done because he now thought it could be done better. He also had the power of concentration. He was looking through a microscope at the Lab once when a bomb exploded nearby. He continued his work at the microscope. He had not noticed the explosion.

Goldberg's ability to develop new designs empirically characterized all his work. His approach was essentially heuristic and experimental. He would think of a need or get a concept and then he would start, or have somebody else start, making some kind of model that would, more or less, do what he wanted it to do. If he could show that it was workable, he could then improve it progressively. His workshop skills enabled him to do this. Shmuel Neumann commented, "In this he was unique in this country in optics. There was nobody else. There were professors who taught optics and there were professors who taught physics, but there was none who [could] take his idea to the lathe and put it into reality in a day to two, not a complete instrument, but he proved that his idea would work."

The modernist dream extended beyond standards, efficiency, and good design to include reliable methods for finding the right information when needed. Goldberg appears to have shared with others the view that within the foreseeable future the amount of recorded knowledge would become so great that it would be practically impossible to use it. This challenge motivated his work on advanced technology for information retrieval. He is quoted as having said, "I don't remember formulas, but I know where I can find them." He wrote to Herbert, "Quick information and solution of problems were always for me of principal interest. But I see the word 'information' in a very much wider sense than the normal scientists."

Goldberg's interests in technology and in the management of information converged in his interest in information technology. An employee recalls him predicting optical computing. "He said, 'Even though computers now use electricity, it is much too slow. They'll have to use light in the future.' He explained to us how sensitive computers will be. That was already 1950 or so and he said, 'Imagine the room and I have a page of a book and I move it, so the light conditions in the room change. That can be calculated and, in the future, we'll be able to calculate it.' "

Goldberg the Educator

Goldberg was a teacher in everything. It was in his character to want to have pupils and to explain. "Of all the different aspects of my life, the education of others was always considered by myself the most gratifying," he wrote in old age. He had a flair for explaining difficult matters. A former apprentice commented, "But what was amazing about him was, first of all, how he explained things. He was a genius. Usually geniuses don't know how to teach, because they learn everything quickly. He had the flair for it. He explained everything in [terms of] the most basic things." The exhibits he developed in Leipzig brought acclaim. All his life he collected teaching materials.

Goldberg's pragmatic problem-solving skill influenced his teaching in three ways. First, he had a flair for providing clear explanations because he had had to work through the problem for himself. In the Lab, he made everything himself first, before he gave a task to the other people. Second, it became clear from his approach that to recall a solution from memory does not in itself provide understanding. Dr Otto Gold, an early employee in the Lab, commented, "I learned one thing: To know it is not enough, you have to understand it. If you know the formulas, chemical or mathematical, you don't know [the subject]. It's not good enough." Third, those whom he taught commented consistently that they were empowered to solve problems that they did not understand. "What I learned from him is this confidence that I can do things which I haven't got the slightest idea about," said Michael Plaot. For Benno Erteshik, "It had enormous influence on my career, not the technical knowledge, but the attitude and the way of thinking." Aviva Kelton never completed high school, but her apprenticeship with Goldberg enabled her later in the United States to supervise engineers with graduate degrees. She explained, "I do all my own repairs, all my own wiring, plumbing, everything, because what's the problem? You look at it, how it works, and find out. Because he taught us not to be afraid of anything. . . . He taught us how to think. Amazing! How to analyze things. What to study. How to look up things. I am eternally grateful to him. . . . Because of him I could approach new problems and find solutions. . . . I think that all who worked with him succeeded, did very well."

Goldberg emphasized the need for close contact between research and industry. "I personally always advocated the union of science and industry," he wrote, and "A designer must be in a close contact with his competitors, customers, etc." He also thought that it was important for creativity to have frequent interaction with other people with quite different ideas and interests. "Even when I was very young in Leipsic, I got many ideas about the possibility of reproduction of nature from painters in the Academy of Graphic Arts, [who had] never even heard that it is possible to measure light emanating from a wall or a tree." He also thought that individuals became less innovative after age 40, but that the solution was for young and old to work together, as in a university.

Goldberg's versatile technical skills and his problem-solving ability increasingly evolved into a preference for doing everything himself, even when it was not necessary. He and his staff repaired his car and painted the Lab. In his home workshop, he preferred to make each component and perform each process himself.

Political, Religious, and Social Views

Goldberg had little interest in politics. His views seem to have been basically liberal and democratic. Like other Russians of his age and background, he was acutely aware of the injustice and inefficiency of the Tsarist regime. He welcomed the Russian Revolution, and he thought that the peasants were better off as a result, despite the later excesses of the U.S.S.R. He and Sophie believed that Russia would have an important future, but they made no attempt to have their children learn Russian. He liked the English way of life, admired British political institutions, and defended the United States against Mees.

Similarly, although consciously Jewish, he was not observant and seems to have had little interest in religion. He went to Palestine because he believed that there should be a place where Jews could live without discrimination or persecution, and he wanted to help make the Jewish state a successful reality. In Palestine, he criticized killings by extremist groups fighting to expel the British.

Although liberal and democratic, he and Sophie had traditional views on the role of women. Women were likely to become housewives and mothers; they needed to be taken care of, but an academic or professional education was unlikely to be justified. Nevertheless, he did accept and train young women as apprentice engineers in his Lab.

After his experience of Russia and Germany, he liked the relatively informal way of life in Israel. A cosmopolitan upbringing, language skills, an affable manner, and a sense of humor seem to have enabled him to establish good relationships with a wide range of people. Unlike Guido Mengel, he had been effective in dealing with the heads of the other firms that were combined into Zeiss Ikon. He was, however, sensitive concerning his status as head of the Lab. He would take it as an insult if an employee took another job without his advice and, in Israel, he tended to consider his employees as students. He seems to have been most comfortable when dealing with independent equals or in a teacher-student relationship. Well-qualified and independent-minded employees found working with him less easy, and he tended to be unappreciative when others improved on his designs.

Gardening was a constant source of pleasure. He liked animals and always had a large dog. He wrote to his grandson Brett, "I myself like very much dogs and think that these animals are in their thinking and behaviour very close to *good* human beings. Just as young men can be educated regarding good manners the dogs learn how to behave themselves."

Those who worked with Goldberg remember him with awe, greatly respecting his talents, and are appreciative of what they learned from him. Usually, there is also affection. A sense of sadness also surfaces when they consider what, with all his talents, he might have achieved if his career had not been destroyed in 1933, or if he had somehow been in circumstances that would have allowed him to continue a serious scientific career. For all his contributions to the development of industry in Israel, there is also a sense of wasted potential.

Goldberg in Context

The late nineteenth century from the 1890s until the mid-twentieth century was a period of renaissance. Among many other changes, there was a pivotal transition in information technology: movies, radio, vacuum tubes, television, sound recording, scientific photography, halftone printing. These and other changes were developed largely in the period of the 1890s through the 1930s. It was a wonderful time to be an engineer. Goldberg was caught up in the exciting but slow and tantalizing transition from "brass and glass" to electronics, from egg whites and asphalt to videocassettes and night vision. He moved to Germany at the beginning of the twentieth century and so was very well placed to participate in these exciting changes, even after the debilitating effects of World War I and its aftermath. But with the move to Palestine, his scientific career was effectively ended by his isolation from the rest of the scholarly world and the need to work on different, more practical problems. A recital of Goldberg's life and work gives an impression of versatility and variety: university researcher, graphics arts teacher, military optics specialist, industrialist, designer, and businessman. There was, however, more unity and coherence than might appear at first sight. All of his work had to do with light, with images, with design, and with improvement, in a career buffeted by the turbulent politics of his time.

Goldberg's ideas epitomize the technological modernism of the early twentieth century, imbued with a strong belief in the potential of technology, standardization, systems, ergonomic design, efficiency, and organized access to recorded knowledge, all marshaled to build a better world in which to live. It was a practical, rather secular idealism, based on thoughtful technological innovation and guided by social and political views that were liberal and pragmatic, valuing peace, reason, good organization, and progress, rather than doctrine or ideology.

History and What Is Remembered

It is useful to distinguish between *the past,* what happened; *history,* accounts of the past; and *heritage,* which consists of those parts of the past that affect us in the present. What is past, what has happened, is passed, and is no longer directly knowable. The past is knowable only indirectly, through histories, descriptions, and narratives of what happened. For any aspect of the past, there may be many narratives or none. Histories are always multiple and incomplete, and many factors influence what histories are or can be written.

Heritage is what we have now from the past: the goods that we inherit from our parents, the residues of toxic wastes, the memories and artifacts that we retain, our genetic inheritance, and such culture as we have absorbed and made our own. Included in our cultural, intellectual, and professional heritage are the historical narratives we know and we accept and which help shape our sense of identity. Our heritage is, in a significant sense, accidental. The legacy that we have, which influences what we do, results not only from past events, but also from past decisions about acceptance and discarding. Our sense of history is doubly accidental, because it depends not only on what narratives happened to be composed, but also on which ones were accepted, received, and incorporated into our sense of the past. The life and work of Emanuel Goldberg is interesting not only in its own right, but also as a case study of the relationships between history, heritage, and the past. It illustrates how accidental received history can be. Internationally known as a scientist and inventor, Goldberg effectively disappeared from sight.

The Statistical Machine was the first electronic document retrieval machine, but it was not developed into a commercial product and very little evidence of it has survived. Like Goldberg himself, his machine dropped out of sight. Neither Goldberg's paper about it in the proceedings of the 1931 Congress in Dresden nor the English translation of it in the *British Journal of Photography* appear to have been cited after 1938, except for once in Israel, until an early version of Chapter 14 was published in 1992. Goldberg's name gradually disappeared from reference works. What happened? There were several causes.

The history of technology tends to be written along national lines, and English-language writings tend to focus on developments in United States. In the vocabulary of the dominant English discourse, one refers to the Gamma Rule, rather than the Goldberg Condition. Historians need resources to work with and are understandably attracted to topics for which resources are available. Bombs in Dresden and flood in Rehovot destroyed archives that historians would otherwise have drawn on. Motivation is also a factor: In Saxony, first Nazi, then Communist, ideology had little sympathy for a Jewish, capitalist inventor, and there was very little interest in history within the field of information science until the 1990s.

Normal science progresses through many small, marginal, and often duplicative contributions. Newer papers gradually replace older ones in the visible literature listed in footnotes and citations. As photographic science advanced, Goldberg's many publications gradually receded from view.

There is also a human need for a narrative of the past, preferably heroic, which can help to explain who we are and how we come to be the way we are. But any retelling of the past involves drastic simplification. A few developments acquire landmark status, some individuals become mythic heroes, and only a very few writings come to be regarded as classics. These simplified accounts arise through mechanisms that are not well understood, but they arise from and through the knowledge and motivations of storytellers. In Goldberg's case, his most striking innovations were directly eclipsed by the actions of three powerful and ambitious men. J. Edgar Hoover, glorifying the FBI, replaced Goldberg with a Professor Zapp as the inventor of microdot technology. Heinz Küppenbender propagated a Küppenbender-centric narrative that became the accepted corporate history of Zeiss Ikon. Vannevar Bush, with his largely unsuccessful Microfilm Rapid Selector and his famous essay, "As we may think," became the iconic pioneer of information systems, filling the niche that Goldberg and other earlier pioneers might otherwise have shared.

Goldberg himself wrote very little after 1933, and, at the end of his life, he systematically destroyed most of his papers, keeping only those few items that had the most significance for him: some photos, some certificates, some offprints of his own publications, and almost no correspondence. The exception was the Statistical Machine. For it, alone among his inventions, he preserved the patent documents. There is no doubt that Goldberg considered his Statistical Machine to be his most important invention, because it had to do with improving access to recorded knowledge. With the destruction of his brilliant career in Germany by Martin Ludwig and others, he had chosen to move away to an underdeveloped Palestine to help build a country in which Jews could live without the discrimination that he himself had experienced. He had little faith in history, but he could, and did, look back with considerable pride in what he had achieved. At the opening ceremony of the new building for El Op in Rehovoth in 1967, Goldberg said, "Standing here and seeing the beautiful and elaborated institution, I am proud to have had the possibility to contribute to some extent to its creation.... I am now an old man and am proud that these boys... are now senior members of this undertaking, following the way their former 'boss' started full 30 years ago."

To the end of his days, Goldberg kept a yellowing clipping from an Egyptian newspaper, the *Cairo Times,* of 1950. It was an account of how an American professor had invented a wondrous mechanical brain. In this way, the media coverage of Vannevar Bush's Memex reached him in the heat and sand of Tel Aviv. Goldberg must have realized that it was unlikely that he would get credit for the invention he was most proud of, the machine he had designed, built, demonstrated, and used, the machine that was important because it provided people with access to knowledge.

Acknowledgments and Sources

Finding out about Goldberg is not easy. His activities took place in distant worlds: Tsarist Russia, the Kingdom of Saxony, World War I, the Weimar Republic, and Palestine under the British Mandate. His activities and the records of them were affected by most of the great turbulent events of the twentieth century: the Russian Revolution, World War I, the Third Reich, and World War II. The records of his firms were destroyed by bombing and fire (Ica, Zeiss Ikon) or by flood (El Op). He did not reminisce, even to his children. In his last days, he destroyed much of his own papers and memorabilia.

I am especially grateful to numerous people who have helped me in many ways, and especially for numerous discussions with Goldberg's son, Dr. Herbert Goldberg; his daughter, Chava (Renate) Gichon; and his son-in-law, Professor Mordecai Gichon. Details of Goldberg's domestic life are based almost entirely on their recollections. Contact with his family in Russia was lost in the 1930s.

The following generously agreed to be interviewed: Moshe Arad, Ramat Chen, Israel, 26 and 27 March 1995; Jacob Beutler, Rehovot, Israel, 25 March 1995; Dr. Russell C. Coile, Pacific Grove, CA, 13 April 1990; Alex Eliraz, Jaffa, Israel, 2 April 1995; Dr. Otto Gold, Haifa, Israel, 4 April 1995; Joseph H. Jaffe, Jaffa, Israel, 27 March 1995; Edward K. Kaprelian, New Jersey, 18 May 1997; Aviva Kelton, Great Neck, NY, 11 May 1998; George Lowy, Silver Spring, MD, 1 November 1997; Shmuel Neumann, Ramat Gan, 29 March 1995; Michael Plaot (of Eschborn, Germany), in Tel Aviv, 12 November 1998; Dr. Walther Riedel, Dresden, Germany, 20 November 2000; George Sorenson, Rishon Le Zion, Israel, 28 November 1998; Martin Strauss, Washington, DC, 18 October 1994; General Israel Tal, Tel Aviv, 24 March 1995.

A series of talented research assistants were most helpful, especially with foreign-language resources and obscure references, including: Brian Kassof, Ziming Liu, Linda-Cathryn Muehlinghaus (formerly Evertz), Vivien Petras, Jan Plamper, and Jacek Purat.

Many others provided invaluable assistance and encouragement, especially Gerald Autler, Berkeley; Julia Blume; the late Dr. Burghard Burgermeister, Dresden; Professor Marc Davis, Berkeley; Dr. Sabine Fahrenbach, Leipzig; Gerald Feldman, Berkeley; Thomas Hapke, Hamburg; Diplom-Ingenieur Edith Hellmut, Jena; Gerhard von Knobelsdorff, Berlin; Dr. Hans-Peter Frei, Zurich; Paul Hamburg, Berkeley; Noam Kaminer,

Tel Aviv; Professor Klaus Mauersberger, Dresden; Kilian Steiner, Munich; Lawrence J. Gubas, Randolph, NJ; H. Keith Melton, Boca Raton, FL; John R. Posniak, Alexandria, VA; Professor W. Boyd Rayward; Professor Dr. Volkmar Richter, Koethen, Germany; Kilian Steiner, Munich; G. P. Zachary; but also many more.

The principal archival sources used were

Goldberg Papers: What survives of Goldberg's personal papers is in the possession of his daughter, Mrs. Chava Gichon, Zahala, Tel Aviv, Israel.

Dresden, Germany: Dresden: Hauptstaatsarchiv. Ernemann / Zeiss Ikon series. For Fernseh AG, see File 154. The corporate records of Ica and Zeiss Ikon in the main works at Schandauerstrasse 76 were destroyed in the 1945 bombing of Dresden. However, copies of some of these records were also in the papers of the Ernemann works, especially after 1926 when Ernemann became part of Zeiss Ikon and survive in Hauptstaatsarchiv.

Jena, Germany: The Betriebsarchiv Carl Zeiss (BACZ) contains material relating to Zeiss Ikon, including File 8145 on Goldberg and File 22413 on Fernseh AG.

Leipzig, Germany: Sächsisches Staatsarchiv, Leipzig. See the series *Staatlicher Akademie für graphische Künste und Buchgewerbe. Leipzig* and its finding list *(Findbuch).* Archiv-Signaturen 6: Einförderung neuer Kürse, 1907–1914; and 37: Goldberg (November 1916–January 1918 only).

Rochester, New York: George Eastman House and Museum contains some personal papers of C.E.K. Mees, including a few items relating to Goldberg.

Three specialized sources are presented in three appendixes: Appendix A contains the original German texts of three documents relating to Goldberg; Appendix B is a checklist of biographical sources; and Appendix C contains a list of Goldberg-related patents.

The bibliography is in two parts: first a checklist of Goldberg's own writings, and then a General Bibliography of works mentioned in the chapters and notes.

Financial support was gratefully received from the Academic Senate Committee of Research, University of California, Berkeley; from Ricoh Silicon Valley, Inc.; and through the Harold Lancour Scholarship for Foreign Study, in 1995, from the Beta Phi Mu International Library and Information Science Honor Society.

Appendix A: Texts in German

A.1. The Glass Library, by Michael Gesell. Quoted in Chapter 10

Michael Gesell. Die gläserne Bibliothek. Zeitungsbuch: Organ der
Deutschen Buch Gemeinschaft, Berlin. *3Jg., Nr. 6 (15 März 1926):*
98–99.

Wenn ich reich wäre, liesse ich mir von Doktor Goldberg eine
Bibliothek bauen.

Doktor Goldberg ist kein Architekt. Doktor Goldberg ist Photograph.
Und dieser Photograph hat die Bibliothek der Zukunft erfunden.

Seine Erfindung gestattet, eine Bibliothek von tausend Bücher zu je
tausend Seiten in der Westentasche bei sich zu tragen. Der gesamte
Brockhaus nimmt nicht einmal fünf Quadratzentimeter Platz ein, und die
gesamten Deutschen Klassiker von Ulsilas bis Klabund lassen sich bequem
auf demselben Raum unterbringen.

Doktor Goldberg hat sein mikrophotographisches Verfahren auf den
Internationalen Photographischen Kongress in Paris vorgeführt. Es ist
technisch erwiesen, und nur die Kostenfrage macht einige Schwierigkeiten.
Doktor Goldberg hat auf einer Glasplatte von neun mal zwölf Zentimeter
den Inhalt von tausend Büchern zu je tausend Seiten mikrophotographisch
untergebracht. Mit Hilfe eines besonders konstruierten Mikroskops kann
man diese Platte im Laufe einiger Zeit, wenn man sie hat, durchlesen.

Wenn ich reich wäre, liesse ich mir von Doktor Goldberg einen
Arbeitsraum bauen. Der müsste achteckig sein, in der Mitte einen beque-
men Drehstuhl haben, an dem das Mikroteleskop angebracht wäre, und die
Bände müssten aus Glasplatten bestehen.

Dieser Arbeitsraum braucht nur ein bescheidenes Raummass von
acht mal fünf Meter und fünf Meter Höhe zu haben. Ich hätte dann genau
200 Quadratmeter Bibliotheksfläche zur Verfügung. Darauf liessen sich,
wie jeder nachrechnen kann, ungefahr zwanzig Millionen Bücher zu je
tausend Seiten unterbringen. Ich wurde mich in meinen Drehstuhl setzen
und zu lesen beginnen. Keine Staatsbibliothek würde mich mehr ärgern
können, ich hätte das Nötigste aus der Weltliteratur zur Hand, wenn nicht
gar ein paar Quadratmeter meiner Bibliothek wegen Mangels an Werken
frei bleiben müssten.

Ernsthaft: was ist Radio und Flugzeug gegenüber dieser Erfindung? . . .
Ist das Verfahren praktisch durchzuführen, darf man von ihm eine Umwälzung
erwarten, deren Wirkung die der Erfindung Gutenbergs weit in den Schatten
stellen muss. Es ist durchaus denkbar und vorstellbar, dass man ganze

Wissenschaftszweige in solchen kleinen gläsernen Bibliotheken zusammen-fasst. Das Original würde eine Riesenarbeit und Riesenunkosten machen. Aber man würde gewiss leicht ein Verfahren finden, dieses Original beliebig zu vervielfältigen, so wie man von photographischen Platten Abzüge ohne Zahlbeschränkung herstellen kann. Man brauchte sich dann nur solch einen Abzug zu kaufen, um das Gebiet bei sich tragen zu können.

Unser Arbeitstisch wird eine kleine Veränderung erfahren. Wir werden mit Mikroskop und Lichtkegel arbeiten. Unsere Bibliotheken werden keine Riesenmagazine mehr brauchen; eine Kartothek, in der von jedem Wissensgebiet ein paar hundert Abzüge der Urplatte vorhanden sind, wird genügen. Ein Griff des Beamten genügte, um dir die gesamte Goetheliteratur zur Verfügung zu stellen, wenn du nicht in der Lage bist, solch einen Abzug zu kaufen. Ein paar Griffe an deinem Mikroteleskop— und das Wunder funktioniert im zischenden Lichtkegel. Ein feines Räderwerk, das mit Hundertsteln und Tausendsteln von Millimetern arbei-tet, lässt dich diese Bibliothek *en miniature* durchblättern. Es wird eine Lust sein, Philologe zu sein.

Freilich: die Bibliophilen werden nicht viel Freude an dieser Art von gläsernen Buchbüchern und Bibliotheksbüchern haben können. Aber die Zeit und die Zivilisation geht über alte Romantik hinweg, um neue Romantik zu schaffen. Diese Erfindung des Dokter Goldberg is notwen-dig. Sie korrespondiert sozusagen mit der des Flugzeugs und des Radios. Wie diese den Planeten aufs engste zusammengerückt haben, so rückt die Mikrophotographie den geistigen und seelischen Niederschlag der Menschheit auf den kleinstmöglichen Raum zusammen und schafft die Möglichkeit, die verloren zu gehen drohte, diesen Niederschlag zu über-schen und zu benutzen. Die Metaphysik blinzelt.

A.2. A National Library in the Vestpocket. Quoted in Chapter 10

*Die Nationalbibliothek in der Westentasche. **Prager Tagblatt** (Prague) Jahrgang 63; Nr. 213. (10 September 1938): 5–6. Did not appear in all editions of that day's paper. Transcribed from Library of Congress Microfilm Np 2876; reel no. 2,560.*

In den lezten Jahren sind in den größeren amerikanischen Bibliotheken neben den auch bei uns schon eingeführten Photokopie-Apparaten auch Schmalfilm-Aufnahmegeräte zur Aufstellung gelangt. Für verhältnismäs-sig geringe Unkosten kann man sich von beliebigen Druckwerken Kopien auf 35-Millimeter-Schmalfilm anfertigen lassen. Die Besteller—vorwieg-end wissenschaftliche Institute und Forschungslaboratorien der Industrie, aber auch bereits viele Privatpersonen—brauchen dann nur die Schmalfilm-Aufnahmen in geeigneter Weise auf eine Leinwand zu projizieren, um die aufgenommene Druckseite bequem lessen zu können. In den meisten

Fällen ist die Anfertigung von beispielsweise 800 Schmalfilmaufnahmen billiger als die Anschaffung eines 800 Seiten starken wissenschaftlichen Werkes. Sehr wesentlich fällt auch die Platzersparnis ins Gewicht. Am bedeutungsvollsten ist aber, dass jetzt jede Bibliothek in der Lage ist, ihren Benutzern auch sehr seltene, manchmal nur noch in einem einzigen Exemplar erhalten gebliebene Werke zugänglich zu machen. Es ist ja bekannt, dass man zur Entzifferung schwer lesbarer Schriften häufig den Umweg über photographische Aufnahmen beschreitet, da die Kamera mehr sieht als das Auge. So ist in manchen Fällen dem Bibliotheksbenutzer mit den Schmalfilm-Aufnahmen besser gedient als mit dem Original. Bei Dissertationen und ähnlichen Schriftwerken, die nur in wenigen Exemplaren vorhanden zu sein brauchen, ist man dazu übergegangen, auf die Drucklegung völlig zu verzichten und statt dessen Aufnahmen vom Sc hreibmaschinenmanuskript herzustellen.

Für den Projektion benutzt man besonders konstruierte Tische, auf deren mit einer Projektionsfläche versehene Platte von unten die Filme projiziert werden. Derartige Tische finden auch bereits in den Konstruktionsbüros der grossen amerikanischen Industriefirmen Verwendung, wo Konstruktionspläne und dergleichen auf Schmalfilmen im Archiv aufbewahrt werden. Für die Industrie spielt die Platzersparnis eine besonders grosse Rolle. Man kann beispielsweise einen Konstruktionsplan, der eine Grösse von 75 mal 100 Zentimeter einnimmt, bequem auf eine Schmalfilm-Aufnahme bringen und dann auf dem Projektionstische in der ursprünglichen Grösse wieder erscheinen lassen. In einzelnen dieser Büros wurden die Projektionstische mit automatischen Schalteinrichtungen ausgestattet, die selbsttätig die jeweils gewünschte Aufnahme aus dem innerhalb des Tisches angebrachten Magazin auf der Projektionsfläche erscheinen lassen. Der Benutzer stellt auf seiner Nummernscheibe eine bestimmte Nummer ein, und alles andere besorgt selbsttätig der Zaubertisch.

Mit der Konstruktion dieser Wundertische, in deren Innerem sich eine ganze Bibliothek auf Filmen befindet, ist der erste Schritt zur Verwirklichung einer Idee vollbracht, die vor sieben Jahren auf dem Dresdener Internationalen Kongreß für wissenschafliche Photographie von dem russischen Forscher Goldberg seinen Fachkollegen vorgetragen wurde. Damals lächelte man über die Träume des Professors, der nicht nur als Photo- und Kinotechniker anerkannt, sondern auch als leidenschaftlicher Bastler bekanntgeworden war.

Die Bibliothek der Zukunft, so erklärte damals Professor Goldberg, wird in ihren Lesesälen nur noch Projektionstische stehen haben, und im Inneren eines jeden einzelnen dieser Tische wird sich auf Filmen der gesamte Bibliotheksbestand befinden. Hunderte von Lesern werden so gleichzeitig in einem Werk studieren können, daß heute nur in einem einzelnen Exemplar vorhanden ist. Man lächelte damals über diese Ankündigung. Als der Professor seinen Kollegen aber in seiner Bastlerwerkstatt das erste Modell des Projektionstisches vorgeführt hatte, wurde man doch nachdenklich.

Immerhin hielt man die Prophezeiung des Professors noch für maßlos über-trieben. Wenn sich wirklich jede Seite eines Buches auf einer Schmalfilm-Aufnahme unterbringen liess—für wieviel solche Aufnahmen konnte dann bestenfalls im Inneren eines Tisches Platz sein? Die Besucher begannen zu rechnen, aber mit einem triumpierenden Lächeln unterbrach sie der Professor. Er führte seine Kollegen zu einem Mikroskop und bat sie, durch das Instrument zu sehen. Im Blickfeld zeigte sich eine komplette Seite einer Veröffentlichung des Professors in der "Zeitschrift für Technische Physik." [Presumably his "Herstellung von starken Verkleinerungen. *Zeitschrift für technische Physik* 7. J., Nr. 10 (1926):500–505, 579–82]. Jeder einzelne Buchstabe war klar erkennbar. Der Professor hatte eine Seite mikroskopisch verkleinert und jetzt—bei der Betrachtung durch das Mikroskop—zeigte sich, daß jede Einzelheit genau zu erkennen war. Die Kollegen des Professors—alle erfahrene Phototechniker—wollten es nicht glauben. Nach all ihren Erfahrungen mußte bei einer mikroskopischen Verkleinerung die Körnigkeit des photographischen Materials jede Einzelheit verwischen und unerkennbar machen. In dem mikroskopischen Bild war aber keine Spur der photographischen Körner zu erkennen. Man bestürmte den Professor mit Fragen. Der kleine Professor mit dem liebenswürdigen, zerknitterten Gesicht kaute am Pappmundstück seiner Zigarette und kostete seinen Triumph mit vollen Zügen. "Sehen Sie nochmal durch das Mikroskop", bat er, verschmitzt lächelnd seine Kollegen, "und lesen Sie meine Veröfentlichung. Dann kennen Sie mein ganzes Geheimnis." Die Veröffentlichung behandelte die Eigenschaften von Kollodium-Schichten und wies nach, daß diese Schichten praktisch kornfrei sind und daher zu beliebigen Verkleinerungen verwandt werden können. Die nur in nassem Zustande verwendbaren Kollodium-Schichten sind den Photographen wohlbekannt, sie wurden vor der Einführung der Gelatine-Trockenplatten allgemein verwandt, sind dann aber unbeachtet geblieben, bis Professor Goldberg auf die neue Verwendungsmöglichkei aufmerksam machte.

Neue optische Apparate sind für die Herstellung der Verkleinerung nicht erforderlich, da dazu lediglich ein umgekehrtes Mikroskop notwendig ist. Ebenso kann, wie Professor Goldberg betonte, die Vergrößerung der mikropisch kleinen Aufnahmen bei der Projektion keine unüberwindbaren Schwierigkeiten bereiten. "Und nun, meine Herren", beendete der Professor eine Ausführungen, "nun können Sie ausrechnen, ob sich eine ganze Bibliothek im Inneren eines Tisches unterbringen läßt oder nicht. Ich kann Ihnen verraten, daß die Druckseite, die Sie durch das Mikroskop gesehen haben, auf dem Film einen Zeilenabstand von einem Tausendstel Millimeter hatte. Eine Druckseite von rund 50 Zeilen läßt sich bequem auf einem Hundertstel Quadradmillimeter unterbringen." Man begann zu rechnen. Eine Seite auf einem Hundertstel Quadratmillimeter—das macht für ein 300 Seiten starkes Buch drei Quadratmillimeter. Auf einen Quadratzentimeter kommen dann 33 Bücher, auf einen Quadratdezimeter 3300 und auf einen

Quadratmeter 330.000. In Rollenform mußte es möglich sein, einen Film von einem Meter Breite und 1000 Meter Länge im Inneren des Tisches unterzubringen; auf diesem Film müßten sich 330 Millionen Bücher unterbringen lassen. Die Herren mußten zugeben, daß in dieser Hinsicht dem Projekt des Professors keine Schwierigkeiten im Wege stehen könnten. Skeptischer blieb man allerdings hinsichtlich der automatischen Einstellung der gewünschten Stelle des Filmes im Projektionstisch. Aber auch in diesem Punkte war der Professor fest von der Durchführbarkeit seines Projektes überzeugt. Durch ein Lochkartensystem in Verbindung mit Photozellen mußte seiner Meinung nach auch dieses Problem lösbar sein. Er führte seinen Besuchern ein kleines Modell vor, daß im Prinzip völlig dem jetzt bei den amerikanischen Projektionstischen verwandten entspricht.

"Daß mein Traum einmal verwirklicht werden wird, daran zweifle ich nicht", erklärte der Professor, "ob ich selbst es aber erleben werde, davon allerdings bin ich nicht überzeugt." Als Professor Goldberg vor drei Jahren anläßlich eines Pariser Kongresses nach den Fortschritten seines Projektes gefragt wurde, war er nicht sehr zuversichtlich.

"Ich habe gehört, daß meine mikroskopischen Verkleinerungen im Spionagedienst verschiedener Mächte Eingang gefunden haben", erklärte er. "Das ist aber schließlich nichts Neues. Die in Paris belagerten Franzosen haben ja schon 1871 mit Brieftauben photographische Verkleinerungen zur Nachrichtenübermittlung benutzt. Neu ist, daß sich die Kriminalschriftsteller auf meine Idee gestürzt haben. Das ist aber auch alles, was ich Ihnen an Fortschritten zu berichten habe."

Auch heute noch ist der Weg zur Erfüllung des Traumes des kleinen Professors weit. Aber durch die Entwicklung in Amerika hat man sich doch dem Ziele um einen großen Schritt genähert.

A.3. Goldberg's Messter Medal Acceptance Speech, April 20, 1932. Quoted in Chapter 15

When the **Deutsche Kinotechnische Gesellschaft** *("German Movie Technology Society") conferred its Messter Medal on Goldberg for contributions to cinematography, his acceptance speech was autobiographical, personal, and—unusually for Goldberg—expressed a political view. The only text found is this summary in* **Kinotechnik** *(20 April 1932):160.*

Ein Weg zur Kinematographie

"... und erteilte das Wort Herrn Prof. Dr. Goldberg, der in der ihm eigenen, mit Humor gewuerzten, das Auditorium immer fesselnden Weise seinen Weg zur Kinematographie schilderte... Prof. Goldberg gelangte auf Umwegen zur Kinematographie. Die erste Eindruck, der ihn auch weiter an die Materie fesselte, war die Funktion der M a c h -i n e als solche—schon von fruehester Zeit her interessierte ihn alles, was mit automatischen Maschinen in Verbindung stand: so hatte es ihm die Jacquard-Maschine ganz besonders angetan, Es sind 25 Jahre vergangen, seit Prof. Goldberg mit der Erfindung eines zuverlaessigen Herstellungsverfahrens fuer die bekannten Graukeile eine wissenschaftliches Instrument schuf, das fuer die Filmindustrie spaeter von groesster Bedeutung werden sollte und gerade wieder in neuester Zeit sich in Verbindung mit dem Tonfilm als sehr wichtig erwiesen hat.... Arbeiten, die spaeter zum R e i h b i l d n e r (Kinomatographie aus Luftfahrzeugen) fuehrten, waren die photographischen Aufnahmen von grossen Drachen aus. Schliesslich gedachte der Vortragende seiner in dem bekannten Werke "Der Aufbau des photographischen Bildes" zusammengestellten Arbeiten auf sensitometrischem Gebiet, aus deren Fuelle die "Goldberg-Bedingung" gerade in juengster Zeit durch den Tonfilm zu aktuellster Bedeutung gelangt ist.

Prof. G o l d b e r g wies dann darauf hin, dass sich die unter seiner Leitung stehende Zeiss Ikon A.-G. in letzter Zeit auch mit Roehren und Verstaerkerbau beschaeftigt habe und zu wichtigen Ergebnissen gelangt sei, die zum Bau neuartiger Tonfilmverstaerker gefuehrt haben.... Schliesslich fuehrte der Vortragende noch eine hoechst interessante, bei Zeiss Ikon entwickelte Maschine vor, die ihn, wie er bemerkte, immer wieder an die alte Jacquard-Maschine erinnere: eine R e g i s t r a t u r a u f k i n e m a t i s c h e r G r u n d l a g e. Die zu registrierenden Schriftstcke werden auf einem Filmband aufgenommen und jedes erhaelt seine Nummer. Zum Aufsuchen eines Schriftstueckes stellt man dessen Nummer an der Maschine ein und laesst diese laufen: das Filmband rollt dann ab, bis das gewuenschte Schriftstueck auf der Projektionsflaeche erscheint.

Abschliessend bemerkte Prof. Goldberg, dass die Techniker in neuester Zeit gaenzlich versagt haetten, indem sie duldeten, dass wieder, wie vor 100 Jahren, Sturm auf die Maschine gelaufen wuerde. Es liessen sich Beispiele in grosser Zahl dafuer anfuehren, dass in Zeitungsartikeln nach Produktionseinschraenkung geschrien werde, weil "Ueberproduktion" vorlaege; im Effekt heisse das aber nichts anderes, als dass soundsoviele Maschinen stillgelegt und entsprechend viele Menschen arbeitlos gemacht wrden. Den Begriff der Ueberproduktion gaebe es nur in gewissen Faellen. Wenn aber gesagt wuerden koenne, dass die Maschine Arbeit wegnaehme, so bedeute das nichts anderes, dass wir Techniker das Heft aus der Hand gegeben haetten. Ein Unding sei es, dass Hunderttausende in Deutschland frieren muessten, waehrend wir Kohlen in Huelle und Fuelle haetten, dass unsere Landwirtschaft aus Mangel an Duengemitteln am Rande des

Abgrundes stehe, waehrend Deutschland die groesste Stickstoffindustrie der Welt besitze. Mit der Ausruf "Techniker an die Front" schloss Prof. Goldberg seine Ausfuehrungen, die von der Versammlung stuermisch applaudiert wurden."

One Path to Cinematography

Professor Goldberg spoke and, holding the auditorium constantly captivated in his own, humor-filled way, described his own path to cinematography. Professor Goldberg arrived at cinematography after some detours. The first impression of machines, which captivated him also further on, was the function of the machine as is—already very early on he was interested in everything that was connected with automatic machines: he was particularly taken with the Jacquard loom. 25 years have passed since Prof. Goldberg created a reliable manufacturing process for the well-known gray wedge–a scientific instrument, which should become of the greatest significance for the film industry and proved itself very important in connection with the sound film. Efforts, which later led to serial imaging (cinematography from aircraft), were photographs taken from large observation balloons. Finally, the speaker commemorated his works on sensitometry (compiled in his known book *Der Aufbau des photographischen Bildes*), of which the Goldberg Condition just recently proved to be very significant for the sound film.

Prof. Goldberg also pointed out that Zeiss Ikon (under his leadership) recently employed itself with the production of tubes and amplifiers and reached important results, which led to the construction of new amplifiers for sound film.

Finally the speaker demonstrated a very interesting machine developed at Zeiss Ikon, which reminds him, he noted, of the old Jacquard loom: A retrieval system based on cinematography. The documents to be recorded were filmed and each has its own number. To search for a document one enters its number into the machine and lets it run: the roll of film unwinds until the desired document appears on a projection screen.

In conclusion, Professor Goldberg noted that in recent times engineers had completely failed, in that they tolerated attacks on machines again, as a hundred years earlier. Examples in great number can be quoted of calls in newspaper articles for reduced production, because of the prospect of "overproduction." In effect that means only that some number of machines are idle and a corresponding number of people are made unemployed. The concept of overproduction would hold only in certain cases. But when it could be said that the machine takes work away, it means nothing less than that we engineers lost control. It is monstrous that hundreds of thousands in Germany are freezing when we have coal in abundance; that our agriculture is on the brink of disaster for lack of fertilizer when German[y] has the largest nitrogen industry in the world. With the call "Engineers to the Front!" Professor Goldberg concluded his remarks, which received a storm of applause from the meeting.

Appendix B: Biographical Sources

This list of published biographical statements concerning Goldberg is in chronological order. The statements are often unreliable, and most contain very little information. The more useful ones are identified with an asterisk: *.

Goldberg, E. 1906. *Beiträge zur Kinetik photochemischer Reaktionen: Inaugural-Dissertation... Universität Leipzig.* Leipzig: Barth. Vita on p. 46.*

Emmerich, G. H., ed. 1910. *Lexikon für Photographie und Reproduktionstechnik (Chemigraphie, Lichtdruck, Heliogravüre).* Wien: A. Hartleben, 250–51.*

Seliger, Max. 1912. Wesen, Ziele und bisherige Tätigkeit der königl. Akademie für graphische Künste und Buchgewerbe in Leipzig. *Original und Reproduktion* 2, Heft 3/4 (?1912):78–90. Photo of Goldberg on p 86.

Original und Reproduktion. [?1912.] on p. 102 of article "Leipziger Kunsthistoriker und Künstler," 91–130.

Degener, H.A.L. 1922. *Wer ist's.* 8. Ausg. Berlin: Herrmann Degener. p. 500; 9. Ausg. (1928):505; 10. Ausg. (1935):513.

Wenzel, Georg, ed. 1929. *Deutscher Wirtschaftsführer: Lebensgänge deutsche Persönlichkeiten.* Hamburg: Direktor u. Vorstmitgl.

Prof. Goldberg 50 Jahre. [Clipping from unidentified newspaper, marked 1930.]

Reichshandbuch der deutschen Gesellschaft: Das Handbuch der Persönlichkeit in Wort und Bild. Berlin: Deutscher Wirtschaftsverlag, 1930–31. 2 Bde. Bd 1:563.

Kürschners Deutscher Gelehrten-Kalender, herausg. Gerhard Lüdtke. 4.Aufl. Berlin de Gruyter, 1931. Col. 862; 2. Aufl. (1926): col. 549; 3. Aufl. (1928/29): col. 687; 5. Aufl. (1935): col. 411.

Lobel, L. 1931. [Nomination of Goldberg for the Peligot Medal.] *Bulletin de la Société Française de Photographie* Ser. 3, t. 18, no. 6 (June 1931):122–24.*

Displaced German scholars. ?1936. Reprinted San Bernardino, CA: Borgo Press, 1993, 9.

J. C. Poggendorffs biographisch-literarisches Handwörterbuch. 1937. Berlin: Verlag Chemie. VI, ii (1937):916; VIIb, 3 (1970):1685; VIII, Teil 2 (2002):1388–91. Self-reported: States that he was a student of

R. Luther, lists his inventions as Densograph 1910; Graukeil 1911; Mikrophot 1921; Spektrodensograph 1927.*

Anon. 1940. [Laboratory for precision instruments in Tel-Aviv.] *Davar* (12 February 1940). Newspaper clipping in Hebrew.

Mechner, Ernst. 1942. Training industrial scientists. *U.P.A. Report,* vol. 3, no. 4 (April 1942):2. New York: United Palestine Appeal.

Scaife, Jos. D. 1945. Bricks without straw. *Machinery* (14 June 1945):647.*

Noted scientist visits son at Park; Renews friendship with Dr. Mees. *Kodakery* (18 July 1946).*

Future for Israel seen in industry: Precision instrument inventor from Tel Aviv describes rapid expansion there. *New York Times,* 27 May 1949, 5, col. 5, 6.*

Busch, Leo. 1953. Die Oskar-Messter-Gedenkmünze—höchste Auszeichnung für deutsche Kinotechniker. *Kino-Technik* 7. Jg., Heft 8 (August 1953):210–11. "... ist vor wenigen Jahren in Tel Aviv gestorben."!

Touch of genius: Goldberg Instruments. *The Israel Export Journal* 6, no. 10 (October 1954):7.

Prof. Emanuel Goldberg 75 Jahre. *Ydiot Hadashot* (Israel) (5 September 1956).

Eggert, John. 1956. Prof. Dr. Emanuel Goldberg zur Vollendung seines 75. Lebensjahres. *Camera* 35 (1956):608.*

Cohen, Harry, and Itzhak J. Carmin. 1956. *Jews in the world of science,* 82. New York: Monde.

Citation at conferral of honorary doctorate, Technion, 21 May 1957.

Neumann, S. 1957. Prof. Emanuel Goldberg. *Bulletin of the Research Council of Israel* 5C (4):iii-v. Also portrait, p. i. "A chemist by learning, a physicist by calling and a mechanic by birth."*

Professor Dr. Goldberg 75 Jahre. *Zeitschrift für wissenschaftliche Photographie, Photophysik und Photochemie* 52, Heft 4–6 (1957):105–6.

H. O. 1957. Prof. Dr Emanuel Goldberg 75 Jahre. *Mitteilungsblatt Irgub Olej Merkas Europa* 25, Heft 4 (1957):7.

Wandersleb, Ernst. 1957. *Einige persönliche Erinnerungen an Prof. Emmanuel Goldberg.* 4pp. Unpublished typescript.*

Encyclopedie voor Fotografie en Cinematografie. 1958. Amsterdam: Elsevier, 418; see also 425.

Karger-Decker, Bernt. 1959. Kameraman Erwin Anders. *Fotografie* 13, Nr. 12 (Dez. 1959):466–469. See 466–67 for Goldberg kidnapping.*

Wentzel, Fritz. 1960. *Memoirs of a photochemist,* ed. Louis Walton Sipley, 96–97. Philadelphia: American Museum of Photography.

Elitzor, Yoval. 1960. Spoiled kids and stepsons in industry. *Ha-Aretz* (15 May 1960). Newspaper clipping in Hebrew, with portrait of Goldberg.*

Skopec, Rudolf. 1964. *Photographie im Wandel der Zeiten.* Prague: Artia. Illus. #188, 189, and 286. Transl. of Czech ed., 1963. *Dejiny fotografie v obrazech od nejstarsich dob k dnesku.* Praha: Orbis.

Sipley, L. W. 1965. *Photography's great inventors,* 58–59. Philadelphia: American Museum of Photography.

Goldberg, Norman. 1969. The other Goldberg: A visit with Zeiss Ikon's practical prodigy. *Popular Photography* 65, no. 5 (November 1969):88–89, 154.*

Jaffe, J. H. 1970. Appeciation: Professor Emanuel Goldberg. *Jerusalem Post,* 18 October 1970, 4. Obituary.

Emanuel Goldberg. *Fernseh- und Kino-Technik* 25, Heft 7 (1971):265. Obituary.

Frieser, H. [Obituary.] *Photographische Korrespondenz* 107, Nr. 5 (1971):86.

Kaprelian, E. K. 1971. In Memoriam. Emmanuel Goldberg. *Photographic Science and Engineering* 15, no. 1:3.

Browne, T., and E. Partnow. 1983. *Macmillan Biographical encyclopedia of photographic artists & innovators,* 234–35. New York: Macmillan.

Kröner, Peter. 1983. *Vor fünfzig Jahren: Die Emigration deutschsprachiger Wissenschaftler 1933–1939.* Münster: Gesellschaft für Wissenschaftsgeschichte. #0599 on p. 44.

Strauss, Herbert A., and Werner Röder. 1983. *International biographical dictionary of central European emigres 1933—1945.* Munich: Saur, 1983. Vol. 2, Pt. 1, 388.*

Gubas, Larry. 1985a. Emmanuel Goldberg. *Zeiss Historica* 7, no. 1 (Spring 1985):14–15.

Brockhaus Enzyklopädie. 1989. 19. Aufl. Mannheim: Brockhaus. v.8. S.v. Goldberg; Goldberg-Emulsion, both on p. 642; and Gamma, p. 117.

Bibliographie Judaica: Verzeichnis jüdischer Autoren deutscher Sprache, bearbeitet von Renate Heuer. Frankfurt: Campus Verlag. 1992. Bd 1:119.

Meyers Neues Lexikon in zehn Bänden. Mannheim: Meyers Lexikonverlag, 1993. 4:126.

Deutsche Biographische Enzyklopädie. 1996. Munich: K .G. Saur, 4:77.

Gilbert, George. 1996. *The illustrated worldwide who's who of Jews in photography,* 204–5. Riverside, NY: Gilbert.

Professor Imanuel Goldberg—Chaluts Madaey Hameda Vehaoptica [Professor Emanuel Goldberg—a Pioneer in Information and Optics Science: The Tenth Meeting on Optical Engineering in Israel was on the topic of 60 years of Electro-Optics in Israel.] *Mehandesim VeTechnologim* [*Engineers and Technologists*] 1997:41, 44–46. In Hebrew.*

Emanuel Goldberg, 1881–1970: Ein Lebensbild. In *75 Jahre Zeiss Ikon AG: Aspekte der Entwicklung des 1926 gegründeten Industrieunternehmens,*

51–54. Thesaurus 3. Dresden: Technische Sammlungen der Stadt Dresden, 2002. Papers presented at the Kolloquium 75 Jahren Zeiss Ikon A.-G., Dresden, 18-19 November 2000.*

Mauersberger, Klaus. 2002. Emanuel Goldberg—ein jüdisches Wissenschaftler und Unternehmer. Hochschulalltag in der NS-Zeit (I). *Dresdner Universitätsjournal* (December 2002):8.*

Appendix C: Goldberg Patents

Russian patents

R 8571. 31 January 1904 (Old style). [Method of galvanizing iron using electrolysis.] Applied for 26 January 1902.

German patents

When Goldberg lived in Germany, inventions by employees were considered "work for hire" and patents were issued to the employer not to the employee inventor. A list of 172 German patents issued to Ica (1919–26) or to Zeiss Ikon (1926–46) was compiled, primarily from the German Patent Office weekly lists (*Auszüge*) indexes, but one cannot tell which reflect Goldberg's inventions, unless corresponding U.S. patents were issued. Only those issued to Goldberg personally are listed below. German patents were effective retroactively to the date of application. *Gebrauchsmuster* are a separate kind of patent used for small mechanical inventions, not issued after 1940.

G 151,336. Issued 21 May 1904. Effective 13 February 1902. Emanuel Goldberg. *Verfahren zur Herstellung von Galvanisierlung Zink- oder zinkhaltigen Niederschlägen mittels der Elektrolyze.* (Klasse 48a). Assigned to Dr. G. Langbein & Co., Leipzig-Sellerhausen. (*Auszüge* 27. Juli 1904, Bd 25, p. A1208.) German abstract: *Zeitschrift für angwandte Chemie* 17 (1904):1216.

G 159,897. Issued 17 April 1905. Effective 14 January 1904. Emanuel Goldberg. *Vorrichtung zur Massengalvanisierung kleiner Gegenstände mit Beweglichen oder festem Kathodenträger und über diesem angeordneter Anode.* (Kl. 48a). Assigned to Dr. G. Langbein & Co., Leipzig-Sellerhausen. (*Auszüge* 10 May 1905: A803–4.) German abstract *Zeitschrift für angwandte Chemie* 18, Heft 34 (25 August 1905):1368.

G 250,062. Issued 6 August 1912. Effective 10 December 1909. Emanuel Goldberg. *Apparat zur selbstättigen Registrierung der örtlichen Unterschiede in der Lichtabsorption oder Lichtemission von Gegenständen.* [Densograph.] (Kl. 57c, Gr. 4.) (*Auszüge* 1912: A1826.) Cancelled and replaced by *Gebrauchsmuster* 527,621.

Gebrauchsmuster 527,621. Issued 23 October 1912. Effective date 26 March 1910. *Photometer zur Auswertung örtlicher Unterschiede von*

Lichtintensitäten, insbesondere zur Messung der Schwärzung pho-tographischer Schichten. [Densograph.] (Kl. 42h.) Application G24,364. (*Patentblatt* 23 October 1912:2019–20.)

G 670,190. 22 December 1938. Effective 12 April 1927. Zeiss Ikon AG. & E. Goldberg. *Vorrichtung zum Aussuchen statistischer und Buchhalterischer Angaben.* (Kl. 43a,41/02.) (*Patentblatt* 22 December 1938:1322.) (Corresponds to Application Z 16,746 [Kl.43a, 41/02] 953 in 1935.)

G-M 1,431,500. 1938. *Photographische Kamera für biegsames lichtemp-findliches Material.* Effective 22 October 1937. (Kl.57a.) (*Patentblatt* 1938:296.) Application G 21,258. (Corresponding Luxemburg patent 23 October 1936.)

G 691,162. 4 April 1940. "Zeiss Ikon A.-G. in Dresden und Dr Emanuel Israel Goldberg in Tel Aviv, Palästina." *Statistiche Machine. Zusatz zum Patent 670,190.* Application Z 22,401. Effective 30 March 1928. (*Patentblatt* 1937. [Kl.43a,41/02] 574. *Namenverzeichnis* 1940, p. 429. *Auszüge* A1104.)

G 697, 265. 12 September 1940. Zeiss Ikon A.-G. in Dresden und Dr. Emanuel Israel Goldberg in Tel Aviv, Palästina. *Vorrichtung zum Aussuchen statistischer Angaben.* Effective 2 August 1931. Application Z 19,459. (*Patentblatt* 1936. [Kl.43a, 41/02] 1214.)

Application Z 19,461. Zeiss Ikon Akt. Ges., Dresden, und Dr. Emanuel Goldberg, Paris. *Vorrichtung zum Aussuchen statistischer und buch-halterischer Angaben.* Zus. z. Anm. Z16,746. 3.8.31. (*Patentblatt* 60. Jg., Nr 36 vom 3.9.36, 1019. [Kl.43a, 41/02].) No copy found. The Deutsches Patentamt, Dienststelle Berlin, stated, September 23, 1998, that the *Konkordanzbuecher* that link applications with resulting pat-ents list no corresponding patent, and that the files of unsuccessful patent applications for that period have been destroyed.

Also: G 332,653. 7 February 1921. Effective 23 June1917. Issued to Firma Carl Zeiss Jena. *Speigel, der dazu bestimmt ist, an der Erzeugung optischer Bilder teilzunehmen.* (Kl 42h–Gr. 8.) BACZ catalog record states: "Goldbergscher Spiegel. Erfinder Goldberg."

British patents

GB 7,923. 5 March 1903. *An improvement in electrolytically coating iron with zinc.* Date of application and provisional specification 4 April 1902.

GB 288, 580. 25 July 1929. *Improvements in or relating to Adding, Sorting, Statistical and like Machines.* Convention date (Germany): 12 April 1927. Application date (in United Kingdom): 11 April 1928. No. 10,732/28. Complete, accepted: 4 July 1929. *Illustrated Official Journal (Patents)* June 7, 1928, p. 2263: *Statistical apparatus.*

French patents

Fr. 657,787. Application: 7 April 1928. Issued 21 January 1929. Zeiss Ikon A.-G. (Société) et Goldberg (E.). (*Machine statistique.* XII-3). [*Table des brevets* 1929, p. 681].

Italian patents

I 268,389. 14 Ottobre 1929. Anno VII. Zeiss Ikon and Emanuel Goldberg. *Macchina per la compilazione di lavori di statistica.* Applied for 10 April 1928.

U.S. patents

US 733,025. 7 July 1903. E. Goldberg. *Electrolytically coating iron with zinc.* Application filed 17 April 1902. (*Gaz.* 105:1112.)

US 1,573,314. 16 February 1926. E. Goldberg and Martin Nowicki. *Enlarging camera.* (Cl. 88–24.) Corresponds to German patents 405,893; 410,991; 417,550.

US 1,667,110. 24 April 1928. E. Goldberg and Martin Nowicki, assigned to Zeiss Ikon. *Film box.*

US 1,704,189. 5 March 1929. E. Goldberg. *Motion picture camera driven by a spring mechanism.* (Cl. 315.)

US 1,713,277. 14 May 1929. E. Goldberg, O. Fischer, ass. to Zeiss Ikon. *Film spool construction.* Cl. 3204.

US 1,747,705. 18 February 1930. E. Goldberg, ass. to Zeiss Ikon. *Film-feeding device.* (Cl. 3101.) Corresponds to German patent 411,417 and French patent 591,435.

US 1,750,401. 11 March 1930. E. Goldberg, O. Fischer, ass. to Zeiss Ikon. *A cinematograph camera with clockwork driving mechanism.* (Corresponds to French patent 645,229.)

US 1,772,774. 12 August 1930. E. Goldberg, ass. to Ica A. G. *Cinema camera.* (Cl. 315.)

US 1,779,468. 28 October 1930. E. Goldberg and O. Fischer. *Cinematographic camera.* (Cl. 88–18.) Filed 12 July 1928. Filed in Germany 25 July 1927.

US 1,789,679. 20 January 1931. E. Goldberg. *Cinematographic camera.*

US 1,802,598. 28 April 1931. E. Goldberg, ass. to Zeiss Ikon. *Film magazine.* (Cl. 3104.) Corresponds to French patent 678,722.

US 1,804,500. 12 May 1931. E. Goldberg and O. Fischer. *Film box.* (Cl. 242–71.)

US 1,830,602. 3 November 1931. Distance releasing mechanism device for moving picture cameras driven by a spring mechanism. (Cl. 88–16.)

US 1,838,389. 29 December 1931. Emanuel Goldberg *Statistical machine.* Application 267,556, filed 5 April 1928 and in Germany 12 April 1927. (Cl. 234–1.5.)

US 1,973,203. 11 September 1934. E. Goldberg, ass. to Zeiss Ikon. *Nipkow disk for television.* (Cl. 178–6.) Applied for 15 September 1932.

US 1,973,213. 11 September 1934. H. Kuppenbender, M. Nowicki, E. Goldberg, and A. Mende. *Photographic camera with finder.* (Corresponds to British patents 386,230, 398,481, 401,328 and French patent 401,328.)

U.S. 2,225,433. 17 December 1940. *Photographic camera for flexible materials sensitive to light.* MAB 27. Applied for 18 October 1937. (In Luxemburg 23 October 1936.) (Cl. 95–31.)

U.S. 2,652,744. 22 September 1953. E. Goldberg, ass. to Bell & Howell, Co. *Photographic copying apparatus.* Filed 1 June 1950.

Notes

Abbreviations

BACZ: Betriebsarchiv Carl Zeiss Jena
CG: Chava Gichon, née Renate Eva Goldberg (Goldberg's daughter)
FG: Frances Goldberg (daughter-in-law)
G: Emanuel Goldberg
GP: Emanuel Goldberg's personal papers in the possession of Ms. Chava
    Gichon, Zahala, Tel Aviv, Israel
HG: Herbert Goldberg (son)
MG: Mordechai Gichon (son-in-law)
SG: Sophie Goldberg (wife)

Bibliographical references are to the General Bibliography, except for Emanuel Goldberg's own writings, indicated with prefix G (e.g., G1957), which are listed separately in the Goldberg Bibliography preceding the General Bibliography. In quotations, emphasis is always in the original, none has been added. Images for the illustrations were kindly made available by Herbert Goldberg or Chava Gichon. The original sources of the drawings and photographs are unknown, except as noted below.

Chapter 1: Origins

1   *The Memex project* Fairthorne (1958, 36; also 1961, 135).
2   *the confession of Moses* In the nuances of German at that time, *mosaische Konfession* ("of the confession of Moses") was considered more positive than *jüdische* ("Jewish") or *isrealitische* ("Israelite").
3   *Colonel Grigorii Goldberg* For Grigorii Goldberg, the only sources found are two photographs and a detailed transcript of his military record, handwritten in Russian, dated 1894, in the Goldberg Papers (GP) in the possession of Goldberg's daughter, Mrs. Chava Gichon.
3   *Order of St. Stanislaus* For Russian orders: *Order* (Undated); Durov (1990; 1993); Hazelton (1932); and Hurley (1935). I thank Dr. F. S. Stych for help.
3   *Kovno Encyclopaedia Britannica*, 11 ed. (1911, 15:921). Kovno Jewish community: Gilbert (1990, viii–ix) and Mendelsohn (1983, 213–17).

4 *Such promotion was very unusual for Jews.* For Jews in the Tsar's Army, see Petrovky-Shtern (2001), and, for Jewish officers, also Raskin (1998), who identified nine practicing Jews who became commissioned officers in combatant ranks between 1874 and 1917, one through merit and eight through influence. Jews who converted were no longer considered Jews; and those who, like Colonel Goldberg, were in a noncombatant corps, would have been considered separately. For Tsarist military officers more generally: Kenez (1973) and Rich (1998). For Jewish doctors in the Tsar's military medical corps, see Gessen (1910).

5 *Joseph Trumpeldor* His father was inducted into the army at age eight, but refused to convert to Christianity and raised his son as a Jew. Trumpeldor was also taken into the army, refused to convert, and become a highly decorated war hero in the Russian-Japanese war, losing an arm. He was promoted to officer rank in the field and in 1904 was later given an officer's commission in the army reserves. A Zionist activist, Trumpeldor moved to Palestine. During World War I, hoping that defeat of the Ottoman Empire would create the opportunity for establishing a Zionist state, he and Vladimir Jabotinsky persuaded the British government to accept a corps of Jews from the Ottoman Empire. He led the Zion Mule Corps, which assisted the British Army in Gallipoli. He and Jabotinsky formed a Zionist political party (Laskov 1972). An informal biography, which cites no sources, wrongly claims that Trumpeldor was the first-ever Jewish officer in the Tsar's Army (Freulich 1968, 48).

6 *Emanuel Goldberg's education* Memory, slow to speak: E. Goldberg letter to F. and H. Goldberg, 16 August 1968. "At age of six" is from his Technion acceptance speech (G1957).

6 *fête... Khodynka field* Ferro (1991, 37); Lieven (1994, vol. 2, 65–67).

Chapter 2: University Studies

9 *The years I spent* "Die Jahre, die ich an der Leipziger alma mater verbracht habe, gehören zu den schönsten Erinnerungen meines Lebens. Es war eine ausergewöhliche Zeit, als ich zum ersten Mal als armer russisch-jüdischer Jüngling im Jahre 1901 die Pforten des physikalisch-chemischen Instituts in der stillen Linné Strasse betrat. Eine neue Wissenschaft war im Enstehen. Junge Gelehrte der ganzen Welt versammelten sich dort, um von Wilhelm Ostwald in die Zusammenhänge zwischen Chemie und Physik eingeführt zu werden und von Wilhelm Wundt über

Zusammenhänge zwischen Leib und Seele zu hören. Die Kolloquien, an denen sich die berümtesten Gelehrten der Welt beteiligt haben, gaben uns die Richtlinie des Schaffens fürs ganze leben." (EG letter to Neef, 3 June 1956, GP).

9   *A quota* Family tradition. University admissions quotas for Jews were introduced in 1887: 10 percent in the Pale; 3 percent in Moscow and St. Petersburg; 5 percent elsewhere (Nathans 2002, 267). The certificate (Figure 2.1) is in GP.

11 *Electro-Plating Zinc* Goldberg's joint paper with Speranskii is G1900. For background, see Trescott (1981, xxiv, 17–19); also Smith (1918, 33) and Haynes (1954, 388).

11 *Alexander W. Speranskii* 1865–1919, graduated from Moscow University in 1888 and taught there before becoming a professor at the University of Kiev in 1907.

12 *Patents* for the solution are: Russia 8571; Germany 151,336; Great Britain 7,923, and U.S. 733,025; and for the vats: Germany 159,897. See Appendix C.

12 *Royalties* N. Goldberg (1969, 88); Beutler interview, 25 March 1995.

12 *Langbein* "Dr. G. Langbein & Co. Elektrochemische Fabrik, Dynamo- und Maschinenbauanstalt. Zweigniederlassungen: Berlin, Solingen, Mailand, Utrecht, Brüssel, Wien. Leipzig-Sellerhausen, den 25. Februar 190[?4]. Herrn Emanuel Goldberg, Physikalisches Institut, Leipzig, Lineestrasse. Hierdurch bestätigen wir Ihnen, dass wir Ihr patentiertes Verfahren zur 'Herstellung von Zinkniederschlägen' erworben haben und dass wir das Verfahren selbst verwenden und die Bäder dazu schon vielseitig an andere Leute geliefert haben. Wir können über die Wirkungsweise des Verfahrens bis dato uns nur lobend aussprechen und sind die Vorteile derart, dass wir unserer Kundschaft stetes die Anschaffung dieser Bäder empfehen. Hochtachtungsvoll!" (GP, with a similar letter from Russische Metallhandelsgesellschaft Isnoskow, Suckau & Co., Moscow, 1 October 1903.)

13 *Studies abroad* For German universities, see Thwing (1928); Johnson, J. A. (1990); and Nachmansohn (1979). Substantial equality: M. Gichon, 14 December 2002. Goldberg's movements have been reconstructed from the vita in Goldberg's doctoral dissertation, an undated resume in GP, official published lists of students for Göttingen and Leipzig, and other clues.

13 *Jewish Russian students* Treatment of Russian Jews see Jarausch (1982, chaps 5 and 6); Kampe (1985); Nathans (2002); and Wertheimer (1982, 1987).

14 *Wilhelm Lossen* 27 July 1900: "Herr Emanuel Goldberg hat während des Monats Juli im hiesigen chemischen

Universitätslaboratorium gearbeitet und sich speziell mit quantitativen Analysen beschäftigt. Er war stets unermüdlich fleissig, hat ein recht gutes Verständnis und Geschick für die sehr [*illegible:* ?aufmerksam] Arbeiten bewiesen." For Lossen: *J. C. Poggendorff's* (1863- :3:835; 4:916–17; 5:768).

14   *Institute for Physical Chemistry* Goldberg was at the Institute for Physical Chemistry headed by Wilhelm Ostwald in 1901, and his doctoral dissertation was approved early in 1906. Leipzig University's official list of students, the *Personal-Verzeichnis der Universität Leipzig,* lists Goldberg as a registered student only in nos. 146 and 147 for the winter and summer semesters of 1904/05. For Ostwald and his interest in the organization of science litera-ture, see Hapke (e.g., 1991, 1997, 1999, 2000, and 2003).

14   *Temperature and photochemical reactions* Goldberg explained the photographic origins of his research of the effects of tempera-ture in an interview with Norman Goldberg (1969, 88). Also mul-tiple personal communications, Herbert Goldberg. For Ostwald and chlorophyll: EG letter to H. Goldberg, 20 December 1966. The factor by which the speed of a chemical process increased with warmer temperature was called the temperature co-efficient.

15   *"A study"* is Beitrag (G1902).

15   *the Jahrbuch… noted* Jahrbuch 17(1903):416.

15   *"the rather detailed summary"* "Die etwas ausführliche Form des Referats mag durch den Wert der vorliegenden Arbeit für die wissenschaftliche Photochemie entschuldigt werden, für welche dieselbe zweifellos eine der ersten systematischen Anwendungen der chemischen Kinetik, jedenfalls auf völlig homogene lich-tempfindliche Systeme darstellt." (*Zeitschrift für wissenschaftli-che Photographie* 1, no. 1 [1903]:32–34). J. Plotnikow, aka I. S. Plotnikov, a fellow student of Goldberg in Moscow and in Leipzig, provides an explanation and a literature review of the effect of temperature on photochemical processes, stating (1921, 128), "E. Goldberg war der erste, der im Jahre 1902 darauf aufmerksam machte, dass die photochemischen Temperaturkoeffizienten einen kleinen, nahe an eins liegenden, Wert besitzen." Also: Bodenstein (1903, 32–34); Plotnikow (1912). For scattered ear-lier observations: Eder (1879).

15   *Robert Luther* Letter, no addressee, 27 July 190[?7], in GP: "Herr Goldberg had sich hierbei als guter Experimentator, mit getiegenen physikalisch-chemischen speziell photochemischen Kenntnissen erwiesen." For Luther: *J. C. Poggendorff's* (1958, 164–65).

16   *the Nernst lamp* was the only incandescent alternative to carbon filament lamps to be produced in quantity. It used a small rod of refractory metallic oxides as the illuminant (Bright 1949, 170–73).

16   *When I was a student* "Während meiner Studienzeit benutzte ich
     alle grösseren Ferien, um mir technische Kenntnisse anzeignen,
     und arbeitete zu diesem Zwecke praktische in elektrochemischen
     und Reproduktionstechnischen Betrieben" (In a typescript cur-
     riculum vitae ["*Lebenslauf*"], probably from 1917, in GP).
     "I was working" quoted in Noted scientist (1946). The London
     County Council School of Lithography and Engraving at 6 Bolt
     St served the newspaper industry in nearby Fleet Street. For A.
     J. Newton, see Amstutz (1906a); A. J. Newton (1932); and
     Collins (1990, 147). For Mees: Sipley (1965, 57–58); Browne
     and Partnow (1983, 410); Collins (1990).

16   *Figure 2.2* portrait of Luther, was kindly supplied by Prof. Klaus
     Mauersberger, Technical University, Dresden.

18   *Co-authored article* Robert Luther and Emanuel Goldberg.
     Beiträge zur Kinetik photochemischer Reaktionen. I.
     Sauerstoffhemmung der Photochemischen Chlorreaktionen in
     ihrer Beziehung zur photochemischen Induktion, Deduktion und
     Aktivierung. *Zeitschrift für Physikalische Chemie etc.* 56 (1906):
     43–56. "Teilweise erweiterter Auszug aus der inzwischen in der
     Zeitschr. für wiss. Photographie 4, 61 (1906) erschienen
     Dissertation von E. Goldberg." p.43, n1. No Part II found. Three
     publications in 1906, all starting with "Beiträge," reported
     Goldberg's dissertation research, see Goldberg Bibliography.
     Plotnikow (1920, 227–29) summarized the dissertation and
     praised it as an important step forward.

18   *reprinted* in Beiträge *ZwP* (G1906) with acknowledgement on
     p. 107: "The present work": "Vorliegende Arbeit wurde im
     physikalische-chemischen Institute von Prof. Ostwald in Leipzig
     ausgeführt. Es ist mir eine angenehme Pflicht, Herrn Subdirektor
     Prof. Luther für die Anregung zu dieser Arbeit und seine vielfachen
     Ratschläge meinen innigsten Dank auszusprechen."

18   *Wilhelm Wundt* Reed (1997). Toulmin (1990, 149–54) explains
     the significance of the research on sensory physiology by Wundt
     and others. Goldberg himself wrote on the physiology of vision:
     Farbenphotographie (G1908) and Physicalische (G1908).

19   *The years* Goldberg letter to Neef, 3 June 1956, GP. For text,
     see quotation note above.

Chapter 3: Berlin

21   *We have conquered* quoted in Cooley (1912, 11).
21   *Nobel prizes . . . articles in chemistry* Richards (1994, chap 1).
22   *Cooley* Cooley (1912).

22 *In Charlottenburg Encyclopaedia Britannica*, 11th ed. (1911, 5:946). For the Technical University in Charlottenburg: Cooley (1912; Emperor is quoted on p. 174); *Encyclopaedia Britannica* (1911, 3:788); and Mauersberger (1993). As technology center: Hall and Preston (1988, 123).

22 *Goldberg went to Charlottenburg* "Um insbesondere auf den Gebieten der Reproduktionstechnik und der wissenschaftlichen Photographie bei Prof. Dr. Miethe zu arbeiten" (Curriculum vitae in GP). For Adolf Miethe (1862–1927), see "Adolf Miethe" (1922); Stenger (1939); Hahn (1962); Baier (1963; 1964, 255–59, 659); Sipley (1965, 124–25); and Browne and Partnow (1983, 417); for his lab: Photochemische Laboratorium (1907).

23 *Photoengraving and halftone printing* Heidtmann (1984) provides a very detailed history of book illustration techniques associated with photography. Goldberg wrote on etching (Studien G1907; Herstellung G1913); on halftone printing (Richters G1907); and a commentary on articles in the *Inland Printer,* March–August 1906 by N. S. Amstutz (Arbeiten G1906); also Production (G1913). Goldberg's early writings on color printing include Physikalische (G1908) and *Farbenphotographie* (G1908).

24 *The moiré effect* Goldberg's initial analysis is Berechnung (G1906; also Etudes G1907). Moiré (G1907) includes revisions based on practical experience. His work is noted by Gasch (1959) and Tollenaar (1992). More generally, Amidror (2000, esp. 60–62); also Indebetouw and Czarnek (1992) and Oster (1965; 1969).

27 *Frederick E. Ives* Sipley (1965, 121–22); *Encyclopedia of Photography* (1984, 269–70).

27 *Military officers:* For the Militärtechnische Akademie see Paszkowski (1910, 142–44). Interviews with CG, MG, and HG, 7 March 1997; CG and MG, 30 November 1998. Goblet inscription: "Ihrem verehrten Lehrer Dr. E. Goldberg in dankbarer Erinnerung an gemeinsame Arbeit 1906–1907."

28 *Miethe . . . testimonial* Miethe memo, 16 May 1907, in GP: "Herr Dr. E. Goldberg ist seit Jahresfrist in meinem Laboratorium tätig. Schon noch wenigen Wochen habe ich erkannt, dass der genannte ein weit über das Mittelmass hinaus befähigter Chemiker von ungewöhnlichem allgemeinen Wissen ist und habe ihm daher sogleich einen Teil meines Unterrichts anvertraut, da er auf dem Gebiet der Photochemie und der Reproduktionstechnik sich als hervorragend tüchtig erwiesen hat. Goldberg hat dann in meinem Laboratorium eine Reihe von sehr schönen und originellen Arbeiten, die seine Fähigkeit, eigene Forschungen anzustellen,

deutlich bewiesen haben, verfasst und durch seine Ideen mir immer wieder Anlass gegeben, seinen vielseitigen und beweglichen Geist schätzen zu lernen. Im letzten Semester hat G. dann den Unterricht der Offiziere der Militärtechnsichen Akademie speziell auf dem Gebiet der Reproduktionstechnik geleitet und dabei gezeigt, dass er ein vorzüglicher Lehrer von unermüdlichem Fleiss ist, der seine Autorität seinen Schülern gegenüber sehr zu wahren weiss und dieselben lebhaft und erfolgreich anregt. Ich halte daher den genannten Herrn für sehr geeignet, eine grössere Versuchsanstalt selbständig zu leiten und dieselbe sowohl als Lehrinstitut fruchtbar zu machen, als auch durch seine Forschungen weiterbildend auf die photochemische und photomechanische Technik einzuwirken. Miethe. Vorsteher des Photochem. Laboratoriums d. Kgl. Technischen Hochschule zu Berlin."

Chapter 4: Sophie Posniak

This chapter draws heavily on discussions with C. and M. Gichon.

29   Ειν το παν Berthelot (1889, 132; 1909,113).
29   *George Posniak* grew up Mohilew, Russia (now Mogil'ov, Belarus) and Koenigsberg, Prussia (now Kaliningrad, Russia). He was sent to boarding school in Koenigsberg because he associated with the wrong people at home (H. Goldberg, 20 December 2002). He completed his doctorate in chemistry at Leipzig in 1910. A vita is in his dissertation (Posnjak 1910, 53).
29   *Nizhnii Novgorod Encyclopaedia Britannica,* 11th ed. (1911, 19:721–22).
31   *went to Leipzig* Chava Gichon and a certificate of completion of studies from the Koenigliche Conservatorium, Leipzig, 15 March 1907, in GP.
32   *Love and Warsaw* The surviving document, in GP, is a notarized German translation of the official declaration, in which her father's forename is given as Wulf, not Wladimir. For marriage laws, see Wertheimer (1987, 83–84).
32   *Koppelmann* Details of the Koppelmann family and the weddings in and near Warsaw are from an undated set of typescript documents in German by Max Koppelmann about his life and his family's history. I thank John Posniak, of Alexandria, VA, grandson of George Posniak, for showing me this typescript. "I know that the families were very upset, both of them, and they both wouldn't agree [to the marriage]"(CG 7 March 1997).

33 *Ouroboros* Cirlot (1971); for Ouroboros in the diagrams of Cleopatra, see Lindsay (1970, Chapter 12, esp. 260–61) and Roob (1997, 422); also Berthelot (1889, 132; 1909,113).

Chapter 5: Graphics

37 *A well-known scholar* Zeitler (1914, 23): "Ein namhafter Gelehrter von lebendigstem Forschergeist."

37 *Graphics and Industrial Design* General background on art and design is taken from Meggs (1983); also Heller and Fili (1998) and Heskett (1986).

38 *Graphic Arts Education* Cooley (1912) and Heskett (1986).

38 *Leipzig ... Academy* See its annual reports (Akademie. *Berichte,* 1906/07 onward); Köhler (1921, 111–13); and Seliger (1912, photo of Goldberg on p. 86). Also Sächsisches Staatsarchiv Leipzig. *Staatliche Akademie für graphische Künste und Buchgewerbe. Findbuch,* 1970; *Zweihundert Jahre* (1964); *Bibliographie zur Geschichte der Stadt Leipzig. Sonderband: Die Kunst* (1964) and *Sonderband: Das Buch* (1967); and Heidtmann (1984). *Buchgewerbe* does not translate well into English. It includes both book technology and the book trade, and so is broader than "bookcraft."

39 *Department of Photography* Emmerich (1910, 799–804) summarizes education programs in photography in the German-language countries.

41 *Figure 5.1* is from Seliger (1912, 90).

41 *Professor Goldberg* For the history of photography in the Leipzig Academy, including Goldberg's role, see Sachsse (1993); e.g., p.10: "Sein immenses publizistisches und didaktisches Talent verschaffte der Leipziger Akademie auf Anhieb Gehör in reprographischen Kreisen; binnen einen Jahres konnte er die Hörerzahl seiner Übungen auf den vierfachen Durchschnittswert von Aarland steigern." See also Photographische (G1912). The professorship was conferred by a royal certificate dated 14 October 1911. See the Akademie's *Berichte ... Schuljahre 1910–1912.*

43 *Offer not a secret* "Die kürzlich in photographischen Kreisen verbreitete Nachricht, daß der auch unseren Lesern als Mitarbeiter unseres Blattes wohlbekannte Forscher und Lehrer seine Stellung verlassen wolle, dürfte damit gegenstandlos geworden sein, was wir mit Vergnügen verzeichnen." (*Photographische Industrie,* Heft 47 [22 November 1911]: first page).

44 *Acquisition of equipment* For controversy over equipment: *Jahrbuch für Photographie* 25 (1911): 265–66).

44 *Dr. Mees Again* Correspondence in Eastman House Museum and Library, Rochester, NY: Mees to Goldberg 26 January 1912; G. Eastman to M. B. Philipp, 29 April 1912; Goldberg to Mees, 4 February 1912: "Lieber Dr. Mees! Ihr heutiger Brief hat auf mich wie 'ein Blitz aus heiterem Himmel' gewirkt. Ich würde alles andere erwarted können, nur nicht die Nachricht, dass Wratten & Wainright ihre Existenz verlassen und sich eine neue Heimat in Amerika suchen wollen. Da wie Sie schreiben Ihre Position eine 'remunerative and satisfactory' sein wird, so muss Ihnen aufrichtig gratulieren, wobei ich allerdings nicht Ihnen verheimlichen kann, dass Ihre Nachricht für all recht betrübend ist, denen unser altes Europa noch etwas lieb ist. Das Gesicht von Callier beim Empfang Ihrer Nachricht möchte ich gerne sehen. Andererseits kann ich rein persönlich Sie nur beneiden, da Amerika mein alter Traum ist, und Sie werden sich noch erinnern können, wie ich die Vorzüge Amerikas Ihnen gegenuber verteidigte habe. Wenn Sie mal dort einen Gehülfen brauchen, so denken Sie auch an mich. Vielleicht wird sich später noch dort unsre Zusammenarbeit ermöglichen lassen. Einer der mir wirklich leid tut ist Mr. Newton, der doch sicher Bolt Hall verlassen hat, um *Ihnen* zu helfen. Ich würde mich sehr interessieren zu hören, wann Sie England verlassen wollen. Mit besten Grüssen auch an Ihre Frau Gemahlin. Ihr E Goldberg." Goldberg to Mees, 3 March 1912: "Lieber Dr. Mees! Leider muss ich heute schreiben, dass ich nicht mit Ihnen jetzt nach Rochester gehen kann. Die Eltern meiner Frau wollen über diesen Plan nichts wissen, so dass jetzt auch meine Frau dagegen geworden ist. Ich hoffe, dass Sie einen viel besseren Mitarbeiter finden werden, als ich es sein könnte, und will aber trotzdem der Hoffnung Ausdruch geben, dass wenn nicht jetzt, so doch vielleicht in spaeteren Jahren wir einmal noch zusammen arbeiten werden können. Es würde mich recht sehr freuen, wenn Sie mir mal schreiben wuerden. wie Sie alles in Amerika gefunden haben. Inzwischen wuensche ich Ihnen glueckliche Reise und bitte mich Ihrer Frau zu empfehlen. Mit besten Grüssen, E. Goldberg." Response, Mees to Goldberg, 7 March 1912.

46 *"Looking back"* Quoted in "Noted scientist..." *Kodakery* (18 July 1946). For Mees and Kodak: Jenkins (1975, 306–18).

46 *Exhibitions* Cooley (1912, 181–84).

47 *"Lessons on vision"* "'Die Lehre vom Lichtsinn und dem Farben als Grundlagen der Photographie.' Sammlung von Apparaten zum Selbstanstellen von versuchen aus den Gebieten der Optik und der Farbenlehre, hergestellt von Schülern der Abteilung für photographischen Reproduktion der Königl. Akademie unter

der Leitung von Dr. E. Goldberg." Goldberg also mounted an exhibit on the moiré effect, and Seliger, very likely with Goldberg's help, mounted an exhibit of 82 images showing comparatively the varied effects of different imaging techniques. Details are in the official exhibition catalog: Dresden. Internationale Photographische Ausstellung (1909, 53–64; also for moiré, 67 and for Seliger, 167–71).

47 *"Perhaps the most eloquent testimony"* British Journal of Photography 56 (1909): 418.

47 *ineligible on bureaucratic grounds* Explained with reproach in: Die photographischen Fachschulen (1909, 501–2).

47 *Oskar von Miller* Letter to Goldberg, 2 November 1909, in GP: "Nach München züruckgekehrt, möchte ich nicht versäumen, nochmals meiner Freude Ausdruck zu geben, dass ich Jhre musterhaft organisierten Demonstrations Einrichtung Über die verschiedenen Erscheinungen der Farbentheorie bewundern konnte." Planetarium: Miller to Goldberg, 14 June 1912, and 1 July 1912. The following year Miller approached Carl Zeiss Jena, who designed and installed a planetarium, opened in 1923.

47 *Numerous guides* included three in 1909 on the Dresden exhibition and, 1914, a guide and four other reports on the Bugra exhibition in Leipzig.

48 *Bugra Bibliographie* (1964, *Sonderband* 3:312–21); *Weltgalerie* (1989, 16–24).

49 *"As is known"* Photographische Rundschau 52 (1915):72–73: "Wie bekannt, hatte Prof. Dr. E. Goldberg cbenso wie in Dresden 1909, so auch der Leipziger Ausstellung im Vorjahre eine höchst beachtenswerte Sammlung aus der Gebieten der wissenschaftlichen und technischen Photographie organisiert. . . . Diese Objekte sollen nunmehr den Grundstock für die Errichtung eines photographischen Museums bilden. Herr Prof. Goldberg ist gewiss eine berufenen Persönlichkeit, ein derartiges Unternehmen ins Werk zu setzen und auch mit Erfolg zu leiten . . . "

49 *Deutsche Bibliotekar- und Museumsbeamten-Schule* see Bekanntmachung (1915). Course titles were "Photographie mit praktischer Einführung in das Photographieren," "Über die öffentliche Kunstplege, das Sammelwesen und die Aufgaben der Kunst- und gewerblichen Museen," "Geschichte des Buches und Buchgewerbekunde," "Geschichte der Schrift," and "Einfuehrung in die deutsche und ausländische Literatur der letzten Jahrzehnte vom Standpunkt des Büchereiverwalters."

49 *3 March 1917* Museum (1917); Museum of Culture: Deutsche (1918); Technical Committee: Verwaltungsrat (1918, 89).

49 *displayed again in 1932* Sachsse (1993, 10n51).

49 *bombing of Leipzig* Lothar Poethe e-mail to V. Petras, 23 August 2002.

50 *entire field of reprographics* Reviews include Reproduktionstechnik (G1909); Photomechanischen (G1912); Photomechanischen (G1913); Graphische (G1914); and a series entitled "Die photomechanischen Vervielfältigungsverfahren im Jahre" (G1908; G1910; G1911). Popular introductions: *Farbenphotographie* (G1908) and *Grundlagen* (G1912). The chapter on photomechanical processes is "Photomechanische Illustrations-Verfahren" (G1910).

50 *Research Institute* A list of contents for a teaching museum in reprographics and a proposal for a research institute (*An das Königliche Ministerium des Innern, IIIte Abteilung, Dresden. Vorschlag und Entwurf für die Errichtung einer graphischen und buchgewerblichen Versuchsanstalt im Anschluss an die Akademie für graphische Künste und Buchgewerbe in Leipzig, 9 April 1913*) are in the Sächsisches Staatsarchiv, Leipzig, Series No 6: *Staatliche Akademie für graphische Kunst und Buchgewerbe.*

51 *Figure 5.4 Minerva* 1 (1914):5. We thank Ms. Julia Blume, Leipzig, for the identifications.

Chapter 6: The Goldberg Wedge

53 *The device* "...dispositif universellement connu sous le nom de 'coin de GOLDBERG.'" (*Formation* G1926, 173).

53 *The Characteristic Curve* Goldberg's writings for a general audience include Photographie (G1912); Möglichkeiten (G1930); and, with H. Socher, Photographie (G1932). Specialized writings include color photography: *Farbenphotographie* (G1908) and *Farbenphotographie* (G1913); lighting: Beleuchtung (G1912); photometry and sensitometry: Photometrie (G1912); Photometrischen (G1918); and Bewertung (G1921); shutters: Ueber (G1907) and Zur Frage (G1927); and lenses: Objectiv (G1917).

54 *Figure 6.1* was kindly drawn by Vivien Petras. See also notes for Chapter 9.

55 *1910...in Brussels* International Congress of Photography. (5th, Brussels, 1910). (1912).

55 *The Goldberg Wedge* Goldberg's papers on his wedge were numerous: In German: Herstellung (G1910); Über (G1910); Herstellung (*ZfwPP* G1911); Herstellung (*Jahrbuch* G1911); and *Aufbau* (G1925, Anhang 2); in English: Preparation (G1910) and Gray (G1923); and in French Préparation (G1910);

Préparation (G1911); Sur (G1911); and Préparation (G1912). Use of a wedge is illustrated in *Führer* (G1914, 5). The Goldberg Wedge is noted in: *Encyclopaedic* (1961, v3:483); *Focal Encyclopedia* (1993, 336); *Handbuch* (1929–33, v4:111–13; v5:162); and other reference works. The history of gelatin wedges is summarized by Formstecher in *Handbuch* (1930, Bd 4:111–13).

56 *"constructed on the principle"* Encyclopaedia Britannica, 11th ed. (1911, 21:531 s.v. Photometry—The wedge photometer).

56 *egg white* On Goldberg's Wedge, and use of fresh egg white as a mold releasing agent: N. Goldberg (1969, 89). Gautier (1902) examined the tendency of egg whites to form membranes. On albumen and albumen coatings: *Albumen Photographs* (2000).

57 *exposed silver grains Aufbau* (G1925, Anhang 2).

57 *editorial note British Journal of Photography* 57 (26 August 1910):648.

58 *"crossed wedge method"* Eder (1920, 25) has a concise explanation and a good illustration. Also Luther (1910); Goldberg, Luther and Weigert (G1910); Mees (1942, 623–25).

59 *detail plate* Haferkorn (1990, 62–63). Aufbau (G1925, 71–77).

59 *The Densograph* Goldberg's accounts of the densograph were widely published. See Goldberg Bibliography for titles beginning with "Densograph" in the years 1910, 1912, 1923, and 1924; also Zeiss Ikon (1935a).

60 *Figure 6.2* Drawings are from G1910 Densograph *Zeitschrift für Reproduktionstechnik* 12, Heft 4 (1910):52, except lower right, which is from G1910 Densograph. *British Journal of Photography* 57, no. 2625 (25 August 1910):649. The same drawings were used in several publications. The curved lines on the graphs are misleading, because the densograph produced only a series of pricked holes.

61 *Figure 6.3* Photograph kindly supplied by Professor Klaus Mauersberger, Technical University, Dresden.

61 *patent* German patent 250,062. 6 August 1912. *Apparat zur selbsttätigen Registrierung der örtlichen Unterschiede in der Lichtabsorption oder Lichtemission von Gegenständen,* and Gebrauchsmuster 527,621. 23 October 1912. *Photometer zur Auswertung örtlicher Unterschiede von Lichtintensitäten, insbesondere zur Messung der Schwärzung photographischer Schichten.*

62 *The Spectrodensograph* Spektrodensograph (G1926 and G1927); and *Jahrbuch für Photographie* 31 (1928–29):I, 251. Callier is known for the "Callier Effect" (*Handbuch* 1929–33, Bd 5:153–54). Goldberg also developed an improved version of

the Martens photometer (Martens 1901), the Martens-Goldberg Schwärzungsmesser, see Umconstruktion (G1916); also *Schwärzungsmesser* (no date).

63   *Paul Otlet and Microfiche:* For Otlet, LaFontaine and the Institute for International Bibliography see Otlet (1934, 1990); Rayward (1976, 1986) and Levie (2002). For microfiche: Goldschmidt and Otlet (1906), English translation in Otlet (1990, 87–95), conveniently summarized in Gradewitz (1910).

63   *serve as catalog cards* This idea was taken up by Bendikson (1933) and Rider (1944).

63   *portable library of "microphotic books"* Goldschmidt and Otlet (1925), English translation in Otlet (1990, 204–10).

63   *Ostwald and Hypertext* Writings by and about Ostwald are extensive. Johnson (1990) provides context. See Behrends (1995) for documentation in Germany; also Buder (1976). For Ostwald and Die Brücke see work by Hapke (1991, 1997, 1999, 2000, and 2003); also Bonitz (1979); Hold (1977); Lewandrowski (1979); Sachsse (1998); and Satoh (1987). Bührer, Ostwald, and Saager wrote numerous publications about Die Brücke in 1911 and 1912, the main manifesto being Bührer and Saager (1911). The world brain idea is in Ostwald (1912). Serres (1995) provides a good concise history of hypertext, identifying five different historical origins and mentioning Goldberg. See also Rayward (1994a; 1994b).

65   *"In 1911"* Eder (1932, 628–29): "Im Jahre 1911 gab Prof. Emanuel Goldberg in Leipzig eine verbesserte Art der Herstellung solcher Graukeile an, die später allgemein Eingang fand und als großer Fortschritt in der Herstellung zu bezeichnen war. Allerdings war die Priorität Stolzes, der längst verstorben war, in Vergessenheit geraten, so daß Eder für den verstorbenen und seine Priorität eintreten mußte." For Eder see Browne and Partnow (1983, 167–69); Sipley (1965, 33–34). For Stolze and his gelatin wedge, see Baier (1964, esp. 347–50), which includes excerpts from Stolze's account (1893), but not the paragraph (Stolze 1893, 18–19) on how Stolze made them.

66   *Eder-Hecht Neutral Wedge Photometer* Eder (1920; also 1921) and Spencer (1973, 185).

66   *It should not go unmentioned Der Aufbau* (G1922, 94, fn 2): "Es soll nicht unerwähnt bleiben, dass Eder und Hecht es vorgezogen haben, das *in der gesamten Fachwelt* unter dem Namen Goldbergkeil bekannte Hilfsmittel mit ihren eignen Namen zu bezeichnen." French ed. (G1926, 173): "L'auteur tient à observer que EDER & HECHT ont préféré donner leurs noms au dispositif universellement connu sous le nom de 'coin de GOLDBERG.'" Also: Response (G1927). Eder-Hecht wedge

widely used: Sipley (1965, 34). Reprinted letter in encyclopedia: Eder (1932, 629).

67 *"But the most important"* Excerpt from the committee recommending conferral of the Peligot Medal: "Mais la plus importante de découvertes du professeur Goldberg qui a rendu son nom populaire parmi les photographes est celle du 'coin' sensitométrique qu'il présenta au Congrès International de Photographie de Bruxelles de 1910. Vous savez tous quelles facilités ce coin a apporté aux études sensitométriques et quel auxiliaire précieux il constitue dans un grand nombre d'appareils photométriques. Une application immédiate du coin dans son 'Densograph' mit à la disposition des laboratoires de sensitométrie une méthode rapide de mesures photométriques et de tracé automatique des courbes caractéristiques des émulsions." *Bulletin de la Société Française de Photographie et de Cinématographie* 3. ser., t. 18 (Juin 1931):123.

68 *Traill Taylor Memorial Lecture* Secretary of the Royal Photographic Society [name illegible] to Goldberg, 7 July 1914, in GP.

68 *Mees wrote* Mees to Goldberg, 5 October 1914, in GP.

Chapter 7: The Great War

69 *enemy alien* On citizenship for Jews in Germany see Wertheimer (1987, 42, 58).

69 *"In the present"* "In der gegenwärtigen ernsten Stunde empfinde ich das Bedürfnis das Kgl. Ministerium ganz ergebenst zu bitten den in meiner Bestallungsurkunde vom 25 November 1911 eingesetzten Vorbehalt, die Nichtaufnahme in die sächsische Staatsangehörigkeit betr., gütigst zurücknehmen zu wollen. Als Sohn einer deutschen Mutter, die ihre preussische Staatsangehörigkeit bei der Verheiratung verloren hatte, habe ich vom 15. September 1907 dem sächsischen Staate treu und nach besten Kräften zu dienen versucht. Schon früher habe ich ... die Ehre gehabt den Unterrricht der Offiziere der Kgl. Militär-Technischen Akademie in der Reproduktionstechnik zu führen. Es ist für mich ausserordentlich schmerzlich trotzdem als ein Angehöriger eines feindlichen Staates betrachtet zu werden." Goldberg to Seliger, 3 August 1914 (Sächsisches Staatsarchiv, Leipzig, Series Staatliche Akademie für graphische Künste und Buchgewerbe, 37).

70 *Robert Luther* For Luther and the Institute for Scientific Photography at the Technical University in Dresden: Luther

(1934); Leubner (1955); Reuther (1955; 1968); Sipley (1965, 49–50); and Mauersberger (2000b).

70 *"a little rivalry"* "Da war immer eine kleine Rivalität zwischen Prof. Luther und seinem Freund Prof. Dr. Goldberg aus Leipzig. Prof. Goldberg war ein vorzüglicher Konstrukteur und Bastler. Und wenn Prof. Goldberg zu besuch ins W.P.I. kam, da fand man die beiden Freunde stets in der Werkstatt, wo sie versuchten, sich durch kleine Finessen an der Werkbank zu übertrumpfen." (Leubner 1955, 32).

70 *Early Aerial Photography* Ives (1920); Hugershoff (1930, 217–22); and Babington Smith (1961). The *Jahrbuch für Photographie und Reproduktionstechnik* included annual survey of advances in aerial photography, especially from 1904. From balloons: Miethe (1909; 1916). White (1990, 181, 221) reports photography from balloons in the Russo-Japanese war in 1904.

72 *aerial photography from a kite* Bois (1906) is a good, detailed account; also *Dictionnaire militaire* (1908–11, s.v. Cerf-volant: *Suppl.* 116–17; Photographie en ballon: *Suppl.* 303–5); and Thiele (1903).

73 *Sallaumines* Peters, 18 January 1916, in GP: "Herr Professor Dr. Goldberg...hat liebenswürdiger Weise kostenlos die von der Firma Braun, Berlin hergestellte und in unbrauchbaren Zustande abgelieferte photographische Drachenkamera wiederhergestellte, sodass sie jetzt ausgezeichnet funktioniert. Um die Drachenkamera praktisch auszuprobiern, hat Herr Professor Dr. Goldberg sich persönlich an die Front zur Feldluftschiffer Abteilung 7 begeben (15.—18. 1.1916). Die Kamera funktionerte in jeder beziehung ausgezeichnet, wie die praktische Versuche beim Drachenaufstieg ergeben haben."

73 *Field Balloon Unit* For military kite balloons, see Christienne and Lissarrague (1986, Chapter 11); United States (1919); and Widmer (1917); also Forty (2002, 60–61); Kennett (1991, photo after p. 116). Christienne (1989) has mainly French sources.

73 *6 × 9 cm camera* N. Goldberg (1969, 89), reporting on an interview with Goldberg, refers to 1917 "during the trench warfare in Belgium," but the contemporary evidence indicates early 1916 in northern France: "The army wanted a better idea of what enemy trench lines looked like. Goldberg lashed a 6 × 9-cm folding camera to a balloon so that it hung down, pointing at the ground. He then devised a clockwork device for it so that after it was aloft, the shutter would be tripped. Although the camera had to be brought down for reloading after each exposure..." Also H. Goldberg (7 March 1997) and E. Kaprelian (18 May 1997).

73 *"serial images (cinematography from aircraft)"* "Arbeiten, die später zum Reihbildner (Kinomatographie aus Luftfahrzeugen) führten, waren die photographischen Aufnahmen von grossen Drachen aus" (Ein Weg [G1932, 160]; reprinted as Appendix A.3). Also: Noted (1946).

74 *Figure 7.1* is from Widmer (1917).

74 *I was called upon* Goldberg "When asked" typescript (GUndated).

74 *Ernst Wandersleb* J. C. *Poggendorff's* (1961, VIIIa, Teil 4:854); Gubas (1999b); and balloon photography: Brogiato and Horn (2003). Portrait (Figure 7.2) kindly supplied by Lawrence J. Gubas.

74 *"In spring 1916"* Wandersleb (1957, [1]): "im Frühjahr 1916, stieß ich auf Goldbergs Spuren in den deutschen Schützengräben an der Westfront in der nähe von Douai, . . . wo man des Lobes unter Anerkennung für wertvolle Ratschläge Goldbergs voll war; kurz vorher war er dort gewesen auf Anregung seines schon langjährigen befreundeten Fachkollegen aus der Ostwaldschule, Prof. R. Luther, damals Unteroffizier in einem Luftschifferbataillon, . . . "

75 *Lens testing device* Méthode (G1926) and New method (G1926); also N. Goldberg (1969, 89).

76 *"From summer 1916"* Resume in GP: "Von Sommer 1916 bis zum Sommer 1917 war ich auf Aufforderung der Carl Zeiss Werke zur Bearbeitung militär-wissenschaftlicher Aufgaben nach Jena beurlaubt, führte aber den Unterricht in Leipzig weiter. Vom Herbst 1915 bis zum Frühjahr 1917 habe ich als Dozent der Hochschule für Frauen in Leipzig [*illegible:* ?Vorlesungen] und praktische Uebungen über wissenschaftliche Photographie und mikrophotographie abgehalten."

76 *Women's University* Köhler (1921, 110–11: "Die Hochschule für Frauen will durch einen auf wissenschaftlicher Grundlage beruhenden Lehrbetrieb Frauen, die sich a) zu Lehrerinnen an Anstalten zur Ausbildung von Kindergärtnerinnen, Jugendleiterinnen und dergl., b) für eine soziale breufstätigkeit, c) für leitended Stellungen in der Krankenpflege, d) zu Assistantinnen an medizinischen und naturwissenschaftlichen Instituten und entsprechenden industriellen Betrieben."); also *Bibliographie zur Geschichte der Stadt Leipzig.* 2. Hauptband, 135.

76 *imperfections on optical surfaces* N. Goldberg (1969, 89); H. Goldberg 7 March 1997 and 13 April 2002.

76 *Goldberg mirror* Gebrauchsmuster 332,653, applied for on 23 June 1917, issued 7 February 1921. Firma Carl Zeiss Jena. *Speigel, der dazu bestimmt ist, an der Erzeugung optischer Bilder teilzunehmen.* (Kl 42h—Gr. 8). The Carl Zeiss Betriebsarchiv

catalog record for this patent has a note: *Goldbergscher Spiegel. Erfinder Goldberg.* ("Goldberg mirror: Inventor: Goldberg."). Gleichen (1918) is a convenient contemporary account of optics and optical instruments.

77 *Moving On* Correspondence on resignation and lathe is in what survives of his personnel file at the academy, now in the Sächsische Staatsarchiv, Leipzig, Series *Staatliche Akademie für graphische Künste und Buchgewerbe, Personal-Akten Nr 37: Professor Dr Goldberg.*

78 *Guido Mengel* Heinrich Ernemann (1935); Zeiss Ikon AG (1937, 125); and Wandersleb (1946).

78 *List on Sylt* Commission interalliée (1922, v1, p. 63); and Sonderkommission (1917).

79 *among the earliest German military aerial photographs* M. Gichon, personal communication, 1994.

Chapter 8: Ica and the Kinamo

81 *He drew on his Greek* N. Goldberg (1969, 89), which has more on the design of Kinamo.

81 *Dresden Encyclopaedia Britannica* 1911, s.v. Saxony, 24:265–73, gives Dresden's population in 1905 as: Town: 514, 283; District: 1,216, 489. Also: Leipzig: Town: 502,570; district: 1,146,423.

82 *Photocity* For the photographic industry in Germany, see Kühn (1928) and History (1956, incl. Carl Zeiss 142–43; Zeiss Ikon 154–55); and in Dresden: Dresden die Photostadt (1935) and Blumtritt (2000).

82 *Hermann Krone* Hesse and Starl (1998) and Krone (1998).

83 *Ica* Kühn (1928) and Blumtritt (2000).

83 *Treaty of Versailles ... restrictions* Whaley (1984).

83 *Innovations* Ica patent information derived from German patent office lists. More than half were Gebrauchsmuster. See Gispen (1989; 2002) for German patent law history.

84 *Figure 8.2 Self-focusing enlarger* U.S. Patent 1,573,314 of 26 February 1926.

85 *The Kinamo* Goldberg published papers on amateur cinematography (Entwicklung G1928); the use of glowlamps (Glühlampe G1923); filming cloud movements (Kinematographische G1926); the illusion of movement (Bewegungssynthese G1926); and movie sound technology (Physikalischen G1931; Grundlagen G1932); and movie gate temperature (Measurement G1926).

85 *Monopol projector* Kinematographische Apparate (2001).

86 *"While we other comrades"* Wandersleb (1957, [2]): "wahrend wir anderen Kameraden uns abends auf der behaglichen Schwarzwasseralphütte mit Essen, Trinken, Rauchen, Singen zugute taten, froh, allen Geschäften fern zu sein, packte Goldberg aus dem Rucksack ein ganzes Arsenal von kleinem Werkzeug aus und bastelte stundenlang an dem mitgebrachten ersten 'Kinamo'-Modell, einer neuen Aufnahmekinokammer, die er gerade in Dresden ausarbeitete."

86 *compact 35 mm movie cameras* The Debrie Sept, a spring-driven 35 mm camera marketed in 1921, held 5 meters of film, enough to film for only 17 seconds. The hand-cranked Kinamo appeared in 1921. Spring-driven cameras included the Kinamo in 1922, the Bell & Howell Eyemo in 1923, and the Cine-Kodak Model B in 1925 (Entwicklung G1928; Zeiss Ikon (1937, 81); Kuball (1980); Coe (1981, 86, 168); Katelle (1986, 51); and Filmmuseum Potsdam (2001).

86 *malfunctioned at very low temperatures* HG, 23 June 2002.

86 *When the camera British Journal of Photography* (23 September 1932):582–83.

87 *Figure 8.4 Kinamo N25* is copied from an undated advertisement.

87 *safety film* At the 1928 International Congress on Photography, Mees announced that Agfa, Kodak, and Zeiss Ikon had agreed that they would make 16 mm film, which was increasingly in use for amateur moviemaking, only of nonflammable "safety film."

87 *Promoting amateur movies* Publicity from an undated sales flyer entitled *Ica Kinamo,* circa 1922–25, issued by the Ica's U.S. agent, Harold M. Bennett, New York, offering the Kinamo models for $85-$135 and from publicity reprinted in Kuball (1980, 61–70).

88 *One can easily take it* Liebhabekinematographie (1923): "Man kann ihn also wie diese bequem auf allen Ausflügen, Spaziergängen und Reisen mitfuhren.... Handhabung is äusserst einfach; man braucht kein erfahrener Amateur zu sein, um gute Aufnahmen zu erzielen, da die Fertigstellung der Filme ja in jeder guten Photohandlung übernommen wird. Welch lockende Ausblicke eröffnet das Arbeiten mit einem Kinamo für den Familienchronik!"

88 *Bezee-Photo-Mitteilungen* was a magazine published monthly by Photohaus Bezee, Leipzig, 1924 onward. The only copy located (Leipzig University Library, Oek u. Techn. 2222s) lacks the pages (II. J. [1926]:145–48) containing Goldberg's paper "Kinematographische Wolkenaufnahmen" (G1926).

88   *short movies* Herbert Goldberg owns 16 mm copies of four
        shorts. Other copies have not been found. Dolomites
        (H. Goldberg, 8 March 1997).

88–96   *Figures 8.5–8.12* are digital copies of frames of Herbert
        Goldberg's 16 mm copies, made with the help of Professor Marc
        Davis, Berkeley.

91   *the kinamo has been credited* "Mit dieser Kamera wurde das
        Filmen unter den wohlhabenden Amateuren populär" (Kuball
        1980, 62).

92   *Joris Ivens* For Ivens in Dresden (Ivens 1969, 17, 26–28); Schoots
        (2000, 29); and Ivens and Destanque (1982, 43: "Dans un atelier
        de mécanique, un homme me fit un grand impression : le profes-
        seur Goldberg. C'était un inventeur et il venait de mettre au point
        un merveilleux petit caméra, la fameuse Kinamo, une caméra pro-
        fessionelle 35 mm à ressort, d'une robustesse and d'une précision
        étonnante pour l'époque. De cet homme j'ai appros le principes
        élémentaires de ce genre de méchanique et j'ai touché aux secrets
        de sa fabrication." And 70–71: "Mais il avait de mieux, avec ma
        caméra à la main, la merveilleuse Kinamo du professeur Goldberg,
        je m'étais naturellement libéré de la rigidité du trépied, et j'avais
        donné le mouvement à ce qui, normalement, aurait dû être une
        succession de plans fixes. Sans le savoir, en filmant en souplesse
        et en continuité, j'avais réalisé un plan séquence. Ce jour-là, j'ai
        pris conscience que la caméra était un oeuil et je me suis dit: 'Si
        c'est un regard, il faut qu'il soit vivant.'").

93   *"To me the Bridge"* Ivens (1969, 26). Also: Ivens and Destanque
        (1982, 71–74) and Schoots (2000, 41–42). Ivens (1996) includes
        a reissue of *The Bridge*.

94   *Other moviemakers* For Erwin Anders's reminiscence of Goldberg,
        see Karger-Decker (1959, 466–67). Bernt Berg: H. Goldberg
        communication (2002). Werner Sell: Kuball (1980, I, 74–77).

94   *Goldberg Mikrophot Microscope Attachment* For illustrated
        accounts: Rikli (1925, 1926). For use of the Kinamo at the
        Amsterdam telephone exchange, see Chapter 14.

95   *popular technical writing* Grundlagen (G1923); Kampmann
        (G1927).

96   *effect of atmospheric haze Aufbau* (G1922, 19–26); Eastman
        Kodak (1923); and Hugershoff (1930, 117).

97   *Figure 8.13 Student's cartoon of Goldberg* from souvenir volume
        *Herrn Prof. Dr. E. Goldberg—aus Dankbarkeit gewidmet. Die
        Ureinwohner vom Vikartal. Alpenskikurs Ostern 1927.* [Dedicated
        to Herr Prof. Dr. Emanuel Goldberg in gratitude [by] the original
        inhabitants of Vikartal, Alpenskikurs, Easter 1927] in GP.

97 *faculty appointment* For Robert Luther, the Institute for Scientific Photography, and local industry: Luther and Staude (1935); Prof. Dr. Robert Luther (1955); Reuther (1968); Schmidt (1968); *Geschichte* (1978, 146); Mauersberger (1998; 2000b; 2002). Inaugural lecture: Kinematographie (G1921).

97 *course on Cinematography* Outlines for the summer semester, 1930, survive in GP.

97 *interests extending broadly across photography* Schmidt (1968).

97 *Bald* Sprung (1927).

Chapter 9: The Goldberg Condition

99 *"The basic reproduction law"* Kaprelian (1971, 3).

99 *The Gamma* For an explanation of the Characteristic Curve, see Chapter 6.

100 *The Goldberg Condition* Mutter (1955, 216–17); Narath (1957, 261–68); Spencer (1973, 267); and Haferkorn (1990, 142). The same principle was also reached, perhaps independently, by L. A. Jones of Eastman Kodak who pioneered graphical solutions known as Quadrant (or Jones') Diagrams (Jones 1920, 61).

101 *Francke's Lexikon* Francke (1969, v1, p. 601): "**Goldberg-Bedingung** betrifft die richtige photographischc Wiedergabe von Leuchtdichten (Helligkeitswerten, Tonwerten) beim Kopierprozeß. Sie lautet $\gamma_N \gamma_P = 1$ oder allgemeiner $G_N G_P = 1$, wo γ_N und γ_P die Gammawerte der Schwärzungskurven des Negative- bzw. Positivprozesses darstellen; G_N, G_P sind die Gradationen (Neigung) dieser Kurve in dem zur Verwendung kommenden Punkte. Qualitativ besagt die G. B., daß zu einem 'weichen' Negativ ein 'hartes' Kopierpapier oder eine harte Entwicklung des Positivs notwendig ist und umgekehrt, damit die vom Positiv remittierten oder vom Diapositiv durchgelassenen Leuchtdichten verschiedener Bildteile sich ebenso verhalten wie die Leuchtdichten in die Natur."

102 *referred to as the Goldberg Constant* e.g., *Jahrbuch für Photographie,* by Eder, 31, I (1929):246; Formstecher (1927, 286–87).

102 *simpler... formulation* Herbert Goldberg's formulation: Draw a right angled triangle ABC on the righthand side of the Characteristic Curve such that a section, C, the straight part of the Characteristic Curve, is the hypotenuse, and the other two

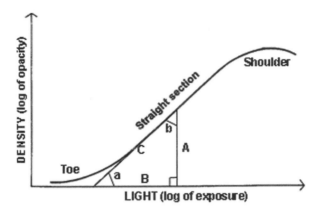

Figure N.1. Trigonometry of the Gamma.

sides, A and B, are parallel to the axis and abscissa respectively. (See Figure N.1.) The Gamma of the slope of C, γ_C, is A / B. Tan_a also = A / B. Because the triangle ABC is right-angled, Tan_b = B / A, so $\text{Tan}_a \times \text{Tan}_b$ = 1 and Tan_b = 1 / Tan_a. The Goldberg Condition for C is satisfied by another slope D when $\gamma_C \times \gamma_D$ = 1, hence γ_D = 1 / γ_C and so = 1 / Tan_a = Tan_b. When Tan_b = 1 / Tan_a, $\angle a + \angle b$ = 90° and $\angle a$ = 90° − $\angle b$ and the angles of the Gammas must average 45°.

102 *Movie Soundtracks* For the Gamma in movie soundtracks, see Kellogg (1945; 1955). It was not relevant to the alternative "variable area" technique. Quotation from Wheeler (1963, 162–63). The reflectance of the screen would be relevant to the Gamma to the extent to which the image is diffused.

103 *efficient high-fidelity reproduction* See *Der Aufbau* (G1922, 7–8, 10–11); and, for sound reproduction, Lastra (2000).

104 *Der Aufbau des photographischen Bildes* Five versions were published: first edition in 1922; second edition, 1925; French translations in 1924 and 1925; and Russian in 1929. Details in Goldberg Bibliography.

104 *Finally the speaker* "Schliesslich gedachte der Vortragende seiner in dem bekannten Werke 'Der Aufbau des photographischen Bildes' zusammengestellten Arbeiten auf sensitometrischem Gebiet, aus deren Fülle die 'Goldberg-Bedingen' gerade in jüngster Zeit durch den Tonfilm zu aktuellster Bedeutung gelangt ist." (Physikalischen Grundlagen G1931).

Chapter 10: Microdots

The principal sources are Goldberg's own papers; White (1992; also 1989 and 1990); and G.W.W. Stevens (1968).

105　*"If I were a rich man"* Gesell (1926, 98).

105　*Sharpness of Details* Goldberg's papers on halation are Lichthof (G1916 and G1917). Other papers relating to resolution are Detailwiedergabe (G1909); Studien (G1909); Unschärfe (G1911); Auflösungsvermögen (Schärfenwiedergabe) (G1912); Auflösungsvermögen von (G1912); and Auflösungsvermögen (G1913); in English, On the resolving power (two papers in G1912); and, in French, Etudes (G1913) and Auflösungsvermögen ... Pouvoir (G1914).

106　*Microphotography* Anfertigung (G1917 and G1919).

107　*Figure 10.1* based on Anfertigung (G1917) was kindly drawn by Vivien Petras.

108　*"Opposite me"* Klemperer (1996, 11–12: "Mir gegenüber, galizisches Deutsch sprechend, ein Professor *Goldberg,* Director der Ica-Werke (photograph.-Unternehmen). Er war erst peinlich durch sein eng positivistisches Wesen—man werde Psyche berechnen lernen wie elektrischen Strom—erzählte dann höchst interessant von Forstchritten der verkleinerungsphotographie u. von der sicheren Zukunft der Bibliotheken. Man bringe heute schon 10 000 Druckseiten in gut lesbarer mikropscopischer Schrift auf dem Durchmesser eines frühstückstellers unter. Man wird eine Bibliothek in der brieftasche tragen. In den Lesesälen werden Mikroscope stehen, man wird durch Kurbeln die betreffenden Seiten einstellen." Other references to Goldberg on p. 347 ("Geradezu galizisch"), 423–24, and 443–44. Klemperer's later diaries (1995; English translation 1998) for 1933–45 mention Zeiss Ikon but not Goldberg.

108　*without any accent* Lack of accent (e.g., Aviva Kelton, 11 May 1998). Grandmother's letter: M Gichon 7 March 1997. Thierfelder (1938, v1, 123–26) discusses German in Poland.

108　*speech by Erich Bethe* Klemperer (1996, 443): "Dann die Clou. Bethe, Leipziger Rector, griff uns, die Kuturwissenschaftlicher Abteilung, mit plumpen Entgleisungen an. Fachschule, Fachbildung! Nicht Allgemeinbildung." Herbert Goldberg remembers his parents discussing Bethe's speech (13 April 2002).

109　*M. G. Labussière* M. G. Labussière, Commission Permanente des Congrès Internationaux de Photographie, Paris, to C.E.K. Mees, 17 January 1925; and C.E.K. Mees, to Labussière, 4 February

1925 (George Eastman House Museum Library, Mees personal correspondence); also VI. Internationaler (G1925).

109 *Mikrat nach Goldberg* For Goldberg's microdot: VI. Internationaler (G1925); Herstellung (G1926); New process (G1926); Obtention...réduites (G1926); L'obtention...réductions (G1926); and Herstellung (G1927). The *New York Times* reported Goldberg as saying that he had applied for a patent for his microdot method, but "after filing the patent, Dr. Goldberg had forgotten about it" (Future 1949), but no such patent has been found. Skopec (1964, 165) reproduces the microdot image as illustrations 188 and 189, reproduced in Figure 10.2, with a diagram adapted from Obtention (G1926). Goldberg's methods are described in G.W.W. Stevens (1957; 1968); and White (1992), a history of microdots; also White (1989 and 1990). For later equipment, Melton (2002, 150–53).

112 *Bibles per square inch* G.W.W. Stevens (1968, 3, 46) and Heilprin (1961, 215). *American Documentation* is now the *Journal of the American Society for Information Science and Technology.* High Resolution (1960) explains and reproduces the microimage of Genesis, but the "50 Bibles" story originated earlier, as it is noted in Baines (1953, 78). Goldberg stated in 1949 that his smallest photograph was 4/1000 of an inch square and that he could photograph 60,000 pages on a negative the size of a postcard (Future 1949).

112 *The Goldberg Emulsion* Born (1972, s.v. Goldberg-Emulsion, p. 271); also Fergg (1957).

112 *"If I were a rich man"* Gesell (1926, 98–99), see Appendix A.1.

114 *H. G. Wells* Wells (1938, 71); also Goldschmidt and Otlet (1925) and Ostwald (1912).

114 *The National Library* Nationalbibliothek (1938), see Appendix A.2.

117 *"Dr Goldberger's cute invention"* Thiess (1931, 288–89).

Chapter 11: Zeiss Ikon and the Contax

119 *"Under his leadership"* Busch (1953, 211).

119 *Zeiss Ikon* Corporate histories of Zeiss include: Zeiss Ikon AG. (1937); 25 Jahre Zeiss Ikon (1951); Schumann (1962); and Walter (2000; reviewed by Steiner [2002]). Buckland (Forthcoming) discusses thes corporate history in relation to Goldberg. Also, 75 Jahre Zeiss Ikon (2002); Gubas (1984b and 1994–95); and Blumtritt (2000, 49–71).

119 *Deckel and Gautier* Blumtritt (2000); Thiele (2000).

120 *Heinrich Ernemann* Heinrich Erneman (1935).

120 *Helmuth Goerz* Helmuth Goerz was the son of Carl Paul Goerz, founder of the Goerz company. See Sipley (1965, 72–73); Browne and Partnow (1983, 233–34); and Gubas (2001).

120 *August Nagel* Gubas (1984a).

121 *a range of nonphotographic products* Seherr-Thoss (1979) has a few notes on Zeiss Ikon automobile accessories.

121 *The flow of patents* Goldberg to Wilkanski 23 October 1940, in GP: "Eine grosse Reihe von Zeiss Ikon Patenten und Konstruktionen stammt von mir."

122 *Goldberg...traveled instead to Jena* The story of Goldberg's late night journey to Jena and Straubel's handwritten addendum is a family tradition. The outcome is corroborated by a more formal, notarized typescript addendum by Straubel, Jena, dated 16 March 1928, increasing Goldberg's salary by 9,000 RM payable half-yearly starting 31 March 1928. Only Straubel had the authority, as *Stiftungsbevollmächtigter,* to make such a change unilaterally.

122 *Sound Movies* Kellogg (1945) explains movie soundtracks and Kellogg (1955) their history; also Sponable (1947).

122 *Triergon* In 1928, Tonbild Syndicate A.G. (Tobis), with capital from Holland, Switzerland, and Germany, acquired the Tri-Ergon patents and began to install sound equipment in German cities. At the same time Siemens and Allgemeine Elektrizitäts Gesellschaft (AEG) produced their own jointly owned system and formed Klangfilm. Tobis and Klangfilm united in the struggle to compete with U.S. companies and their sound systems: Tobis made films and Klangfilm made the sound apparatus. Then Tobis signed an agreement with Dutch firm NV Kuchenmeisters Internationale Ultraphon Mij, based in Holland, but with a production center in Germany. A new company, NV Kuchenmeisters Internationale Mij voor Sprekende Films, was formed, to which Tobis apportioned a third of its capital. The result was a huge, German-based multinational trust, Tobis-Klangfilm-Kuchenmeister, with, later, an agreement with Universum-Film AG ("UFA"), a major German studio and distributor. As a result, the sound movie field in Germany was completely controlled by a small group of companies. Sponable (1947, 414–16); Kellogg (1955, 294); Neale (1985, 82–84).

123 *Oskar Messter* Messter (1936); Sipley (1965, 97–98).

123 *Messter Medal* For the Messter Medal and quotation: L. Busch (1953, 210–11): "Die Filmtechnik hatte bald auch der Photochemie wichtige Aufgaben zugewiesen. Um ihre Loesung machte sich ein Mann besonders verdient, an dessen Arbeiten

kein Tonmechniker und kein Bildtechniker bei der Leistung des Kopier- und Entwicklungsprozesses vorbeikomment. Professor Goldberg war es, der als Wissenschaftler und spaeter als Leiter der Zeiss Ikon AG die grundlegenden Bedingungen fuer die sensitometrische Kontrolle in den Kopieranstalten gelegt hat. Daneben setzte er sich ebensosehr als Konstrukteur, beispielsweise des Kinamo, des Zeiss Ikon-Tonfilmkoffers und vieler andere Konstructionen erfolgreich ein. Unter seiner Leitung wuchs die Zeiss Ikon AG zu einem der fuehrenden deutschen Werke auf."

125 *Figure 11.1* (a)–(c) are adapted from Zeiss Ikon AG (1937, 53, 60); (d) is from a Carl Zeiss, Inc. advertisement from *Photo Art Monthly* (October 1934) reproduced in *Zeiss Historica* 20, no. 2 (Fall 1998):24.

125 *The Contax* Wandersleb (1946, 3) notes Barnack's proposal to Mengel. The Contax, having become a collector's item, has a specialized literature of its own (e.g., Pacific Rim Camera (2001). Note Kuč (1992); Photographie und Forschung (1935–60); and the Contax-Leica comparison by Helm (1988). The innovations listed are mostly from N. Goldberg (1992, 260) and H. Goldberg. Gubas (1985b) analyzes who was named as (co)inventor in the Contax-related U.S. patents.

126–27 *Figures 11.2 and 11.3 Contax I and II* were kindly supplied by Lawrence J. Gubas.

128 *"Among the many cameras"* N. Goldberg (1969, 154). *Products of Vision* (1988) is a guide to Zeiss Ikon cameras.

128 *Heinz Küppenbender* Gubas (2000, 2002); Berthel (2000); and Schumann (1962).

129 *Oeserstrasse 5* Kurze (1998, inside back cover) has 360° panoramic views from the Ernemann tower that show many buildings of Goldberg's period and the area where Oeserstrasse 5 was located (horizon, near Nord Ost 7).

130 *Figure 11.4* is copied from a pen and watercolor original drawn by an unidentified artist, probably in the 1920s, in GP.

131 *Blue Wonder bridge* Haufe and Säckel (1993).

Chapter 12: Television

An early version of this chapter appeared as Buckland (1995b).

133 *An economic-technological move* "Ein ökonomisch-technischer Schachzug erster Güte, denn die verschiedenen Firmen konnten so ihre Erfahrungen aus unterschiedlichen Bereichen gemeinsam

verwerten...Die Zeit der individuellen Tüftelei im kleinen Privatlabor war damit endgültig vorbei." Zielinski (1989, 146).

133 *Loewe* For Siegmund Loewe, 1885–1962, David Ludwig Loewe, 1882–1935, and their company, see the corporate history of Loewe Radio by Steiner (1998; 2003) and the Loewe Opta corporate Web site www.loewe.de. Also Loewe and Goerz (1929). Visit (1929) has an aerial photo of the Goerz works in Berlin-Zehlendorf. The papers of Radio AG D. S. Loewe are in the Loewe Opta archives in Kronach, Germany.

134 *Fernseh AG* For early German television seen Burns (1998, 241–70, 321–25); Fisher and Fisher (1997); and History of German Television (1990); also Bruch (1967); Eckert (1963); Fuchs (1931); Geschichte (1993); Goebel (1953); and Karolus (1984). For Fernseh AG: Hoppe (1995); Rudert (1979); and Steiner (1998); also Abrahamson (1955); Bruch (1967); Bulow (1987); Everson (1949, 149); Günther (1938); Möller (1954); Zielinksi (1989); and Wilson (1937). The July 1939 issue of Fernseh AG's technical journal, *Fernseh GmbH,* contains, on pages 109–22, a well-illustrated review of the firm's activities and products during its first 10 years, precisely the period of Zeiss Ikon's involvement by Möller and Schubert (1939). Fernseh AG's corporate records are said to have destroyed in the war, but some archival material on Zeiss Ikon's involvement in Fernseh AG survive in the Hauptstaatsarchiv, Dresden: Ernemann / Zeiss Ikon Series, File 154; in the Carl Zeiss Jena, Betriebsarchiv, File 22413; and in the Bosch archives in Stuttgart.

135 *Figure 12.1* is from U.S. Patent 1,973,203 of 11 September 1934.

135 *Robert Bosch company* Robert Bosch GmbH (1979) and Heuss (1994, 433–34).

135 *"With this"* Zielinski (1989, 146): "Die Zeit der individuellen Tüftelei im kleinen Privatlabor war damit endgültig vorbei."

135 *Paul Görlich* Mütze (1986).

136 *"Yesterday in Berlin"* Goldberg "an die Geschäftsleitung der Firma Carl Zeiss," 13 June 1929, in BACZ 22413.

136 *Erich Rassbach...letter* Rassbach letters to A. Kotthaus, 1 September 1932, and to Goldberg, 4 February 1932, are in BACZ Jena, File 22413.

137 *Galloping after* Dunlap (1932, 54–55). The text purports to be from 25 April 1926, but this paragraph is a later addition, not in his *New York Times* article (25 April 1926, sec. 9, p. 17), from which the ensuing text (about Baird) is taken.

137 *Intermediate technology* Fernseh AG's "intermediate" technology combining film and television technologies is noted in

Anwendung (G1933) and in contemporary books on television technology, e.g., Günther (1938) and Myers (1936, 235–38). See also Bruch (1967); Burns (1986, 98, 158; 1998, 254–56, 321–25); Fuchs (1931); Goebel (1953); Görlich (1954, photos on 465–67) and Zielinski (1989, 146–58 and 168).

138 *Figure 12.2* Günther (1938, Abb. 168, p. 107). For additional images, see Burns (1998, 322–25).

139 *Some use of intermediate technology...1940s* Hodgson (1949); Abrahamson (1955).

Chapter 13: The 1931 Congress

141 *"At the end of the evening"* International (1932, 5): "Als Abschluss des Abends fand auf der Dachterrasse des Restaurants einer Vorstellung im Stile des altdeutschen Puppenspieles statt, in der die Persönlichkeiten, Ereignisse und Ergebnisse des tages in dem von 'Dr. Aurimontanus' verfassten Stück 'Sensitometrica Diabolica' oder 'Kasperle im Normenausschuss' in launiger Weise persifliert wurden."

141 *The 1931 Congress* The proceedings were published in International (1932) in German and also, selectively, in French (International 1933). Reports on the congress include Harrison (1931); Kongress (1931); Sheppard (1932); Stiebel (1931); and Versammlungsberichte (1931). Newspaper coverage includes *Basler Nachrichten* 15–16 August 1931; *Dresdner Anzeiger* 4–9 August 1931; *Dresdner Nachrichten* 3, 4, 6 and 7 August 1931; and *Dresdner Neueste Nachrichten* 4–9 August 1931.

141 *Eggert* For John and Margarete (Ettisch) Eggert, see Gill and Löhnert (1997, 39–46).

141 *"the gracious kindness"* International (1933): "L'aimabilité gracieuse et l'activité inlassable de Mme Luther, Mme Goldberg, et de Mme Eggert, qui avaient prévu pour elles un programme chargé de réunions, de visites et de distractions, leur a rendu le séjour aussi intéressant qu'agréable."

141 *Standard Film Speeds* For congress, discussions are reported extensively in the proceedings (International 1932, esp. 100–1, 122–30, 424–25). Also in English in Neblette (1938, 203). The proposal by Goldberg and Luther is Deutscher (G1932).

142 *Goldberg...Ausschuss für Phototechnik* Fischer (1957, 2).

143 *described in Der Aufbau* G1925 Aufbau, 85.

144 *DIN 4512:1934* Deutsches Institut für Normung (1934).

144 *test equipment* Apparat (G1933); Zeiss Ikon (1935b).

144 *By 1936 British Journal of Photography* 83 (14 August 1936):515.

144 *Goldberg dazzled his audience* For his lecture "Fundamentals of Talking Films," see the proceedings (International 1932, 213–14); Sheppard (1932); Versammlungsberichte (1931, 878: "mit verblüffend einfachen Experimenten"); *Bulletin de la Société Française de Photographie et de Cinématographie* 3. ser., t. 18, no. 11 (November 1931):242: "de remarquables expériences"; also Stiebel (1931, 813–14); and *Dresdner Neueste Nachrichten* Nr. 182 (7 August 1931): 4. An earlier version of his lecture, presented to the Deutsche Kinotechnische Gesellschaft, 9 March 1931, is summarized in Physikalischen (G1931) and Prof. Goldberg (G1931).

145 *Punch and Judy show* International (1932, 5) and Harrison (1931, 418).

145 *Figure 13.1* was kindly supplied by Professor Klaus Mauersberger, Technical University, Dresden.

146 *Peligot Medal* French Photographic Society committee report recommending conferral of the Peligot medal on Goldberg is in the *Bulletin de la Société Française de Photographie et de Cinématographie* 3. ser., t. 18 (Juin 1931):123. An excerpt is quoted in Chapter 6.

146 *documentary* A brittle, deteriorated copy of the 16 mm documentary film is in GP.

Chapter 14: The Statistical Machine

147 *He was telling us* George Lowy (formerly Ze'ev Levi), 1 November 1997, Silver Spring, MD.

147 *microfilming business records* Cady (1994, 1999).

147 *Banks found* Johnson (1932) and Schwegmann (1940).

148 *Giro...Amsterdam* For Zeiss Ikon's microfilm-based office equipment with its code-line marks, see Joachim (1935). For the Amsterdam Giro check equipment, see also Keegstra (1933); Asperen (1934); Ergänzungen (1935); Joachim (1936); Munters (1936); Goebel, J. (1952, 3). A photo of the machine is in *I.I.D. Communicationes* 1, Fasc. 3 (1934): Plate XLV.

148 *Amsterdam city telephone system* Maitland (1931); Harrison (1931, 417); and Joachim (1935). A photo appears in *I.I.D. Communicationes* 1, Fasc. 3 (1934): Plate XLIV.

149 *The Development of Workstations* Based mainly on U.S. patents. The *History of personal workstations,* edited by A. Goldberg (1988), includes only digital computer workstations from 1950 on.

149   *Alexander Rudolph* Miksa (1978: 449–50) and Alexander's U.S. patents 473,345; 473,348; 483,312; and 499,443.

149   *Figure 14.1* is from U.S. patent 473,348. Continuous Revolving File and Index. Alexander J. Rudolph, 1892.

150   *Georges Sebille* Otlet (1934a) and Sebille (1932, U.S. patent 1,889,575, the source of Figure 14.3).

150   *Figure 14.2* U.S. patent 1,845,410 (Harding 1932).

151   *Leonard G. Townsend* Burke (1994, 194 and 414,n69) and Townsend (1938).

152   *basic functional requirements* Otlet (1990, 25–26); French original is La Fontaine and Otlet (1895).

153   *"We should have"* Otlet (1934b, 391; in English, Otlet (1990, 1). The wording in the translation has been lightly modernized: "Nous devons avoir un complexe de machines associées qui réalise simultanément ou à la suite les opérations suivantes: 1° transformation du son en écriture; 2 multiplication de cette écriture tel nombre de fois qu'il est utile; 3° établissement des documents de manière que chaque donnée ait son individualité propre et dans ses relations avec celles de tout l'ensemble, qu'elle y soit rappelée là où il est nécessaire; 4° index de classement attaché à chaque donnée; perforation du document en corrélation avec ces indices; 5° classement automatique de ces documents et mise en place dans les classeurs; 6° récupération automatique des documents à consulter et présentation, soit sous les yeux ou sous la partie d'une machine ayant à y faire des inscriptions additionnelles; 7° manipulation mécanique à volonté de toutes les données enregistrées pour obtenir de nouvelles combinaisons de faits, de nouveaux rapports d'idées, de nouvelles opérations à l'aide des chiffres. La machine qui réaliserait ces sept desiderata serait un véritable *cerveau mécanique et collectif.*"

153   *... that all knowledge* Otlet (1934b, 428); in English, Otlet (1990, 1): "Une hypothèse moins absolue, mais très radicale encore, supposerait que toutes les connaissances, toutes les informations pourraient être rendues assez compactes pour être contenues en un certain nombres d'ouvrages disposés sur la table de Travail même, donc à distance de la main, et indexés de manière à rendre la consultation aisée au maximum. Dans ce cas le Monde décrit dans l'ensemble des Livres serait réellement à portée de chacun. Le Livre Universel formé de tous les Livres, serait devenu très approximativement une annexe du Cerveau, substratum lui-même de la mémoire, méchanisme et instrument extérieur à l'esprit, mais si près de lui et si apte à son usage que ce serait vraiment une sorte d'organe annexe, appendice exodermique.... Cet organe aurait fonction de rendre notre être 'ubique et éternel'."

153 *microfiche* Goldschmidt and Otlet (1906). Otlet (1990, 87–95) is an English translation with a note on Goldschmidt.

153 *portable "microphotographic" library* Goldschmidt and Otlet (1925) and, in English, Otlet (1990, 204–10).

154 *The Statistical Machine* Goldberg's paper (Registrierproblem G1932) is in International Congress of Photography (8th, Dresden, 1931) (1932, 317–20), summarized in Stiebel (1931, 813) and Versammlungsberichte (1931, 876). English translations are Methods (G1932); and Retrieval (G1992). Figures 14.4 and 14.6 were kindly drawn by Dr. Samia Benidir. Figures 14.5 and 14.8 are reproduced from Registrierproblem (G1932). Figure 14.7 is from Goldberg's U.S. patent 1,838,389, 29 December 1931. *Statistical machine.* Buckland (1992; summarized in Buckland [1995a]) includes an earlier discussion..

157 *After London… Paris… Berlin* Demonstrations were reported in London on 27 October 1931 (Photocell G1931; Royal 1931); in Paris on 3 November 1931 (Cellule G1932); and in Berlin on 20 April 1932 (Weg G1932, see Appendix A.3).

157 *Refinements* Explanation is based on German supplementary patent applications and non-German patents: Great Britain 288,580, 25 July 1929. *Improvements in or relating to Adding, Sorting, Statistical and like Machine.* France 657,787, 21 January 1929. Zeiss Ikon A.-G. (Société) et Goldberg (E.). *Machine statistique;* Italy 268,389, 14 Ottobre 1929. Zeiss Ikon and Emanuel Goldberg. *Macchina per la compilazione di lavori di statistica.*

161 *He was telling us* George Lowy, 1 November 1977; confirmed by Dr. Walter Riedel, Dresden, 20 November 2000.

161 *Goldberg… suggested* Schantz (1982, 4); also Schantz (1979).

162 *Paul W. Handel* See his U.S. patent 1,915,993, 27 June 1933, *Statistical Machine.*

162 *German patent law* Gispen (1989; 2002).

Chapter 15: Ludwig, Killinger, and Mutschmann

165 *"The Workers' Council"* "Der Betriebsrat behandele nicht dei Frage 'Prof. Dr. Goldberg als wissenschaftler und Mensch,' sondern sehe in ihm lediglich den 'Wissenschaftler, den Juden.'" (*Oeffentliche Betriebsversammlung am 24. April 1933.* Minutes of the meeting, quoting Herr Zobler, in BACZ 8145).

165 *Oskar Messter Memorial Medal* For Messter, see Messter (1936). Busch (1953) provides an account of the Messter Medal and its award to Goldberg: "Die Filmtechnik hatte bald auch der

Photochemie wichtige Aufgaben zugewiesen. Um ihre Loesung machte sich ein Mann besonders verdient, an dessen Arbeiten kein Tonmechniker und kein Bildtechniker bei der Leistung des Kopier- und Entwicklungsprozesses vorbeikommt. Professor Goldberg war es, der als Wissenschaftler und spaeter als Leiter der Zeiss Ikon AG die grundlegenden Bedingungen fuer die sensitometrische Kontrolle in den Kopieranstalten gelegt hat. Daneben setzte er sich ebensosehr als Konstrukteur, beispielsweise des Kinamo, des Zeiss Ikon-Tonfilmkoffers und vieler andere Konstructionen erfolgreich ein. Unter seiner Leitung wuchs die Zeiss Ikon AG zu einem der fuehrenden deutschen Werke auf."

165 *Engineers* For the ideology of German engineers and how right-wing Germans were able to reconcile acceptance of technology with rejection of rationalism, see Herf (1984); Gispen (1989); and Hård (1998).

166 *One path* The published summary of Goldberg's acceptance speech "Ein Weg zur Kinematographie" is Weg (G1932) and is reprinted as Appendix A.3. H. Goldberg attended and remembers the speech.

167 *economists did not really understand* H. Goldberg, 8 March 1997.

167 *As the Nazis came to power* For a vivid account of how the Nazis consolidated their power at the local level, see Allen (1965); also Victor Klemperer's diary (1995; 1998). The play *Professor Mamlock,* written in 1933 by Konrad Wolf, a refugee from Germany, tells a dramatic story of a famous Jewish surgeon forced out of his position as head of a clinic. The circumstances and the outcome differ from Goldberg's, but the movie versions of 1938 and 1961 provide a vivid depiction of a rather similar situation.

167 *"We should leave now"* Chava Gichon, 23 March 1995.

167 *By 1925 Dresden* Based mainly on Bramke (1989) and on information and exhibits in the Stadtmuseum Dresden, visited 2–4 June 1995. Zeiss Ikon details from Carl Zeiss Jena Betriebsarchiv File 8145.

167 *Jews living in Dresden* Hagemeyer (2002); and, for Nazi period, Haase and Jersch-Wenzel (1998) and Strauss (1980, I, 321).

167 *Fritz Busch New Grove's* (2001, 4:653–54) and Busch (1949, 196–97; English edition, 1953, 200–201): "Ein schwerer, dicker SA-Offizier in blendend neuer Uniform ... Dem nebensitzenden SA-Offizier konnte kein Wort unseres Gespräches entgehen, das von Sympathien für die Nazibewegung, den Erfolg Hitlers und die Zukunft Deutschlands unter dem neuen Regime nicht getragen war."

168 *Killinger Encyclopedia* (1991, 615).

168 *"On the basis"* "Auf der Grundlage der Verordnung des Reichspräsidenten zum Schutz von Volk und Staat."

168 *"an impossible situation"* Sächsischen *Verwaltungsblatt* 31 (1933):233; quoted in Bramke (1989, 482).

168 *1. Immediate dismissal* "1. Fristlose Entlassung von Dr. Bondi und allen jüdischen Arbeitnehmern bis 10.30 h im Filmwerk. Begrundung: Lt. Anordnung der Reichsleitung ist jeder Jude in leitender Stellung fristlos zu entlassen. Als Jude ist auch der zu betrachten, der eine andere Konfession angenommen hat; die Zugehörigkeit zur jüdischen Rasse ist allein massgebend. 2. Prof. Goldberg als Generaldirektor hat sofort zurüruckzutreten, damit der jüdische Einfluss sich auf das Filmwerk nicht mehr ausbreiten kann. Dieser Forderung sind auch alle bei der Zentralleitung Dresden unterworfen. 3. Beseitigung aller jüdischen Aufsichtsräte. 4. Bis 13 h fordern die N.S.B.O. [= Nationalsozialistische Betreibsobmänner] und der Betriebsrat von der Direktion die Erklärung, dass alle Forderungen restlos durchgeführt sind. Unterschrift: Der Kommissarische Betriebsrat." (Original in BACZ 8145).

169 *120 hourly workers* "120 Arbeiter / 100 Angestellte / sollen entlassen werden! / Aber eine Viertelmillion schluckten / die Herren Vorstandsmitglieder im / Jahre 1932/33. So sieht die Judendik / tatur bei Zeiss Ikon aus! / Arbeitskameraden! Heraus zum Protest! / Heute Abend 16.30 Uhr / Belegschaft-Versammlung im / Volkshaus. Schandauer Strasse. / Es sprechen: / Kollege Heinrich—Filmwerk Berlin / Kollege Ludwig—Dresden / außerdem Kollegen aus Stuttgart und Jena. / Erscheint in Massen! Es geht um euern / Arbeitsplatz, um eure Zukunft. / Ludwig— Henke—Heinrich / Komissarische Betriebsräte." (Original in BACZ 8145).

170 *Martin Ludwig and Comrades* The kidnapping was one of the few experiences Goldberg did talk about. Carl Zeiss Jena corporate archives File BACZ 8145 contains material about the kidnapping, including both the draft and final pencil-written letters of resignation and two contemporary, unsigned, undated, typescript accounts of the kidnapping. The longer, more detailed one reads as if written by Heyne or Simader. The second was by someone who arrived in Dresden early Tuesday morning, 4 April, and went with Ernemann and Simader to visit Killinger and so was, very likely, a senior manager from Carl Zeiss Jena, almost certainly August Kotthaus (1884– 1941), Manager of Production. Also W. Riedel interview 20 November 2000.

171 *taken to a nearby bar* "...wo er vor einer Hakenkreuzfahne strammstehn und die menschenunwürdigste Behandlung über sich ergehen lassen muß." Erwin Anders, quoted in Karger-Decker (1959, 466).

173 *Figure 15.1* Original is in BACZ 8145.

173 "*I hereby declare*" Ich erkläre hiermit freiwillig, dass ich meine sämtlichen Aemter im Zeiss Ikon Konzern einschl. aller Tochtergesellschaften niederlege, dass ich von sämtlichen Aussichtsrats- und Verwaltungsratsposten, die ich innehabe, zurücktrete, dass ich die mir noch zustehenden Gehälter, Aufwandsentschädigungen und sonstige Einkünfte aus meiner wirtschaftlichen Tätigkeit der Arbeiterschaft der betreffenden Werke für soziale Zwecke abtrete, dass die freie Verfügung über diesen Wohlfahrtsfonds den Arbeitsräten der betreffenden Werke zusteht, dass die Behandlung und Verpflegung während meiner Haft in jeder Beziehung einwandfrei war, dass ich für die durch meine sowie Herrn Grentz's Haft enstandenen Unkosten voll und ganz aufkomme und den bei mir gefundenen Geldbetrag einschl. Devisen usw. restlos dafür zur Verfügung stelle, dass ich die Rechtsgültigkeit dieser Erklärung niemals anfechten werde, dass ich verständigt worden bin, dass mir im Falle meiner Freilassung die abgenommenen Kleidungsstücke und Wertgegenstände (mit Ausnahme des Geldes usw.) zugestellt werden, dass ich mich im Falle meiner Freilassung gegenüber der Regierung der nationalen Erhebung loyal verhalten werde. Dresden am 4.4.1933.

174 *A young man* The role of the unidentified young man is a family tradition from Goldberg himself. The Dresden police files that might have helped are presumed to have been destroyed in the bombing of Dresden.

174 *Dresdner Neueste Nachrichten* Fiedler (1939, 270–73). Editorial statements are from Nr. 124 and Nr. 133 of 1933, as quoted in Fiedler, p. 271: "...stolzen und selbstbewussten Aufmarsch einer Nation, der sich entschlossen frei macht von den schwarz-roten Verführern." "Den Kritikern der nationaler Revolution aber muss mit besonderem Ernst die Frage vorlegt werden: Habt ihr schon wieder vergessen, was geschehn wäre, wenn die nationale Revolution nicht gründlichen Wandel geschafft hätte?—Darüber darf man von jedem guten Deutschen nicht nur Verständnis, sondern auch tiefe Dankbarkeit dafür erwarten, dass die natio-nale Revolution den Bolschewismus in letzter Minute niederge-halten hat."

175 *no mention of his kidnapping* I thank Professor Klaus Mauersberger and his staff for having looked for me in the

Dresdner Nachrichten, Dresdner Neueste Nachrichten, and the *Sächische Volkszeitung.*

175   *two cryptic statements* The statements by Detten and Mutschmann were published in the *Dresdner Neueste Nachrichten* Nr. 84 (8 April 1933):4. Detten's statement was also printed in the *Sächische Volkszeitung* 8 April 1933, p. 2, under the heading *"Unberechtigte Verhaftungen"* ("Unlawful arrests").

175   *Irresponsible Elements* "Unverantwortliche Elemente. Die Nachrichtenstelle der Staatskanzlei teilt mit: Am Donnerstag sind verschiedene Innungsvorstände in Dresden verhaftet worden. Der neuernannte Oberpräsident für die sächsische Polizei, v. Detten, weist nachdrücklich darauf hin, dass diese Verhaftungen weder von der kommissarischen Regierung oder einer ihr nachgeordeneten Stelle, noch von der SA-Führung oder von der politischen Leitung der NSDAP. veranlasst worden sind. *Völlig unverantwortliche Elemente* haben sich den guten Glauben der SA-Leute zunutze gemacht. Die Inhaftierten konnten nach kurzer Zeit wieder auf freien Fuss gesetzt werden. Es sind alle Massnahmen getroffen worden, um eine Wiederholung derartiger Vorkommnisse zu unterbinden." [Emphasis in original].

175   *Ban on individual actions* "Verbot aller Einzelaktionen. Ein Gaubefehl Mutschmanns. Der sächsische Gauleiter der NSDAP. hat im 'Freiheitskampf' folgenden Befehl an seine Parteigenossen erlassen: Im Verlauf der von der Reichsleitung gewünschten Gleichschaltung des gesamten öffentlichen Lebens werden mir immer wieder Fälle gemeldet, in denen Parteigenossen sind durch Einzelaktionen amtliche Funktionen anmassen. Ein solches Verhalten entspricht nicht der Würde, mit der die nationale Revolution nach dem ausdrücklichen Wunsch des Führers durchgeführt werden soll. Das sie noch nicht beendet ist, hat Dr. Goebbels in seiner gestrigen Rundfunkrede zum Ausdruck gebracht mit der Worten: Sie wird nicht eher zum Stillstand kommen, als bis sie das ganze deutsche Gemeinschaftsleben überflutet und bis in die letzte Faser durchtränkt hat. Diese Vollendung wird sich aber nunmehr nach Uebernahme der Macht planmässig von oben vollziehen. Ich ordne deshalb hiermit noch einmal an, dass *jede selbständige Einzelaktion unbedingt verboten ist.* Wer dieses Verbot trotzdem übertritt, stellt sich von nun an selbst ausserhalb der Reihen der Partei." [Emphasis in original].

175   *Martin Mutschmann Encyclopedia* (1991, 615); Höffkes (1986, 242–44).

176   *embarrassment of Killinger . . . motivation* H. Goldberg, 8 March 1997. For SA and political motivation in the Spring of 1933: Strauss (1980, I, 330).

176 *Hitler praised* Hitler (1992, 1:445): "Dort [Saxony] hat der Führer Mutschmann augenblicklich Sachsen fest in die hand genommen, geschlossen in der die N.S.D.A.P. hinübergeführt und mustergültig in der Hand behalten, so dass eine gegenströmung nicht entstehen konnte (Heilrufe, Beifall)."

176 *Goebbels diaries* Goebbels (1987–2001, e.g., I, v3:353: "richtige Gangstermethoden"; 664: "ein richtiger alter Gauleiter von echtem Schrot und Korn.")

176 *statements by Killinger* Killinger issued a series of strongly worded official statements asserting his authority and trying to restrain unauthorized activities by SA, SS, and Nazi Party leaders: *Sächsisches Verwaltungsblatt* Nr. 20 (10 March 1933):139: "Soweit die SA. und SS. von sich aus es für notwendig gehalten hat, in Verwaltung, Polizei und Verkehr einzugreifen, damke ich ohr für die von ihr getroffenen vorbeugenden Massnahmen. Sie sind nunmehr jedoch durch den mir gewordeu Auftrag hinfällig geworden.... Ich erwarte von der Disziplin der SA., dass sie im vertrauen darauf, dass ich Herr der Lage sein werde, allen meinen Befehlen pünktlich nachkommt." *Sächsisches Verwaltungsblatt* Nr. 27 (28 March 1933):199: "In neuester Zeit werden mir wieder Fälle gemeldet, in denen eigenmächtig in den Gang der Verwaltung eigegriffen, insbesondere dir Verhaftung unschuldiger Personen und die Absetzung von beamten verfügt worden ist. Es hat den Anschein, als würden von unverantwortlichen Stellen Führen der SA. und SS. oder der politischen leitung der NSDAP. Befehl zugleitet, die von diesen als ordnungsmässig erteilt angesehen und dann auch befolgt werden.... Glieder der politischen Leitung, SA. und SS., haben sich künftighin jedes Eingriffs in fremde Verwaltungszweige zu enthalten. Wenn sie zu einem solchen Eigriff von dritter Seite uafgefordert werden, haben sie sofort mich oder die von mor eingesetzten zuständigen Stellen der Staatsverwaltung davon inKenntis zu setzten und Entschliessung einzufordern." *Sächsisches Verwaltungsblatt* Nr. 31 (10 April 1933):233: "Erlass an die Beamtenschaft. 7. April 1933.... Es is ein unmöglicher Zustand, dass Beamte Beschwerden über ihre Vorgesetzen und Anzeigen gegen sie und andere Beamte unmittlebar bei mir oder bei den von mir eingesetzten Kommissionen der einzelnen Minister anbringen.... In den gegenwärtigen schweren Notzeiten hat sich der Beamte durch verstärkten Diensteifer und eiserne Disziplin auszuzeichnen."

176 *organized...Zeiss Ikon employees* Schumann (1962, 495): "Goldberg wurde am 3. April 1933 von SA-Banditen unter der Führung der Nazibetriebsräte des Ikon-Werkes...verhaftet und verschleppt."

176 *Anna Schütz* Simader memo "Aktennotiz," 20 February 1935, in BACZ 8145.

176 *Flight* Based on surviving letters in BACZ 8145 and GP. Goldberg's departure from Zeiss Ikon is sometimes given in error as 1932.

177 *"The Workers' Council"* See the first note for this chapter.

177 *such people thought* Chava Gichon, 23 March 1995.

177 *Mees* C.E.K. Mees letter to Goldberg, 11 May 1933, is in GP.

178 *thunderous applause of the students* Wandersleb (1957, 3–4) was an eyewitness: "Luther hatte in dem Auditorium trotz zahlreicher auf den vorderen Bänken sitzender uniformierter SA-Leute den Mut gefunden, Goldbergs entscheidenden Anteil an den Vorlesungen und Übungen des Instituts mit warmen Worten zu erwähnen, und dies führte, nach einem Augenblick des Schweigens, zur Verblüffung der SA-Leute zu einem stürmischen Beifall der anwesenden Studenten als Dank für Goldberg."

178 *Luther drew attention* Robert Luther to Sächsisches Ministerium für Volksbildung: *Bericht über die Bedeutung und die Tätigkeit des Wissenschaftlich-Photographischen Instituts an der Technischen Hochschule Dresden,* 30 März 1934.

Chapter 16: Paris

179 *Étape* Merriam-Webster's French English Dictionary. Springfield, MA: Merriam-Webster, 2000:137.

179 *"I only want one thing"* "Ich will nur eins, und zwar so bald wie moeglich: Eine Arbeitstaette, wo ich ein Ziel vor die Augen habe, dessen Erreichen nur von *meiner* Kraft abhaengt. Ich weiss, dass mir hierzu meine fruehere Energie und Initiative immer noch zur verfuegung stehen." (Goldberg, in Milan, to Henrichs, 1 July 1933, in BACZ 8145).

179 *employment contract...terms were amended* A copy of Goldberg's 1933 contract with Zeiss is in GP.

179 *Ikonta...Optica* Schumann (1962, 495–96). The Archives Nationales, Paris, Series 104AQ1–123 *Zeiss Ikonta et entreprises allemandes diverses* includes Ikonta business records, 1935–45, but nothing relating to Goldberg was found.

182 *A Copying Camera* Rhodes and Streeter's *Before Photocopying* (1999, Chapter 6) provides a convenient introduction to copying technology.

183 *3. A small knife blade* The Kine Exakta 35 mm camera, marketed by Ihagee, Dresden, in Spring 1936, incorporated a sliding knife to cut film.

183 *World Congress* Rayward (1983). There are several contempo-
rary accounts. World Congress (1937) *Proceedings* states
(p. 72) that Goldberg presented a paper on a special camera for
recording documents on film, but does not include the text.
A copy of the German text of Goldberg's paper, entitled
*Eine Spezialkamera zur Herstellung von dokumentarischen
Filmaufmahmen,* is in the Science Museum Library, London,
Archive BSIB/11.

183 *World Brain* Wells (1938, 89–93).

184 *a patent... in Germany and in the United States* Gebrauchsmuster
1,431,500 *Photographische Kamera für biegsames lichtemp-
findliches Material* (1938). U.S. patent 2,225,433 *Photographic
camera for flexible materials sensitive to light,* 17 December
1940, from which Figure 16.1 is taken.

185 *Figure 16.2 is* from Goldberg's U.S. patent 2,652,774
Photographic Copying Apparatus, 22 September 1953, which
provides a very detailed mechanical description.

186 *More Negotiations* Documentation has survived on both sides,
Goldberg's, seemingly incomplete, in GP, and Zeiss' in BACZ
8145.

186 *He annotated a copy... with pointed remarks* e.g., "Es kann mir
nicht zugemutet werden auf jede Beschäftigung mit lichtemp-
findlichen Material zu verzicheten. Unter solches verbot würde
Z. I. jedes verfahren für Reproduktionstechnik (Druckverfahren)
fallen, also Gebiete, die vollkommen ausscrhalb der
Z. I. liegen.[Sic]" "Warum denn nicht so nennen wie es in der
ganzen Welt üblich ist? ('Goldbergkeile')." "Was wird davon
Zeiss Ikon eigentlich hergestellt?" "Warum denn nicht so nennen
wie es in der ganzen Welt üblich ist? ('Goldbergkeile')." "Da für
mich unentbehrlich."

Chapter 17: Palestine

This chapter and the next draw primarily on numerous and lengthy
discussions with Goldberg's daughter and son-in-law, Chava (Renate) and
Mordechai Gichon, and son, Herbert Goldberg, and on interviews with
others who worked with Goldberg in Palestine / Israel: Moshe Arad, Ramat
Chen, 26 and 27 March 1995; Jacob Beutler, Rehovot, 25 March 1995;
Alex Eliraz, Jaffa, 2 April 1995; Dr.Otto Gold, Haifa, 4 April 1995;
J. H. Jaffe, Jaffa, 27 March 1995; Aviva Kelton, Great Neck, NY, 11 May
1998; George Lowy, Silver Spring, MD, 1 November 1997; Shmuel
Neumann, Ramat Gan, 29 March 1995; Michael Plaot, of Eschborn,
Germany, in Tel Aviv, 12 November 1998; George Sorenson, Rishon Le
Zion, 28 November 1998; Martin Strauss, Washington, DC, 18 October 1994;

General Israel Tal, Tel Aviv, 24 March 1995; and a reunion in Zahala on 2 April 1995. Also miscellaneous memos in the GP.

189 *"It is my intention"* Goldberg to Wilkanski, 23 October 1937, in GP: "Da ich seit etwa 20 Jahren Mitglied der Zionistischen organisation bin und immer schon mein Arbeitsfeld nach Palästina verlegen wollte, habe ich im vergangen Jahre meine Beziehungen zum Zeiss Konzern gelöst und beschloss nach Palästina überzusiedeln. Meine Absicht ist es, der palästinenschen Wissenschaft und Technik meine Erfahrungen auf der Gebiete der Instrumentenkunde, Optik und praktischen Feinmechanik zur Verfügung zu stellen."

189 *Weizmann* Rose (1986, 3).

190 *Some time ago I succeeded* G., Paris, to C.E.K. Mees, 22 April 1937.

190 *A British government report* The Palestine Royal Commission Report (1937) includes substantial historical and contemporary description of Tel Aviv (pp. 13, 114, 352–54) and of Palestine.

190 *immigration from Germany* For German immigrants and their influence in Palestine: Eliav (1985); Nicosia (1979); Strauss (1980); and Worman (1970).

190 *Koppelmann* Typescript autobiography and family history by Max Koppelmann in the possession of John Posniak, Arlington, VA; also C. and M. Gichon, 9 March 1997.

191 *"My aim now"* Quoted in Mcchner (1942).

191 *The Laboratory* I am grateful for the guidance of Shmuel Neumann, 29 March 1995, concerning the development of the Lab. Published accounts of the Lab, all brief, include: Precision Instruments (1945); Touch (1954); and Israel Electro-optical Industry (1967, 1969).

191 *"Whatever I do"* quoted by unidentified speaker at a reunion of Goldberg's former employees, Zahala, 2 April 1995.

191 *prepaid rent* C. Gichon, 7 March 1997, and lease agreements in GP.

192 *Standards Institute* Jakob Beutler, 25 March 1995.

192 *van Leer* For Bernhard and Oscar van Leer: Fortune (1967, 187–89). Conversation with Leer as Goldberg reported it to S. Neumann.

192 *Weizmann had encouraged* M. Gichon, 24 March 1995.

192 *Marks and the Sieff family* Rees (1969).

192 *precision instruments industry was a shrewd move* Goldberg summarized his views on education, technology, human

resources, and industrial policy in Precision (G1946) and Precision (G1950).

192 *"Such an industry"* Precision (G1946, 239).

193 *micrometer... in Budapest* Otto Gold, 4 April 1995.

194 *"It was very nice"* Jakob Beutler, 25 March 1995.

194 *"He was part of it"* Aviva Kelton, 11 May 1998.

194 *"Professor Goldberg needs"* Moshe Arad, 26 March 1995.

194 *"I was supposed"* Jakob Beutler, 25 March 1995.

195 *journals...books* Otto Gold, 4 April 1995.

196 *"I feel very well"* "Ich fuehle mich sehr gut und meine Energie ist ungebrochen. Reich bin ich nicht geworden, wir leben sehr bescheiden, aber wir hungern nicht. Das einzige was ich vermisse, ist die freie Natur, Berge, Schnee, usw. Zu Hause ist alle in Ordnung. Meine Frau muss schwer arbeiten, da alles schwer zu beschaffen ist und Hilfe ja nicht zu bezahlen ist. Sie ist auch nicht juenger (und leider nicht duenner) geworden und das Klima vertraegt sie nicht so gut wie ich." Goldberg letter from New York, 22 July 1946, addressee unknown, in GP.

197 *Comfortable Housing Bericht* (G1940).

197 *"I have no aspirations regarding patents"* G. To H. Z. Tabor, 6 November 1958, in GP.

198 *an improved refractometer* N. Goldberg (1969, 154) and discussions with H. Goldberg. Boiler refractometers are described in Continuously (1955); and shown in Figure 17.2 and in Alexander (1957, 368). The American Optical Company marketed Goldberg handheld refractometers from 1953 to 1960; a temperature-compensated model until 1979; and, from 1953, boiler refractometers marketed as Goldberg Process Refractometers.

198 *Figure 17.2* is from Precision (G1946, 240).

199 *portable copying camera* U.S. patents are 2,225,433. *Photographic camera for flexible materials sensitive to light,* 17 December 1940; and 2,652,744. *Photographic copying apparatus,* 22 September 1953.

200 *optical comparator for microscopic objects (Messmikroskop)* An undated draft patent application in GP was probably not submitted.

200 *aglar* M. Arad, 26 March 1995.

200 *Bricks without straw* Scaife (1945, 647).

201 *Syrian asphalt* Moshe Arad, 26 March 1995; also Gamble (1938, 205–10).

201 *Vera Salomons* The "In Jerusalem" quotation from *Vera Frances Bryce Salomons 1888–1969* (1970), which has a portrait; also Vera Salomons (1983); Brown (1990); Nellhaus (2000); and

Canterbury Christ Church University College. Salomons. (2002), which includes portraits. Vera Salomons appears, lightly fictionalized, in *The Grand Complication,* a novel by Allen Kurzweil (2001, 160–61).

202 *Eastern Group Conference* Goldberg's participation is noted in Tuning (1940).

203 *Freedom Village Minutes of the First Meeting of the Committee for the establishment of the "Freedom Village" held ... September 13, 1943.* In GP.

203 *A visit to the United States* Noted scientist (1946).

204 *"Professor Goldberg visited Rochester"* T. H. James to S. Kitrosser, endorsing the nomination of Goldberg to Honorary Membership in the Society of Photographic Scientists and Engineers, 22 October 1969, in GP.

204 *"One visit was in 1946"* H. Goldberg in a talk at the American Society for Information Science Annual Meeting, Washington, DC, 31 October 1991: Session: Information Science before 1945. Tape D251–57, produced by InfoMedix for the American Society for Information Science and Technology, Silver Spring, MD, Side B, at about 500th inch.

204 *Forty years later* VCR household data from *Leisure Time Industry Surveys* (11 March 1993), p. L25.

205 *"Optics is finished"* Quoted in a letter from Harry Z. Tabor to H. Goldberg, 5 November 1985, in GP.

Chapter 18: Military Needs

Chapter 18 is based on the interviews noted for Chapter 17 and documents in GP.

207 *"The small Hebrew seal"* Quoted in Laboratory (1940).

207 *report on the capacity of the Jewish community* Concise (G1941).

208 *Haganah* The British Mandate authority's relationship with the Haganah varied (Hoffman 1983).

208 *Martin Strauss* Interview, 18 October 1994. Strauss in the United States: Schwartz (1983).

209 *continue working* Aviva Kelton was required to continue working in the Lab.

209 *Compasses* Otto Gold, 4 April 1995, and others. The prismatic compass is shown in Alexander (1957, 368).

209 *Goldberg rectifiers* Rectifiers are based on Scheimpflug's principle. Articles on Scheimpflug's principle by "Ingenieur

Goldberg" in *Prometheus* (1913) and *Dinglers Polytechnisches Journal* (1914) are by a different Goldberg, an Austrian.

210 *handheld cameras for aerial photography* were Fairchild KT241825 (Shmuel Neuman 29 March 1995).

210 *Clinometers* Interview with General Israel Tal, 24 March 1995. Goldberg reverse engineered a British clinometer shown in Plate II of a British government pamphlet, *Notes on Repairs to Fire Control Instruments. Part 45. Clinometers.* 2nd ed.1941. The Lab reportedly also built clinometers for the British Army and for the French Army in Syria.

211 *Sniper sights* Alex Eliraz, 2 April 1995, at the Collection Houses defense museum, Jaffa, where a Goldberg sniper scope, a reengineered British Enfield L1A1 rifle no. 32 scope, 2-1/2 × magnification, is on display. Another account mentions use of crystal glass from a broken Belgian mirror.

212 *The Ktina* GP contains: a letter from R. S. Schultze, Kodak Ltd, Wealdstone, Kent, to Chief Inspector Roman Kirschner, Tel Aviv Police Department (ref 48/R33/JME; 3 October 1956) acknowledging receipt of Goldberg portrait; a memorandum dated 6 June 1956, in Hebrew on "Dotting-pen. Memo to Sum Up Structure," marked Top Secret; and what appears to be a diagram, dated 22 June 1959. Interview J. Beutler, 25 March 1995. White (1990), an encyclopedic guide to subminiature photography, notes cameras disguised as pens (pp. 135–38 and 211), but does not mention the Ktina.

213 *Advisory Services* For Grisha Schapiro, who died in 1963, Gershon Sorenson interview 28 November 1998.

214 *The details...remain classified* M. Gichon, former Deputy Director of Military Intelligence, letter to M. Buckland, 16 July 1995.

214 *List of products* El Op mounted a display of products made by Goldberg's Lab at the 10th Meeting on Optical Engineering in Israel, Jerusalem, 2–6 March 1997.

Chapter 19: The Microfilm Rapid Selector

217 *"A Top U.S. Scientist"* Bush (1945b, 112).

217 *microdots... in Dresden* Frieser (1941; also 1957).

217 *wrote to Zeiss Ikon* Simader and Küppenbender, Zeiss Ikon, to Goldberg, 3 February 1940 (in GP), which was in reply to a letter from Goldberg dated 1 July 1939 (not found).

218 *Zeiss-Dokumator-System* Pescht (1953) and Wendel (1955).

218 *Ralph Shaw Dictionary of American Library Biography* (1978, 476–81) and N. D. Stevens (1975), which includes, pp. 6–14, "Shaw and the machine" by Theodore C. Hines (1975). Photo in Photoelectric librarian (1949, 122). For Shaw and the Rapid Selector: Varlejs (1999) also Burke (1994).

218 *"Not long after"* For Goldberg's visit: Bello (1960, 166–67); also personal communications from Herbert Goldberg.

218 *Two patent searches* Bello (1960, 166–67). *Electronics* magazine: Statistical (1932). Other patents for "Statistical machines" include Handel (1933) and Bryce (1938); also Morse (1942).

219 *Statistical machine. Use of light beam* Statistical (1932).

219 *Vannevar Bush* The only biography of Bush is Zachary (1997a; also 1997b). Colin Burke's *Information and secrecy: Vannevar Bush, Ultra, and the other Memex* (Scarecrow Press, 1994) is an excellent, detailed account of Bush's work on the Microfilm Rapid Selector for document retrieval and the Comparator for cryptanalysis. Buckland (1992) discusses Bush in relation to Goldberg. For Bush and Shaw: Burke (1994, 348).

219 *at 1,000 codes per second* Bush (1970, 187–88).

220 *copies... without stopping* Shaw (1950).

220 *Zeitlupe cameras* Zeiss Ikon (1937, 116–21); Gubas (1996); Blumtritt (2000, 48). Jungnickel (1934) reports on use of stroboscopic light with the Zeitlupe. Continuous-flow movie equipment was also developed by Emil Mechau (Krueger 2002.).

220 *Engineering Research Associates (ERA)* Shurkin (1984, 213–14); Tomasch (1980). The numerous reports on the ERA Rapid Selector include: Green (1949); Optical punched card (1949); Royal Society (1948, 158–59); Shaw (1949; 1950; 1951a, 58–69; 1951b); also New machine (1948). Shaw (1949) and Photoelectric librarian (1949) provide a convenient introduction to microfilm selectors. Technical report PB 97 313 on the ERA microfilm rapid selector (Engineering Research Associates 1949) is sometimes wrongly cited as PB 97 535. Bagg and N. D. Stevens (1962), although incomplete with respect to Goldberg, provide the best historical accounts of microfilm selector development and can be supplemented by Alexander and Rose (1964). G.W.W. Stevens (1968, Chapter 12) provides a summary, as does the International Federation for Documentation (1964, Chapter 9).

220 *$75,000* Green (1950, 67).

220 *skepticism* e.g., Vickery (1951) and Urquhart (1951).

220 *criticism* The Rapid Selector coding system is described and criticized by Wise and Perry (1950).

220 *became more cautious* Shaw (1951b).

220 *Bureau of Ships* Bagg (1963); Ball (1961); Murray (1962). For related rapid selector development work at the National Bureau of Standards and at Yale University: Ordung and Bagg (1957); Pike and Bagg (1962); and Bagg (1963).

220 *The Paradoxical Memex* The original text of "As we may think" is in Bush (1945a; 1945b; and various reprints). Associate Press issued a news release and *Time* printed a news item (Machine 1945). Nyce and Kahn (1991) is a useful, though rather uncritical, resource for "As We May Think;" also Nyce and Kahn (1989).

221 *"Dr Bush does not seem"* Fairthorne (1948, 211, emphasis in original) reviewing Bush's *Endless Horizons,* Chapter 11, a reprint of "As we may think"; also Fairthorne (1958).

221 *an image of potentiality* "An image of potentiality in information retrieval research and development" is the phrase used by Linda C. Smith (1981; updated and extended in Smith 1991), who analyzes as a cultural phenomenon the iconic role of Bush's essay and the fashion of citing it.

221 *an inspiration for many readers* Zachary (1997b).

222 *little or no relevance* Chalmers (1999, 1108) notes that "The hypermedia and retrieval systems that declare an origin in Bush's work generally do not work with the phenomena of context and person as Bush proposed..."

222 *they had not read it* e.g., J.C.R. Licklider (1965, xii–xiii): "Perhaps the main external influence that shaped the ideas of this book had its effect indirectly, through the community, for it was not until Carl Overhage noticed its omission from the References that I read Vannevar Bush's 'As we may think.' (*Atlantic Monthly,* 176, 101–8, July 1945). I had often heard about Memex and its 'trails of references.' I had hoped to demonstrate Symbiont to Dr. Bush as a small step in the direction in which he had pointed in his pioneer article. But I had not read the article. Now that I have read, I should like to dedicate this book, however unworthy it may be, to Dr. Bush."

222 *striking absence of references* On Bush's nonciting of related work: Zachary (1997a, 265).

222 *Wilhelm Ostwald* Hapke (1991; 1997; 1999; 2000; and 2003).

222 *Paul Otlet* Otlet (1934b, 389–91; 1990, 1, 8 and 9); Rayward (1976; 1994a; 1994b).

222 *Watson Davis* Farkas-Conn (1990); also Burke (1994); and Zachary (1997a, 74–75).

222 *James Bryce* Basche and others (1986, 5–6, 30–31); Light (1949); and Pugh (1995).

222 *H. G. Wells* Wells (1938) and Rayward (1999).

222 *distributed to Bush* Bush was a member of National Research Council's Committee on Scientific Aids to Learning that received an extensive (and widely read) report on microphotography prepared in 1937 by Vernon Tate (1938, 48), which notes the rapid selector design of Merle C. Gould (1941).

222 *in the air* e.g., Carruthers (1938, 266–67); Davis (1934; 1935, WD9); Farkas-Conn (1990, 19–20, 23n25); Schürmeyer (1936).

222 *inventions... occur duplicatively* Douglas 1986, (74–75).

222 *Russell C. Coile* Personal communication, 1990.

222 *When Bush came to know* Burke (1994, including 348, 413n46, 443n98); John C. Green to Vannevar Bush, 22 September 1949, in Library of Congress. Bush Papers, Box 44.

223 *"In 1931, a patent was"* United States. Advisory Committee (1954, 54).

223 *comparator renamed "Goldberg"* Burke (1994, 315).

223 *quick to acknowledge Goldberg's priority* Shaw (1949, 164; repeated by Hawkins [1960, 145]).

223 *Walter Schürmeyer* Schürmeyer (1933; 1936, 8). For Schürmeyer, see Habermann, Klemmt and Siefkes (1985, 315-16).

223 *Frits Donker Duyvis* at IID conference, Oxford 1936: 35th Conference (1938, 139).

224 *In 1957 Shmuel Neumann* Neumann (1957, v).

224 *Although Goldberg's patents were known* His U.S. patent is also mentioned by Mooers (1959, 117, 122) and Shaw (1951a, 58n18).

224 *in a European bibliography* Schürmeyer and Loosjes (1937, 25).

224 *in a U.S. bibliography* Berthold (1938).

224 *credited Shaw* e.g., Hines (1975, 6).

224 *Bush continued* Bush's "Memex revisited" (Bush 1967, 75–101) states, p. 76, "...the rapid selector, which first appeared some twenty years ago." Also Zachary (1997a, 51 and 265).

225 *A Networked Search Machine* The undated "search photo" patent diagram and draft text is in GP. The use of New York hotel stationery and use of the phrase "Rapid Selector" suggest that it was stimulated by his visit to Shaw in 1949.

226 *The development of photo-optical machines* Verry (1963, 71–83); also Becker and Hayes (1963, 200–217); Burke (1994, 360–65); Coblans (1957); Doyle (1975, 40–42, 268–71); several papers in Western Reserve (1957); and contemporary articles in *American Documentation.* For the Eccetron machine: (Grangeon and others 1962); Locquin (1960); Pun and Mitter (1962); Roger and Locquin (1962).

227 *Russian design* Kliachkin (1964). I thank Professor Ruggero Giliarevskii, Moscow, for contacting Mr. Kliachkin for me.

227 *chips of film* Goldberg: Neumann (1957, v); Beutler interview 26 March 1995. Kodak Minicard (Tyler, Myers and Kuipers 1955; Kuipers, Tyler, and Myers 1957). IBM's Walnut: Bradshaw (1962). Less complex chip systems included the Filmorex system (Samain 1956).

227 *first recorded online search* Bourne and Hahn (2003, 15).

228 *"A strip of 35 mm film 100 feet long"* yler (1948, 146); also O'Neal (1948).

228 *making biscuits* Berkeley (1949, 181).

Chapter 20: Finale

This chapter draws on personal letters, 1953–70, in the possession of Herbert Goldberg, written to him and his wife Frances by Emanuel Goldberg, Sophie Goldberg, and Chava (Renate) Gichon.

229 *"I must work"* E. Goldberg to F. and H. Goldberg, 16 August 1968.

229 *Difficulties* "Training new people" E. Goldberg to H. Goldberg, 1 April 1959. "For us": Goldberg to unidentified "Dear Friends," 9 December 1953 (in GP). "I continue": E. Goldberg to H. Goldberg, 19 January 1956. "I have": E. Goldberg to H. Goldberg 20 September 1957. "It is simply": E. Goldberg to F. and H. Goldberg 19 January 1956. "Aside of": E. Goldberg to H. Goldberg, undated, probably late 1955.

231 *El Op* Shmuel Neumann, who was directly involved in all these developments, interviewed 29 March 1995; and Israel Electro-Optical Industry Ltd. (1967).

231 *"I am in a real spider web"* E. Goldberg to H. Goldberg, 2 March1959.

231 *"Mr. Kapilow suddenly appeared"* Goldberg to A. Baroway, 1 May 1961, in GP.

232 *Oscar van Leer* Fortune (1967, 187–89).

233 *"for his contributions"* "zum Verdienste um die Klärung grundsätzlicher Fragen in der wissenschaftlen un angewandten Photographie." (Certificate, Leipzig, 21 April 1956, in GP).

233 *"Now please allow me"* Copies of acceptance speech and correspondence with Ben Gurion are in GP.

234 *"I made a short speech"* E. Goldberg to F. and H. Goldberg, 25 May 1957.

235 *Old Age* "I can only": Jakob Beutler, 25 March 1995. "… lonely": S. Goldberg to F. and H. Goldberg, 15 October 1967. "We are happy.": E. Goldberg to H. Goldberg, 23 October 1968.

"Very important": E. Goldberg to F. and H. Goldberg, 13 January 1968. "Well, I know": S. Goldberg to H. and F. Goldberg, 30 September 1967. "Mutti's strength": E. Goldberg to H. and F. Goldberg, 24 June 1968. "For all of us": C. Gichon to H. and F. Goldberg, 1 October 1970.

Chapter 21: After Goldberg

The notes below supplement the notes on these topics in earlier chapters.

237 *"the famous Professor Zapp"* Hoover (1946, 3).
237 *Tamara Grigorevna Goldberg* Russkoe zolotoe (1967), which also cites six other works by her on p. 289. For her medal, see Zaks (1988, 89).
238 *Leipzig* For the later history of the academy, see Pachnicke (1990) and a chronology by Hübscher (1990).
238 *Fernseh AG* Hoppe (1995) and Hempel (1990); also Rudert (1979). Also the notes for Chapter 12. Fernseh AG equipment was on display in the Berlin Technikmuseum as of June 1998.
238 *Volksempfänger* Wagenführ (1990) gives a nontechnical description.
239 *Wilhelm Ohnesorge* Deutsche Verkehrs-Zeitung (1937, esp. 9–18, 124–26); Ohnesorge (1938, 83–85); and *Encyclopedia of the Third Reich* (1991, 666).
239 *did not coordinate wartime scientific research* Grösse (1953).
240 *"Seeing Bomb"* For Fernseh's TV-guided bombs, see Hempel (1990); Hoppe (1995); Münster (1957); and Rudert (1979); also British Intelligence Objectives Subcommittee (1946, which includes German texts, selectively translated into English in Uricchio [1990]); and Feigel-Farnholz (1948, 594–96).
240 *Erich Rassbach* Scholtyseck (1999).
240 *Siegmund Loewe* Steiner (1998). S. Loewe, Berlin, to Goldberg, 17 October 1953, in GP.
240 *Zeiss and Zeiss Ikon* Carl Zeiss Jena liked to project a strong corporate image. Zeiss' use of professors and of theory was a marketing asset (Feffer 1994; 1996). The corporate histories of Zeiss and Zeiss Ikon most relevant to Goldberg's period are Zeiss Ikon AG. (1937); 25 Jahre (1951); Schumann (1962); and Walter (2000). Cohen (2000) is a detailed Zeiss chronology 1846–1997. Recent writings on Goldberg include *International* (1983); Gubas (1985a) and Mauersberger (2002a). See also Appendix B: Biographical Sources.

241 *Eduard Grentz... Walter Riedel* K. Mauersberger to Buckland, 22 December 1999; Interview, W. Riedel, Dresden, 20 November 2000.

241 *Joachim... office products* Joachim (1935; 1936).

241 *Contax* Kuč (1981, 1992) and numerous articles in *Zeiss Historica.*

241 *Rudolf Straubel* Gubas (1999a) and Müller (1998).

242 *Küppenbender advocated...forced labor* Herbert (1985, 278, 280; 1997, 305, 307), Schumann (1962, 568).

242 *Ernst Wandersleb* Gubas (1999b) and Müller (1998). Mrs. Wandersleb: H. Goldberg, 20 December 2002.

242 *removed...as reparations* Nuttall (2002); Widder (2003). Blumtritt (2000) describes developments in Dresden.

242 *Contax...at Carl Zeiss, Jena* Widder (2003).

242 *Heinz Küppenbender* Gubas (2000, 2002). His "spring" comment was made to Michael Plaot circa 1955 (M. Plaot, 11 November 1998).

242 *Die Leistung* 25 Jahre (1951).

243 *Interview* Küppenbender (1981), Berthel (2000).

243 *Armin Hermann* Hermann (1989).

243 *two Goldbergs* Walter (2000, 208, 216, 346).

243 *Zeiss went into a steady decline* Kuč (1993).

243 *Ikon AG* Finnische Wärtsilä (1989); IKON GmbH Präzisionstechnik (2003).

244 *Saxony* Bramke (1989). *Encyclopedia of the Third Reich* (1991: Killinger, p. 497; Mutschmann, p. 615). Mutschmann as King Mu: Bergander (1977, 59); Goebbels (1987–2001, Part II, v7:52): "Ich möchte nichts als Privatmann in sächsichen Bereich tätig sein. Man ist hier seiner Freiheit und seines Lebens nicht sicher. Irgendwann muss der Führer ja auch hier einmal helfen eingreifen." Saxon jokes, e.g.: II, v3:357).

244 *Killinger* Fiery (1937); German (1944).

244 *Hellerberg* Haase, Jersch-Wenzel, and Simon (1998), which includes some 60 stills from the film, *Zusammenlegung der letzten Juden in Dresden in das Lager am Hellerberg am 23. und 24. November 1942,* which is briefly described by Hirsch (2002). Klemperer (1998, see index) makes several references to Zeiss Ikon and to the Hellerberg barracks.

244 *forced labor from other camps* Nationalsozialistische Lagersystem (1990).

245 *Microdots* I am very grateful for the help of H. Keith Melton and the late William White.

245 *boastful article* Hoover (1946, 3). For discussion of "this concoction of semitruths and overt disinformation," see White

(1990, 191–95; 1992, 49–56). White (1992, 151), who searched for a Zapp who worked on microdots in Dresden but did not find one, cites and criticizes numerous authors as careless "retellers of the Zapp-Myth."

245 *Hoover... Pearl Harbor* Bratzel and Rout (1982); Young and others (1983).

245 *Kurt Zapp* United States. Federal Bureau of Investigation (1946, 8–10). I thank Professor K. Mauersberger, of Dresden, for contacting Professor Rudolf Reuther, who was at the Institute when Kurt Zapp was there and who kindly confirmed Zapp's activity, 25 August 2003.

246 *Cold War Russian spies* Personal communication, 26 June 2003, from H. K. Melton, author of *Ultimate Spy* (2002), who is preparing a book of microdots in espionage.

247 *Goldberg's Vision for Israel* This section is largely based on Autler's thesis (2000a, esp. 34–38, 61–62), which is summarized in Autler (2000b), and informal communications. Evron (1992, 25) notes Goldberg's contributions to military research and development prior to the creation of the state. The index confuses Professor Emanuel Goldberg with Professor Alexander ("Sacha") Goldberg. Also: Professor Imanuel Goldberg (1997).

247 *"Twelve years ago"* Future (1949).

247 *El-op, through its work* Autler (2000a, 62).

248 *billions* = milliards.

Chapter 22: Goldberg in Retrospect

249 *"I have no trust"* "Hoffnung, Erinnerungen oder Reminiszenzen aufzuschreiben, habe ich nicht. Ich war immer ein sehr schlechter Geschichtschüler, und meine Lebenserfahrungen haben mich gelehrt, dass es immer anders kommt, als man auf Grund der Vergangenheit annehmen möchte." (Goldberg to Otto M. Lilien, 13 November 1955, in GP.)

249 *Memory and Method* Sources: Best craftsman: Benno Erteshik, 2 April 1995. Two right hands: S. Neumann, 29 March 1995. Contax: Michael Plaot 12 November 1998. Sanding and Gilbreth: Moshe Arad, 26 March 1995. "I could say": EG "When asked ... " (GUndated, after 1947). Radio sets, M. Gichon, 14 August 1994. Wundt: see Chapter 2. "Pure mathematics": EG letter to Bret Golann, 18 September 1967. "I always considered": EG letter to HG and FG, 30 September 1967. "Goldberg's knowledge": M. Gichon, 14 August 1994; HG, 7 March 1997. "He knew everything": Aviva Kelton, 11 May 1998. "I learned": EG letter to FG

and HG, 16 August 1968. "I had bad": EG letter to HG, 16 November 1967. "Thought and worked constantly": M. Gichon, 14 August 1994 and 24 March 1995. "He would often come": Martin Strauss, 18 October 1994. "Energy and will-power: Martin Strauss, 18 October 1994. "Bomb": Aviva Kelton, 11 May 1998. "Heuristic and experimental": HG, 15 August 1994; also Moshe Arad, 26 March 1995. "He was unique": Shmuel Neuman, 29 March 1995. "Finding recorded knowledge": M. Gichon, 15 August 1994. "I don't remember formulas": quoted by Martin Strauss, 18 October 1994. "Quick information": EG letter to HG, 8 August 1967. "Optical computing": Aviva Kelton, 11 May 1998; also Jakob Beutler 25 March 1995.

251 *Goldberg the Educator* Moshe Arad, 26 March 1995: "He was a teacher in everything." "Character": Michael Plaot, 12 November 1998. "Of all": EG letter to HG and FG, 30 September 1967; also EG letter to Bret Golann, 18 September 1967. "But what was amazing": Aviva Kelton, 11 May 1998. For exhibits, see Chapter 5. "Teaching materials": MG, 7 March 1997. "Made everything first": Otto Gold, 4 April 1995. "I learned one thing": Otto Gold, 4 April 1995; Michael Plaot, 12 November 1998; Benno Erteshik, 2 April 1995; and Aviva Kelton, 11 May 1998. "I personally always advocated": EG letter to HG, 16 November 1967. "A designer": EG letter to FG and HG, 27 February 1961. "Even when": EG to HG, 15 August 1966. "Doing everything himself": Jakob Beutler, 25 March 1995.

252 *Political, Religious, and Social Views* Goldberg left little evidence of his political, religious, or social views. This section draws primarily on comments by HG, CG, and MG. "He liked the English way of life": MG, 30 November 1998. "Not observant, but supported a Jewish state, criticized killings": Jakob Beutler, 25 March 1995; Michael Plaot, 12 November 1998; Martin Strauss, 18 October 1994. "Dogs": EG letter to Bret Golann, 2 September 1966. "Those who worked": See list of interviewees in Appendix B.

254 *Goldberg in Context* J. H. Jaffe suggested the phrase "'brass and glass' to electronics."

254 *History and What Is Remembered* Buckland (2004).

256 *look back with considerable pride* Precision (G1946).

256 *Standing here* Standing (G1967).

Bibliography of Emanuel Goldberg's Writings

This list is probably not complete. Items are arranged by year, then alphabetically by title, disregarding initial articles, with separately published summaries by others appended. Many were also separately distributed as offprints.

1900

Speranskii, Alexander W., and Emanuel G. Goldberg. 1900. [Electrolysis of some metallic salts in organic solutions.] Злектролизъ растворовъ металлическихъ солей въ органическихъ растворителяхъ. *Russkoe Fiziko-Khimicheskoe Obshchestvo. Zhurnal.* [*Journal of the Russian Physical-Chemical Society*, St. Petersburg] 32 (1900): 797–804. Paper presented at a meeting of the Russian Physical-Chemical Society, St. Petersburg, November 15 (Old Style November 2), 1900. A manuscript in Goldberg's writing is in GP. Brief German summaries in *Zeitschrift für angewandte Chemie* 13 (18 Dezember 1900):1292, and *Zeitschrift für physikalische Chemie* 39 (1902):369–70.

1902

Beitrag zur Kinetik photochemischer Reaktionen. Die Oxydation von Chinin durch Chromsäure. *Zeitschrift für physikalische Chemie.* 41 (1902):1–10. Extended summary with data in *Zeitschrift für wissenschaftliche Photographie, Photophysik und Photochemie* 1, no. 1 (1903):32–34. Also summary in *Jahrbuch für Photographie* 17(1903):416.

1906

Die Arbeiten von Amstutz über Autotypie. *Zeitschrift für Reproduktionstechnik* 8, Heft 11 (1906):171–74. Continuation intended, but none found. Comments on the first six of a series of articles by N. S. Amstutz entitled "Physical characteristics of relief engravings, especially relating to half-tones" in *Inland Printer,* starting with 36, no. 6 (March 1906):842–45.

325

Beiträge zur Kinetik photochemischer Reaktionen: Inaugural-Dissertation ... Universität Leipzig. Leipzig: Barth, 1906. Repr. as next item.

Beiträge zur Kinetik photochemischer Reaktionen. *Zeitschrift für wissenschaftliche Photographie, Photophysik und Photochemie.* 4, Heft 3 (1906):61–107. Repr. of previous item. Summary in *Jahrbuch für Photographie.* 20(1906):374 and 397. Discussed on pp. 227–29 of J. Plotnikow, Die mathematische Theorie der photographischen Kinetik *Zeitschrift für wissenschaftliche Photographie, Photophysik und Photochemie* 19 (1920):225–74.

Robert Luther and Emanuel Goldberg. Beiträge zur Kinetik photochemischer Reaktionen. I.. Sauerstoffhemmung der Photochemischen Chlorreaktionen in ihrer Beziehung zur photochemischen Induktion, Deduktion und Aktivierung. *Zeitschrift für Physikalische Chemie* 56 (1906):43–56. No Part II found. Develops part of Goldberg's dissertation. Abstract in *Jahrbuch für Photographie* 21 (1907): 383–84.

Die Berechnung der Moiré-Erscheinungen. *Zeitschrift für Reproduktionstechnik.* 8, Heft 12 (1906):189–95.

1907

Etudes géométriques sur la formation des moirages en similigravure polychrome. (Extraits) *Procédé* 4 (Avril 1907):51–55. French transl. of G1906 Berechnung.

Das Moiré. *Deutscher Buch- und Steindrucker.* 13, Heft 5 (Februar 1907):457–59.

Richters Kombinationsraster. *Archiv für Buchgewerbe* 44, Heft 11/12 (November–Dezember 1907):479–84.

Studien über Metallätzung. *Zeitschrift für Reproduktionstechnik* 9, Heft 7 (Juli 1907):98–102. Intended continuation not published.

Ueber die Einstellung der Schlitzblende. *Zeitschrift für Reproduktionstechnik* 9, Heft 3 (März 1907):39–40.

1908

Farbenphotographie und Farbendruck. Leipzig: Verlag des deutscher Buchgewerbevereins, 1908. (Monographien des Buchgewerbes, 2). 84 pp. plus 30 pp. of illustrations. Also published in instalments in *Archiv für Buchgewerbe* (next item). Reviews in *British Journal of Photography. Monthly Supplement on Colour Photography* 3, no. 36 (3 December 1909):96, and *Photographische Industrie* 56, Nr. 2587 (13 Oktober 1909):1394.

Farbenphotographie und Farbendruck. *Archiv für Buchgewerbe* 45, Heft 4 (April 1908):142–49; Heft 5 (Mai 1908):186–95; Heft 6 (Juni 1908):230–35. Also published separately, see previous item.

Die photomechanischen Vervielfältigungsverfahren im Jahre 1908. *Archiv für Buchgewerbe* 45, Heft 11/12 (November–Dezember 1908): 474–78.

Physikalische Grundlagen des Dreifarbendruckes. *Zeitschrift für Reproduktionstechnik.* 10 (1908):Heft 4:50–54: "Einleitung"; Heft 6:82–86: "Das Auge"; Heft 7:98–100: "Beziehung zwischen Grundlagen des Dreifarbendruckes"; Heft 8:120–22; Heft 11:162–64: "Die Gesetze der Farbenmischung I"; 11, Heft 10 (Oktober 1909):147–50: "I. Apparate zur Ermittlung der Detailwiedergabe"; 12 (1910):21–23: "Die Gesetze der Farbenmischung IV." "Fortsetzung folgt," but no continuation found.

1909

Die Detailwiedergabe und Beziehung zur Sensitometrie. *Photographische Industrie.* Heft 45 (10 November 1909):1527–30. "Fortsetztung folgt," but no continuation found.

Die internationale photographische Ausstellung Dresden 1909. *Archiv für Buchgewerbe* 11, Heft 6 (1909):159–61; Heft 7:190–93; Heft 8:230–34.

Internationale photographische Austellung Dresden 1909. Original und Reproduktion: Zeitschrift für Kunsthandel und Kunstsammlungen 1 (1909):79.

Reproduktionstechnik. Original und Reproduktion: Zeitschrift für Kunsthandel und Kunstsammlungen 1, Heft 1 (1909):52.

Studien über die Detailwiedergabe in der Photographie. *Zeitschrift für Reproduktionstechnik* 11, Heft 10 (1909):147–50.

Die Wissenschaft auf der Internationalen Photographischischen Ausstellung Dresden 1909. *Photographische Chronik* 16, Nr. 54 (4 Juli 1909): 333–35; Nr. 64 (8 August 1909):397–99.

1910

The densograph: An instrument for obtaining automatically the characteristic curve of a plate. *British Journal of Photography* 57, no. 2625 (26 August 1910):649–51. Editorial comment p. 648.

Densograph. Ein Registrierapparat zur Messung der Schwarzung von photographischen Platten. *Jahrbuch für Photographie* 24 (1910):226–33.

Densograph, ein Registrierapparat zur Messung der Schwärzung von photographischen Platten. *Photographische Korrespondenz* 47, Nr. 596 (Mai

1910):226–32; Nr. 597 (Juni 1910):266–69. Also in *Photographische Industrie* 8 (20 April 1910):529–30; (4 Mai 1910):596–98.

Densograph, ein Registrierapparat zur Messung der Schwärzung von photographischen Platten. *Zeitschrift für Reproduktionstechnik* 12, Heft 4 (1910):49–55.

Densographe, appareil enregistreur pour le mesure du noircissement sur les plaques photographiques. (Résumé de la communication faite au Congrès International de Photographie, Bruxelles, août 1910). *Bulletin de la Société Française de Photographie* 3e ser., tom. 1, no.10 (1910):336.

Herstellung neutral grauer Keile und verlaufender Filter für Photometrie und Photographie. *Jahrbuch für Photographie* 24 (1910):149–55.

Die photomechanische Illustrations-Verfahren. [Chapter, pp. 219–46, in:] *Das moderne Buch,* ed. Ludwig Volkermann. Stuttgart: Krais, 1910, which is Band 3 of *Die graphischen Künste der Gegenwart.* Herausg. von Theodor Goebel. Stuttgart: Krais. Bd 1, 1895; Neue Folge [= Bd 2] 1908; Bd 3, 1910. Sections titled "Die Reproduktionsphotographie," "Fortschritte der photographischen Reproduktionstechnik in den letzten 10 Jahren," and "Die Herstellung von Druckplatten," followed by about 35 illustrative plates by different printers.

Die photomechanischen Vervielfältigungsverfahren im Jahre 1910. *Archiv für Buchgewerbe* 47, Heft 11/12 (November–Dezember 1910):350–55.

Préparation de prismes et d'écrans de ton gris neutres pour usages photométriques. *Bulletin de la Société Française de Photographie* 3e ser., tom. 1, no.10 (1910):326–29. A version of paper at Brussels conference, 1910.

The preparation of prismatic wedges of neutral colour for photometric work. *British Journal of Photography* 57 (26 August 1910):648–49. Editorial comment p. 643.

Über die Herstellung neutralgrauer Keile und Schichten für photographische Zwecke. *Chemiker Zeitung* 34, Nr. 109 (1910):964–65. Paper presented at the 5th International Congress of Photography. Brussels, 1–6 August 1910. English abstract: *Chemical Abstracts* 5 (1910):3543. Summary in *Zeitschrift für angewandte Chemie* 23, Heft 41 (14 Oktober 1910):1945–46.

1911

Herstellung neutral-grauer Keile und verlaufender Filter für Photometrie und Photographie. *Zeitschrift für wissenschaftliche Photographie, Photophysik und Photochemie.* 10, Heft 7 (1911):238–44.

Herstellung neutral-grauer Keile und verlaufender Filter für Photometrie und Photographie. *Jahrbuch für Photographie* 25 (1911):149–55.

Die photomechanischen Vervielfältigungsverfahren im Jahre 1911. *Archiv für Buchgewerbe* 48, Heft 11/12 (November–Dezember 1911):340–45.

Préparation de prismes et écrans de ton gris neutres pour usages photométriques. *La photographie des couleurs et la revue des sciences photographiques* 5, no. 1 (1911):40–41. Summary G1912 Préparation.

Studien über die Detailwiedergabe in der Photographie. *Zeitschrift für wissenschaftliche Photographie, Photophysik und Photochemie* 9, Heft 10 (1911):313–23. Extended abstract in French: *Bulletin de la Société Française de Photographie* 3. ser., tom. 4, no. 9 (Septembre 1913):286–88.

Sur la préparation de prismes gris-neutres et d'écrans à teintes croissante pour la photométrie et la photographie. *La photographie des couleurs et la revue des sciences photographiques* 5, no. 12 (Décembre 1911):248–53.

Goldberg, Emanuel, Robert Luther, and Fritz Weigert. Über die automatische Herstellung der charaktischen Kurve. *Zeitschrift für wissenschaftliche Photographie, Photophysik und Photochemie.* 9, Heft 10 (1911):323–31. English abstract *Chemical Abstracts* 5 (1910):3767.

Unschärfe in Reproduktionen. *Zeitschrift für Reproduktionstechnik* 13, Heft 8 (1911):114–20.

1912

Auflösungsvermögen (Schärfenwiedergabe) der photographischen Platten. *Zeitschrift für Reproduktionstechnik* 14, Heft 9 and 10 (1912):130–35, 146–53. A continuation of G1912 Unschärfe and G1912 Auflösungsvermögen von. English abstract *Chemical Abstracts* 7 (1912):310. Extended French summary in *Bulletin de la Société Française de Photographie* (1914):72–74.

Auflösungsvermögen von photographischen Platten. Zeitschrift für Reproduktionstechnik 14, Heft 1 (1912):4–9. Summary in Zeitschrift für wissenschaftliche Photographie, Photophysik und Photochemie 15 (1915):62.

Beleuchtung in der Photographie und Reproduktionstechnik. *Helios. Exportzeitschrift für Elektrotechnik* 18 (1912):512–19. Numerous illustrations of equipment.

Le densographe. Appareil enregistreur pour le mesure de la densité des clichés photographiques. In International Congress of Photography. (5th, Brussels, 1910). 1912. *Ve Congrès International de Photographie [, 1910]. Compte rendu, procès-verbaux, rapports, notes et documents.* [Ed. by] C. Putttemans, L. P. Clerc et E. Wallon, 144–51. Brussels: Établissements Émile Bruylant, 1912.

Die Grundlagen der Reproduktionstechnik: In gemeinverständlicher Darstellung. Halle: Knapp, 1912. (Enzyklopädie der Photographie und Kinematographie. Heft 80). Reviews in *Zeitschrift für wissenschaftliche Photographie, Photophysik und Photochemie.* 14, Heft 9 (1915):313, and *Jahrbuch für Photographie.* 27 (1913):451. 2nd ed. in 1923.

On the resolving power of the photographic plate. *British Journal of Photography* 59, no. 2743 (November 29, 1912):920–23; no. 2744 (December 6, 1912):936–38; and no. 2745 (December 13, 1912):958–60. "A paper read before the Royal Photographic Society." Abstract in French: *Bulletin de la Société Française de Photographie* 3. ser., tom. 5, no. 3 (Mars 1914):104.

On the resolving power of the photographic plate. *Photographic Journal* 36 (November 1912):300–19. Translated and read by A. J. Newton. Original manuscript in German is at Eastman House Library, Rochester, NY, in vertical file under Goldberg.

Photographie. In *Handwörterbuch der Naturwissenschaften.* Hrsg. Eugen Korschelt, 7:737–54. Jena: Fischer, 1912. Later version in 1932.

Die photographische Reproduktionstechnik als Erganzungsunterricht, vornehmlich der Kunstschüler in der Akademievorschule. In *Die technische Kurse der Vorschule der Königlichen Akademie für graphische Künste und Buchgewerbe zu Leipzig,* vom M. Seliger, K. Berthold, A. Schelter, A. Kolb, F. Naumann. E. Goldberg, G. Belwe und H. Dannhorn. Hrsg. von der Akademie gelegentlich des Internationalen Kongresses für Kunstunterricht in Dresden, 1–12. Leipzig: Akademie, 1912.

Die photomechanischen Vervielfältigungsverfahren im Jahre 1912. *Archiv für Buchgewerbe* 49, Heft 11/12 (November–Dezember 1912):349–51.

Photometrie: Photographische Photometrie. In *Handwörterbuch der Naturwissenschaften.* Hrsg. Eugen Korschelt, 7:779–81. Jena: Fischer, 1912.

Préparation de prismes et de couches de ton gris neutres pour usages photométriques. In International Congress of Photography. (5th, Brussels, 1910). 1912. *Ve Congrès International de Photographie [, 1910]. Compte rendu, procès-verbaux, rapports, notes et documents.* [Ed. by] C. Putttemans, L. P. Clerc et E. Wallon, 152–55. Brussels: Établissements Émile Bruylant. German summary "Über die Herstellung neutralgrauer Keile und Schichten für photographische Zwecke." *Zeitschrift für angewandte Chemie* 33, Heft 41 (14. Oktober 1910):1945–46.

1913

Das Auflösgsvermögen von photographischen Platten. Zeitschrift für wissenschaftliche Photographie, Photophysik und Photochemie.

12, Heft 3 (1913):77–92. Reviewed in *Jahrbuch für Photographie* 27(1913):385–86. German abstract in *Zeitschrift für angewandte Chemie* 26 (15 Juli 1913):425. Summary in *Zeitschrift für wissen-schaftlichen Photographie, Photophysik und Photochemie* 1915 (15):62.

Études sur la précision des images photographiques: La cause de manque de netteté dans les reproductions. *Le Procédé* 15, No. 7 (Juillet 1913):98–103; No. 8 (Août 1913):117–24; Le pouvoir résolvant de la plaque photographique. No. 9 (Septembre 1913):133–41; [Cont.] No. 10 (Octobre 1913):154–58. Translation of G1911 Studien and closely related materials in G1909 Studien; G1911 Unschärfe; G1912 Auflösungsvermögen (Schärfenwiedergabe); G1912 Auflösungsvermögen von; and G1912 On the resolving.

Farbenphotographie: Eine Sammlung von Aufnahmen in natürlichen Farben. Hrsg von Fritz Schmidt. Leipzig: Verlag von E. A. Seemann, 1913. Issued in 12 Hefte by different authors, including, by Goldberg: Heft 10:73–76: Das Licht und die Farben; Heft 10:77–80: Das Auge des Menschen; Heft 11:81–83: Das Sehen der Farben; Heft 11:83–87: Die Rolle der Einbildung und des Kontrastes beim Betrachten von Farbenphotographien; Heft 12:88–91: Nebenwirkung der Anordnung des Kornes in der Farbenphotographie.

Herstellung von Aetzungen mit Hochlicht. *Zeitschrift für Reproduktionstechnik* 15 (1913):2–6.

Die photomechanischen Vervielfältigungsverfahren im Jahre 1913. *Archiv für Buchgewerbe* 50, Heft 11/12 (November–Dezember 1913): 300–301.

La production des similigravures à blanc purs. *Procédé* 15 (May 1913): 73–74. Abstract in French in *Bulletin de la Société Française de Photographie* 3. ser., tom. 4, no. 7 (Juillet 1913):240.

1914

Auflösungsvermögen der photographische Platte (Le pouvoir résolvant de la plaque photographique). *Bulletin de la Société Française de Photographie,* ser. 3, tom 5, no. 2 (Février 1914):72–74. Summary of G1912 Auflösungsvermögen (Schärfenwiedergabe); G1912 On the resolving; and G1913 Études: 133–41, 154–58.

Führer durch die Gruppe: Wissenschaftliche Photographie der internation-alen Ausstellung für Buchgewerbe und Graphik. Halle: Knapp, 1914. Separate printing of G1914 Die wissenschaftliche.

Graphische Technik. *Zeitschrift für Elektrochemie und angewandte physi-kalische Chemie* 21, Heft 7/8 (1915):122–28. Paper presented at the 21st conference, Deutsche Bunsengesellschaft für angewandte physikalische Chemie, 21–24 May 1914. German summary: *Zeitschrift für angewandte Chemie* 27 (1914):527.

Die Reproduktionstechnik auf der Internationalen Ausstellung für Buchgewerbe und Graphik. *Zeitschrift für Reproduktionstechnik* 16 (1914):82–88.

Die Reproduktionstechnik auf der Internationalen Ausstellung für Buchgewerbe und Graphik, Leipzig 1914. *Archiv für Buchgewerbe* 51, Heft 7–9 (1914):261–66.

Der Tiefdruck an der Internationalen Ausstellung für Buchgewerbe und Graphik. *Zeitschrift für Reproduktionstechnik* 16 (1914):98–100.

Die wissenschaftliche Photographie auf der Internationalen Austellung für Buchgewerbe und Grafik. *Photographische Rundschau* 51 (1914): Heft 14:213–20; Heft 15:231–37. Also publ. separately as G1914 Führer.

1916

Lichthof bei photographischen Platten. *Zeitschrift für Reproduktionstechnik* 18, Heft 11 (November 1916):82–85; Heft 12 (Dezember 1916): 90–92. Paper presented at 29th conference of the Verein deutscher Chemiker, Leipzig, October 1916. German summaries: *Zeitschrift für angewandte Chemie* Pt I, 29 (31 Oktober 1916):394; *Zeitschrift für wissenschaftliche Photographie, Photophysik und Photochemie.* 17, Heft 11 and 12 (1918):258; and also in *Photographische Korrespondenz* 53, Nr. 674 (1916):368 (English version: *Journal of the Society of Chemical Industry* 35 (1916):1236). English abstracts: *Chemical Abstracts* 11:1607; and Eastman Kodak Company. Research Laboratories. *Monthly Abstracts Bulletin* 3 (1917):92.

Eine Umkonstruktion des Martensschen Schwärzungsmessers. *Photographische Korrespondenz* 53, Nr. 374 (September 1916):368–69. Brief summary of paper presented at 29th conference of the Verein deutscher Chemiker, Leipzig, October 1916. German abstract *Zeitschrift für angewandte Chemie* Pt I, 29 (31 Oktober 1916):394 and English versions of this abstract: *Journal of the Society of Chemical Industry* 35 (1916):1236, and *Chemical Abstracts* 11:1607. Also *Photographische Rundschau* 54 (1917):21. See also G1917 Umkonstruction.

1917

Anfertigung von stark verkleinerten Photographien. *Photographische Industrie* Heft 29 (18 Juli 1917):448–50.

Lichthof bei photographischen Platten. *Photographische Rundschau* 54 (1917):73–79. Preceded by German abstract, 21–22.

Eine neue Methode zur Messung des Lichthofes. *Photographische Korrespondenz* 54, Nr. 678 (March 1917):81–86. Summary of paper at the Leipzig meeting of the Verein Deutscher Chemiker.

Objektiv und Platte in ihren Beziehungen zu einander. *Deutsche Optische Wochenschrift* 11 (18 März 1917):108–9.

Eine Umkonstruktion des Martensschen Schwaerzungsmessers. *Photographische Korrespondenz*. 54, Nr. 684 (September 1917):321–24.

1918

Die photometrischen Grundlagen der Sensitometrie. *Chemiker Zeitung* 42, Nr. 119/120 (1918):485–86.

1919

Anfertigung von stark verkleinerten Photographien. Das Neue Universum; Die interessanten Erfindungen und Entdeckung auf allen Gebieten, sowie Reiseschilderungen, Erzählungen, Jagden und Abenteuer. Ein Jahrbuch für die reifere Jugend. Mit einem Anhang zur Selbstbeschaftigung "Häusliche Werkstatt". Stuttgart: Union Deutsche Verlagsgesellschaft. 40 [1919]:462–65.

1921

Bewertung der charakterischen Kurve von Platten und Papieren für die naturtreue photographischen Abbildung. *Zeitschrift für angewandte Chemie* 34 (1921):228. Brief summary of paper presented at the 34th conference of the Verein deutscher Chemiker, Fachgruppe für Photochemie und wissenschaftliche Photographie, 20 May 1921.

Die Kinematographie als technisches Problem. Inaugural lecture, Technical University Dresden. Cited in Sächische Hauptstaatsarchiv, Dresden, MfV No. 15266, Bl.56, 19 May 1921. Copy of text not located.

1922

Der Aufbau des photographischen Bildes. Teil I: Helligkeitsdetails. Halle: Knapp, 1922. (Enzyklopädie der Photographie und Kinematographie. Heft 99). Extended review by F. Weigert. Ein photographisches und optisches Standardwerk. *Die Naturwissenschaft* 10, Heft 39 (29 September 1922):861–67. Also review in *British Journal of Photography* 69 (28 July 1922):450. Review in French: *La revue française de photographie. Science Sup.* 3 (1 Mai 1922): 46, transl. in Eastman Kodak Company. Research Laboratories. *Monthly Abstracts Bulletin* 8 (1922):331. Also 2nd ed. 1925, French eds. 1924 and 1926, and Russian ed. 1929.

1923

Densograph, ein Registrieapparat zur Messung der Schwärzung von photographischen Platten und Papieren. *Kinotechnik* 5, 23/24 Heft (15 Dezember 1923):529–31. English abstract in Eastman Kodak Company. Research Laboratories. *Monthly Abstracts Bulletin* 10 (1923):312.

Die Glühlampe im Dienste der Projektionstechnik. *Zeitschrift des Vereines deutscher Ingenieure* 67, Nr. 42 (20 Oktober 1923):991. Summary of paper presented at the Jahresversammlung der Deutschen Beleuchtstechnischen Gesellschaft, Dresden, 1 September 1923.

The gray wedge and its use in sensitometry. *Transactions of the Faraday Society* 19 (1923):349–54. Also discussion 383–85. Paper presented at meeting on The Physical Chemistry of the Photographic Process, London, 23 May 1923. Summary in French: Emploi des coins gris-neutre en sensitometrie; détermination du halo. *Science et industries photographiques* 4, no. 2 (Février 1924):19. English abstract *Chemical Abstracts* 18 (1924):1846; also Eastman Kodak Company. Research Laboratories. *Monthly Abstracts Bulletin* 10 (1924):366–67.

Die Grundlagen der Reproduktionstechnik: In gemeindverständlicher Darstellung. Zweite Auflage. Halle: Knapp, 1923. (Enzyklopädie der Photographie und Kinematographie. Heft 80). First ed. 1912.

1924

Le densographe: Appareil enregistreur pour les mesures de densités sur négatifs et sur épreuves photographiques. *Science et industries photographiques* 4, no. 3 (1 Mars 1924):25–26.

La formation de l'image photographique. *Science et industries photographiques* 4 (1924) and 5 (1925). Transl. of 2nd German ed. of *Der Aufbau* in numerous installments starting 4:25.

1925

VI. Internationaler Kongreß für Photographie in Paris. *Photographische Industrie,* 23, Heft 29 (20 Juli 1925):785.

Der Aufbau des photographischen Bildes. Teil I: Helligkeitsdetails. Zweite, erweiterte Auflage. Halle: Knapp, 1925. (Enzyklopädie der Photographie und Kinematographie. Heft 99). Reviewed in *Photographische Industrie* 24, Heft 2 (11 Januar 1926):26, and *British Journal of Photography* 73 (25 June 1926):361.

Eine neue Methode zur Prüfung photographischer Objective. Undated typescript, probably 1925, in GP, presumably the original of G1926 Méthode.

1926

Bewegungssynthese in der Kinematographie. *Kinotechnik* 8. J., Nr. 13 (10 Juli 1926):333–36. Summary in French: Le mécanisme de la synthèse cinématographique. *Science et Industries Photographiques* 6, no. 9 (Mars 1926):171.

La formation de l'image photographique: Considérations photométriques et sensitométriques. Paris: Paul Montel, 1926. (Bibliothèque de "La Revue Française de Photographie"). French ed. of the 2nd German ed. of *Der Aufbau*, 1925. Review in *British Journal of Photography* 73 (25 June 1926):361.

Herstellung von starken Verkleinerungen. *Zeitschrift für technische Physik* 7. J., Nr. 10 (1926):500–505. German abstracts in *Jahrbuch für Photographie* 30 (1928):1073; *Zeitschrift für Instrumentenkunde* 48, no. 4 (April 1926):195–97; and by B. Fergg in *Zeitschrift für technische Physik* 52, nos. 1–3 (1957):24–54.

Kinematographische Wolkenaufnahmen. *Bezee-Photo-Mitteilungen.* II. J. (1926):145–48. Monthly published by Photohaus "Bezee," Leipzig. No copy found. Leipzig University Library's copy lacks these pages.

[The measurement of temperature in projector gates]. *Science et industries photographiques* 6A (1 June 1926):60] [Not seen]. Abstract in *Bildwerfer* (Januar 1926):32. English abstract Eastman Kodak Company. Research Laboratories. *Monthly Abstracts Bulletin* 13 (1927):10.

Une méthode nouvelle pour l'essai des objectifs. In *VIe Congrès International de Photographie: Décisions, Procès-Verbaux, Rapports et Mémoires [1925].* Ed. L. P. Clerc and G. Labussière, 186–93. Paris: Société française de photographie, 1926. Sample test photo pasted on p. 191. Extended summary in *Science et industries photographiques* 6, no. 5 (Mai 1926):87–88. Review: *British Journal of Photography* 73 (30 July 1926):440. English transl.: G1926 New.

A new method of lens testing. *British Journal of Photography* 73, no. 3467 (15 October 1926):598–600. Abstract in Eastman Kodak Company. Research Laboratories. *Monthly Abstracts Bulletin* 12 (1926):633.

A new process of micro-photography. *British Journal of Photography* 73, no. 3458 (13 August 1926):462–65. English transl. of G1926 L'obtention. Summarized as: Micro-photographs with extreme reduction. *British Journal Photographic Almanac and Photographer's Daily Companion* 1927:234–35. Abstract in Eastman Kodak Company. Research Laboratories. *Monthly Abstracts Bulletin* 12, no. 11 (November 1926):575.

L'obtention photographique de très fortes réductions. In *VIe Congrès International de Photographie: Décisions, Procès-Verbaux, Rapports et Mémoires [1925]*. Ed. L. P. Clerc and G. Labussière, 236–45. Paris: Société française de photographie, 1926. Reviewed in *Photographische Industrie* 24, Heft 2 (11 Januar 1926):32, and *British Journal of Photography* 73, (30 July 1926):440. English translation: G1926 New process. See also next item.

Obtention photographiques d'images très réduites. *Science et Industries Photographiques* 6M, no. 3 (1 Mars 1926):9–12. Corrigenda in 6, no. 5 (1924):24. Preprint of previous item. Summary in *Photographische Industrie*. 24, Heft 19 (10 Mai 19\26):484–85; also Eastman Kodak Company. Research Laboratories. *Monthly Abstracts Bulletin* 12 (1926):402.

Spektrodensograph, ein Registrierapparat zür Ermittlung von Absorptionskurven von Farbstoffen. *Zeitschrift für angewandte Chemie.* 39 (1926):835.

1927

Kampmann, Carl. *Die graphische Kunste.* Vierte, vermehte und verbesserte Auflage. Neubearbeitet von Prof. Dr. E. Goldberg in Dresden. Berlin and Leipzig: Walter de Gruyter & Co., 1927. (Sammlung Goschen, 75). Other eds. in 1898, 1906, 1909, 1932, and 1941.

Herstellung von starken Verkleinerungen. *Die Linse: Monatschrift für Photographie und Kinematographie* 23, Nr. 4 (April 1927):116–18; Nr. 5 (Mai 1927):152–54.

[Response to J. M. Eder, Zur Geschichte des Graukeiles in seiner Anwendung zur Sensitometrie photographischer Platten] *Photographische Industrie* 25, Heft 11 (14 März 1927):264; also Heft 18 (2 Mai 1927):444–46.

Spektrodensograph, ein Registrierapparat zür Ermittelung der Absorptionskurven von Farbstoffen. *Melliand-Textilberichte* (Heidelberg) 8 (1927):447–49. Abstract: *Chemical Abstracts* 21(1927):3002.

Zur Frage der Blendennormung. *Photowoche* 18, Heft 5 (6 Dezember 1927):185–86.

1928

Entwicklung der amateur Kinematographie. *Kinotechnik* 10, Heft 22 (20 November 1928):575–76. An historical review of amateur movie equipment, based on paper entitled "Schmalfilmaufnahme" presented at the Deutsche Kinotechnische Gesellschaft, Berlin, 8 November 1928. Brief German summary "Schmalfilmaufnahme." *Zeitschrift für angwandte Chemie* 42 (1929):31. Abstract in Eastman Kodak Company. Research Laboratories. *Monthly Abstracts Bulletin* 15 (1929):58.

1929

Образование фотографического изображения. [Obrazovaniye fotografichcskogo izobrazheniya. Transl. of *Der Aufbau des photographischen Bildes*]. Пер. с нем. К. Л. Колособа. Лод. ред. А. И. Рабинобича. М., акц. изд-ске о-во "Огонек", тип. "Гудок". 1929. (Б-ка ?урн. "Советское фото".) Not seen. Entry from *Knizhnaia letopis'* 1930, no. 14, p. 1254.

1930

Möglichkeiten und Grenzen der Photographie. Paper presented at the first meeting of the Deutsche Gesellschaft für photographische Forschung, 23 and 24 May 1930, Berlin. Noted in *Zeitschrift für wissenschaftliche Photographie, Photophysik und Photochemie* 28, Heft 2 (Mai 1930):72.

1931

The photocell in photography. Traill Taylor Memorial Lecture, Royal Photographic Society, London, 27 October 1931. Summarized in *British Journal of Photography* 78 (30 October 1931):655–56. Draws on Dresden conference "Tonfilms" and "Registrier" papers.

Die physikalischen Grundlagen des Tonfilms. *Kinotechnik* 13, Heft 7 (5 April 1931):132–33. Summary of paper at the 94th session of the Deutsche Kinotechnische Gesellschaft, 9 March 1931, Berlin. Brief earlier summary in Heft 6 (20 März 1931):118.

Prof. Goldberg über die physikalischen Grundlagen des Tonfilms. *Filmtechnik* 7, Heft 7 (4 April 1931):12–13. Summary of lecture at the 94th meeting of the Deutsche Kinotechnische Gesellschaft, 9 März 1931.

1932

La cellule photo-électrique et ses applications à la photographie. *Bulletin de la Société Française de Photographie* Ser. 3, tom 19, no. 1 (Janvier 1932):7–9. Brief summary of lecture, 3 Novembre 1931, Paris.

Deutscher Vorschlag zur sensitometrischen Normung: Bericht des Deutschen Normenausshusses für Phototechnik. In International Congress of Photography. 8th, Dresden, 1931, 101–102. See G1932 International Congress. Also in *Zeitschrift für wissenschaftliche Photographie, Photophysik und Photochemie* 31, Heft 3 (1932):81–83, followed by detailed description by Robert Luther, 83–95. English abstract: Eastman Kodak Company. Research Laboratories. *Monthly Abstracts Bulletin* 19 (1932):150. Abstract: *Chemical Abstracts* 27 (1933):1833; also *Photographic Abstracts* 12, Part 4, no. 48 (1932):218.

Die Grundlagen des Tonfilms. In *International Congress of Photography. 8th, Dresden, 1931,* 213–14. See G1932 International Congress. Brief German summary *Zeitschrift für angewandte Chemie.* 44, Nr. 43 (1931):877.

International Congress of Photography. 8th, Dresden, 1931. *Bericht über den VIII. internationalen Kongress für wissenschaftliche und angewandte Photographie, Dresden, 1931.* Herausg. von J[ohn] Eggert und A[rpad] von Biehler. Leipzig: J. A. Barth, 1932. Contains G1932 Vorschlag (101–102), G1932 Registerproblem (213–214), and G1932 Grundlagen (317–20). French ed. see G1933 International Congress. Summary of proceedings (noting G1932 Grundlagen) in *British Journal of Photography* 79 (1932):773. Brief French summary in *Bulletin de la Société Française de Photographie* 18, no. 11 (Novembre 1931) notes Registerproblem (p. 241) and Grundlagen (p. 242).

Goldberg, Emanuel, and Heinrich Socher. Photographie. In *Handwörterbuch der Naturwissenschaften.* 2. Aufl. Hrsg. Von R. Dittler [et al.]. Jena: Fischer, 1931–35. 7. Bd (1932):934–47. First ed. G1912 Photographie.

Methods of photographic registration. *British Journal of Photography* 79, no. 3774 (2 September 1932):533–34. English transl. of G1932 Registrierproblem. English abstract Eastman Kodak Company. Research Laboratories. *Monthly Abstracts Bulletin* 18 (1932):475–76.

Das Registrierproblem in der Photographie. In *International Congress of Photography (8th: 1931: Dresden),* 317–20. Title when presented: Neue Wege der photographische Registriertechnik. For English transl. G1932 Methods and G1992 Retrieval. German abstract *Zeitschrift für angewandte Chemie* 44, Nr. 43 (1931):876. English abstract: Eastman Kodak Company. Research Laboratories. *Monthly Abstracts Bulletin* 18 (1932):477.

Akeman, W, . . . E. Goldberg, [et al.]. Vorschlag zur Vereinheitlichung einiger Ausdrücke aus dem Gebiete der Tonphotographie. *Kinotechnik* 14, Heft 16 (20 August 1932):300–301.

Ein Weg zur Kinematographie. *Die Kinotechnik* 14, Heft 8 (20 April 1932):160. Extended summary of Goldberg's presentation to the 104. ordentliche Sitzung, Deutsche Kinotechnischen Gesellschaft when presented with the Messter-Medaille.

1933

Anwendung der Fernsehmethoden in der photographischen Technik. *Zeitschrift für angewandte Chemie* 46, Nr. 1 (1933):27–28. Summary of paper presented at the 3rd conference of the Deutsche Gesellschaft für photographische Forschung, Berlin, 29 October 1932.

Apparat für die Bestimmung der DIN-Zahl. *Zeitschrift für angewandte Chemie* 46, Nr. 1 (1933):26–27. Summary of paper presented at the 3rd conference of the Deutsche Gesellschaft für photographische Forschung, Berlin, 29 October 1932.

International Congress of Photography. 8th, Dresden, 1931. Huitiême congrès international de photographie scientifique et appliqué. Dresde. 1931. *Comptes rendus des séances et mémoires présentés.* Documents receuillis par L. P. Clerc. Paris: Editions de la Revue d'Optiques théoriques et instrumentales, 1933. Record of the daily proceedings and full text of French language papers. Goldberg's lectures described (p. 9). Official proceedings: G1932 International.

1937

Eine Spezialkamera zur Herstellung von dokumentarischen Filmaufnahmen. [Special camera for the production of documentary photographs.] Typescript in Science Museum Library ARCH BSIS/11. Paper presented at the World Congress for Universal Documentation, 1937, the proceedings of which state (p. 72): "M. Goldberg présente un appareil spécial pour l'enregistrement de documents sur film." See: World Congress, 1937. *La documentation...* Paris, 1937, 72.

1940

Bericht über eine klimatische Untersuchung im Jordantal. [Tel Aviv]:1940. Typescript. Report on climate research in the Jordan Valley in relation to building specifications for Jewish settlements.

1941

Concise survey of the Jewish industry in Palestine and its contribution to the war effort. Tel Aviv, 28 February [1941?].

1946

Precision instruments industry. In *Palestine's economic future,* ed. J. B. Hobman, 238–42. London: Percy Lund Humphries, 1946.

The scope of the optical industry. [?1946]. Typescript report based on visit to United States and U.K.

1950

Precision instruments. *Technion Yearbook* (1950):280–81.

1957

Acknowledgment by Professor E. Goldberg, upon receipt of the degree of Science in Technology at Technion City, 21 May 1957. [Typescript in GP.]

Late 1950s

When asked about my profession . . . [Untitled autobiographical statement. Typescript, undated, after 1947, probably late 1950s.]

1960

[Synopsis of the A. M. Arnan Memorial Lecture. Summary in Hebrew of speech at memorial meeting to honor A. M. Arnan, Tel Aviv, 13 October 1960. Typescript. In GP.]

1967

Standing here and seeing the beautiful and elaborated institution . . . [Untitled handwritten manuscript of speech at opening of new El Op building, Rehovot, 21 September 1967.]

1992

The retrieval problem in photography (1932). *Journal of the American Society for Information Science* 43, no. 4 (May 1992):295–98. Transl., with notes, by M. K. Buckland of G1932 Registrierproblem.

General Bibliography

Anonymous books and articles are filed by the title, excluding initial articles. See also Bibliography of Emanuel Goldberg's Writings and Appendix B: Biographical Sources for material *about* Goldberg.

25 Jahre Zeiss Ikon Aktiengesellschaft 1926–1951. 1951. *Die Leistung: Illustrierte Zeitshrift für die Wirtschaft* 2, Heft 7:1–59.

35th Conference of the International Federation for Documentation. 1938. *IID Communicationes* 5, Fasc. 4:131–46.

75 Jahre Zeiss Ikon AG: Aspekte der Entwicklung des 1926 gegründeten Industrieunternehmens. Thesaurus 3. 2002. Dresden: Technische Sammlungen der Stadt Dresden, 2002. Papers presented at the Kolloquium 75 Jahren Zeiss Ikon A.-G., Dresden, 18–19 November 2000.

A. J. Newton. 1932. *The British Journal Photographic Almanac* 1932:332.

Abrahamson, Albert. 1955. A short history of television recording. *SMPTE Journal* 64 (February):72–76. Repr. in *A technological history of motion pictures and television,* ed. R. Fielding, 250–54. Berkeley: University of California Press.

Adolf Miethe. 1922. *Zeitschrift für wissenschaftliche Photographie, Photophysik und Photochemie* 21:192–96.

Akademie für graphische Künste und Buchgewerbe. *Berichte der königlichen Akademie für graphische Künste und Buchgewerbe zu Leipzig. Schuljahre 1906/08,* etc. Leipzig: Akademie.

Albumen photographs: History, science and preservation. 2000. Available at http://albumen.stanford.edu. Accessed 24 January 2004.

Alexander, E. 1957. Some fine mechanical instruments produced in Israel. *Bulletin of the Research Council of Israel* 5C:365–68.

Alexander, S. N., and F. C. Rose. 1964. The current status of graphic storage techniques: Their potential application to library mechanization. In *Libraries and automation,* ed. B. E. Markuson, 111–40. Washington, DC: Library of Congress.

Allen, William Sheridan. 1965. *The Nazi seizure of power: The experience of a single German town, 1930-1935.* Chicago: Quadrangle Books.

Amidror, Isaac. 2000. *The theory of the moire phenomenon.* Computational imaging and vision,15. Dordrecht; Boston: Kluwer Academic.

Amstutz, N. S. 1906a. Mr. A. J. Newton. *Inland Printer* 37, no. 2 (May):229.

Amstutz, N. S. 1906b. Physical characteristics of relief engravings, especially relating to half-tones. [Series of articles in] *Inland Printer* 36, no. 6 (March):842–45 onward.

Asperen, J.P.C. 1934. Neuzeitliche photographische Reproduktionsverfahren. *IID Communicationes* 1, Fasc. 3:1–12; Fasc. 4:2–24; 2, Fasc. 1:16–19.

Autler, Gerald. 2000a. *Global networks in high technology: The Silicon Valley-Israel connection.* MA thesis, Department of City and Regional Planning, University of California, Berkeley. Available at http://www.geocities.com/gerald_autler/ Accessed 10 August 2003.

———. 2000b. *Territorially-based learning in a global economy: The semiconductor industry in Israel.* 23 pp. Paper based on Autler (2000a). Available at http://www.geocities.com/gerald_autler/ Accessed 10 August 2003.

Babington Smith, Constance. 1961. *Evidence in camera.* Harmondsworth, U.K.: Penguin.

Bagg, Thomas C. 1963–64. The Rapid Selector as currently used for information search and replica copy retrieval. In American Documentation Institute. *Automation and scientific communication; short papers contributed to the theme sessions of the 26th Annual Meeting of the American Documentation Institute at Chicago, Pick-Congress Hotel, October 6-11, 1963,* ed. H. P. Luhn, Part 2:227–28. Washington, DC: American Documentation Institute.

———, and M. E. Stevens. 1962. *Information selection systems retrieving replica copies: A state-of-the-art report.* National Bureau of Standards Technical Note 157. Washington, DC: Government Printing Office.

Baier, Wolfgang. 1963. Adolf Miethe. *Fotografie* 17 (February):60–61.

———. 1964. *Quellendarstellung zur Geschichte der Fotografie.* Halle: Fotokinoverlag.

Baines, H. 1953. Document copying. *Journal of Photographic Science* 1B (March–April):78–80.

Ball, Howard R. 1961. Bureau of Ships Rapid Selector. *Bureau of Ships Journal* 10, no. 11 (November):6–7.

Bashe, C. J., and others. 1986. *IBM's early computers.* Cambridge, MA: MIT Press.

Becker, Joseph, and Robert M. Hayes. [1963]. *Information storage and retrieval: Tools, elements, theories.* New York: Wiley.

Behrends, Elke. 1995. *Technisch-wissenschaftliche Dokumentation in Deutschland von 1900 bis 1945: unter besonderer Berucksichtigung des Verhaltnisses von Bibliothek und Dokumentation.* Wiesbaden: Harrassowitz.

Bekanntmachung [Deutsche Bibliotekar- und Museumsbeamten-Schule]. 1915. *Archiv für Buchgewerbe* 52, Hefte 9/10 (September–Oktober 1915):271–72.

Bello, Francis. 1960. How to cope with information. *Fortune* 62, no. 3 (September):162–67, 180, 182, 187, 189, 192.

Bendikson, Ludowyk. 1933. When filing cards take the place of books. *Library Journal* 58:911–13.

Bergander, Götz. 1977. *Dresden im Luftkrieg.* Cologne: Böhlau.

Berkeley, E. C. 1949. *Giant brains; or, Machines that think.* New York: Wiley.

Berthel, Fridolin. 2000. Heinz Küppenbender's role in the Contax history. *Zeiss Historica* 22, no. 2:6–8. Based on an interview with Küppenbender. Transl. of German summary in the Zeiss Ikon internal magazine *Im Bild,* 1981.

Berthelot, Marcellin. 1889. *Introduction a l'étude de la chimie des anciens et du moyen âge.* Paris: Steinheil.

———. 1909. *Die Chemie im Altertum und im Mittelalter.* Leipzig: F. Deuticke.

Berthold, Arthur. 1938. Selected bibliography on photographic methods of documentary reproduction. *Journal of Documentary Reproduction* 1:87–123.

Bibliographie zur Geschichte der Stadt Leipzig. 1964–1977. Weimar: Historische Kommission der Sächsche Akademie der Wissenschaft. 5 Bde.

Blumtritt, Herbert. 2000. *Die Geschichte der Dresdner Fotoindustrie.* Stuttgart: Verlag der H. Lindemanns Buchhandlung.

Bodenstein, M. 1903. [Review of Goldberg 1902 *Beitrag* with detailed summary]. *Zeitschrift für wissenschaftliche Photographie* 1, Heft 1:32–34.

Bois, Théophile. 1906. *Les cerfs-volants et leur applications militaires.* Paris: Berger-Levrault. Repr. from the *Revue du génie militaire* (Août–Décembre 1905).

Bonitz, M. 1979. Gedanken Wilhelm Ostwalds zum Informationsproblem in der wissenschaftlichen Forschung. In *Internationales Symposium anläßlich des 125. Geburtstages von Wilhelm Ostwald,* 142–48. Sitzungsberichte der Akademie der Wissenschaften der DDR. Jg. 1979, Nr. 13/N. Berlin: Akademie-Verlag.

Born, Ernst. 1972. *Lexikon für die graphische Industrie.* 2. Ausg. Frankfurt am Main: Polygraph Verlag.

Bourne, Charles, and Trudi Bellardo Hahn. 2003. *A history of online information services, 1963-1976.* Cambridge, MA: MIT Press

Bradshaw, P. D. 1962. The Walnut system: A large capacity document storage and retrieval system. *American Documentation* 13, no. 3 (July):270–75.

Bramke, Werner. 1989. Unter der faschistischen Diktatur (1933–1945). In *Geschichte Sachsens,* ed. Karl Czok, 480–517. Weimar: Hermann Böhlaus Nachfolger.

Bratzel, John F., and Leslie B. Rout. 1982. Pearl Harbor, microdots, and J. Edgar Hoover. *American Historical Review* 87, no. 5:1342–51.

Breuer, William B. 1989. *Hitler's undercover war.* New York: St. Martin's.

Bright, Arthur A. 1949. *The electric-lamp industry: Technological change and economic development from 1880 to 1947.* New York: Macmillan.

British Intelligence Objectives Subcommittee. [?1946]. *Television development and application in Germany.* BIOS Report 867. London: BIOS.

British Journal of Photography. Liverpool: Greenwood. 1(1854).

Brogiato, Heinz-Peter, and Katarina Horn. 2003. The "eagle eye of your camera" in the balloon age. *Innovation: The Magazine from Carl Zeiss* no. 12 (February):30–37. E. Wandersleb's aerial photographs. Summary in *Zeiss Historica* 26, no. 1 (Spring 2004):12–13.

Brown, Malcolm. 1990. Vera Bryce Salomons. *Journal of the Sir David Salomons Society* 3, no. 21 (January):1–3.

Browne, T., and E. Partnow. 1983. *Macmillan biographical encyclopedia of photographic artists & innovators.* New York: Macmillan.

Bruch, Walter. 1967. *Kleine Geschichte des deutschen Fernsehens.* Berlin: Haude and Spenersche.

Bryce, James W. 1938. *Statistical Machine.* U.S. patent 2,124,906. 26 July.

Buckland, M. K. 1992. Emanuel Goldberg, electronic document retrieval, and Vannevar Bush's Memex. *Journal of the American Society for Information Science* 43, no. 4 (May):284–94. Available at http://www.sims.berkeley.edu/~buckland/goldbush.html. Accessed 23 March 2003.

———. 1995a. Zeiss Ikon's "Statistical machine." *Zeiss Historica* 17, no. 1 (Spring):6–7. Available at http://www.sims.berkeley.edu/~buckland/statistical.html. Accessed 15 July 2003.

———. 1995b. Zeiss Ikon and television: Fernseh AG. *Zeiss Historica* 17, no. 2 (Autumn):17–19. Available at http://www.sims.berkeley.edu/~buckland/television.html. Accessed 23 March 2003.

———. 1996. Documentation, information science, and library science in the U.S.A. *Information Processing and Management* 32, no. 1:63–76. Available at http://www.sims.berkeley.edu/~buckland/20THCENT.pdf. Accessed 23 March 2003.

———. 2002. Emanuel Goldberg (1881–1970)—Ein Lebensbild. In *Zeiss Ikon AG Dresden: Aspekte der Entwicklung des 1926 gregründeten Industrieunternehmens,* 51–54. Thesaurus 3. Dresden: Technische Sammlungen der Stadt Dresden. Available at http://www.sims.berkeley.edu/~buckland/goldbergleben. Accessed 23 March 2003.

———. 2002. *Emanuel Goldberg, 1881-1970: Pioneer of information science.* Available at http://www.sims.berkeley.edu/~buckland/goldberg.html. Accessed 23 March 2003.

————. 2004. "Histories, heritages, and the past: The case of Emanuel Goldberg." In *The History and Heritage of Scientific and Technical Information Systems. Proceedings of the 2002 Conference,* Philadelphia, Nov. 15–17, 2002, eds., W. B. Rayward, M. E. Bowden, 39–45. Medford, N.J.: Information Today. Available at http://www. sims.berkeley.edu/~buckland/goldchf.pdf. Accessed 23 March 2003.

Buder, Marianne. 1976. *Das Verhältnis von Dokumentation und Normung von 1927 bis 1945 in nationaler und internationaler Hinsicht. Ein Beitrag zur Geschichte der Dokumentation.* DIN Normungskunde 7. Berlin: Beuth Verlag.

Bührer, Karl Wilhelm, and Adolf Saager. 1911. *Die Organisierung der geistigen Arbeit durch die Brücke.* Ansbach: Seybold. Also published in Esperanto as *La organizado de la intelekta laboro per la Ponto.*

Bulletin de la Société Française de Photographie [et de Cinématographie]. Paris, 1(1855).

Bulow, Rolf. 1987. Ich sehe dich! Fernsehen, Fernsprechen und die Fernseh AG. *Kultur & Technik* 11:29–35, 38–40.

Burke, Colin. 1994. *Information and secrecy: Vannevar Bush, Ultra, and the other memex.* Metuchen, NJ: Scarecrow Press.

Burns, R. W. 1986. *British television: The formative years.* London: Peter Peregrinus.

————. 1998. *Television: An international history of the formative years.* London: Institution of Electrical Engineers.

Busch, Fritz. 1949. *Aus dem Leben eines Musikers.* Zurich: Rascher Verlag. English translation: *Pages from a musician's life.* London: Hogarth, 1953.

Busch, Leo. 1953. Die Oskar-Meßter-Denkmünze—höchste Auszeichnung für deutsche Kinotechniker. *Kinotechnik* 7, Nr. 8:210–211.

Bush, Vannevar. 1945a. As we may think. *Atlantic Monthly* 176, 101–8. Available at http://www.theatlantic.com/unbound/flashbks/computer/ bushf.htm. Accessed 24 July 2004.

————. 1945b. As we may think: A top US scientist foresees a possible future world in which man-made machines will start to think. *Life* 19, no, 11, pp. 112–14, 116, 118, 123–24.

————. *Endless horizons.* Washington, DC: Public Affairs Press.

————. 1967. *Science is not enough.* New York: Morrow.

————. 1970. *Pieces of the action.* New York: Morrow.

Cady, Susan A. 1994. *Machine tool of management: A history of microfilm technology.* PhD diss., Lehigh University. University Microfilms o/no 94–30952.

————. 1999. Microfilm technology and information systems. In Conference on the History and Heritage of Science Information Systems (1998: Pittsburgh). *Proceedings,* ed. M. E. Bowden, T. B. Hahn, and R. V. Williams, 177–86. Medford, NJ: Information Today.

Canterbury Christ Church University College. Salomons. 2002. *The Salomons family gallery.* Available at http://www.salomonscentre. org.uk/history/gallery_family/index.htm. Accessed 23 March 2003.)

Carruthers, R. H. 1938. The place of microfilm in public library reference work. *Journal of Documentary Reproduction,* 1:263–68.

Chalmers, Matthew. 1999. Comparing information access approaches. *Journal of the American Society for Information Science* 50, no.12:1108–18.

Christienne, Charles, and Pierre Lissarrague. 1986. *A history of French military aviation.* Washington, DC: Smithsonian Institution Press. Originally *Histoire de l'aviation militaire française.* Paris: Charles-Lavauzelle, 1980.

———, and others. 1989. *French military aviation: A bibliographical guide.* New York: Garland.

Cirlot, J. E. 1971. *A dictionary of symbols.* 2nd ed. New York: Barnes and Noble.

Clelland, Catherine Taylor, Viviana Risca, and Carter Bancroft. 1999. Hiding messages in DNA microdots. *Nature* 399 (10 June):533–34.

Coblans, Herbert. 1957. New methods and techniques for the communication of knowledge. *Unesco Bulletin for Libraries* 11, no. 7 (July):153–79.

Coe, Brian. 1981. *The history of movie photography.* Westfield, NJ: Eastview Editions.

Cohen, Martin C. 2000. *Carl Zeiss—A history of a most respected name in optics.* Available at http://www.company7.com/zeiss/history.html. Accessed 22 July 2003.

Collins, Douglas. 1990. *The story of Kodak.* New York: Abrams.

Commission interalliée de contrôle aeronautique en Allemagne. [1922?]. *Rapport technique.* Chalais Meudon: Atelier de Reproductions.

Continuously reading in-line refractometer for difficult measurements. 1955. *Food Processing* 16, no. 7 (January):54–56.

Cooley, Edwin G. 1912. *Vocational education in Europe.* 2 vols. Chicago: Commercial Club.

Davis, Watson. 1934. Optical problems involved in a comprehensive system of bibliography. *Journal of the Optical Society of America* 24, no. 2 (February):58.

———. 1935. Scientific publication and bibliography. Documentation Institute of Science Service. *IID Comunicationes* 3: cols. WD1-WD12.

Deutsche Verkehrs-Zeitung. 1937. *Festausgabe der Deutschen Verkehrs-Zeitung, aus Anlass des 65. Geburtages des Reichspostministers Ohnesorge am 8. Juni 1937.* Hrsg. vom Staatstekretar im Reichspostministerium Nagel. Berlin: Koenig.

Deutsches Institut für Normung. 1934. *Negativmaterial für bildmässige Aufnahmen: Bestimmung der Lichtempfindlichkeit. DIN 4512.* [?Berlin]: Reichsverband der Deutschen Photoindustrie.

Das Deutsche Kulturmuseum zu Leipzig. 1918. *Zeitschrift des Deutschen Vereins für Buchwesen und Schifttum* 1, Nr. 7/8:90–93.

Dictionary of American library biography, ed. B. S. Wynar. 1978. Littleton, CO: Libraries Unlimited.

Dictionnaire militaire. Encyclopédie des sciences. 1898, 1910. [?Paris]: Librairie Berger-Levrault. 1898, 1910. 2v. Also *Supplément général,* 1911.

Douglas, Mary. 1986. *How institutions think.* Syracuse, NY: Syracuse University Press.

Doyle, Lauren B. 1975. *Information retrieval and processing.* Los Angeles: Melville.

Dresden. Internationale photographische Austellung. 1909. *Offizieller Katalog der internationalen photographischen Austellung, Dresden, 1909.* Dresden: Baensch, [1909]. Repr. in *History of photography.* [1980–82?] [Microfilm]. Woodbridge, CT: Research Publications, Reel 51, no. 589.

Dresden die Photostadt. 1935. Special issue, *Photo-Fachhändler* 6 Jg, Heft 20:663–79.

Dresdner Neueste Nachrichten. Dresden: Huck, 1(1903)–51(1943).

Dunlap, Orrin E. 1932. *The outlook for television.* New York: Harper.

Durov, Valerii A. 1990. *Russian and Soviet military awards.* Moscow: Vneshtorgizdat.

———. 1993. *The orders of Russia.* Moscow: Voskresenie.

Eastman Kodak Company. 1923. *Aerial haze and its effect on photography from the air.* Monographs on the theory of photography, 4. New York: Van Nostrand.

Eckert, Gerhard. 1963. *Von Nipkow bis Telstar: 80 Jahre Fernsehen in Daten und Tabellen.* Frankfurt am Main: Verlag für Funk- und Fernsehpublizistik Fritz Niehaus.

Eder, Josef Maria. 1879. Ein neues chemisches Photometer mittelst Quecksilber-Oxalat zur Bestimmung der Intensität der ultravioletten Strahlen des Tageslichtes und Beiträge zur Photochemie des Quecksilberchlorides. *Sitzungberichte. Akademie der Wissenschaften in Wien.* 80, 2. Abt.:636–60. Repr. in Eder, J. M., and Eduard Valenta. 1904. *Beiträge zur Photochemie und Spectralanalyse,* II:1–15. Vienna: Graphischen Lehr- und Versuchsanstalt.

———. 1920. *Ein neues Graukeil-photometer für Sensitometrie, photographische Kopierverfahren und wissenschaftliche Lichtmessungen.* Halle: Knapp.

———. 1921. Die Graukeil. *Jahrbuch für Photographie und Reproduktionstechnik* 29:215–25.

———. 1932. *Geschichte der Photographie.* 2 vols. Ausführliches Handbuch der Photographie, Bd 1. Halle: Knapp, 1932. English ed.: *History of photography.* New York: Columbia University Press, 1945.

Eliav, M. 1985. German Jews' share in the building of the national home in Palestine and the state of Israel. *Leo Baeck Institute Year Book* 30:255–63.

Emmerich, G. H. 1910. *Lexikon für Photographie und Reproduktionstechnik (Chemigraphie, Lichtdruck, Heliogravüre)*. Leipzig: Barth.

Encyclopaedia Britannica. 1911. 11th ed. New York: Encyclopaedia Britannica Co.

Encyclopaedic dictionary of physics. 1961. Ed. J. Thewlis. Oxford: Pergamon.

Encyclopedia of photography. 1984. [Comp. by] ICP, International Center of Photography. New York: Crown.

Encyclopedia of the Third Reich. 1991. Ed. C. Zentner and F. Bedurftig. New York: Macmillan.

Engineering Research Associates, Inc. 1949. *Report for the Microfilm Rapid Selector*. PB 97 313 [often miscited as 97 535]. St. Paul, MN: Engineering Research Associates.

Ergänzungen und Verbesserungen zu dem Artikel von Dipl. Ing. J. P. C. van Asperen über moderne photographische Reproduktionsverfahren. 1935. *IID Communicationes* 2, Fasc. 2:16–19.

Everson, George. 1949. *The story of television: The life of Philo T. Farnsworth*. New York: Norton.

Evron, Joseph Abbo. 1992. [*Shield and spear: The story of Israel military industries.*] Tel Aviv. In Hebrew.

Fairthorne, Robert A. 1948. [Review of Bush, *Endless horizons*]. *Journal of Documentation* 4, no. 3 (December):210–11.

————. 1958. Automatic retrieval of recorded information. *Computer Journal* 1:36–41. Repr. in Fairthorne (1961, 135–46).

————. 1961. *Towards information retrieval*. London: Butterworths.

Farkas-Conn, Irene. 1990. *From documentation to information science: The beginnings and early development of the American Documentation Institute–American Society for Information Science*. New York: Greenwood.

Feffer, Stuart M. 1994. *Microscopes to munitions: Ernst Abbe, Carl Zeiss, and the transformation of technical optics, 1850–1914*. PhD diss., University of California, Berkeley. University Microfilms o/no 95–04797.

————. 1996. Ernst Abbe, Carl Zeiss, and the transformation of microscopic optics. In *Scientific credibility and technical standards in 19th and early 20th century Germany and Britain*, ed. Jed Z. Buchwald, Archimedes 1996. 23–66. Dordrecht: Kluwer Academic Publishers.

Feigel-Farnholz, Richard von. 1948. Fernsehen zwischen bewegten Objekten: Die Reportageanlagen der Fernseh GmbH. *Radiotechnik* 11:593–98.

Fergg, B. 1957. Untersuchungen über den Einfluss der verschiedenen Komponenten von photographischen Auskopieremulsionen auf

Bildentstehung. *Zeitschrift für wissenschaftliche Photographie* 52, nos. 1–3:24–54.

Fernseh A.G.: Hausmitteilungen aus Forschung und Betrieb der Fernseh A.G. later *Fernseh G. m. b. H.,* 1–2 (1938–43). Berlin: Fernseh A.G.

Ferro, Marc. 1991. *Nicholas II: The last of the tsars.* London: Viking.

Fiedler, Helmut. 1939. *Geschichte der "Dresdner Nachrichten" von 1856—1936.* Inaugural-dissertation. University of Leipzig. Olbernhau i. Sa.: Fiedler.

Fiery Nazi [Manfred von Killinger] named consul on coast. 1937. *New York Times* (25 June):12, cols. 3–5.

Filmmuseum Potsdam. 2001. *Kinematographische Apparate aus 100 Jahren: Bildband zur technischen Sammlung im Filmmuseum Potsdam.* Hrsg. Filmmuseum Potsdam, Red. Christian Ilgner. Berlin: Parthas-Verlag.

Finnische Wärtsilä übernimmt Zeiss Ikon. 1989. *Frankfurter Allgemeine Zeitung* Nr. 148 (30 June):22, cols.5–6.

Fischer, O. 1957. Entwicklung und Arbeiten des Fachnormenausschusses "Phototechnik." *DIN-Mitteilungen* 36, Heft 1 (15 Januar):2–5.

Fisher, David F., and Marshall Jon Fisher. 1997. *Tube: The invention of television.* San Diego: Harcourt Brace.

The Focal encyclopedia of photography. 1993. 3rd ed. Boston: Focal Press.

Formstecher, Felix. 1927. Die Beziehung zwischen photographischer und visueller Unterschiedsempfindlichkeit. *Photographische Industrie* 25 (21 März):286–87.

Fortune. 1967. *Businessmen around the globe.* Englewood Cliffs, NJ: Prentice-Hall.

Forty, Simon, ed. 2002. *World War 1: A visual history.* London: PRC Publishing.

Francke, Hermann, ed. 1969. *Lexikon der Physik.* 3. Auf. Stuttgart: Franckh'sche Verlagshandlung.

Frank, Peter R., ed. 1978. *Von der systematischen Bibliographie zur Dokumentation.* Wege der Forschung 144. Darmstadt: Wissenschaftliche Buchgesellschaft.

Freulich, Roman. 1968. *The hill of life.* New York: T. Yoseloff. [Biography of Joseph Trumpeldor].

Frieser, H. 1941. Mikrate für Dokumentation. *Dokumentation und Arbeitstechnik* (November):1–2. Repr. from *Zeitschift für angewandte Photographie* Jg 39, Heft 4:57–79.

———. 1957. On some properties of photographic layers for the production of mikrats. *Bulletin of the Research Council of Israel. Section C: Technology* 5C, no. 4:285–88.

Fuchs, F. 1931. *Die Entwicklung des Fernsehens.* Deutsches Museum Abhandlungen und Berichte, 3 Jg. Heft 5. Berlin: VDI Verlag.

Future for Israel seen in industry: Precision instrument inventor from Tel Aviv describes rapid expansion there. 1949. *New York Times* (27 May):5, cols. 5–6.

Gamble, Charles William. 1938. *Modern illustration processes.* 2d ed. London: Pitman.

Gasch, Bernhard. 1959. *Moiré-Erscheinungen in Farbendrucken.* Leipzig: Institut für Grafische Technik.

Gautier, Armand. 1902. Existence, dans l'albumin de l'oeuf d'oiseaux, d'une substance fibrigène pouvant se transformer, in vitro, en membranes pseudo-organisées. *Comptes rendus hebdomadaires des seances de l'Academie des Sciences* (Paris) 135, no. 3:133–39.

German slays his staff: Von Killinger said to have run amok in Rumanian legation. 1944. *New York Times* (8 September):6, col. 4.

Geschichte des Fernsehens in der Bundesrepublik Deutschland, hg. von Helmut Kreuzer und Christian W. Thomsen. 1993. Munchen: Fink.

Geschichte der Technischen Universität Dresden: 1828-1978. 1978. Autorenkollektiv, Rolf Sonnemann [et al.]. Berlin: Deutscher Verlag der Wissenschaften. Also 2nd ed., 1988.

Gesell, Michael. 1926. Die gläserne Bibliothek. *Zeitungsbuch: Organ der Deutschen Buch Gemeinschaft, Berlin.* 3Jg., Nr. 6 (15 März):98–99.

Gessen, Iulius. 1910. K sud'be evreev-vrachei v Rossii. [On the fate of Jewish doctors in Russia]. *Evreiskaia Starina* 3:612–23.

Gilbert, Martin. 1990. Introduction. In Tory, Avraham. *Surviving the Holocaust: The Kovno ghetto diary.* Cambridge, MA: Harvard University Press.

Gill, Manfred, and Peter Löhnert. 1997. *Jüdische Chemiker aus Dessau in der Filmfabrik Wolfen: ein Beitrag zum Schicksal der jüdischen Wissenschaftler und der jüdisch verheirateten Wissenschaftler der Filmfabrik Wolfen in der Zeit des Nationalismus.* Schriftenreihe der Moses-Mendelssohn-Gesellschaft Dessau, 5. Dessau: Moses-Mendelssohn-Gesellschaft.

Gispen, K. 1989. *New profession, old order: Engineers and German society, 1815–1914.* Cambridge: Cambridge University Press.

Gispen, Kees. 2002. *Poems in steel: National socialism and the politics of inventing from Weimar to Bonn.* New York: Berghahn Books.

Gleichen, Alexander Wilhelm. 1918. *The theory of modern optical instruments: A reference book for physicists, manufacturers of optical instruments, and for officers in the Army and Navy.* London: H. M. Stationery Office. 2nd ed. 1921. Transl. of *Die Theorie der modernen optischen Instrumente.* Stuttgart: F. Enke, 1911.

Goebbels, Joseph. 1987–2001. *Die Tagebücher von Joseph Goebbels.* Munich: Saur.

Goebel, Gerhard. 1953. Das Fernsehen in Deutschland bis zum Jahre 1945. *Archiv für das Post- und Fernmeldewesen* 5. Jg, Nr. 5:259–393.

Goebel, Joseph. 1952. Mikrodokumentation in den Niederlanden. *Nachrichten für Dokumentation* 3:128–32. Also published separately: *Mikrodokumentation in den Niederlanden.* The Hague: Mikrokopie Verlag.

Goldberg, Adele, ed. 1988. *A history of personal workstations.* New York: ACM Press; Reading, MA: Addison-Wesley.

Goldberg, Emanuel. *See* Bibliography of Emanuel Goldberg's Writings.

Goldberg, Norman. 1969. The other Goldberg: A visit with Zeiss Ikon's practical prodigy. *Popular Photography* 65, no. 5 (November): 88–89, 154.

———. 1992. *Camera technology: The dark side of the lens.* Boston: Academic Press

Goldschmidt, Robert B., and Paul Otlet. 1906. *Sur une forme nouvelle du livre: Le livre microphotographique.* (IIB publ. 81). Brussels: Institut International de Bibliographie. English transl. in Otlet (1990, 87–95).

———. 1925. *La conservation et la diffusion de la pensée: Le livre micro-photique.* (IIB publi. 144). Brussels: Institut International de Bibliographie. English transl. in Otlet (1990, 204–10).

Görlich, Paul. 1954. *Die Anwendung der Photozellen.* Technisch-physikalische Monographien 7. Leipzig: Akademische Verlagsgesellschaft.

Gould, Merle E. 1941. *Identifying means.* U.S. patent 2,231,186. 11 February 1941.

Gradewitz, A. 1910. La bibliothèque microphotographique. *La Nature* 39, no. 1962 (31 Decembre):68–70.

Grangeon, M., Ch. Greber, M. Locquin, and J. Roger. 1962. Réalisation d'une machine taxinomique dans une branche des sciences naturel-les: la palynologie. *Bulletin du Bureau de Recherches Geologiques et Minières* 2, no. 1:1–15.

Green, John C. 1949. The Rapid Selector—An automatic library. *Military Engineer* 41 (September–October):350–52.

———. 1950. The Rapid Selector—An automatic library. *Revue de la Documentation* 17, n 3:66–68.

Grösse und Verfall der deutschen Wissenschaft im Zweiten Weltkrieg. 1953. In *Bilanz des Zweiten Weltkrieges: Erkenntnisse und Verpflichtungen für die Zukunft,* 249–64. Oldenburg: Gerhard Stalling.

Gründung eines photographischen Museums. 1915. *Photographische Rundschau* 52:72–73.

Gubas, Larry. 1984a. Zeiss Ikon and Dr. August Nagel. *Zeiss Historica* 6, no. 1 (Spring):[4].

———. 1984b. The birth of Zeiss Ikon. *Zeiss Historica* 6, no. 1 (Spring): [8–11].

———. 1985a. Emmanuel Goldberg. *Zeiss Historica* 7, no. 1 (Spring): 14–15.

Gubas, Larry. 1985b. Who invented the Contax? *Zeiss Historica* 7, no. 1 (Spring):7–11.

———. 1994–95. Zeiss Ikon: The golden age. Part I. *Zeiss Historica* 16, no. 2 (Autumn 1994):3–7. Part II. 17, no. 1 (Spring 1995):10–16.

———. 1996. Zeiss Ikon's Zeitlupe: A photographer of moment. *Zeiss Historica* 18, no. 1 (Spring):8–10.

———. 1999a. Dr. Rudolph Straubel (1864–1943). *Zeiss Historica* 21, no. 1 (Spring):16.

———. 1999b. Ernst Wandersleb (1879–1963). *Zeiss Historica* 21, no. 1 (Spring):17.

———. 2000. Heinz Küppenbender (1901–89). *Zeiss Historica* 22, no. 1 (Spring):10–11.

———. 2001. Carl Paul Goerz (1854–1923) *Zeiss Historica* 23, no. 1 (Spring):6–7.

———. 2002. *Dr. Heinz Küppenbender 1901-1989*. Available at http://www.zeisshistorica.org/Keup.html. Accessed 22 July 2003.

Günther, Hanns. 1938. *Das grosse Fernsehbuch: Die Entwicklung des Fernsehens von Grundlagen bis zum heutigen Stand.* Stuttgart: Frankh.

Haase, Norbert, Stefi Jersch-Wenzel, and Hermann Simon. 1998. *Die Erinnerung hat ein Gesicht: Fotografien und Dokumente zur nationalsozialistischen Judenverfolgung in Dresden.* Schriftenreihe der Stiftung Sächsische Gedenkstätten zur Erinnerung an die Opfer Politischer Gewaltherrschaft 4. Leipzig: Kiepenheuer.

Habermann, A., R. Klemmt, and F. Siefkes. 1985. *Lexikon deutscher wissenschaftlicher Bibliothekare 1925–1980.* Zeitschrift für Bibliothekswesen und Bibliographie Sonderheft 42. Frankfurt: Klostermann.

Haferkorn, Heinz, ed. 1990. *Lexikon der Optik.* Hanau: Werner Dausien.

Hagemeyer, Kerstin. 2002. *Jüdisches Leben in Dresden: Ausstellung anlässlich der Weihe der neuen Synagoge Dresden am 9. November 2001.* Schriftenreihe der Sachsischen Landesbibliothek—Staats- und Universitatsbibliothek Dresden (SLUB) 7. Dresden: Sachsische Landesbibliothek—Staats- und Universitatsbibliothek.

Hahn, W. 1962. Adolf Miethe: Zum hundertsten Geburtstag am 25. April 1962. *Bild und Ton* 15, Heft 5 (May):157.

Hall, Peter G., and Paschal Preston. 1988. *The carrier wave: New information technology and the geography of innovation, 1846–2003.* London: Unwin Hyman.

Handbuch der wissenschaftlichen und angewandten Photographie. 1929–33. Hg. von Alfred Hay. Vienna: Springer.

Handel, Paul W. 1933. *Statistical machine.* U.S. patent 1,915,993, 27 June.

Hapke, Thomas. 1991. Wilhelm Ostwald über Information und Dokumentation. *Mitteilungen, Gesellschaft Deutscher Chemiker, Fachgruppe Geschichte der Chemie* 5:47–55.

————. 1997. Wilhelm Ostwald und seine Initiativen zur Organisation und Standardisierung nuturwissenschaftlicher Publizistik: Enzyklopaedismus, Internationalismus und Taylorismus am Beginn des 20. Jahrhunderts. In Meinel, Christoph, ed. *Fachshriftum, Bibliothek und Naturwissenschaft im 19. und 20. Jahrhundert,* 157–74. Wolfenbuetteler Schriftern zur Geschichte des Buchwesens 27. Wiesbaden: Harrassowitz.

————. 1999. Wilhelm Ostwald, the "Brücke" (Bridge), and connections to other bibliographic activities at the beginning of the twentieth century. In Conference on the History and Heritage of Science Information Systems (1998: Pittsburgh). *Proceedings,* ed. M. E. Bowden, T. B. Hahn, and R. V. Williams, 139–47. Medford, NJ: Information Today. Also Powerpoint slides available at http://www.tu-harburg.de/b/hapke/ostwald/ostwald.htm Accessed November 16, 2005.

————. 2000. *Wilhelm Ostwald's activities to improve scholarly information and communication seen as part of the bibliographic movement in the first half of the 20th century.* Powerpoint slides available at http://www.tu-harburg.de/b/hapke/ostwald/leipzig.htm. Accessed 1 October 2002.

————. 2003. *From the world brain to the first transatlantic information dialogue: Activities in information and documentation in Germany in the first half of the 20th century.* Paper presented at the 69th IFLA General Conference, 1–9 August 2003, Berlin. Available at http://www.ifla.org/IV/ifla69/papers/057e-Hapke.pdf Accessed November 16, 2005.

Hård, Mikael. 1998. German regulation: The integration of modern technology into national culture. In *The Intellectual appropriation of technology: Discourses on modernity, 1900–1939,* ed. Mikael Hård and Andrew Jamison, 33–67. Cambridge, MA: MIT Press.

Harding, Brooks B. 1932. *Cataloguing device.* U.S. patent 1,845,410. 16 February.

Harrison, G. B. 1931. The VIIIth International Congress of Photography, Dresden, 1931. *Photographic Journal* 71 (September):417–19.

Haufe, Fritz, and Rolf Säckel. 1993. 100 Jahre "Blaues Wunder:" Zur Geschichte der Loschwitz-Blasewitzer Brücke. *Dresdner Hefte* 34:5–13.

Hawkins, R. R. 1960. *Production of micro-forms.* State of the library art, ed. R. Shaw, v. 5, part 1. New Brunswick, NJ: Graduate School of Library Service, Rutgers–The State University.

Haynes, Williams. 1954. *American chemical industry: Background and beginnings.* Toronto: Van Nostrand.

Hazelton, Alan Weaver. 1932. *The Russian imperial orders.* Numismatic notes and monographs [No. 51]. New York: The American Numismatic Society.

Heidtmann, Frank. 1984. *Wie das Photo ins Buch kam: Der Weg zum photographisch illustrierten Buch.* Berlin: Berlin Verlag Arno Spitz.

Heilprin, L. B. 1961. Communications engineering approach to microforms. *American Documentation* 12:213–18.

Heinrich Ernemann und Guido Mengel, zwei Pioniere der Dresdner Photoindustrie. 1935. *Der Photo-Fachhändler* 6. Jg, Heft 20 (1 Oktober):678.

Heller, Steven, and Louise Fili. 1998. *German modern: Graphic design from Wilhelm to Weimar.* San Francisco: Chronicle Books.

Helm, Robert A. 1988. Comparing the prewar Leica and Contax. *Zeiss Historica* 10, no. 1 (Spring):10–14; no. 2 (Fall):3–7.

Hempel, Manfred. 1990. German television pioneers and the conflict between public programming and wonder weapons. *Historical Journal of Film Radio and Television* 10, no. 2:123–62.

Herbert, Ulrich. 1985. *Fremdarbeiter: Politik und Praxis des "Ausländer-Einsatzes" in der Kriegswirtschaft des Dritten Reiches.* Berlin: J.H.W. Dietz.

———. 1997. *Hitler's foreign workers: Enforced foreign labor in Germany under the Third Reich.* Cambridge: Cambridge University Press. English ed. of *Fremdarbeiter.*

Herf, Jeffrey. 1984. *Reactionary modernism: Technology, culture, and politics in Weimar and the Third Reich.* Cambridge. Cambridge University Press.

Hermann, Armin. 1989. *Nur der Name war geblieben.* 2. Aufl. Stuttgart: Deutsche Verlags-Anstalt.

Heskett, John. 1986. *German design 1870–1918.* New York: Taplinger.

Hesse, Wolfgang, and Starl, Timm, eds. 1998. *Der Photopionier Hermann Krone—Photographie und Apparatur: Bildkultur und Phototechnik im 19. Jahrhundert.* Marburg: Jonas Verlag.

Heuss, Theodor. 1994. *Robert Bosch: His life and achievements.* New York: Henry Holt. Transl. of *Robert Bosch: Leben und Leistung.* 1946. Tübingen: Wunderlich.

High resolution camera. 1960. *National Bureau of Standards. Technical News Bulletin* 44 (12 December):204–5.

Hines, Theodore C. 1975. Shaw and the machine. In *Essays for Ralph Shaw,* ed. Norman D. Stevens, 6–14. Metuchen, NJ: Scarecrow.

Hirsch, Ernst. 2002. Filmdokument "Zusammenlegung der letzten Juden in Dresden in das Lager am Hellerberg am 23. und 24. November 1942." In *75 Jahre Zeiss Ikon AG: Aspekte der Entwicklung des 1926 gegründeten Industrieunternehmens,* 99. Thesaurus 3. Dresden: Technische Sammlungen der Stadt Dresden.

History of the German photo industry. 1956. Special section, *Popular Photography* 38, no. 5 (May):119–66.

The history of German television, 1935–1944. 1990. Special issue, *Historical Journal of Film Radio and Television* 10, no. 2:113–240.

Hitler, Adolf. 1992–1998. *Reden, Schriften, Anordnungen: Februar 1925 bis Januar 1933*. Munich: K. G. Saur.

Hodgson, Richard. 1949. Theater television system. *Journal of the Society of Motion Picture and Television Engineers* 52:540–48.

Höffkes, Karl. 1986. *Hitlers politische Generale: Die Gauleiter des Dritten Reiches; Ein biographisches Nachschlagewerk.* Tubingen: Grabert.

Hoffman, Bruce. 1983. *The failure of British military strategy within Palestine, 1939–1947.* [Ramat-Gan, Israel]: Bar-Ilan University Press.

Hold, Niles R. 1977. Wilhelm Ostwald's "The Bridge." *British Journal of the History of Science* 10:146–50.

Hoover, J. E. 1946. The enemy's masterpiece of espionage. *Reader's Digest* 48 (April):1–6. Also in French: Le chef-d'oeuvre de l'espionage allemand. *Sélections du Readers Digest* 1 année, no. 3 (Mai 1947): 19–25.

Hoppe, Joseph. 1995. Fernsehen als Waffe: Militär und Fernsehen in Deutschland 1935–1950. In *Ich diente nur der Technik: Sieben Karrieren zwischen 1940 und 1950,* 53–88. Berliner Beiträge zur Technikgeschichte und Industriekultur. Schriftenreihe des Museums für Verkehr und Technik Berlin, Bd 13. Berlin: Nicolaische Verlagsbuchhandlung.

Hübscher, Anneliese. 1990. Die Jahre des Neubeginns: 1945–1959: Dokumentation zur Geschichte der Hochschule für Grafik und Buchkunst. In *Leipziger Schule: Malerei, Grafik, Fotragrafie: Lehrer und Absolventen der Hochschule für Graphik und Buchkunst,* 235–40. [Berlin: Staatliche Kunsthalle Berlin].

Hugershoff, R. 1930. *Photogrametrie und Luftbildwesen.* Handbuch der wissenschaftlichen und angewandten Photographie, hersg. Von Alfred Hay, Bd 7. Vienna: Julius Springer.

Hurley, Christopher. 1935. *Russian orders, decorations and medals... under the monarchy.* London: Harrison.

I.I.D. Communicationes. The Hague: International Institute for Documentation, 1(1934)–5(1938).

Ikon GmbH Präzisionstechnik. 2003. *Chronik der IKON GmbH Präzionstechnik.* Available at http://www.ikon.de/unternehmen/IKONStory.asp. Accessed 11 July 2003.

Indebetouw, Guy, and Robert Czarnek, eds. 1992. *Selected papers on optical moiré and applications.* SPIE Milestone Series MS 64. Bellington, WA: SPIE Optical Engineering Press.

International biographical dictionary of Central European emigrés, 1933–1945. 1983. Munich: Saur.

International Congress of Photography. (5th, Brussels, 1910). 1912. *Ve Congrès International de Photographie [1910]: Compte rendu, procès-verbaux, rapports, notes et documents.* [Ed. by] C. Putttemans, L. P. Clerc et E. Wallon. Brussels: Établissements Émile Bruylant.

International Congress of Photography. (8th, Dresden, 1931). 1932. *Bericht uber den VIII. internationalen Kongress fur wissenschaftliche un angewandte Photographie, Dresden, 1931.* Hg. von J. Eggert und A. von Biehler. Leipzig: J. A. Barth.

International Congress of Photography. (8th, Dresden, 1931). [1933]. *Huitième congrès international de photographie scientifique et appliqué. Dresde. 1931. Comptes rendus des séances et mémoires présentés. Documents receuillis par L. P. Clerc.* Paris: Editions de la Revue d'Optiques théoriques et instrumentals.

International Federation for Documentation. 1964. *Manuel practique de reproduction documentaire et de sélection.* FID Publ. 353. Paris: Gauthiers-Villars.

Internationale Photographische Ausstellung, Dresden, 1909. März–Oktober. 1909. *Offizielle Katalog.* Illustrierte Ausgabe. Dresden: Baensch. Also on microfilm In Smithsonian Institution Libraries. *The Books of the fairs: Materials about world's fairs, 1834–1916, in the Smithsonian Institution Libraries.* Chicago: American Library Association, 1992.

Israel Electro-Optical Industry Ltd. 1967. [Typescript news release dated 21 November 1967, Rehovoth.]

The Israel Electro-optical Industry Ltd. 1969. *Optical Spectra* 3, no. 4 (July/August):29.Ivens, Joris. 1969. *The Camera and I.* New York: International Publishers. Early version of first part was published as: Apprentice to films. *Theatre Arts Monthly* 30, no. 3 (March 1946):179–86; no. 4 (April 1946):245–51.

———. 1996. The Bridge. In *Rare Dutch and Belgian experimental program.* Burbank, CA: Hollywood's Attic. VHS videocassette.

Ivens, Joris, and Robert Destanque. 1982. *Joris Ivens; ou, La mémoire d'un regard.* [Paris]: Editions BFB.

Ives, H. E. 1920. *Airplane photography.* Philadelphia: Lippincott.

Jahrbuch für Photographie und Reproduktionstechnik, ed. J. M. Eder. v1–31 (1887–1929).

Jarausch, Konrad H. 1982. *Students, society and politics in imperial Germany: The rise of illiberalism.* Princeton University Press.

J. C. Poggendorff's biographisch-literarisches Handwörterbuch. 1863–. Berlin: Barth.

Jenkins, Reese V. 1975. *Images and enterprise: Technology and the American photographic industry, 1839–1925.* Baltimore: Johns Hopkins University Press.

Joachim, Hermann. 1935. La copie sur film et la comptabilité. In Office International de Chimie. 1935. *L'utilisation du film comme support de la documentation: Conférences présentées au Symposium, 31 mars 1935, Paris,* 35–40. Paris: Office International de Chimie.

————. 1936. Die photographische Registrierung im Dienste der Betriebesorganisation. *IID Communicationes* 3, Fasc. 1: Jo.1-Jo.12 and plate.

Johnson, Jeffrey Allan. 1990. *The Kaiser's chemists: Science and modernization in imperial Germany.* Chapel Hill, NC: University of North Carolina Press.

Johnson, W. E. 1932. Protection and profits through photography. *Bankers Magazine* 125:537–40.

Jones, L. A. 1920. On the theory of tone reproduction, with a graphic method for the solution of problems. *Journal of the Franklin Institute* 190:39–90.

Jungnickel, Hans. 1934. Ein Gerät zur unmittelbaren Zeitlupenbeobachtung von periodischen Vorgängen. *Zeitschrift für wissenschaftliche Photographie* 32, Heft 9:231–32.

Kampe, Norbert. 1985. Jews and antisemites at universities in imperial Germany (I): Jewish students; Social history and social conflict. *Leo Baeck Institute Year Book* 30:357–94.

Kampmann, Carl. 1898. *Die graphische Kunste.* Sammlung Goschen, Bd. 75. Berlin: Walter de Gruyter. Later eds. in 1906, 1909, 1927, 1932, and 1941.

Kaprelian, E. K. 1971. In memoriam: Emmanuel [sic] Goldberg, 1881–1970. *Photographic Science and Engineering* 15:3.

Karger-Decker, Bernt. 1959. Kameramann Erwin Anders. *Fotographie* 13, Nr. 12 (Dezember):466–69.

Karolus, August. 1984. *Die Anfänge des Fernsehens in Deutschlands.* Berlin: VDE-Verlag.

Katelle, A.D. 1986. The evolution of amateur motion picture equipment, 1895–1965. *Journal of Film and Video* 38, nos. 3–4 (Summer–Fall):47–57.

Keegstra, H. 1933. Die Photographie in der Gemeinde-Giroverwaltung. In International Institute for Documentation. *XIIe Conférence. Rapports,* 130–34. IID Publ. 172a. Brussels: IID.

Kellogg, Edward W. 1945. ABC of photographic sound recording. *Journal of the Society of Motion Picture Engineers* 44 (March):151–94.

Kellogg, Edward W. 1955. History of sound motion pictures. *SMPTE Journal* 64:291–302, 356–74, 422–37.

Kenez, Peter. 1973. A profile of the prerevolutionary officer corps. *California Slavic Studies* 7:121–58.

Kennett, Lee. 1991. *The first air war 1914–1918.* New York: The Free Press.

Kinematographische Apparate aus 100 Jahren: Bildband zur technischen Sammlung im Filmmuseum Potsdam. 2001. Hrsg. Filmmuseum Potsdam, Red. Christian Ilgner, ParthasVerlag, Berlin.

Klemperer, Victor. 1995. *Ich will Zeugnis ablegen bis zum letzten.* 2 vols. Berlin: Aufbau-Verlag. Transl. as Klemperer (1998).

Klemperer, Victor. 1996. *Leben sammeln, nicht fragen wozu und warum: Tagebücher 1925–1932.* 2 vols. Berlin: Aufbau-Verlag.

———. 1998. *I will bear witness: A diary of the Nazi years.* 2 vols. New York: Random House. Transl. of Klemperer (1995).

Kliachkin, Iu. Ia. 1964. Poisk mikrofil'mirovannoi informatsii. In *Sozdanie I ispol'zovanie tsentral'nogo otraslevogo spravochno-informatsionnogo fonda,* 86–91. Moscow: Institut Nauchnoi i Tekhnicheskoi Informatsii.

Köhler, A. 1921. *Academikus: Leipziger Studentenführer Auskunftsbuch: Leipziger Hochschulen und sonstige Institute für Wissenschaft und Kunst.* Leipzig: Lorentz.

Der Kongress der Photographie. 1931. *Filmtechnik* 7, Heft 17:10–14.

Krone, Hermann. 1998. *Historisches Lehrmuseum für Photographie: Experiment. Kunst. Massenmedium.* Hg. von Wolfgang Hesse. Dresden: Verlag der Kunst.

Krueger, Helmut. 2002. *Emil Mechau: A brilliant, virtually unknown inventor in the field of motion-picture projectors and television; A short biography.* Available at http://www.bbctv-ap.co.uk/mechau2. htm. Accessed 26 August 2004.

Kuball, Michael. 1980. *Familienkino: Geschichte des Amateurfilms in Deutschland.* 2 vols. Hamburg: Rowohlt.

Ku, Hans-Jürgen. 1992, 1997. *Auf der Spuren der Contax.* 2 vols. Hückelhoven: Rita Wittig Fachbuchverlag.

———. 1981–82. *Contax Geschichte.* 2 vols. Hamburg: H.-J. Ku_.

———. 1993. Reminiscences of Zeiss Ikon with Wolf Wehran. *Zeiss Historica* 15, no. 2 (Autumn):3–8.

Kühn, Willy. 1928. *Die photographische Industrie Deutschlands wissenschaftlich gesehen in ihrer Entwicklung und ihren Aufbau.* Inauguraldissertation. Vorgelegt der hohn rechts- und staatswissenschaftlichen Fakultät der Albert-Ludwigs-Universität zu Freiberg i. B[reisgau]. Schweidnutz: Berthold Köhn. Repr. New York: Arno Press, 1979.

Kuipers, J. W., A. W. Tyler, and W. L. Myers. 1957. A Minicard system for documentary information. *American Documentation* 8, no. 4:246–68.

Küppenbender, Heinz. 1981. *Die Contax-Geschichte: Interview von Fridolin Berthel.* [Transcript dated October, 1981. Copy in "Pressarchiv,"Carl Zeiss AG, Oberkochen.]

Kurze, Bertram. 1998. *Die Industriearchitectur der Ernemann-Werke in Dresden 1898–1945.* Thesaurus 1/98. Dresden: Technische Sammlungen der Stadt Dresden.

Kurzweil, Allen. 2001. *The grand complication.* New York: Hyperion.

[Laboratory for precision instruments in Tel-Aviv]. 1940. *Davar* [Tel Aviv] (12 February). In Hebrew.

La Fontaine, Henri, and Paul Otlet. 1895. Création d'un Répertoire Bibliographique Universel: note préliminaire. *IIB Bulletin* [Institut Internationale de Bibliographie] 1:15–38.

Laskov, Shulamit. 1972. *Trumpeldor: Sipur hayav* [Trumpeldor: The story of his life]. Haifa: Shikmonah. In Hebrew.

Lastra, James. 2000. *Sound technology and the American cinema: Perception, representation, modernity.* Columbia University Press.

Leubner, A. 1955. Erinnerungen an das alte Wissenschaftlich-Photographische Institut 1909–1913. *Veröffentlichungen der Deutschen Gesellschaft für Photographie* 1:29–33.

Levie, Françoise. 2002. *The man who wanted to classify the world: From the index card to the World City, the visionary life of a Belgian utopian, Paul Otlet (1968–1944).* Brussels: Sofidoc. Documentary film.

Lewandrowski, P. 1979. Der Kampf Wihelm Ostwalds um die Schaffung eines einheitlichen Informations- und Dokumentationssystems der Wissenschaft—"Die Brücke." In *Internationales Symposium anlässlich des 125. Geburtstages von Wilhelm Ostwald,* 149–56. Sitzungsberichte der Akademie der Wissenschaften der DDR, 1979, Nr. 13/N. Berlin: Akademie-Verlag.

Licklider, J. C. R. 1965. *Libraries of the future.* Cambridge: MIT Press.

Liebhabekinematographie. 1923. *Neue Universum* 44:433–36.

Lieven, Dominic. 1994. *Nicholas II: Twilight of the empire.* New York: St. Martin's Press.

The light he [James Brycc] leaves behind. 1949. *Think* (April):5–6, |30–31.

Lindsay, Jack. 1970. *The origins of alchemy in Graeco-Roman Egypt.* London: Frederick Muller.

Locquin, Marcel. 1960. Identification d'une structure complexe dans une collection. *Comptes rendus hebdomadaires des seances de l'Academie des Sciences* (Paris) 120:659–60.

Loewe, Siegmund, and Paul Goerz. 1929. Forward! The progress of televison. *Television* (London) 2, no. 21 (November):428–30.

Loewe Opta GmbH. [Corporate Web site]. http://www.loewe.de. Accessed 23 March 2003.

Luther, Robert. 1910. An automatic method of obtaining the characteristic curve of a plate. *British Journal of Photography* 57 (2 September): 664–66.

———. 1934. *Bericht über die Bedeutung und die Tätigkeit des Wissenschaftlich-Photographischen Instituts an der Technischen Hochschule Dresden.* [Typescript submitted to the Sächsische Ministerium für Volksbildung. Sächsisches Hauptstaatsarchiv (Dresden) 15678.]

———, and Emanuel Goldberg. 1906. Beiträge zur Kinetik photochemischer Reaktionen. I. Sauerstoffhemmung der Photochemischen

Chlorreaktionen in ihrer Beziehung zur photochemischen Induktion, Deduktion und Aktivierung. *Zeitschrift für Physikalische Chemie* 56:43–56.

———, and H. Staude. 1935. Die Bedeutung der Dresdner photographischen Industrie für die Wissenschaft. *Der Photo-Händler* 6. Jg, Heft 20 (1 Oktober):676–77.

A Machine that thinks. 1945. *Time* 46, no. 4 (July 23):93–94.

Maitland, C.E.A. 1931. Die photographische Gesprächszahlerablesung und die optisch-mechanische Auswertung der Zählerstände. *Zeitschrift für Fernmeldetechnik, Werk- und Gerätebau*, 12. Jg, 2. Heft (28 February):17–20.

Martens, F. F. 1901. Ueber einen Apparat zur Bestimmung der Schwärzung photographischer Platten. *Photographische Korrespondenz* 38:528.

Mauersberger, Klaus. 1993. The development of German engineering education in the nineteenth century—A comparison with Great Britain and France. In *European historiography of technology,* ed. Dan C. Christensen, 111–24. [Odense]: Odense University Press.

———. 1998. Hermann Krone und die Etablierung des Lehrstuhls für Fotografie an der Technischen Hochschule Dresden. In *Der Photopionier Hermann Krone—Photographie und Apparatur: Bildkultur und Phototechnik im 19. Jahrhundert.* Herausg. von Wolfgang Hesse und Timm Starl, 177–87. Marburg: Jonas Verlag.

———. 2002a. Emanuel Goldberg—ein jüdisches Wissenschaftler und Unternehmer. Hochschulalltag in der NS-Zeit (I). *Dresdner Universitätsjournal* 12/2002:8.

———. 2002b. Wissenschaftskooperation zwischen der TH Dresden und der Zeiss Ikon AG. In *75 Jahre Zeiss Ikon AG: Aspekte der Entwicklung des 1926 gegründeten Industrieunternehmens,* 37–49. Thesaurus 3. Dresden: Technische Sammlungen der Stadt Dresden.

Mechner, Ernst. 1942. Training industrial scientists. *U.P.A. Report* 3, no. 4 (April):2. New York: United Palestine Appeal.

Mees, C.E.K. 1942. *The theory of the photographic process.* New York: Macmillan.

Meggs, Philip B. 1983. *A history of graphic design.* New York: Van Nostrand Reinhold.

Melton, H. Keith. 2002. *Ultimate spy.* 2nd ed. New York: DK Publishers.

Mendelsohn, Ezra. 1983. *The Jews of east central Europe between the world wars.* Bloomington, IN: Indiana University Press.

Messter, Oskar. 1936. *Mein Weg mit dem Film.* Berlin: Max Hesses Verlag.

Miethe, Adolf. 1909. *Photographische Aufnahmen vom Ballon.* Halle (Saale): W. Knapp.

———. 1916. *Die Photographie aus der Luft.* 2. Aufl. von *Photographische Aufnahmen vom Ballon.* Halle (Saale): W. Knapp.

Miksa, Francis L. 1978. Rudolph, Alexander Joseph. In *Dictionary of American library biography,* ed. B. S. Wynar, 449–50. Littleton, CO: Libraries Unlimited.

Minerva: Auch eine Festschrift zum hundertfünfzigjährigen Jubelfest der Akademie zu Leipzig. Heft 1, 1914. [Leipzig: n.p.].

Mitteilungen der Deutschen Kinotechnischen Gesellschaft E.V. 104. ordentliche Sitzung...Sitzungsberichte. 1932. *Die Kinotechnik* 14, Heft 8 (20 April)·160.

Möller, Rolf. 1954. *25 Jahre Fernseh GmbH.* Darmstadt: [?Fernseh GmbH].

————, and Georg Schubert. 1939. 10 Jahre Fernsehtechnik. *Fernseh G. m. b. H.* 1, no. 4:109–22.

Mooers, Calvin. 1959. Informations-Erschliessung in den nächsten zwanzig Jahren. *Nachrichten für Dokumentation* 10:116–22.

Morse, R. S. 1942. *Rapid selector-calculator.* US patent 2,295,000. 8 September.

Müller, Gisela. 1998. Jüdische Mitarbeiter in der Leitungsebene der Firmen Carl Zeiss und Otto Schott. In Stiebert, Martin, ed. *Juden in Jena: Eine Spurensuche.* Hrsg. vom Jenaer Arbeitskreis Judentum, 152–73. Jena: Glaux.

Münster, Fritz. 1957. A guiding system using television. In North Atlantic Treaty Organization. Advisory Group for Aeronautical Research and Development. *History of German guided missiles development: AGARD First Guided Missiles Seminar, Munich, Germany, April, 1956,* ed. Th. Benecke and A. W. Quick, 135–61. AGARDograph 20. Brunswick, Germany: Appelhans; Published for The Advisory Group for Aeronautical Research and Development, North Atlantic Treaty Organization by Wissenschaftliche Gesellschaft fur Luftfahrt E. V., 1957.

Munters, M. C. 1936. Photomikrophotographie in der Verwaltung. *IID Communicationes* 3, Fasc.1: Mu.1-Mu.6.

Murray, J. P. 1962. The Bureau of Ships rapid selector system. *American Documentation* 13, no. 1:66–68.

Ein Museum für Buchwesen und Schrifttum. 1917. *Zeitschrift des Österreichischen Ingenieur- und Architekten-Vereines* 69. Jg., Heft 20 (18 Mai):320. Summarized in *Urania: Wochenschrift für Volksbildung* (Vienna) 10, Nr. 25 (23 Juni):300.

Mutter, Edwin. 1955. *Die Technik der Negativ- in Positivverfahren.* Die wissenschaftliche und angewandte Photographie, 5. Vienna: Springer.

Mütze, Klaus. 1986. 80th birthday of Professor Paul Görlich. *Jena Review* 30, no. 4 (1985):203–4.

Myers, L. M. 1936. *Television optics: An introduction.* London: Pitman.

Nachmansohn, David. 1979. *German-Jewish pioneers in science 1900–1933.* Berlin: Springer-Verlag.

Narath, A. 1957. On the quality of photographic reproductions. *Bulletin of the Research Council of Israel. Section C: Technology* 5C, no. 4:257–84.

Nathans, Benjamin. 2002. *Beyond the pale: The Jewish encounter with late imperial Russia.* Berkeley: University of California Press.

Die Nationalbibliothek in der Westentasche: Ein Professoren-Traum und die ersten Schritte zu seiner Verwirklichung. 1938. *Prager Tagblatt* 63, Nr. 213 (10 September):5–6.

Das Nationalsozialistische Lagersystem (CCP), hrsg. von Martin Weinmann. 1990. Frankfurt: Zweitausendeins.

Neale, Steve. 1985. *Cinema and technology: Image, sound, color.* Bloomington: Indiana University Press.

Neblette, C. D. 1938. *Photography: Its principles and practice.* 3rd ed. New York: Van Nostrand.

Nellhaus, Arlynn. 2000. Letter from Jerusalem: Israel's Museum of Islamic Art. *The Idler: A Web periodical* 2, no. 149 (22 November). Available at http://www.geocities.com/dcjarviks/Idler/vIIn149.html. Accessed 18 February 2002.

Neumann, S. 1957. Prof. Emanuel Goldberg. *Bulletin of the Research Council of Israel. Section C: Technology* 5C, no. 4:iii-v.

New Grove's dictionary of music and musicians. 2001. 2nd ed. New York: Grove's Dictionary.

New machine will scan, select and copy research data at high speed. 1948. *Library Journal* 73, no. 10 (15 May):797, 806.

Nicosia, Francis R. J. 1979. Weimar Germany and the Palestine question. *Leo Baeck Institute Year Book* 24:321–45.

Noted scientist visits son at Park: Renews friendship with Dr. Mees. 1946. *Kodakery* (18 July).

Nuttall, Bob. 2002. Americans and Russians at Jena. *Zeiss Historica* 24, no. 2 (Fall):11–16.

Nyce, J. M., and P. Kahn. 1989. Innovation, pragmaticism, and technological continuity: Vannevar Bush's Memex. *Journal of the American Society for Information Science,* 40:214–20.

Nyce, J. M., and P. Kahn, eds. 1991. *From Memex to hypertext: Vannevar Bush and the mind's machine.* Boston: Academic Press.

Ohnesorge, Wilhelm. 1938. *Deutsche Reichspost und Staatshoheit: Aufsätze und Vorträge.* Post und Telegraphie in Wissenschaft und Praxis 8. Berlin: Decker.

O'Neal, R. D. 1948. Photographic methods for handling input and output data. *Annals of the Computation Laboratory of Harvard University* 16:260–66.

Optical punched card: Electronic brain searches literature with combination of microfilm and punched-card technique. 1949. *Chemical Industries* 65, no. 2:189–90.

The Order of Saint Anna. [1940?]. [United States.?]: Committee of the Imperial Orders.

Ordung, Philip F., and Thomas C. Bagg. [1957?] *Status report on the Rapid Selector.* Paper on Computing Devices for the AIEE Summer General Meeting, Montreal, Quebec, June 24–28, 1957. N.p.

Oster, Gerald. 1965. Moiré optics: A bibliography. *Journal of the Optical Society of America* 55:1329–30.

———. 1969. *The science of moiré patterns.* 2nd ed. Barrington, NJ: Edmund Scientific.

Ostwald, Wilhelm. 1912. Das Gehirn der Welt. *Nord & Süd* 36:63–66.

Otlet, Paul. 1934a. Le livre microphotographique: Notice sur les brevets de Georges Sebille. *IID Communicationes* 1, Fasc. 2:21–23.

———. 1934b. *Traité de documentation.* Brussels: Palais Mondial. Repr. Liège, Belgium: Centre de lecture publique de la communauté Française, 1989.

———. *Monde: Essai d'universalisme.* Brussels: Editiones Mundaneum, Van Keerberghen.

———. 1990. *International organization and dissemination of knowledge: Selected essays,* trans. and ed. W. Boyd Rayward. Amsterdam: Elsevier.

Pachnicke, Peter. 1990. Traditionslinie der Hochschule. In *Leipziger Schule: Malerei, Grafik, Fotogragrafie; Lehrer und Absolventen der Hochschule für Graphik und Buchkunst,* 13–26. [Berlin: Staatliche Kunsthalle Berlin].

Pacific Rim Camera. 2001. *Photographica pages: An online guide to collectable cameras and related stuff. Zeiss Ikon Contax.* Available at http://www.pacificrimcamera.com/pp/zeiss/contax/contax.htm. Accessed 2 February 2003.

Palestine Royal Commission. 1937. *Report.* Cmd 5479. London: H. M. Stationery Office.

Paszkowski, Wilhelm. 1910. *Berlin in Wissenschaft und Kunst: Ein akademisches Auskunftsbuch nebst Angaben über akademische Berufe.* Berlin: Weidmannsche Buchhandlung.

Personal-Verzeichnis der Universität Leipzig für das Winter-Semester 1904/05. 146, 1905. Also *Sommer-semester 1905.* 147. 1905.

Pescht, Willi. 1953. Das Zeiss-Dokumentator-System: Ein Mittel moderne Dukumentation. *Documentation* 1, Heft 1/2:17–25.

Petrovsky-Shtern, Yohanan. 2001. *Jews in the Russian army: Through the military to modernity, 1827–1914.* PhD diss., Brandeis University. (UMI AAT 3004975).

Das photochemische Laboratorium der Technischen Hochschule Berlin zu Charlottenburg. 1907. *Zeitschrift für Reproduktionstechnik* 9, Heft 12 (Dezember):178–91.

Photoelectric librarian. 1949. *Electronics* 22, no. 9 (September):122, 158, 160, 162, 164, and 166.

Photographie und Forschung: Die Contax-Photographie in der Wissenschaft. Dresden, later Stuttgart: Zeiss Ikon, 1–8 (1935–60). Also English ed. with subtitle: *The Contax in the service of science.*

Photographische Chronik. Organ des Photographischen Vereins zu Berlin. 1(1894)–50(1943).

Photographische Industrie. Berlin: Union, 1(1903)–41(1943).

Photographische Rundschau. Halle a.S.: Wilhelm Knapp, 1(1892).

Die photographischen Fachschulen bei der Dresdener Austellung. 1909. *Photographische Korrespondenz* Nr. 589:501–2.

Pike, J. L., and T. C. Bagg. 1962. The Rapid Selector and other NBS document retrieval studies. In National Microfilm Association. *Proceedings of the Eleventh Annual Meeting,* ed. V. D. Tate, 213–27. Annapolis, MD: National Microfilm Association.

Plotnikow, Johannes [Plotnikov, Ivan Stepanovich]. 1912. Photochemische Studien. IV. Über den photochemichen Temperaturkoeffizienten von Brom. *Zeitschrift für physicalische Chemie* 78:573–81.

———. 1920. Photochemische Studien. X. Die mathematische Theorie der photochemischen Kinetik. *Zeitschrift für wissenschaftliche Photographie, Photophysik und Photochemie* 19, Heft 9 and 10:225–74.

———. 1921. Photochemische Studien. XII. Einfluss der Temperature auf die photochemischen Vorgänge. *Zeitschrift für wissenschaftliche Photographie, Photophysik und Photochemie* 20, Heft 6–8:125–39.

Posnjak, Georg. 1910. *Das Metastyrol und die beide Distyrole.* Weida: Thomas and Hubert.

Precision instruments. 1945. *U.P.A. Report* 6, no. 5 (May), penultimate page.

Products of vision: The Zeiss Ikon company and its cameras. 1988. *CMP [California Museum of Photography] Bulletin* 7, no. 2.

Prof. Dr. Robert Luther zum Gedenken. 1955. Veroff. 1. Cologne: Deutsche Gesellschaft für Photographie e.V.

Professor Dr. Goldberg 75 Jahre. 1957. *Zeitschrift für wissenschaftliche Photographie* 52:105–6.

Professor Imanuel Goldberg—Chaluts madaey hameda vehaoptica [Professor Emanuel Goldberg—a Pioneer in Information and Optics Science: The Tenth Meeting on Optical Engineering in Israel was on the topic of 60 years of Electro-Optics in Israel.] 1997. *Mehandesim VeTechnologim [Engineers and Technologists]* 1997:41, 44–46. In Hebrew.

Pugh, Emerson W. 1995. *Building IBM: Shaping an industry and its technology.* Cambridge: MIT Press.

Pun, L., and S. Mitter. 1962. Processor for graphical information. *Control* 5, no. 43 (January):115–17.

Raskin, D. 1998. Evrei v sostave rossiskogo ofitserskogo korpusa v XIX— nachale XX veka. In *Evrei v Rossii. Istoriia i kultura. Sbornik nauchnykh trudov,* ed. E. Eliashevich, 170–74. St. Petersburg: Petersburgskii evriskii universitet.

Rayward, W. Boyd. 1976. *The universe of information: The work of Paul Otlet for documentation and international organisation.* FID Publ. 520. Moscow: VINITI.

———. 1983. The International Exposition and the World Documentation Congress. *Library Quarterly* 53:254–68.

———. 1986. Otlet, Paul-Marie-Ghislain. In *ALA encyclopedia of library and information services.* 2nd ed., 626–28. Chicago: American Library Association.

——— 1994a. Some schemes for restructuring and mobilising information and documents: A historical perspective. *Information Processing and Management* 30:163–75.

———. 1994b. Visions of Xanadu: Paul Otlet (1868–1944) and hypertext. *Journal of the American Society of Information Science* 45:235–50.

———. 1999. H. G. Wells' idea of a world brain: A critical reassessment. *Journal of the American Society of Information Science* 50:557–73.

Reed, E. S. 1997. *From soul to mind: The emergence of psychology, from Erasmus Darwin to William James.* New Haven: Yale University Press.

Rees, Goronwy. 1969. *St Michael: A history of Marks and Spencer.* London: Weidenfeld and Nicolson.

Reuther, Rudolf. 1955. Das Wissenschaftlich-Photographische Institut der TH Dresden. *Veröffentlichungen der Deutschen Gesellschaft für Photographie* 1:17–22.

———. 1968. Robert Luther und das Wissenschaftlich-Photographische Institut der Technischen Universität Dresden. *Bild und Ton* 21. Jg., Heft 9:271, 274–76.

Rhodes, Barbara J., and William Wells Streeter. 1999. *Before photocopying: The art & history of mechanical copying, 1780–1938.* New Castle, DE: Oak Knoll Press.

Rich, David Alan. 1998. *The Tsar's colonels: Professionalism, strategy, and subversion in late imperial Russia.* Cambridge, MA: Harvard University Press.

Richards, Pamela Spence. 1994. *Scientific information in wartime: The Allied-German rivalry, 1939–1945.* Westport, CT: Greenwood.

Rider, Fremont. 1944. *The scholar and the future of the research library.* New York: Hadham.

Rikli, M. 1925. Ein wichtiger technische Fortschritt auf der Gebiete der Mikro-kinematographie und Mikro-momentphotographie. *Phototechnik* 12 (Mai):212–15.

Rikli, M. 1926. Mikromentphotographie und Mikrokinematographie. *Photographische Korrespondenz* 62, Nr. 3:139–43.

Robert Bosch GmbH. 1979. *Bosch Fernseh 1929–1979.* [Stuttgart?: Bosch?]. Leaflet for 50th anniversary event, Schloß Chillon,

Montreux, Switz., 31 May 1979. Includes Otto R. Oechsner "50 Jahre Fernsehtechnik bei Bosch," and Hans R. Groll, "Fernsehtechnik—gestern, heute aund morgen."

Robinson, Douglas. 1994. *The Zeppelin on combat.* Atglen, PA: Schiffer.

Roger, Jean, and Marcel Locquin. 1962. Le développement de l'information en géologie et ses perspectives. *Bulletin des Bulletin des Bibliothèques de France* 7:147–57.

Roob, Alexander. 1997. *The hermetic museum: Alchemy and mysticism.* Cologne: Taschen.

Rose, Norman. 1986. *Chaim Weizmann: A biography.* New York: Viking Penguin.

Royal Photographic Society. 1931. *British Journal of Photography* 78 (October):655–56.

Royal Society (Great Britain) Scientific Information Conference. 1948. *Report and papers submitted.* London: Royal Society.

Rudert, Frithjof. 1979. 50 Jahre "Fernseh," 1929–1979. *Bosch Technische Berichte* 6 (1979) 5/6:236–67.

Rudolph Alexander J. 1892. *Continuous Revolving File and Index.* U.S. patent 473,348. 19 April.

Russkoe zolotoe i serebrianoe delo XV-XX vekov, T. Goldberg [and others]. 1967. Moscow: Nauka.

Sächsisches Staatsarchiv Leipzig. 1970. *Staatliche Akademie für graphische Künste und Buchgewerbe. Findbuch.* Unpublished note.

Sachsse, Rolf. 1993. Beginnen wir! Die photographischen Abteilungen der Hochschule fuer Graphik und Buchkunst in Leipzig zwischen 1890 und 1950. In *Austellung Katalog Leipziger Schule Fotografie, Arbeiten von Absolventen und Studenten 1980–93: 100 Jahre Fotografie an der Hochschule für Grafik und Buchkunst Leipzig,* 7–15. Leipzig: Hochschule.

———. 1998. Das gehirn der Welt,1912: Die Organisation der Organisationen durch die Bruecke: Ein vergessenes Kapitel mediengeschichte. *Telepolis.* Available at http://www.heise.de/tp/deutsch/inhalt/co/2481/1.html. Accessed 29 March 2003.

Samain, J. 1956. Filmorex: Une nouvelle technique de classement et de sélection de documents. *L'onde électrique* 36 (156):671–75.

Satoh, Takashi. 1987. The Bridge movement in Munich and Ostwald's treatise on the organization of knowledge. *Libri* 37:1–24.

Scaife, Jos. D. 1945. Bricks without straw. *Machinery* 66 (14 June):647.

Schantz, Herbert F. 1979. *Optical character recognition: The key to increased productivity in data entry for yesterday, today and tomorrow.* [Manchester Center, VT: Recognition Equipment Inc.]

———. 1982. *The history of OCR: Optical character recognition.* [N.p.]: Recognition Technologies Users Association.

Schering, H. 1941. Professor Dr. Hermann Joachim 60 Jahre alt. *Kinotechnik* 23, Heft 12 (Dezember):193–94.

Schmidt, Irene. 1968. 60jähriges Jubiläum des Wissenschaftlich-Photographischen Instituts der Technischen Hochschule Dresden und 100. Geburtstag von Professor Dr. Robert Luther. *Zeitschrift für Wissenschaftliche Photographie* 62, Hefte 5–8:147–49.

Scholtyseck, Joachim. 1999. *Robert Bosch und die liberale Widerstand gegen Hitler 1933 bis 1945.* Munich: Verlag C. H. Beck.

Schoots, Hans. 2000. *Living dangerously: A biography of Joris Ivens.* Amsterdam: Amsterdam University Press.

Schumann, Wolfgang. 1962. *Carl Zeiss Jena: Einst und jetzt.* Von einem Autorenkollektiv unter Leitung von Wolfgang Schumann. Berlin: Rutten and Loening.

Schürmeyer, Walter. 1933. Die Photographie im Dienste der bibliothekarischen Arbeit. *Zentralblatt für Bibliothekswesen* 50:580–83.

———. 1935. Aufgaben und Methoden der Dokumentation. *Zentralblatt für Bibliothekswesen* 52:533–43. Repr. in Frank (1978, 385–97).

———. 1936. Mitteilungen über einige technische Neuerungen und Anwendungsmethoden fotographischer Hilfegeräte für das Dokumentarische Arbeiten. *IID Communicationes,* 3, Fasc. 1: cols. Schü. 1–10.

———, and T. P. Loosjes, T. P. 1937. Literatur ueber die Anwendung von photographischen Reproduktionsverfathren in der Dokumentation. *IID Communicationes,* 4, Fasc. 3:23–9.

Schwartz, Adele C. 1983. Martin Strauss just can't rest on laurels. *Washington Times* (22 July): Bus. Sect.:1.

Schwärzungsmesser nach Martens-Goldberg. [N. d.] Berlin: Schmidt and Haensch. Leaflet.

Schwegmann, G. A. 1940. Microfilming in business and industry. *Journal of Documentary Reproduction* 3:147–52.

Sebille, G. 1932. *Method and apparatus for reading books and the like.* US patent 1,889,575. 29 November.

Seherr-Thoss, Hans Christoph, Graf von. 1979. *Die deutsche Automobilindustrie: Eine Dokumentation 1886 bis 1979.* 2. Aufl. [Stuttgart]: Deutsche Verlags-Anstalt.

Seliger, Max. 1912. Wesen, Ziele und bisherige Tätigkeit der königl. Akademie für graphische Künste und Buchgewerbe in Leipzig. *Original und Reproduktion* 2, Heft 3/4:78–90.

Serres, Alexandre. 1995. Hypertexte: Une histoire à revisiter. *Documentaliste—Sciences de l'information* 32, no. 2:71-83.

Shaw, Ralph R. 1949. *The Rapid Selector. Journal of Documentation* 5:164–71.

———. 1950. High speed intermittent camera. *American Documentation* 1:194–96.

———. 1951a. Machines and the bibliographical problems of the twentieth century. In *Bibliography in an age of science,* 37–71. Urbana: University of Illinois Press.

Shaw, Ralph R.1951b. Management, machines, and the bibliographic problems of the twentieth century. In *Bibliographic organization,* ed. J. H. Shera and M. E. Egan, 200–225. Chicago, University of Chicago Press.

Sheppard, S. E. 1932. Resumé of the proceedings of the Dresden International Photographic Congress. *Journal of the Society of the Motion Picture Engineers* 18:232–41.

Shurkin, Joel. 1984. *Engines of the mind: A history of the computer.* New York: Norton.

Sipley, L. W. 1965. *Photography's great inventors.* Philadelphia: American Museum of Photography.

Skopec, Rudolf. 1964. *Photographie im Wandel der Zeiten.* Prague: Artia. Transl. of *Dejiny fotografie v obrazech od nejstarsich dob k dnesku.* Praha: Orbis, 1963.

Smith, Ernest Alfred. 1918. *The zinc industry.* London: Longmans, Green.

Smith, Linda C. 1981. "Memex" as an image of potentiality in information retrieval research and development. In *Information retrieval research,* ed. R. N. Oddy et al., 345–69. London: Butterworths.

———. 1991. Memex as an image of potentiality revisited. In *From Memex to hypertext: Vannevar Bush and the mind's machine,* ed. James M. Nyce and Paul Kahn, 261–86. Boston: Academic Press.

Sonderkommission Technische Abteilung. Seeflugstation List auf Sylt. 1917. *Berichte über zwei Konferenzen zwischen den Mitgliedern der Sonderkommission und dem Direktor der Ica-Werke und dem Abteilungsvorsteher der Photo-Abteilung Zeiss am 30. Und 21. September 1917 zu List.* [Typescript, 22 September 1917].

Spencer, D. A. 1973. *The focal dictionary of photographic technology.* London: Focal Press.

Speranskii, A. W., and E. G. Goldberg. 1900. Злектролизъ растворовъ металлическихъ солей въ органическихъ растворителяхъ. [Electrolysis of some metallic salts in organic solutions.] *Russkoe Fiziko-Khimicheskoe Obshchestvo. Zhurnal.* [Journal of the Russian Physical-Chemical Society, St. Petersburg] 32:797–804.

Sponable, E. I. 1947. Historical development of sound film. *Journal of the Society of Motion Picture and Television Engineers* 48 (April 1947):275–303; (May):407–22.

Ein Sprung—Eine Traum. 1927. *Dresdner Hochschulblatt* 3, Nr. 2 (Juni):25–27.

Statistical machine. 1932. *Electronics* 4, no. 1 (January):35.

Steiner, Kilian. [1998]. *75 Jahre 1923–1998 Loewe: Und die Zukunft geht weiter.* [Kronach, Germany: Loewe Opta GmbH].

Steiner, K. 2002. [Review of R. Walter. *Zeiss 1905–1945.* (Köln: Böhlau 2000)] *H-Soz-u-Kult* 8 January 2002. Available at http://hsozkult.

geschichte.hu-berlin.de/rezensionen/id = 1019&type = rezbuecher. Accessed 11 July 2002.

Steiner, Kilian. 2003. *Alfred D. Chandler's Konzept der learning base und seine Anwendung auf den Unterhanltungselektronikhersteller Loewe.* Munich: Universität München, Volkswirtschaftsliche Fakultät. (Discussion Paper 2003–7). Available at http://epub.ub.uni-muenchen. de/archive/00000047/ Accessed 13 August 2003.

Stenger, Erich. 1939. *The history of photography: Its relation to civilization and practice.* Easton, PA: Mack. Transl. of *Geschichte der Photographie.* Deutsches Museum Abhandlungen und Berichte 1, Heft 6. Berlin: VDI-Verlag, 1929.

Stevens, G.W.W. 1957. *Microphotography: Photography at extreme resolution.* London: Chapman and Hall.

———. 1968. *Microphotography: Photography and photofabrication at extreme resolution.* 2nd ed. New York: Wiley.

Stevens, Norman D., ed. 1975. *Essays for Ralph Shaw.* Metuchen, NJ: Scarecrow.

———. 1978. Shaw, Ralph Robert (1907–1972). In *Dictionary of American library biography,* ed. B. S. Wynar, 476–81. Littleton, CO: Libraries Unlimited.

Stewart, J., and D. Hickey. 1960. *Reading devices for micro-images.* State of the library art, v. 5, part 2. New Brunswick, NJ: Graduate School of Library Service, Rutgers–The State University.

Stiebel, Fritz. 1931. Achter Internationaler Kongress für Photographie. *Die Naturwissenschaften* 19, Heft 39:810–14.

Stolze, Franz. 1893. Ueber eine Methode der Untersuchung von Emulsionsplatten auf Empfindlichkeit und harmonische Wirking. *Photographisches Wochenblatt. Zeitschrift und Repertorium für Photographie und verfielfältigende Künste* 9, Nr. 3:17–22.

Strauss, Herbert A. 1980–81. Jewish emigration from Germany: Nazi policies and Jewish responses. *Leo Baeck Institute Year Book* 25:313–61; 26:343–409.

Tate, Vernon D. 1938. The present state of equipment and supplies for microphotography. *Journal of Documentary Reproduction* 2:3–62. Reprint of a report submitted to the National Research Council Committee on Scientific Aids to Learning.

Die technische Kurse der Vorschule der Königlichen Akademie für graphische Künste und Buchgewerbe zu Leipzig, [1912] vom M. Seliger, K. Berthold, A. Schelter, A. Kolb, F. Naumann. E. Goldberg, G. Belwe und H. Dannhorn. Hrsg. von der Akademie gelegentlich des Internationalen Kongresses für Kunstunterricht in Dresden. Leipzig: Akademie.

Thiele, Hartmut. 2000. Aufstieg und Niedergang der deutschen Photoindustrie durch Monopolisierung der Zubehoerindustrie von

Zeiss Ikon Dresden am Beispiel des Verschlussbaues. In *75 Jahre Zeiss Ikon AG: Aspekte der Entwicklung des 1926 gegründeten Industrieunternehmens*, 71–77. Thesaurus 3. Dresden: Technische Sammlungen der Stadt Dresden.

Thiele, R. 1903. Ueber präzise Aufnahmen von Plänen der Niederungen großer Flüsse, ihrer Mündungen und Deltas mit Hilfe der Photographie und Drachenphotographie. *Jahrbuch für Photographie und Reproduktionstechnik* 17:131–40.

Thierfelder, Franz. 1938. *Deutsch als Weltsprache*. Berlin: Verlag fur Volkstum, Wehr und Wirtschaft, Hans Kurzeja.

Thiess, Frank. 1931. *Der Zentaur.* Stuttgart: T. Engelshorns Nchf.

Thwing, Charles Franklin. 1928. *The American and the German university: One hundred years of history.* New York: Macmillan.

Tollenaar, D. 1992. Moiré interference phenomena in halftone printing. In *Selected papers on optical moiré and applications,* ed. Guy Indebetouw and Robert Czarnek, 618–23. SPIE Milestone Series MS 64. Bellington, WA: SPIE Optical Engineering Press. Originally published in Dutch, 1945.

Tomasch, E. 1980. The start of an ERA: Engineering Research Associates, Inc., 1946–1955. In *A history of computing in the twentieth century,* ed. N. Metropolis, J. Howlett, and G.-C. Rota, 485–95. New York: Academic Press.

Touch of genius: Goldberg Instruments. 1954. *The Israel Export Journal* 6, no. 10:7.

Toulmin, Stephen. 1990. *Cosmopolis: The hidden agenda of modernity.* New York: Frcc Press.

Townsend, L. G. 1938. *Method of and apparatus for the indexing and photo-transcription of records.* US patent 2,121,061. 21 June.

Trescott, Martha M. 1981. *The rise of the American electrochemicals industry, 1880–1910: Studies in the American technological environment.* Westport, CT: Greenwood.

Tuning local industries to war-time needs: Mr Walsh broadcasts on Delhi talks. 1940. *Palestine Post* (15 December):3.

Tyler, Arthur W. 1948. Optical and photographic storage techniques. *Annals of the Computation Laboratory of Harvard University* 16: 146–50.

———, W. L. Myers, and J. W. Kuipers. 1955. The application of the Kodak Minicard system. *American Documentation* 6:18–30.

United States. Advisory Committee on Application of Machines to Patent Office Operations. 1954. *Report.* Washington, DC: Department of Commerce.

United States. Federal Bureau of Investigation. 1946. *Johannes Rudolf Christina Zuehlensdorff.* New York, 29 January 1946, 10 pp. Typescript report, declassified 1986.

United States. Navy Department. Bureau of Construction and Repair. 1919. *The type "M" kite balloon handbook.* Washington, DC: Government Printing Office.

Uricchio, William. 1990. High-definition television, big screen television and television-guided missiles, 1945. *Historical Journal of Film, Radio and Television* 10, no. 3:311–15. Translated excerpts from BIOS Report 867 (British Intelligence Objectives Subcommittee 1946).

Urquhart, D. J. 1951. American impressions. *American Documentation* 2:102–7.

Varlejs, Jana. 1999. Ralph Shaw and the Rapid Selector. In Conference on the History and Heritage of Science Information Systems (1998: Pittsburgh). *Proceedings,* ed. M. E. Bowden, T. B. Hahn, and R. V. Williams, 148–55. Medford, NJ: Information Today.

Vera Frances Bryce Salomons 1888–1969: In Memoriam. 1970. Jerusalem: Published by Arthur Berger for the L. A. Thayer Memorial Association. In English and Hebrew.

Vera Salomons and Jerusalem. 1983. *The Sir David Salomons Society Newssheet* No. 3 (March):[1–3].

Verry, H. R. 1963. *Microcopying methods.* London: Focal Press.

Versammlungsberichte: VIII. Internationale Kongress für Photographie. 1931. *Zeitschrift für angwandte Chemie* 44:875–78.

Verwaltungsrat des Deutschen Vereins für Buchwesen und Schifttum. 1918. *Zeitschrift des Deutschen Vereins für Buchwesen und Schifttum* 1, Nr. 7/8:86–89.

Vickery, B. C. 1951. Some comments on mechanized selection. *American Documentation* 2:102–7.

A visit to the Goerz works. 1929. *Television* (London) 2, no. 21 (November):430–31.

Wagenführ, Kurt. 1990. Developmental possibilities of television, 1939. *Historical Journal of Film, Radio and Television* 10, no. 3:305–9. Transl. of "Entwicklungsmöglichkeiten des Fernsehens." *Deutsche Rundschau* 65, no. 10 (1939):184–91.

Walter, Rolf. 2000. *Zeiss 1905–1945.* Vol. 2 of Mühlfriedel, Wolfgang, and Rolf Walter. 1996- *Carl Zeiss: Geschichte eines Unternehmens in drei Bände.* Köln: Böhlau.

Wanderleb, Ernst. 1946. [Memo beginning:] In einem Brief. [Unpublished typescript dated 25 January 1946.]

———. 1957. *Einige persönliche Erinnerungen an Prof. Emmanuel Goldberg.* 4pp. Unpublished typescript.

Wells, H. G. 1938. *World brain.* Garden City, NY: Doubleday, Doran & Co..

Weltgalerie des schönen Buches: zur Geschichte der Internationalen Buchkunst-Ausstellungen in Leipzig. 1989. [Herausg. von Hans Baier]. 2. Aufl. Leipzig: Fachbuchverlag.

Wendel, Rudolf. 1955. Das Zeiss-Dokumentator-System, ein wirksames Hilfsmittel moderner Dokumentation *Documentation* 2. Jg, Heft 5:94–97.

Wertheimer, Jack. 1982. The "Ausländerfrage" at institutions of higher learning: A controversy over Russian-Jewish students in Imperial Germany. *Leo Baeck Institute Year Book* 27:187–218.

———. 1987. *Unwelcome strangers: East European Jews in imperial Germany.* New York: Oxford University Press.

Western Reserve University. School of Library Science. 1957. *Information systems in documentation; based on the Symposium on Systems for Information Retrieval, held at Western Reserve University, Cleveland, Ohio, in April 1957.* Advances in documentation and library science, 2. New York: Interscience Publishers.

Whaley, Barton. 1984. *Covert German rearmament, 1919–1939: Deception and misperception.* Frederick, MD: University Publications of America.

Wheeler, L. J. 1963. *Principles of cinematography: A handbook of motion picture technology.* 3rd ed. London: Fountain Press.

White, William. 1989. The microdot: Then and now. *International Journal of Intelligence and Counterintelligence* 3:249–69.

———. 1990. *Subminiature photography.* Boston: Focal Press.

———. 1992. *The microdot: History and application.* Phillips Publications, Box 168, Williamstown, NJ.

Widder, Werner. 2003. The early postwar years at Carl Zeiss Jena. *Zeiss Historica* 25, no. 1 (Spring):2–6.

Widmer, Emil Joseph. 1917. *Military observation balloons (captive and free): A complete treatise on their manufacture, equipment, inspection, and handling, with special instructions for the training of a field balloon company.* New York: D. Van Nostrand.

Wilson, J. C. 1937. *Television engineering.* London: Pitman.

Wise, Carl S., and James W. Perry. 1950. Multiple coding and the Rapid Selector. *American Documentation* 1, no. 1:76–83.

World Congress of Universal Documentation, Paris, 1937. [Congrès Mondial de la Documentation Universelle, 1937]. *La documentation.* Paris, 1937. Also *Proceedings* (Paris, 1937).

Worman, K. 1970. German Jews in Israel: Their cultural situation since 1933. *Leo Baeck Institute Yearbook* 15:73–103.

Yost, Graham. 1985. *Spy-tech.* New York: Facts on File.

Young, Roger S., et al. 1983. Once more: Pearl Harbor, microdots, and J. Edgar Hoover: Letters and replies [by] Roger S. Young, John F. Bratzel, Leslie B. Rout, Jr., Otto Pflanze, John Toland. *American Historical Review* 88, no. 4:953- 60.

Zachary, G. Pascal. 1997a. *Endless frontier: Vannevar Bush, engineer of the American century.* New York: Free Press.

————. 1997b. The Godfather [Vannevar Bush]. *Wired* 5 (November): 152–60.

Zaks, A. B., ed. 1988. *Gosudarstvennyi Istoricheskii Muzei v Gody Velikoi Otechestvennoi Voiny, 1941–1945gg. Sbornik vospominanii sotrudnikov muzeia.* Moscow: Gosudarstvennyi ordena Lenina Istoricheskii muzei.

Zeiss Ikon. [?1935a]. *Densograph.* In 720 E. Dresden: Zeiss Ikon. 12 pp., leaflet.

————. [?1935b] *Sensitometer for measuring the sensitivity of photographic emulsions.* In 599 E. [Dresden]: Zeiss Ikon. 8 pp., leaflet.

Zeiss Ikon AG. 1937. *75 Jahre Photo- und Kinotechnik; Festschrift herausgegeben anlässlich der Feier des 75-jährigen Bestehens der Zeiss Ikon AG. und ihrer Vorgängerfirmen 1862–1937.* [?Dresden: Zeiss Ikon].

Zeiss Ikon AG, and E. Goldberg. 1938. *Vorrichtung zum Aussuchen statistischer und Buchhalterischer Angaben.* [German] Patentschrift 670 190. 22 December.

Zeitler, Julius. 1914. *Der Lehrkörper der königl. Akademie für Graphische Künste und Buchgewerbe zu Leipzig im Jubiläumjahre 1914.* [N.p.]

Zielinski, Siegfried. 1989. *Audiovisionen: Kino und Fernsehen als zwischenspiele in der Geschichte.* Reinbeck bei Hamburg: Rowohlts Taschenbuch Verlag.

Zweihundert Jahre Hochschule für Grafik und Buchkunst Leipzig. 1964. Leipzig: Die Hochschule.

Index

About the Author

MICHAEL BUCKLAND is Emeritus Professor, School of Information Management and Systems, and Co-Director of the Electronic Cultural Atlas Initiative, at the University of California, Berkeley. He has degrees in History from Oxford and Librarianship from Sheffield University. He has been Dean of the School of Library and Information Studies at Berkeley and President of the American Society for Information Science. Previous books include Library Services in Theory and Context (1983) and Information and Information Systems (Praeger, 1991).

Recent Titles in New Directions in Information Management